A Place at the
Multicultural Table

A Place at the Multicultural Table

The Development of an American Hinduism

PREMA A. KURIEN

RUTGERS UNIVERSITY PRESS

NEW BRUNSWICK, NEW JERSEY, AND LONDON

Library of Congress Cataloging-in-Publication Data

Kurien, Prema A., 1963–
A place at the multicultural table : the development of an American Hinduism / Prema A. Kurien.
    p.   cm.
  Includes bibliographical references and index.
  ISBN-13: 978-0-8135-4055-9 (hardcover : alk. paper)
  ISBN-13: 978-0-8135-4056-6 (pbk. : alk. paper)
  1. Hinduism—United States. 2. Hindus—United States. I. Title.
  BL1168.U532K87 2007
  294.50973—dc22

                                                        2006027316

A British Cataloging-in-Publication record for this book is available from the British Library.

Manufactured in the United States of America

For Kofi, in gratitude

Contents

PART III
The Relationship between Popular and Official Hinduism

Preface

This book is part of a larger project on ethnicity and religion among Indian immigrants and their children in the United States. Hindus are the largest religious group among Indian Americans, and the bulk of my work has focused on them, but I have also studied Christians and conducted a short study of Muslims. My interest in the relationships between ethnicity, religion, and migration developed out of my earlier research that looked at the impact of temporary migration to Middle Eastern countries on sending communities in Kerala, south India (Kurien 1993, 2002). Although I had planned on studying rural-urban variations, I ended up focusing on the way in which ethnicity based on religious background organized the migration and was transformed by it, since I discovered that there were striking differences in patterns of out-migration, remittance use, and migration-induced social change between Mappila Muslims, Ezhava Hindus, and Syrian Christians (Kurien 2002).

With the exception of some groups of Indian Christians, Indian immigrants from different religious backgrounds do not show major variations in patterns of migration to the United States. But religion is an important factor differentiating patterns of ethnic formation, since religious institutions often come to define and sustain ethnic life in the immigrant context. I have found that Hindu, Muslim, Christian, and Sikh Indian Americans have very different constructions of "Indianness" and, correspondingly, different patterns of identity construction and activism.

My personal background has affected this study in a variety of ways. I spent the first twenty-three years of my life in India before coming to the United States for graduate study. Although I am an immigrant from India, I am not a Hindu, but hail from a south Indian Christian background. This is obvious from my last name and has been a source of some discomfort for many of the people I talked to during the course of this research. After the centuries of mockery and harassment that Hindus have had to endure from Christians, particularly Western Christian missionaries, and the negative stereotypes that exist in American society regarding Hinduism, many of those I interviewed were understandably wary of my intentions and the purpose of my study. To put people at ease and to "prove" that I did not come from a fundamentalist background, on at least two occasions I had to resort to invoking the fact that my brother-in-law is a Hindu.

My being a non-Hindu certainly affected many of the statements that people made to me regarding their ideas and feelings about religion. Being aware of this, I used the help of two research assistants, both of Hindu background, for parts of my study (but those who were interviewed still knew that the research was for my project). My awareness also meant that I often had to be cautious about the questions I asked and how I phrased them. I have felt at a disadvantage many times during the course of my research, since I did not have an insider's perspective and experience of lived Hinduism, particularly as it related to familial and household practices. But I also came to realize that this experience is extremely diverse and depends on the region, time period, caste, class, and religiosity of the particular family. Because of the difficulty involved in studying the private devotions and rituals practiced within the home, in this book I focus primarily on Hindu associations and organizations.

Christians in India are a very small minority (less than 2.5 percent of the population), so many of my friends, classmates, and neighbors were Hindu when I was growing up, and I have always had an admiration for many aspects of Hinduism. I participated fully in the devotions of the Hindu American groups that I studied, and as my knowledge of Hindu doctrines and practices increased, so did my appreciation, something I hope comes through in the pages of this book.

However, as I discovered a few years after I had started my research, there was another, more hidden side to the institutionalization of Hinduism in the United States. Even before I started on this project in 1994, I was aware of scholarship showing that some of the financial support for the Hindu nationalist Hindutva (literally, "Hinduness") movement came from Hindu Indian Americans. But I felt that the behavior of a small group of individuals had little relevance to understanding what Hinduism and Hindu institutions meant for the mass of Hindu Americans. I wanted to focus on the new forms, practices, and interpretations that were developing in the American context and was not interested in Hindu nationalism or politics. But over time I began to realize that in the United States, Hindutva supporters were becoming the central authority and hegemonic voice that Hinduism had so far lacked, defining Hinduism, Indian identity, Indian history and culture, and the obligations of good Hindus. Thus many elements of the Hindutva discourse were manifesting themselves in the self-definitions and explanations of lay Hindu Indian Americans, even those who were uninterested in or opposed to Hindu nationalism. I also began to see how the American context and the functioning of Hindu organizations within this environment was indirectly responsible for this development. In this way, I was drawn into studying immigrant politics, much the way that apolitical Hindu Indian Americans have been drawn into the Hindutva movement.

Reading and hearing about the death threats and harassment that scholars (many practicing Hindus themselves) who have been critical of the Hindutva movement or aspects of Hinduism have received has made me pause during the course of my research to ponder whether I should stop and turn to a less controversial project, whether I should write a book and thus risk drawing unwanted negative attention to myself and my family or play safe and write articles for scholarly journals (read primarily by other scholars), and whether I should focus on only the more innocuous aspects of American Hinduism.[1]

What convinced me that I could not ignore how profoundly the Hindutva movement had penetrated American Hinduism was my study of second-generation Hindu Americans in a Hindu Student Council (HSC) chapter toward the middle of my research on this project. Earnest, passionate, and often wonderfully articulate, these students were wrestling with issues of identity (racial, cultural, and religious) that for the most part their parents and others of the first generation could not even begin to comprehend. Even more interesting, however, was the fact that these struggles seemed to have pushed some members of the group toward the Hindutva platform. Certainly it was a numerical minority of members who expressed Hindu chauvinistic and anti-Muslim sentiments, but they were also the most vocal of the membership. Most of this "hard-core" group (as they were often described by others in the organization) had not spent much time in India, and none kept in regular touch with Indian news and events. All were in highly competitive academic programs and from all indications were doing very well. From my interviews I gathered that they came from affluent, well-educated, liberal, Westernized families.

This then was the puzzle. Why were these highly successful, privileged youngsters who espoused liberal American politics (on race and affirmative action, for instance) and who strongly defended their right to maintain and celebrate their religion and culture in the United States, adopting a reactionary stance when it came to the rights of minorities in India? Why were they so vehement about their dislike for individuals and groups they had little (if any) contact with, and passionate about events that took place hundreds, even thousands of years ago in a country they barely knew? As Dhoolekha Sarhadi Raj (2000, 538) points out, the Hindu politics of second- (and later) generation Indians in the West challenges conventional paradigms of religion, ethnicity, and religious nationalism. It was this research on the second generation that finally persuaded me that the dual nature of American Hinduism was a valuable topic to focus on and understand.

Long before my research was completed, several Hindu Americans questioned my ability and right as a non-Hindu to write on the topic of Hinduism in the United States. An anonymous e-mail of March 25, 2001, titled "The Emergence of American Hinduism's Latest Scholar," was widely circulated on Indian American Internet groups to alert Hindus about my research and portrayed me as a sinister figure—an Indian Christian who had made the journey from India to the United States to study about Hinduism, and who was being funded and groomed by "Christian" organizations in the United States[2] to be one of their "next generation of intellectual samurais."[3] With some help from friends, I was able to trace the source of the e-mail to the founder (and list-owner) of an Internet discussion group focusing on Indian issues, a group that I subsequently joined.

When I signed up to join the discussion list-serv, I was introduced to the group by the list-owner (an unusual procedure) as a Christian from Kerala (a south Indian state) and a Ph.D. in sociology specializing in "Hinduism in America."

In reply, I posted a message to describe my research and to correct several mischaracterizations in the list-owner's introductory e-mail. This message, however, failed to allay the concerns of many of the members about myself and my research; another person wrote that my undertaking to do research on Hindus raised the "troubling question" of whether "converts to a religion depend on denigrating and demeaning their source religion/world view for their continued self esteem in their new community?"[4] Specifically, he wondered whether Indian American Christians needed to present Hinduism in a negative light in order "to obtain a favored place for themselves in America."

To those who question whether I should have studied Hinduism and Hindus at all, I offer as justification for my research and my writing the fact that understanding the many types of immigrant Hindu institutions and expressions in the United States today is an important topic, so far largely neglected by both Hindus and non-Hindus. Whether I have done justice to this very complex issue, I will leave to my readers to decide.

Portions of the material presented in this book have been published elsewhere. Chapter 4 is an amalgamated and revised version of two earlier publications: "Becoming American by Becoming Hindu: Indian Americans Take Their Place at the Multi-cultural Table," pp. 37–70 in *Gatherings in Diaspora: Religious Communities and the New Immigration,* ed. R. Stephen Warner and Judith G. Wittner (Temple University Press, 1998), and "Gendered Ethnicity: Creating a Hindu Indian Identity in the U.S.," *American Behavioral Scientist* 42 (4) (1999):648–670. Chapter 10 is largely from "Being Young, Brown, and Hindu: The Identity Struggles of Second Generation Indian Americans," *Journal of Contemporary Ethnography* 34 (4) (2005):434–469 and is reproduced here with kind permission from Sage Publications. Four other publications—"Multiculturalism and Ethnic Nationalism: The Development of an American Hinduism," *Social Problems* 51 (3) (2004):362–385; "'We are Better Hindus Here': Religion and Ethnicity among Indian Americans," pp. 99–120 in *Building Faith Communities: Asian Immigrants and Religions,* ed. Jung Ha Kim and Pyong Gap Min (Altamira Press, 2002); "Reinventions of Hinduism," pp. 116–120 in *Encyclopedia of Religion and American Cultures,* vol. 1, ed. Gary Laderman and Luis Leon (ABC-CLIO, 2003); and "Hinduism," pp. 881–885 in *Encyclopedia of American Immigration,* ed. James Ciment (M. E. Sharpe, 2001)— foreshadow some of the arguments presented here.

This book is the product of more than a decade of work, and I have accumulated many debts over the course of it. I am particularly grateful to the many Hindu Americans in various parts of the country who welcomed me into their organizations and their homes and patiently answered my many questions. Some of these individuals and many others read and commented on drafts of chapters or earlier articles that form parts of this book. Others provided assistance or information that was important in the development of the project. I especially thank Jon Miller and Don Miller, directors of the Immigrant Congregations project of the Center for the Study for Religion and Civic Culture at the University of Southern California;

Sujatha Ramesh and Dipa Gupta, my research assistants for this project; Stephen Warner, Judith Wittner, and members of the New Ethnic and Immigrant Congregations Project (NEICP) team; Robert Wuthnow, Penny Edgell, and the 2000–2001 fellows at the Center for the Study of Religion at Princeton University; students in my Sociology 880 class at Syracuse University; as well as Gwendolyn Alexis, Subho Basu, Edwin Bryant, José Casanova, Leela Fernandes, Ann Gold, Mathew Guterl, John Stratton Hawley, Pierrette Hondagneu-Sotelo, David Ludden, Michael Moffat, Rajani Natarajan, Stephen Prothero, Arvind Rajagopal, Jishnu Shankar, Robert Thurman, Susan Wadley, Joanne Waghorne, and Mary Waters. I also thank Emera Bridger for her painstaking editorial and bibliographic work, and two reviewers of Rutgers University Press for helpful feedback that aided me in my revisions. During the long process of writing, I worked with three editors at Rutgers University Press. I owe David Myers an immense debt of gratitude for acquiring the manuscript before I had even started writing it, Kristi Long for careful reading of an early draft and extremely helpful suggestions on how to reorganize the book, and Adi Hovav for her patience, support, and advice. I also thank Elizabeth Gilbert for her very careful copyediting. My parents and husband acted as a sounding board for many of my ideas, were a crucial source of support, and also read and critiqued several sections. Lest any of the individuals named above be blamed for the orientation of the book or for parts where I may have misunderstood or misinterpreted the data, let me make clear that no one else is in any way responsible for this final product and that all errors of whatever nature are mine alone.

I gratefully acknowledge that this research was funded by fellowships from the New Ethnic and Immigrant Congregations Project, the Pew Charitable Trusts, and the Center for the Study of Religion at Princeton University. Additional support was provided by the University of Southern California through the Center for Religion and Civic Culture, the Southern California Research Center, and the Zumberge Fund. Because the agenda of my funding agencies has come into question, I emphasize that these organizations are in no way responsible for the content or interpretation of the book or any of the chapters. Other than providing general guidelines for the types of research that they would fund, none of them specified a particular topic or group for study. Moreover, I received the funding early in the research process and my project evolved significantly after that, so the substance and focus of the original proposals which these organizations and centers funded were very different from what is contained in this book.

A Place at the Multicultural Table

CHAPTER 1

The Transformation of Hinduism in the United States

A typical weekend in a U.S. suburb sees several Hindu Indian families toting their children to educational groups known as *bala vihars,* some located in a temple or religious center, others at various member homes, to learn about Hinduism and Indian culture. A variety of Hindu organizations in the United States also run summer camps for the same purpose. Hindu student organizations have now sprung up in colleges and universities around the country, and members earnestly debate the "central beliefs of Hinduism" or the joys and burdens of being Hindu in the United States. Unlike temples in India, which are the abode of a primary deity and his or her consorts, and where most worship is performed by priests at times when few devotees are around, many temples in the United States house a variety of deities, often from opposing traditions, and are community-centered religious institutions with membership lists and congregational worship services on weekends. A variety of independent Hindu organizations such as American Hindus against Defamation (AHAD) and the Hindu International Council against Defamation (HICAD) are another U.S. phenomenon, with the mission of protecting Hinduism against defamation, commercialization, and misuse, particularly by American businesses and the entertainment industry. Another organization, the Hindu American Foundation, whose mission is to "provide a voice for the . . . Hindu American community," took part in a court case challenging the public display of the Ten Commandments in Texas. The group's amicus curiae brief argued that the monument expressed an inherent government preference for Judeo-Christian religions over non–Judeo-Christian ones, since Hindu beliefs regarding the nature of God and the relationship between man and God differed from those enshrined in the monument (www.hinduamericanfoundation.org). All of these are Hindu institutions and activities not seen in India.

This book, based on research on five different types of Hindu Indian organizations in the United States, examines the new forms, practices, and interpretations characteristic of American Hinduism.[1] In addition to new congregational forms and formal mechanisms to transmit culture and religion to the younger generation and newly formed regional and national associations to unite Hindus and represent their interests, Hinduism in the United States is now explicitly interpreted in comparison with Abrahamic religions (Christianity, Judaism, and Islam). Many Hindu American leaders are interested in transforming Hinduism into a global, universal religion, instead of an ethnic religion tied to India.

American Hinduism has developed in response to two interrelated processes, the institutionalization of Hinduism in the United States as a repository of Indian culture, and its politicization as it becomes the means to obtain recognition and validation in multicultural America. Some U.S. modifications of Hinduism attempt to adjust the religion to its new environment by making it more compatible with American culture and society. Other changes derive from the political struggles associated with being nonwhite immigrants and a religious minority, and are often attempts to challenge American practices or to resist assimilation by emphasizing the distinctness of Hinduism and Indian culture. The contradiction between these two intertwined strategies is embedded in the emerging American Hinduism.

Both the institutionalization and the politicization of U.S. Hinduism depend on transnational connections (psychological, social, religious, and economic) with India. The process of institutionalizing Hinduism in the United States requires the help of experts and sacred objects from the homeland, and the politicization of Hinduism in the United States draws on Hindu nationalist ideologies and networks first articulated in India. Ideas and practices of Hinduism that are made or remade in the United States are also exported back to India.

This book addresses two seeming paradoxes: (1) why the institutionalization of Hinduism as the means to maintain and express an ethnic American identity has led to the religion's politicization; and (2) why the settlement and ethnic formation of Hindu Indians in the United States have generated deeper emotional bonds with the homeland and new transnational connections.

Within the social science literature on immigrants, scholars have generally focused on the role immigrant religion plays in creating a subcultural ethnic identity *or* on the transnational political and social involvement of immigrants. Few studies systematically analyze the relationships between the two dimensions and how one draws on the other. The first type of study generally looks at religion's role in the creation of a subcultural identity in pluralistic societies and does not deal with the political or transnational implications of immigrant religion and ethnicity (Hurh and Kim 1990; Min 1992; Warner and Wittner 1998; Yang 1999). The second type draws on transnational theory, which focuses on the home country connections and practices of immigrants but fails to adequately recognize that such practices, rather than merely being maintained by immigrants as a means to resist assimilation and counter marginality, are instead reinterpreted and selectively used, precisely in order to manufacture an "American" ethnic identity and strategy suitable to their new context. Here I analyze the relationships between the institutionalization of immigrant religion, its politicization, and the development of transnationalism. In the Hindu American case as well as in others, these relationships may have contradictory implications for the ethnic community, for the wider society, and for the home country.

MULTICULTURALISM AND IMMIGRANT ETHNICITY

The ideology and practice of multiculturalism play an important role in creating and explaining the contradictions of American Hinduism. Although multiculturalism was never formally adopted as a national policy in the United States (unlike in Canada and Australia), the recognition that the country is made up of citizens from diverse backgrounds, whose identities and cultures need to be publicly acknowledged and valued, has been a "policy rubric" in a variety of arenas for over a decade (Newfield and Gordon 996, 76–77). The philosopher Charles Taylor points out (1992) that Western multiculturalism is premised on the positive valuation of others as a vital human need. This belief is in turn based on a set of related notions: first, that all human beings and cultures have an inner "authentic" essence that gives them their individuality; second, that being "in touch with" and "true" to this inner self allows individuals and groups to develop their full potential; and finally, that such personal and moral development is possible only through interaction with people who recognize and respect this uniqueness. Thus the multiculturalist movement asserts that democratic societies, which are based on the assumption of the equality of their citizens, also have the obligation to publicly acknowledge the distinctness and value of the cultures and peoples contained within them (Taylor 1992).

Multiculturalism permits, even demands, the construction of a public ethnic identity, as opposed to a purely private one. In the postassimilationist era, having an "exotic" national heritage and a "hyphenated" American identity is deemed acceptable, even fashionable (see Walzer 1999). In the words of one of my second-generation interviewees, "Now, ethnicity is no longer a dirty word, something to be ashamed about or to be hidden in the closet. It is to be flaunted. You need to 'come out' and show that you are proud of your heritage." Joshua Fishman (1985, 344) talks about the "sidestream ethnicity" (or "symbolic ethnicity"; Gans 1979) that has become chic in the aftermath of the ethnic revival in the United States. He argues that it is

> recognized as being not only natural but humanizing and strengthening in some very general sense. . . . Americans now expect one another to have some sidestream ethnicity; any sidestream ethnicity will do . . . because their role is no longer to help or hinder "being a success in America" but to provide "roots"— that is, give meaningful cultural depth to individual and family life. Thus, a sidestream ethnicity as part of one's background . . . has become part of an enriched and overarching American experience.

According to Fishman, to have a sidestream ethnicity is now to be mainstream American. Mary Waters (1990) similarly vouches for the trendiness of "symbolic ethnicity" and its widespread adoption, while providing a more detailed and critical analysis of its content and implications.

The relationships between U.S. Hinduism's institutionalization, politicization, and transnationalism are mediated through multiculturalism. Multiculturalism leads to the institutionalization of ethnicity and to ethnic formation among immigrant groups as individuals face pressure (both from the wider society and from within the ethnic community) to organize into groups on the basis of cultural similarity and to have ethnic representatives "speak for the community" and its concerns. Multiculturalism has also made ethnic identification an important source of cultural capital in contemporary Western societies, contributing to ethnicity's politicization. Because official "recognition" can secure a group social, economic, and political resources, the "struggle for recognition" is now becoming a central form of political conflict in multicultural societies (Fraser 1997, 11), spurring ethnic mobilization among a range of groups. Finally, the "authenticity" demanded by multiculturalism requires the transnational legitimation of ethnicity by traditional sources of authority and products from the home country. Again ethnic entrepreneurs work to obtain official recognition for their group by making their homelands and ethnic cultures visible to the public. They do this through cultural displays and parades (Basch, Glick Schiller, and Szanton Blanc 1994, 74–75), by sponsoring academic area studies programs and endowed chairs (Dekmejian and Themelis 1997, 42–43), and by forming political lobbies to promote the image and interests of their homeland and influence foreign policy decision makers (Dekmejian and Themelis 1997; Smith 2000). The pivotal role that national origin plays in community formation, ethnic pride, and individual identity in the United States also provides a strong incentive for members of ethnic groups to get involved, directly or indirectly, in social and political activism in the homeland.

MULTICULTURALISM, IMMIGRANT ACTIVISM, AND SOCIAL CHANGE

Hindu Americans are one of the post-1965 immigrant groups whose activism is reshaping the contours of religion, society, and politics in the United States as well as in the international arena in the twenty-first century. Since the passage of the Immigration and Nationality Act of 1965, which dramatically liberalized immigration policies, the United States has witnessed a second period of mass immigration.[2] By the late 1980s almost three-quarters of a million legal immigrants were entering the country every year (Bean and Stevens 2003, table 2.1), and the number of immigrants admitted in the 1990s (9 million) exceeded the number admitted between 1901 and 1910 (8.8 million), the peak decade of the first mass immigration period (Min 2002, 2). The beginning of the contemporary wave of immigration coincided with a fertility decline in the United States, making immigration now the primary factor contributing to U.S. population growth. In 2000 foreign-born residents numbered 31.1 million, or over 11 percent of the population, and this proportion is projected to increase over time. Even more significant, almost one in every five births in this country now occurs to a foreign-born woman (Bean and Stevens 2003, 5).

The large-scale European immigration from the end of the nineteenth to the early twentieth century resulted in a transformation of the self-definition and identity of the United States. The definition of "white persons" was expanded from a category that included only Anglos to one that included first people from northern or western Europe and then those from southern and eastern Europe as well. The religious identity of the United States was expanded from "Protestant" to "Christian" (including Catholics) and finally in the 1950s to "Judeo-Christian" (including Jews). Post-1965 immigrants, who are largely from Latin America, Asia, and the Caribbean, are likely to bring about even more dramatic shifts in American culture and identity. Scholars have noted, for instance, that these immigrants and their children have been transforming the United States "from a largely biracial society . . . into a multiracial, multi-ethnic society consisting of several racial and ethnic groups" (Bean and Stevens 2003, 20) and that the United States has gone from being a "Christian country" to becoming the "world's most religiously diverse nation" (Eck 2001). The very presence of today's immigrants calls into question traditional conceptions of Americanness as white, Christian, and Anglocentric (e.g., Huntington 2004), and many newcomers are also challenging these conceptions directly by confronting American institutions, practices, and norms that they consider to be hostile to their cultures.

Most studies of post-1965 immigration have focused on the reception and integration of immigrants (Reitz 2002). This orientation has a long tradition in American sociology and is a legacy of the assimilationist lens through which early American sociologists examined the impact of the country's large-scale European immigration. This assimilationist orientation in turn is a product of a static model of identity that views national culture as given or already accomplished, usually at origin. According to this view, the cultural essence of a nation is defined at its birth and then needs to be maintained and safeguarded through its history. Immigrants' adaptation to their host society and their incorporation within it are indeed important issues, but the almost exclusive adoption of the assimilationist paradigm has meant that immigrant agency, particularly the ways in which immigrants have been able to have an impact on the United States, has been overlooked.

Anthony Orum (2002b, 6) argues that contemporary international migration takes place under circumstances very different from those of earlier European immigration, "[circumstances] that are likely to affect the capacity of immigrants, and ethnics to reshape American institutions." The fact that immigrants today hail from well-defined nation-states, and usually arrive in search of better economic opportunities, means that assimilation or "becoming American" is often not their goal. New transportation and communication technologies facilitate the maintenance of ethnicity by permitting immigrants to return to their home countries frequently and to stay in close and even instantaneous contact with friends and relatives. The Internet and satellite television enable one to quickly learn about events taking place in one's homeland, and to research one's identity, culture, and religion. These new technologies have also strengthened ethnicity by increasing the ability of ethnic groups to develop, mobilize, and move resources in support of their causes. Norms of multiculturalism that are in place today, moreover, often work to encourage the maintenance and cultivation of ethnicity.

Norms of multiculturalism, unlike those of assimilation, are based on a processual model of identity that views national culture as constantly in the making, shaped both by significant national and international events and, most important, by the backgrounds and actions of the people who make up the nation. Consequently, multiculturalism sees immigrants as agents who can and should recraft

national identity. This paradigm therefore provides immigrant groups with a justification for seeking and receiving national membership as valued contributors to
the pluralist fabric. At the same time, it also provides the rationale for such groups
to demand an end to demeaning portrayals and a lack of positive acknowledgment
by arguing that such treatment is discriminatory and harmful. Multiculturalism
not only has resulted in "grievances being addressed through the apparatus of the
state" (Berbrier 2002, 556) but has also permitted ethnic groups to demand fundamental changes in American society and culture (see Kurien 2004). In part II we
will see how Hindu American groups have been mobilizing on the basis of a pan-
Hindu identity to challenge and rectify their racial and social marginality in the
United States.

Religion, Ethnicity, and Multiculturalism in the United States

Tariq Modood (1998, 387) argues that there has been a "theoretical neglect of the role
of religion" in multicultural societies, which "reflects a bias of theorists that should
be urgently remedied." Although religion is often overlooked in the literature on
immigrants and multiculturalism, within the sociology of religion, it is now well
understood that religious institutions often play a central role in the process of
migration and ethnic formation, particularly for immigrants to the United States. As
the sociologist Stephen Warner (1993, 1058) points out, even in the assimilationist
era of American history, immigrants were able to hold on to their religious identity
and practices, since Americans have traditionally viewed religion as the most acceptable and nonthreatening basis for community formation and expression. Reflecting
on the patterns of European immigration to the United States at the turn of the
twentieth century, Will Herberg, in his now classic formulation, writes:

> Of the immigrant who came to this country it was expected that, sooner or later,
> either in his own person or through his children, he would give up virtually
> everything he had brought with him from the "old country"—his language, his
> nationality, his manner of life—and would adopt the ways of his new home.
> Within broad limits, however, his becoming an American did not involve his
> abandoning the old religion in favor of some native American substitute. Quite
> the contrary, not only was he expected to retain his old religion . . . but such was
> the shape of America that it was largely in and through his religion that he, or
> rather his children and grandchildren, found an identifiable place in American
> life. (Herberg 1960, 27–28)

Writing about contemporary immigrants from India and Pakistan, Raymond
Williams makes the same claim. "In the United States, religion is the social category
with clearest meaning and acceptance in the host society, so the emphasis on religious
affiliation is one of the strategies that allows the immigrant to maintain self identity
while simultaneously acquiring community acceptance" (Williams 1988, 29). The literature on immigrant religion indicates that religious organizations become the

means of maintaining and expressing ethnic identity not just for non-Christians like the Hindus but also for groups such as Chinese Christians (Yang 1999), Korean Christians (Hurh and Kim 1990; Min 1992), and Maya Catholics (Wellmeier 1998).

Since religion in immigrant contexts also defines and sustains ethnic life, religion and religious institutions become more important for immigrants. As Raymond Williams (1988, 11) notes, "immigrants are religious—by all counts more religious than they were before they left home—because religion is one of the important identity markers that helps them preserve individual self-awareness and cohesion in a group." Immigrant religion, as the repository of ethnicity, also becomes transformed in turn (Yang and Ebaugh 2001). Timothy Smith (1978, 1178) describes immigrant congregations as "not transplants of traditional institutions but communities of commitment and, therefore, arenas of change. Often founded by lay persons and always dependent on voluntary support, their structures, leadership and liturgy . . . [have] to be shaped to meet pressing human needs." He continues, "Pastors, rabbis, and lay officers respond . . . to this challenge to make religion more personal by reinterpreting scriptures and creeds to allow ancient observances to serve new purposes." In becoming primary ethnic and community centers for immigrants, religious institutions manifest increasing congregationalism and lay leadership (Ebaugh and Chafetz 2000; Warner 1993, 1994, 1998; Yang and Ebaugh 2001). As de facto ethnic institutions, most immigrant religious organizations also develop regional and national associations to represent their interests.

Because of the importance of religion and ethnicity in defining personal identity in the United States, immigrants find that they are frequently forced to explain the meaning of their beliefs and practices to American friends and coworkers and to their own children, a process that encourages the recasting of religious doctrines to fit in with American culture and society. Non-Christians often find themselves having to legitimize their religion by drawing parallels to Christian concepts and practices. Religious beliefs have to be simplified to be easily understandable, and summarized to be presented in "sound bite" versions. Immigrants may also face the burden of having to confront and correct the negative stereotypes and misrepresentations of their culture and religion that prevail in the wider society.

In addition, as religious organizations become the means to create community in the diaspora, bonds between coreligionists belonging to the same ethnic group are strengthened while, correspondingly, less interaction occurs between members of the same nationality belonging to different religious backgrounds. This reduced interaction is reinforced by the fact that different religious groups frequently develop definitions of nationality from their own perspective, resulting in differences in the construction of homeland culture and identity along religious lines (Min 1992; Yang 1999). Secular organizations representing the ethnic group often tend to be weak or are de facto religious organizations largely representing one (usually the dominant) religious group. For all of these reasons, the religious organizations of contemporary immigrants are vital crucibles of change where new identities, practices, and politics are forged (Ebaugh and Chafetz 2000; Warner and Wittner 1998; Yang 1999; Yang and Ebaugh 2001).

Hinduism in the United States

As is true for many other immigrant groups, religion seems to have become more important for Hindus as a marker of identity in the United States than it was for them in India. Many of the American Hindus I interviewed mentioned that they had become more religious since immigrating, when for the first time they had to think about the meaning of their religion and religious identity, something they could take for granted in India. Others, who claimed that they were not especially religious, nevertheless participated in Hindu organizations for social and cultural reasons, and "for the sake of the children." According to Arvind Rajagopal (1995), Hinduism also becomes important in the United States because identifying as Hindus allows the predominantly upper-caste immigrants to sidestep their problematic racial location. For similar reasons, Hinduism and "Indianness" also seem to become significant for the second generation during their coming-of-age process (Maira 2002).

Unlike most other established religions, Hinduism does not have a founder, an ecclesiastical structure of authority, or a single canonical text or commentary. Consequently Hinduism in India consists of an extraordinary array of practices, deities, texts, and schools of thought. Because of this diversity, the nature and character of Hinduism have varied greatly by region, caste, and historical period. It is also a religion that stresses orthopraxis over theological belief. For all these reasons, the average Hindu immigrant is often unable to explain the "meaning" of Hinduism and its "central tenets," something that she or he is repeatedly asked to do in the American context. As the scholar of religion Vasudha Narayanan, herself a Hindu, points out, "We are forced to articulate over and over again what it means to be a Hindu and an Indian to our friends and to our children, and one feels ill-equipped for the task. . . . [In India] one was never called upon to explain Deepavali or Sankaranti [Hindu festivals], and least of all, 'Hinduism' " (Narayanan 1992, 172).

A variety of Hindu organizations have developed in the United States to address the needs of immigrants and their children. Some of these groups seek to provide community and support, others focus on maintaining and reproducing Hindu traditions, and yet another group of organizations aims to unite, educate, and mobilize Hindu Indians of different backgrounds in support of Hindu interests. The five Hindu organizations on which I focus—satsangs (local worship groups), bala vihars (educational groups for children), temples, Hindu student organizations, and Hindu umbrella groups—represent this diversity. Leaders of these organizations have been trying to recast and reformulate Hinduism to make it a suitable vehicle for Hindu Americans to use in assimilating into multicultural America. Organizers have taken upon themselves the task of simplifying, standardizing, and codifying the religion to make it easier to understand, articulate, and practice. Hindu Web sites summarize the "central beliefs" of Hinduism or the "basic principles of Hindu dharma." Speakers at Hindu student organizations give talks about the "essence of the *Bhagavad Gita*," generally defined as the central Hindu text. In the process, an encapsulized, intellectual Hinduism is created, very different from the diversity of ritual practices and caste observances that are characteristic of everyday Hinduism in India.

Although turning to Hinduism and seeking to maintain Indian culture and values are ways of resisting Americanization, they are also particularly American ways of making the transition from immigrant sojourners to ethnic Americans for the first generation, and of expressing individualism and taking their place "at the multicultural table" for the second. Waters (1990) points out that unlike the symbolic, costless, and voluntarily chosen ethnicity of third- and fourth-generation white ethnics, the ethnicity of immigrants of color such as Indians shapes most aspects of their everyday life and behavior. The prevalence and acceptance of a multiculturalist discourse, however, allow room for groups like Indian Americans to use it to legitimize their own brand of ethnicity, although different in content and nature from that of most other Americans.

Following Steven Vertovec (2000), I make a distinction between "popular" and "official" Hinduism in the United States. By "popular" Hinduism, I mean the beliefs and practices of the mass of Hindus in the United States. For the most part, popular Hinduism focuses on re-creating, maintaining, and transmitting religion, culture, and values. "Official" Hinduism, in contrast, refers to the articulation of Hinduism by leaders of organizations that claim to speak for all Hindus. "Official" in this sense does not mean "governmental," but recognized or self-proclaimed representatives. "Official" Hinduism is most directly concerned with formulating what Hinduism and being Hindu mean, particularly in the American context. This book examines both popular and official Hinduism and the relationship between the two.

American Hindu Organizations
Organizations of Popular Hinduism

Bala vihars and satsangs have proliferated among the immigrant Hindu Indian community in the United States, but both are institutions that are not typical in India.[3] Bala vihars conduct religious education classes for children and are largely a diasporic invention. Satsang groups in the United States meet periodically (typically monthly, but occasionally more frequently) and conduct a *puja* (worship) generally led by lay leaders, consisting of prayers, chants, the singing of *bhajans* (devotional songs), and frequently a discussion of sacred texts. Satsangs are practiced by a few Hindu sects and by several Hindu groups in some parts of India, particularly in the north-central regions and Tamil Nadu State (Babb 1975; Singer 1972, 199–241; Weightman 1997, 290). Middle- and upper-middle-class housewives in urban India may attend bhajan sessions on a fairly regular basis. Local worship groups involving the whole family of the type that exist in the United States (and in other diasporic contexts), however, are not a traditional form of Indian Hinduism.[4] Group religious activity is not generally a part of Hinduism in India except during temple and village festivals. In India, Hindus worship largely as families or as individuals, in their homes or in a temple.[5] This practice continues in the diaspora as well. Because Hindu immigrants often feel the need for community, many of them also develop congregational forms of worship and learning. Even temples frequently adopt a congregational format, offering special Saturday or Sunday puja and bhajan "worship services." A survey by Pyong Gap Min of Hindu Indians in Queens, New York, indicated that 53 percent participated in a "religious congregation" at least once a month (Min 2000), a large number considering that the practice is not common in India.

Hindu Americans whom I interviewed identified several interrelated reasons for the development of congregationalism. Immigration is often a profoundly disruptive experience. Indian immigrants to the United States are uprooted from the social and cultural context that they are familiar with and thrust into a radically new and alien environment. Although quick to appreciate the economic and educational benefits they obtain through immigration, most Indian immigrants also tend to be highly critical of many aspects of American culture and society, which they believe is characterized by unstable and uncaring families, lack of close community ties, sexual promiscuity, violence, drug and alcohol abuse, and teenage delinquency. Immigration generally results in the isolation of the family from relatives and friends who would have provided social support at home. Hindu immigrants to the United States also face negative racial, cultural, and religious stereotypes. For all of these reasons, re-creating an Indian community and maintaining ethnic traditions become very important. Indians are also the most dispersed new immigrant group in the United States (Portes and Rumbaut 1990, 39), and thus in most cases, the only way they can meet other Indians on any regular basis is through attending the meetings and functions of religious organizations.

The desire to teach children Indian culture and values is an important reason for the formation of satsangs and the primary reason for the formation of bala vihars. In India, children "breathe in the values of Hindu life" (Fenton 1988, 127). In the United States, in contrast, parents realize that unless they make a deliberate effort, children will never learn what being Hindu or Indian means. Many Indian parents, however, find themselves unable to explain a range of Hindu customs, practices, and doctrines. Bala vihars and satsangs capitalize on the expertise of knowledgeable people in the community and help children and parents cope with many of the issues they confront in their everyday lives.

Hindu student organizations are another diasporic invention, for many of the reasons already mentioned. As several of the young people I talked to indicated, it is often in college that issues of identity become important, particularly for minority groups. Faced with multiculturalism on campus, minority students have to be able to articulate "who we are and what we are about." Hindu student organizations provide the second generation (and sometimes Hindu students from India) a forum where they can discuss these issues in a safe space. Now prevalent in many of the universities and college campuses around the country, they are the counterparts of the typical campus religious organizations of other groups and denominations. They generally meet at least a few times a semester (some of the more active organizations meet weekly) for discussions about various Hindu and Indian concepts and practices, presentations on various aspects of the religion by knowledgeable Hindus in the community, and celebrations of Hindu festivals. Hindu student groups also organize periodic trips to local temples and other Hindu venues. Many Hindu student organizations are campus specific, but there is also a national organization, the Hindu Student Council, which was formed in 1990; as of 2005, it had over seventy active chapters nationwide. Most of these chapters are located in the leading universities of the country. The Hindu Student Council runs the Global Hindu Electronic Network (GHEN), "the largest and most frequently visited site on Hinduism available on the web" (www.hscnet.org/news.shtml), with links to over a thousand other Hindu Web sites.[6] The council also supports the activist group American Hindus against Defamation in its protests against the commercialization and misuse of Hindu deities, icons, and texts by American businesses and the advertising and entertainment industries.

Hindu temples have now mushroomed all over the United States. While temples are of course widespread in India, American Hindu temples manifest unique features. Most tend to be more "ecumenical" (Williams 1992, 239) than temples in India. In India, many temples are devoted to a single regional deity, and often the local language is used for rituals and worship. Because of the enormous expense involved, usually Hindu groups from different backgrounds have to unite to build a temple in the United States. Thus American Hindu temples commonly house only the major Indian deities, and enshrine deities from several, and sometimes opposing, traditions. Rituals and worship in ecumenical temples are generally conducted in Sanskrit and, in the American context where the meaning of religious practice becomes important, frequently explained in Hindi or English for the benefit of the eclectic audience. As religious institutions become de facto ethnic institutions, American temples also become cultural and social centers for Hindu Americans and perform a range of services not performed by temples in India. Besides classes on Hinduism, many temples also offer Indian language, music and dance classes, and have a central hall where dance, drama, and music recitals can be held.

Organizations of Official Hinduism

Several Hindu umbrella organizations have sprung up in the United States. In India there are two major interlinked Hindu umbrella groups—the Rashtriya Swayamsevak Sangh (RSS, or National Volunteer Corps) and the Vishwa Hindu Parishad (VHP, or World Hindu Council)—along with militant activist groups like the Bajrang Dal, and a political party, the Bharatiya Janata Party (BJP, or Indian People's Party), all known collectively as the Sangh Parivar, or the family of (Hindu) organizations, with branches all over the country. In the United States, however, a greater number and variety of such groups exist.

The VHP of America (VHPA), a branch of the VHP in India, was the earliest Hindu American umbrella organization and was founded in 1969 on the East Coast. It now has chapters in more than forty states (Rajagopal 2000, 473). Although the VHP in India is militantly nationalistic (see its Web site at www.vhp.org), the VHPA has officially remained devoted to promoting Hinduism and pursuing cultural and social activities (see its Web site at www.vhp-america.org). This focus is perhaps in part because it is registered in the United States as a nonprofit, tax-exempt religious organization, which is therefore forbidden to pursue political activities. The VHPA claims that its central focus is to help the Hindu American family to face the challenges of living in the United States.[7] One of the VHPA's founding members and longtime president, Mahesh Mehta, indicated in an interview with the sociologist Arvind Rajagopal that the VHPA was able to provide parents and children with information about their religion and values, so that parents could socialize their children appropriately and the children would not "go astray" (Rajagopal 2000, 474). The VHPA organizes bala vihars and youth camps under its auspices throughout the country. It also founded the Hindu Student Council, as its student wing, in 1990.[8] Unofficially, VHP members and activists are networked with a range of Hindu organizations and groups around the country and thus, as Rajagopal points out, "its influence extends well beyond its enrollment" (2000, 473).

In addition to organizations like the VHPA, there is an organization parallel to the RSS, the Hindu Swayamsevak Sangh (HSS), with chapters around United States, and there are also support groups for the BJP. All of these are branches of Hindu organizations based in India. What is different about the American context is that there are also several regional Hindu groups, such as the Federation of Hindu Associations (FHA) in Southern California, which are not directly under the control of the Sangh Parivar. Typically they consist of a small core of dedicated, largely male activists who disseminate their message through speeches and writings, conferences, and Hindu celebrations. Claiming to represent Indian American Hindus, umbrella organizations act as the watchdogs and defenders of Hinduism and have been involved in campaigns against negative portrayals of Hindu deities, icons, and music. They also sponsor the visits of politicians and Hindu leaders from India, meet with American public officials to discuss concerns of Indian Americans, and frequently raise money to support causes in India.

DATA AND METHODS

As I have indicated, Hindu organizations provide Hindu Indians the structure to develop a Hindu American community and identity and to make the transition from sojourners to ethnic Americans. To understand this process, I decided to focus on Hindu organizations rather than on a random group of Hindu Americans. As part of this project I conducted ethnographic research over a period of eight years in the 1990s and the early 2000s in twelve Hindu organizations, representing the five major categories of Hindu Indian American organizations: satsangs, bala vihars, temples, Hindu student organizations, and Hindu umbrella groups. I conducted a detailed case study of one organization and supplementary studies of at least one other within each of these five categories. All of the five primary case studies and some of the supplementary ones were of organizations in Southern California. By studying different Hindu American organizations in one geographical region, I was able to see the interconnections among them and the impact such organizations and their leaders had on the Indian American community and the wider society in the area. I also carried out studies of some Hindu organizations in New Jersey. In addition to participating in the activities and programs of the organizations, I conducted detailed interviews with leaders and many of the members (over 120 first- and second-generation Hindu Indian Americans in all), most of the time at their homes. I supplemented my fieldwork with a few months of research in India in 1997, studying the connections between Hindu American organizations and Indian groups. To maintain confidentiality, I use pseudonyms for the organizations and the members (except when they are easily recognizable institutions or public figures), change some identifying details, and also do not reveal exactly when my research on a particular organization was conducted.

In addition to this ethnographic research, I have also been following the activities of the Hindu Indian community around the country for the past ten years by reading several Indian American newspapers and the international magazine *Hinduism Today*, published from Hawaii. From the year 2000 on, the Internet became a major site of Hindu American activity, adding a new and important source of data. The composition and dynamics of virtual communities were often different from the "real" communities I had studied until then. The anonymity of the Internet (most participants wrote under fictitious names) also meant that the substance and tone of cyberspace discussions varied considerably from those conducted publicly.

Indian Americans are one of the wealthiest and most highly educated groups in the United States, with large numbers working in IT (information technology) industries. Given this educational and occupational profile, it is not surprising that this group has such a large presence on the Internet. The Internet makes it possible for Indian Americans to disseminate information around the country and the world within a matter of minutes and provides a forum for discussion, agenda planning, group mobilization, and the rapid formulation of responses. Through the Internet even isolated individuals and small groups can be closely networked to provide support for people and issues that are not mainstream. I joined several Internet discussion groups devoted to Hindu and Indian topics in 2000 and kept up with the daily discussions on one until it closed down in 2003 and on three others until 2005. I checked the discussions on three more discussion groups sporadically over the same period. The four discussion groups that I focused on had 150 to 900 members each, and five to fifty messages were posted on these boards every day. The postings included news items and articles from a variety of sources (newspapers, magazines, other Internet sites, books); commentary and discussion about past, current, or upcoming events and member e-mails; and reports on actions individuals and groups had taken or were going to take in support of Hindu and Indian causes (copies of letters sent to newspapers, politicians, and other organizations, speeches given or to be given, and meetings and conferences that were being organized). These discussions informed my understanding of the concerns and activities of Hindus in the United States. Over the same period I also monitored two popular Internet magazines for the Indian diaspora—*Sulekha.com* (hosted in the United States) and *Rediff.com*—and periodically examined several major Internet Web sites devoted to Hinduism. I draw on several articles posted on these Web sites to make my arguments, particularly about official Hinduism, in subsequent chapters.

My research thus provided me with information about the practices and interpretations of Hinduism at four different sites or analytical levels—the household, local Hindu associations (of both the immigrant and the second generation), regional and national Hindu umbrella organizations, and finally the Internet. Migration, settlement, and ethnic formation result in distinct developments at the four different levels, which are interrelated in complicated and contradictory ways. The contradictions are manifested in the construction and practice of American Hinduism.

Plan of the Book

This book is divided into three parts: chapters 2–5 focus on popular Hinduism, chapters 6–9 focus on official Hinduism, and chapters 10 and 11 examine the relationship between the two. To set the context for the emergence of an American Hinduism, chapter 2 provides a brief introduction to the religion, its history and reformulation under British colonialism, and concludes with a discussion of everyday Hindu ideas and practices in India. Because Hinduism is such an ancient, diverse, and complex religion, the summary presented here is of necessity simplified. Scholars of Hinduism and others who are familiar with the religion should therefore feel free to skip this chapter. In chapter 3, I turn to an overview of Hinduism in the United States, focusing particularly on the history of the religion in America and the development of Hindu American communities and institutions over the last few decades. This chapter provides a template for the case studies in the rest of the book.

Typically, satsangs and bala vihars are the first types of Hindu organizations that are formed in a community. A case study of these two organizations is presented in chapter 4. Relying largely on ethnographic vignettes, the chapter paints a picture of the social and religious activities of these local associations. It shows why these associations were founded, how these organizations become the means to develop an ethnic community and identity and reproduce professional status, and the implications of these developments. The chapter also demonstrates the way in which the contradictory effect of immigration on gender relations is reflected in the gendered practices and interpretations of Hinduism of such groups.

The next stage in the institutionalization of Hinduism is the building of temples. Chapter 5 provides a case study of an ecumenical temple, enshrining a variety of deities, and a sectarian temple, focusing on one deity and tradition. I describe the formation, organization, and patterns of worship in the two temples, the importance of the temple for the devotees, and some of the differences between the two types of temples. The case studies are located within the larger literature on temples in India and the United States. Issues discussed include some of the compromises and modifications the American setting required in the construction of the temple, organizational structure, and practices; the differences in the role of the temple, its board members, priests, and volunteers when compared with similar temples in India; and the relationship between these temples and the "home" temple and denomination.

Part II, the section on official Hinduism, begins with chapter 6, which provides an overview of the development of official Hinduism in India. Organized Hinduism emerged with the Hindu reform movement and subsequent Hindu nationalist or Hindutva movements in the colonial period. In the postcolonial period Hindu nationalism resurged with the founding of new organizations and agendas. Some of the Hindu umbrella groups that were formed in the colonial and postcolonial periods have become spokespersons for Hindu interests in contemporary India. Chapter 7 focuses on the development, platform, and activities of American Hindu umbrella groups. We will see that while a great deal of overlap between official Hinduism in India and the United States is evident, differences also exist as American Hindu leaders locate Hinduism within the multicultural American context. This theme is further expanded in chapters 8 and 9, which detail some of the issues around which Hindu American leaders have mobilized.

The conventional historiography of India and of Hinduism is a hot-button issue that has become a central focus of Hindu umbrella organizations both in India and in the United States. Practically everything about the history of India is now contested by spokespersons for Hindu groups, and their critiques are disseminated widely within Hindu communities in the United States and around the world through the Internet. In chapter 8 I focus on the issues that have become controversial and discuss the competing versions of Indian history provided by most mainstream historians, on the one hand, and by revisionist Hinducentric scholars, on the other. Here again, I have of necessity compressed and somewhat simplified the data and the arguments. This chapter also shows the ways in which Hindu Americans are trying to rewrite the history of India and of Hinduism. Readers who are not particularly interested in the details of Indian history may want just to glance through the chapter at the outset and then return to it if they feel they need more background to understand some particular controversy discussed in subsequent pages. The revisionist historical enterprise has provided the impetus for a variety of Hindu American mobilizations over the past decade and for the emergence of Hindu Americans in the American public sphere. Chapter 9 examines these activities, the ways in which these mobilizations have been shaped by American multiculturalism, and the difference between the strategies of Hindu groups before and after September 11, 2001. The role of Hindu nationalism and of the Internet in this mobilization will also be discussed.

To what extent has the definition of Hinduism, Hindu history, and Hindu interests by Hindu American spokespersons affected the average Hindu American? How has it affected the maintenance, re-creation, and transmission of Hinduism by Hindu American groups and organizations? These topics are discussed in part III. Chapter 10 provides a case study of a Hindu Student Council chapter consisting almost entirely of second-generation Hindu Americans. Relying largely on direct quotes from interviews, weekly discussion meetings, and the Internet forum, this piece of the book examines the extent to which the Hindutva ideology has penetrated the chapter and the ways in which this ideology results in cleavages and tensions between supporters and more moderate members. The effect of official Hindu ideologies on the second generation gives us a glimpse into the future of American Hinduism. This chapter also discusses the struggles of the second generation with issues of identity and race and the ways in which these struggles brought many of them to Hinduism and the HSC; the reformulations of Hinduism of the second generation; gender differences in participation and viewpoints regarding Hinduism and Indian culture; and finally, the goals of these youth for India, Indian Americans, and Hinduism. Chapter 11 provides an overview of the relationship between popular Hinduism and official Hinduism in the United States, the contradictions embedded in American Hinduism, and the interrelationship between multiculturalism, ethnic mobilization, and ethnic nationalism.

PART I

Popular Hinduism

CHAPTER 2

Hinduism in India

Although many of the beliefs and practices of Hinduism are at least several thousand years old (exactly how ancient is a controversial matter), the term "Hinduism" was only introduced in the late eighteenth century (Sweetman 2001, 219). The British colonialists who coined the term used it to refer to the religion and culture of the non-Islamic people of the Indian subcontinent, the "Hindus." The term "Hindu" had first been used by Persians (at least as early as 500 B.C.E.) to designate the people living in the region of the river Indus and had subsequently been adopted by the Muslim rulers of India (von Stietencron 1989, 12). Thus "Hindu" at that time really meant "Indian." By about the fourteenth century, as the number of Muslim converts in the region increased, "Hindu" came to mean "non-Muslim Indian" (Narayanan 1996, 14), a usage that was taken over by the British. Frykenberg (1989, 31) notes, however, that the British later used the term more narrowly to refer to the culture and religion of Vedic origin, interpreted and propagated by the Brahmins. As we shall see, this narrower use of the term gave rise to attempts by different groups, from the colonial period up to the present, to argue that they were not "Hindu."

INTRODUCTION TO HINDUISM
Is Hinduism a Religion?

Because Hinduism does not have a unified belief system or canonical text, in recent years some have disputed whether Hinduism can even be called a religion. Two types of arguments are put forth to make this claim. There are scholars (e.g., Balagangadhara 1994) and lay Hindus who argue that Hinduism is not a "religion" in the Western (particularly the Christian) sense of the term. By this, they mean variously that there is no single belief system that is accepted as "true," that correct practice (i.e., the meticulous observance of rituals) is more important than theology, or that Hinduism is a "way of life" (i.e., that it is difficult to make the distinction between sacred and secular aspects of life). Support for this position is provided by the fact that Hindus do not even have an indigenous term that is the equivalent of "religion." The closest equivalent is the term *dharma*, which means righteousness, duty, or a moral and social obligation. So some Hindus prefer to use the term Sanatana Dharma (eternal, universal dharma) or Hindu dharma to refer to the panoply of their beliefs and practices.

The second objection comes from scholars like Heinrich von Stietencron (1989, 20), who question whether there is one unitary religion called "Hinduism" at all, arguing instead that "what we call 'Hinduism' is a geographically defined group of distinct but related religions." Other scholars, including Robert Frykenberg (1989) and Daniel Gold (1991), agree that in precolonial times there was never a "single 'Hinduism'... for all of India" (Frykenberg 1989, 20), but claim that during the colonial period, Hindu revivalist movements developed and in the process created "modern" and "organized" pan-Indian versions of Hinduism. According to this perspective, the contemporary Hindu nationalist Hindutva movement is a continuation of such an effort (Frykenberg 1993; Gold 1991).

Definitions of Hinduism

Nothing can be said definitively about Hinduism that is not contradicted by the beliefs and practices of one or more of the major groups that are officially classified as "Hindu." Many Hindus believe in the sanctity of the Vedas, described below, but not all. Some believe in other texts either exclusively, or believe that they are equivalent to the Vedas. Most Hindus believe in one or more deities. The primary deities worshipped by Hindus are the male deities Vishnu or Shiva, or a mother Goddess, Devi. Each of these deities in turn has multiple names and forms. But some sects reject the conception of a theistic being altogether. Hinduism is often described as polytheistic, because several deities are revered and worshipped within the tradition. But many Hindus say that all of these deities are manifestations of a supreme being. Many Hindus also believe in a transcendent God who is immanent within all living beings. Most Hindu traditions believe in reincarnation, which is determined by how a person carries out his or her dharma (prescribed duties) in a previous life, and in a concept of salvation, which is liberation from the endless cycle of rebirth *(samsara)*. However, these beliefs are not exclusively Hindu, since they are shared by Buddhism and Jainism. I will return to a more detailed discussion of Hindu theology later in the chapter.

Who Is a Hindu?

Difficulties with the concept and definition of Hinduism also lead to problems in defining who is a Hindu. Official definitions of Hinduism are often negative, defining Hindus as Indians who are not members of other religions. For instance, India's Hindu Family Act defines a Hindu as anyone who belongs to one of the Hindu denominations and any other person living in India who is not a "Muslim, Christian, Parsi, or Jew by religion" (Narayanan 1996, 16). According to the Hindutva perspective, Hindus are those whose beliefs and practices are based on religious and spiritual principles that originated in the Indian subcontinent. The key factor here is whether the religion is indigenous or not, and thus the term Hindu includes groups like the Sikhs, Buddhists, and Jains but excludes Muslims and Christians. Many of the groups classified as Hindu according to the above definitions have challenged this designation, and thus Sikhs, Buddhists, and Jains frequently resist being labeled Hindu. From the colonial period on, several sects have also gone to court to argue against being classified as Hindu, often to benefit from affirmative action provisions for minority religions. Most official definitions include former Untouchable or slave castes and tribal groups under the Hindu umbrella, even though these groups were traditionally considered to be outside the pale of the Hindu *varna* system of caste categories (Brahmins or priests, Kshatriyas or warriors, Vaishyas or merchants, and Sudras or service workers). In the past few decades, several prominent Dalit (members of former Untouchable castes) leaders have stated publicly that they do not consider themselves Hindu (e.g., Iliah 1996) and have been trying to radicalize their constituencies on this basis. It must be noted that the concept of Hinduism as the religion of the majority of Indians can only be sustained if Dalits and tribal groups are counted as Hindu.

Sruti, or Primary Scripture. Hindu texts are vast and very ancient. There are two main types of texts—*sruti,* or "revealed" scripture (which is considered to be authorless and thus to enshrine eternal truth) and *smriti,* or "remembered" scripture (human authorship is acknowledged here, but these are still considered to be inspired texts). The earliest texts of the sruti literature are the Vedas. There are four collections of Vedas—the Rig, Sama, Yajur, and Atharva—each divided roughly chronologically into four sections: (1) Vedic samhitas (containing hymns); (2) Brahmanas (containing rituals and prayers to guide priests); (3) Aranyakas (treatises concerning worship and meditation); and (4) *Upanishads* (containing mystical and philosophical teachings). Sometimes the term *Veda* is used in a restricted sense to refer only to the four Vedic samhitas. In other contexts, the term Veda refers to all the texts in the Vedic corpus described above. Most of this vast corpus has not been translated into English or any other Western language.

The earliest and most important of the Vedas is the *Rig Veda.* The Rig Vedic samhita consists of 1,028 hymns to various deities, organized in ten books, each composed by sages of different families. It was compiled over a period of several hundred years and was transmitted through oral tradition for up to three thousand years before it was written down (Flood 1996, 39). The Rig Vedic samhita had elaborate rules of memorization to ensure that it was transmitted exactly, even down to the pronunciation, accent, rhythm, and pitch. It was believed that a single mispronounced syllable could have dire consequences. Each of the other Vedas also had samhita texts that were passed down through oral tradition. Different priestly schools affiliated with each of the four Vedic collections preserved and transmitted the texts in their particular tradition. Much of Hindu philosophy and doctrines originate in the *Upanishads,* which are the last section of the Vedas. Thus the *Upanishads* are also called Vedanta, the end of the Veda.

In addition to the Vedas, there are the Agamas (scriptures), a class of literature considered as authoritative and as ancient as the Vedas by Hindus who follow

Vaishnavism (the tradition which worships Lord Vishnu as the primary deity), Shaivism (the tradition which worships Lord Shiva), and Shaktism (those traditions that worship Devi, the mother goddess). The majority of Hindus fall into one of these three traditions. Each of these traditions has its own type of Agama or scripture.

Smriti, or Secondary Scriptures. Over the ages, sages and saints have tried to analyze, explain, and expand on Vedic ideas in smriti, or secondary scriptures. There are several types of smriti, the most important being the two great epics—the *Mahabarata* and the *Ramayana*—the Puranas, or ancient stories, and the Dharma Shastras, or the codes of law. One of the best-known and most popular Hindu texts, the *Bhagavad Gita,* is a portion of the *Mahabarata* that is frequently printed separately. There are large numbers of Puranas and several types of Dharma Shastras. All of these smriti texts were originally written in Sanskrit, but as in the case of the epics, vernacular versions also exist. In addition to these four types of texts, there are also some later vernacular texts, such as the *Tiruvaymoli* in Tamil, which many Tamilian Hindus believe to be equivalent in status to the Sanskrit Vedas (Carman and Narayanan 1989). These Hindus believe that the saints who composed the *Tiruvaymoli* distilled the truth from the Vedas and made it accessible to the ordinary person. There are also other types of vernacular smriti texts in several other Indian languages.

THE DEVELOPMENT OF HINDU THEOLOGY

The history of Hinduism has become an important issue in the current Hindu renaissance, and of particular importance to Hindu Americans. Practically every aspect of that history is now contested. This section provides only a quick overview of some of the main stages in the theological development of Hinduism. Issues regarding the history of Hinduism that have become prominent or particularly controversial within Hindu American groups are discussed in chapter 8. The development of Hindu reform movements and the emergence of Hindu nationalism beginning in the colonial period are discussed in chapter 6.

The Vedic Period (Antiquity–1000 B.C.E.)

One of the best-known early hymns of the Rig Vedic samhitas, "The Hymn of Creation" (*Rig Veda* 10.129), demonstrates the conceptual sophistication and tolerance for ambiguity of the Vedic people.

> There was neither non-existence nor existence then; there was neither the realm of space nor the sky which is beyond. What stirred? Where? In whose protection? Was there water, bottomlessly deep?
>
> There was neither death nor immortality then. There was no distinguishing sign of night nor of day. That one breathed, windless, by its own impulse. Other than that there was nothing beyond.

Darkness was hidden by darkness in the beginning; with no distinguishing sign, all this was water. The life force that was covered with emptiness, that one arose through the power of heat. . . .

Who really knows? Who will here proclaim it? Whence was it produced? Whence is this creation? The gods came afterwards, with the creation of this universe. Who then knows whence it has arisen?

Whence this creation has arisen—perhaps it formed itself, or perhaps it did not—the one who looks down on it, in the highest heaven, only he knows—or perhaps he does not know. (O'Flaherty 1981, 25–26)

However, most of the Rig Vedic samhitas consist of hymns that praise the various deities or divine powers *(devas)* and were used during the performance of religious rites. The central religious practice described in the *Rig Veda* is the propitiation of the deities by the ritual of fire sacrifice, conducted by a priestly class. More common than the sacrifice of animals was the offering of milk, ghee (clarified butter), and grains into the sacred fire. The sacrificial rites were complex, involving several categories of priests.[1] There were also domestic and life-cycle rites, to be performed by the householder in the home.

The next stage in the development of Vedic religion can be seen in the Brahmanas, which emphasize ritualism. Weightman (1997, 266) observes that "no longer was it the response of the devas to human praise and offerings that ensured the welfare of man and the order of the cosmos, but rather the correct performance of the sacrifice itself." The importance of the *mantra*, or chant, that is performed during the sacrifice is also emphasized. According to Klostermaier (1989, 71), "a mantra need not have an intelligible word meaning; it is the sound equivalent of some reality and, at the same time, the medium by which this otherwise transcendent reality is reached. OM [the most powerful of all mantras] is not a concept of something but the ... Supreme Being in the form of sound." *Vac*, or speech, is addressed as a (female) deity in the *Rig Veda*, and attains a magical power in the Brahmanas, which were composed at least a few centuries before the Christian era.[2] The one great cosmic power comes to be identified as Brahman in these texts. The practices of meditation and asceticism are referred to in the Brahmanas and also in the Aranyakas.

The final stage of the Vedic religion can be found in the *Upanishads*. Here the emphasis is away from the ritualism of the Brahmanas, toward a personal and mystical experience of the Brahman. Most important, the doctrine of samsara or the cycle of birth and rebirth that individual souls go through until they attain *moksha*, or liberation, by merging with the Brahman, and the concept that one's *karma*, or actions in the previous life, affect the present life are developed. The *Upanishads* also discuss techniques of yoga and some of the magic powers obtained by the yogi.

The Period of Classical Hinduism (500 B.C.E. to 500 C.E.)

It is in the period of classical Hinduism that the codification of Hindu dharma took place. Vedic literature began to be described as sruti, or eternal truths that were revealed, in distinction to the later literature, which was described as smriti—historical texts that were remembered or passed down. Allegiance to the Vedas became the touchstone of orthodox Hinduism, in opposition to newly formed sects like Buddhism and Jainism, which rejected the authority of the Vedas and were therefore treated as heterodox (Hiltebeitel 1987, 342; Weightman 1997, 262). Both Hinduism and the heterodox traditions developed in mutual interaction with each other. Buddhism and Jainism evolved out of ideas and practices in the Upanishads such as the doctrine of karma and samsara and practices such as meditation and asceticism. At the same time, Hinduism reformed in response to the criticisms of the two traditions against the caste system as well as the excessive spending and cruelty of brahminical animal sacrifices. An important corpus of smriti texts from this period were the Dharma Sutras and the Dharma Shastras, the religious law books that prescribed the duties of Hindus. The central concept of these texts was the notion of *varnashrama dharma*, or the dharma, the moral code governing the behavior of men of the four varnas in the four stages of life (*ashramas*)—the celibate student, the householder, the forest dweller, and the renunciant. This was of course an ideal-type model; few individuals actually relinquished their householder status to become hermits and even the texts exalted the householder stage, because it supported the other three. What is of importance to note is the context-sensitivity of dharma, since a person's duties varied according to sex, varna, and stage of life (in addition to other factors, such as family and region). The most famous and earliest of the Dharma Shastras was the *Manusmriti*, or the *Manava Dharma Shastra*. Manu, the law giver, has come to be known for his emphasis on the importance of maintaining caste hierarchy and male supremacy. Other codes of laws existed, however (in fact, it was the British who "discovered" and canonized the *Manusmriti*), and as is true today, there was always a disjuncture between the brahminic, androcentric ideals enshrined in the texts and everyday practice (Narayanan 1999a, 34–36).

Two male deities, Vishnu and Shiva, who were relatively unimportant in the Vedas, became preeminent in this period. Vishnu is depicted as a benevolent god, who descends to the world in various incarnations when dharma has disappeared, in order to restore righteousness. Conventionally ten such *avatars* (incarnations) are depicted. The earlier ones are in the form of animals—the Fish, the Boar, and the Tortoise, followed by the Man-lion and the Dwarf. The next four incarnations took human male form, the most important of whom are Krishna and Rama, the heroes of the epics. The last incarnation is the only one in the future. Kalki, the White Horse, is said to descend at the end of the *kali yuga* (evil age) to liberate the world from immorality.

Shiva is a more complex deity with both benevolent and fearsome attributes. He embodies the unity of opposites—ascetic and householder, celibate yogi and seducer, male and female, the Lord of the (cosmic) Dance who creates, maintains, and destroys the cosmos. He is represented iconographically in all of these forms, but most commonly as the *linga*, a cylindrical stone, often set within a *yoni*, a hollowed stone. The linga represents a phallus within a vulva (the yoni), symbolizing the union of Shiva, the male principle, with his dynamic energy, Shakti, conceptualized as a female principle.[3]

A mother goddess deity also emerges as the focus of an independent tradition of worship toward the end of this period. Both Vishnu and Shiva have their own consorts (Lakshmi and Parvati, respectively), who are worshipped along with their husbands. But for the Shakta traditions, the Devi, or the mother goddess, is the central power in the universe. In the contemporary period, the Shaktas are strongest in eastern India, particularly in Bengal, where the goddess in the form of Durga is worshipped in her powerful but benevolent form and as Kali in her violent and bloodthirsty manifestation. Innumerable local or village goddesses are also identified with the mother goddess.

Although the three traditions of Vaishnavism, Shaivism, and Shakta are often described as independent and even monotheistic from roughly medieval times, the texts from the classical period often represent their deities as interacting and complementary. Another theological development in the classical period was the formulation of the concept of *bhakti,* or loving devotion to the deity of one's choice *(ishtadevata)* as the most effective path to salvation (compared with the other two paths of seeking enlightenment through meditation and asceticism or through the punctilious performance of religious rites). This formulation, first enunciated by Lord Krishna in the *Gita,* subsequently became central to the belief and practice of many Hindu traditions. A theological shift also took place in the understanding and portrayal of deities, represented by the shift from traditional Vedic sacrifices, which were based on the notion that the gods could be controlled by the proper performance of rituals, to the puja (a ritual honoring the deity by offering gifts of flowers and fruits), which acknowledged that the gods were in control and could only be supplicated by humans (Stein 1998, 85). Temple building and worship were introduced in this period.

Itihasa is the collective name for the two great epics, the *Mahabharata* and the *Ramayana,* which were composed in the classical period, although they referred to events that took place much earlier. The term *itihasa* has no direct English equivalent and refers to the English concepts of both "myth" and "history." The epics contain characters who are humans as well as characters who are gods and demons, so it is unlikely that all of the incidents took place as described. But it is possible that some of the characters and events referred to real people and occurrences, and that the stories were subsequently embellished and elaborated. As we will see later, the question of whether the epics describe actual historical people and events is an issue that has become controversial today.

At the heart of the *Mahabharata,* an epic poem comprising over 100,000 verses, is the story of the war between the five Pandava brothers (aided by Krishna), and their cousins, the hundred Kauravas. It was probably compiled over several centuries from around 500 B.C.E. By the medieval period, there were two major recensions of the text, one northern and one southern. There are also several regional variations of the text (Flood 1996, 105). In addition, a supplement to the epic, the *Harivamsa,* deals with the life of Krishna.

The much loved text the *Bhagavad Gita* is part of the *Mahabharata* and occurs on the eve of the battle, when Arjuna, one of the Pandavas, has deep misgivings about having to kill his relatives. Lord Krishna tells him that even if the body is killed, the soul is eternal and moves from body to body in a series of reincarnations. He therefore counsels Arjuna to follow his duty *(svadharma)* as a warrior, since, "there is no greater good for a warrior than to fight a righteous war" (*Gita* 2:31). Krishna also emphasizes the importance of performing one's duty with detachment from the end result. "Set thy heart upon thy work, but never on its reward" (*Gita* 2:47).

The *Ramayana* tells the story of Rama, heir-apparent to Dasaratha, the king of Ayodhya. Dasaratha is forced to send his beloved son into exile in the forest for fourteen years because of an earlier promise he had made to his second wife (to grant her any two wishes). As an obedient son, Rama agrees to go without protest. He is accompanied by his loyal wife, Sita, and brother, Lakshmana. While in the forest, Sita is abducted by Ravana, the demon king of Sri Lanka. With the help of Hanuman, the monkey-general, whose army builds a bridge between India and Sri Lanka, Rama rescues Sita. When the fourteen years of exile are over, Rama returns to Ayodhya and is crowned king. But because the people of Ayodhya suspect that Sita might have lost her virtue while in the custody of Ravana, Rama banishes her to the forest to fulfill his duty to his subjects. This is despite the fact that Sita has proved to Rama's satisfaction (by going through a fire ordeal at his request) that she had remained faithful. Sita gives birth to twin boys in the forest and when Rama finds out about them, he wants to take back Sita along with his sons. But Sita demonstrates her purity in a final test of virtue (she asks the mother earth to receive her to prove her faithfulness to Rama), and disappears into the earth.

The story of *Ramayana* is a favorite in India, since Rama is seen as the ideal man and Sita, the ideal woman. Rama is obedient and brave and fulfills his ethical responsibilities, while Sita is devoted to her husband, while also being strong in herself. The rule of Rama *(Ram-raj)* is believed to have restored justice, order, and prosperity to his kingdom and is frequently invoked by Hindus as a model for contemporary governance. While the Sanskrit version attributed to Valmiki is considered by many to be the oldest and most widespread version of the *Ramayana*, many vernacular traditions exist. The vernacular renditions differ in significant ways from one another and from the Valmiki text. Versions of the story are also found in the Buddhist Jataka tales and in Jain texts (Thapar 2000b, 1061–1063).

The Puranas, which began to be composed during this period, are a vast compendium of texts dealing with a variety of topics such as the genealogies of deities and kings, narratives about their exploits, cosmology, and ritual. There are eighteen major Puranas. Those that have Vishnu as the central deity are called *Vaishnava Puranas* and those that have Shiva as the central deity are called *Shaiva Puranas*. The *Markandeya Purana* has Devi as the central deity. There are also Puranas that belong to other traditions. This collection of texts, the *Itihasa-Purana*, is often called the fifth Veda, because of the central place it plays in popular Hinduism.

The Medieval Period (600–1500 C.E.)

During the medieval period, the three theistic traditions (Vaishnavism, Shaivism, and Shaktism) developed further, and each produced its own body of literature (the *Vaishnava Samhitas*, the *Shaiva Agamas*, and the *Shakta Tantras*). Hindu philosophy obtained a major fillip with the articulation of the doctrine of Advaita, or nonduality, by Sankara;[4] Vishishtadvaita, or differentiated nonduality, by Ramanuja;[5] and Dvaita, or dualism, by Madhva.

The bhakti tradition developed and flourished in this period. Tamil devotional poets belonging to the Vaishnava and Shaiva traditions (the Alvars and Nayanars) expressed their passionate devotion to their deity in hymns composed in Tamil. Similarly, several bhakti sects sprang up in different parts of the country to worship Krishna, Rama, and the goddess with hymns and poetry in vernacular languages. *Sants* (saints) like Kabir, Raidas, Dadu, Nanak, and Mirabai (many from the lower castes) rejected the caste system and many forms of institutionalized religion (both Hindu and Muslim), and preached about the importance of personal experience and devotion to a transcendent God without attributes. The tradition founded by one such sant, Guru Nanak, later developed into Sikhism.

The East India Company and British Colonialism (1660–1947)

Colonialism led to a reformulation of Hinduism. The activities and interventions of two groups of Britishers—scholars and administrators—first set this process in motion. British scholars were very interested in understanding the origin and history of Hinduism and in relating it to the conception of history with which they were familiar. British administrators, in contrast, wanted to codify Hinduism and Hindu "laws" to aid in the effort to understand and govern the country. Colonial scholars and colonial administrators together with their indigenous informants played a central role in creating the Hinduism religion that we know of today. As we have seen, even the term *Hinduism* was a British creation.

Because Hinduism relied on an oral tradition for a long time, little is known definitively about its origin and early history. One of the earliest studies of Hinduism, aimed at understanding its conception of the origin of the universe and of human history, was undertaken by British scholars of the East India Company, the trade company that over the course of two centuries would establish British colonialism in India. They discovered that Hindu sources described a universe that went through a timeless cosmic cycle of creation and dissolution and that in its current cycle was almost two billion years old.[6] This conception, however, contradicted the prevailing theory about the peoples of the world (subscribed to by Jews, Christians, and Muslims), which was based on the Old Testament story of the Flood and the subsequent scattering of the descendants of the three sons of Noah, believed to be the progenitors of the "three branches of the human family."[7] Integral to this conception of history was a time framework that dated the creation of the world by God to a few thousand years B.C.E.—for instance, according to British Protestants who adopted the time framework of Archbishop James Ussher, creation took place in 4004 B.C.E. and the Flood in 2349 B.C.E. (see Trautmann 1997, 57). The Hindu theory of time obtained the support of disaffected Christians, such as Voltaire, who were looking for sources to undermine the historicity of the Bible (Bryant 2001, 14).

Further studies of the chronology of Hinduism were carried out by Sir William Jones, who founded the Asiatic Society at Calcutta in 1784. But because he subscribed to the Old Testament version of history, he saw the flood narrative in the Puranas, which describes how the Hindu deity Vishnu first incarnated as a fish and carried Manu, the first man, his family, and seven sages, together with "the seeds of all the animals" in a ship fastened to a horn on his head (Narayanan 1996, 44), as confirmation of the flood of Noah. At the same time he rejected the Hindu conception of immense cycles of time and the conception of the universe as two billion years old. Instead, following the Ussherian time frame, he dated the flood to 2349 B.C.E. and the beginning of the reign of King Rama of Ayodhya (who is identified with the biblical Raamah, the descendant of Ham, mentioned in Genesis) to 2028 B.C.E. (Jones 1807, 4:24, 48, cited in Trautmann 1997, 59).

However, what Sir William Jones is now remembered for is his much-cited presidential address to the Asiatic Society in 1786, in which he pronounced, "The Sanscrit [sic] language, whatever be its antiquity, is of a wonderful structure; more perfect than the Greek, more copious than the Latin, and more exquisitely refined than either, yet bearing to them a stronger affinity, both in the roots of verbs and in the forms of grammar, than could possibly have been produced by accident; so strong indeed, that no philologer could examine them all three, without believing them to have sprung from some common source, which perhaps, no longer exists" (1807, 3:34–35, cited in Trautmann 1997, 38). Jones went on to argue that the Germanic, Celtic, and Old Persian languages were also likely to belong to the same family tree of languages. This idea was to subsequently become central in the development of the theory of an Indo-European or Aryan people by Friedrich Max Müller, on which more below.

The Development of Orientalism. The work of the scholars of the Asiatic Society stimulated the interest of several Britons in the second half of the eighteenth century. According to Trautmann (1997), these "Orientalists" manifested a breathless enthusiasm for Indian civilization and particularly for the religion and laws of the "Hindoos" or the "Gentoo," believing that their "benevolence . . . made India a prosperous and peaceful country before foreign conquest" (Trautmann 1997, 65). Thus the shortcomings of contemporary Hindu society were attributed to Muslim domination, and it was believed that enlightened British rule would soon restore India to her original glory (Trautmann 1997, 104). Some Europeans in this period were also ardent admirers of ancient India. In 1777, even before William Jones's statement about an Indo-European family of languages, the French astronomer Bailly stated on the basis of his deliberations that the earliest humans lived on the banks of the Ganges and therefore that, "the Brahmans are the teachers of Pythagoras, the instructors of Greece and through her of the whole of Europe" (Bailly 1777,

51, cited in Bryant 2001, 18). Other eminent European figures such as Voltaire and Friedrich von Schlegel also argued that India was the homeland of the human race and therefore the cradle of European civilization (Bryant 2001, 18–19).

Friedrich Max Müller was a German scholar who studied Sanskrit and then became a professor at Oxford from 1846 to the end of his life in 1900. He translated most of the important Hindu scriptures, and his two best-known works are the standard edition of the *Rig Veda with Commentary* (6 vols., 1849–1873) and the *Sacred Books of the East* (51 vols., 1875–1900). He was the most celebrated scholar of Sanskrit and of Hindu texts during the Victorian period, and his work was enormously influential in his day. Müller had a great admiration for the Vedic civilization of India and described India as a land where "the human mind has most fully developed some of its choicest gifts, [and] has most deeply pondered on the greatest problems of life" (1883, 6, cited in Bryant 2001, 22). He believed that this civilization had been corrupted in subsequent periods, however, and that the real-life India that his contemporaries encountered was thus far removed from India of the golden age. According to Nicholas Dirks (2001, 39), this view of Müller's was picked up by Gandhi and others (including the early Hindu nationalists), who also came to identify the "soul of Indian civilization as that of the Vedic age."

Müller is probably best known today for his development of the theory of the Aryan invasion. By the mid-nineteenth century, the similarity between Sanskrit and many European languages had been established. It had also been established that most of the south Indian languages were derived not from Sanskrit but from a family of languages unrelated to Sanskrit called "Dravidian." The theory of India's being the original homeland of the human race had largely been discarded and the popular consensus situated the site of human origins back somewhere in the Middle Eastern region, in accordance with biblical ideas. On the basis of these ideas, Müller developed a theory of an Aryan homeland to the west of India, from which some branches migrated to the west (to Europe) and another to the east, to India. From descriptions in the Vedas of numerous battles between Aryans (a term which the Brahmana texts seemed to use to refer to the top three caste groups—the Brahmins, Kshatriyas, and Vaishyas—but not the Sudras) and the apparently darker-skinned non-Aryans, Müller concluded that the Aryans were a light-skinned warrior people who invaded India with horse-drawn chariots and vanquished the indigenous darker race in north India between 1500 and 1200 B.C.E. (a time frame based on conjectural calculations regarding the minimum time needed to develop the different genres of texts in the Vedas). These indigenous groups, according to Müller, became the Sudra castes. He argued that some of the Aryans (the Brahmins) moved gradually south, but there they adopted the language of the natives, the Dravidians, and conveyed "through its medium their knowledge and instruction to the minds of [these] uncivilized tribes" (Müller 1847, quoted in Trautmann 1997, 176). In the process, Müller believed that the Aryans had refined the Dravidian languages to an extent that they even rivaled Sanskrit and that they had made the south the repository of brahminical science and culture (Trautmann 1997, 176). Müller's theory of Aryan invasion became enormously influential, since it helped to explain several puzzles of ancient Indian history—the sharp distinction between the three "twice-born" upper castes and the Sudras, along with the servile position of the latter; the similarities between European languages and Sanskrit; and the similarities and differences between north and south Indian languages and cultures.[8]

Just as the concept of Aryanism came to be co-opted by a range of groups in Europe in the nineteenth and twentieth centuries for their own, often differing, purposes (see Bryant 2001), the idea of the Aryan invasion into India developed by Müller was also used to support a variety of agendas in the Indian context. Some Indian leaders of late-nineteenth-century Bengal were ecstatic over Müller's formulation, since "the belief that the white masters were not very distant cousins of their brown Aryan subjects provided a much needed salve to the wounded ego of the dependent elite" (Raychaudhuri 1988, 8, cited in Trautmann 1997, 219). Other leaders used the theory to point to the superiority and greater antiquity of the Hindu civilization when compared with the European (since the ancient undivided Aryans were believed to have spoken Sanskrit and to have practiced an early form of Vedic Hinduism). The concept of the Aryan/Dravidian dichotomy became firmly entrenched in the consciousness of the average educated Indian, and even today, many upper-caste individuals in the north (those who consider themselves to be Brahmins, Kshatriyas, or Vaishyas) and those believing themselves to be descendants of Brahmin groups in the south believe themselves to be Aryan. The same theory, however, has also provided the ammunition for the Dravidian and the Dalit (lower caste) movements against the upper castes, with both the Dravidianists and the Dalits arguing that they are the indigenous Indians whose culture was colonized and corrupted by alien Aryan invaders.

Once British colonial rule was well established in India, the admiration for Hinduism was soon replaced by what Trautmann (1997) describes as "Indophobia," which emphasized the moral depravity of the Hindus and the role of Hindu religion and laws in causing this depravity and went hand in hand with an aggressive Christian evangelicalism. One of the chief architects of this new colonial policy, Charles Grant, went on to argue that the Hindus could be rescued from their moral "darkness" by being exposed to British thoughts and ideas through education in English. This Anglicist policy was subsequently implemented by Lord Macaulay in 1835.

The body of knowledge about India and Hinduism created by colonialists and their Indian collaborators, now described as "Orientalism," fundamentally shaped the perceptions of Hinduism and Indian history of Hindu leaders from the colonial period onward. In fact, Carol Breckendridge and Peter van der Veer (1993, 11) argue that even today, "it is very difficult for both Indians and outsiders to think about India outside of orientalist habits and categories." Van der Veer (1994, 133) summarizes the central elements of the orientalist framework:

> Inspired by the Enlightenment, orientalists brought modern philological methods and concepts to bear on India's past. By producing critical editions of Hindu scriptures they replaced a largely fragmented, oral tradition with an unchanging,

homogenized written one. In that way a "history" as established by modern science, came to replace a traditional "past." They also canonized certain scriptures such as the Bhagavad Gita, which prepared the ground for Mahatma Gandhi to make this Sanskrit work into a fundamental scripture of modern Hinduism. By looking for the roots of Western (Aryan) civilization in Vedic and later Hindu scriptures, they created an image of the decline of Hindu society after "the Muslim invasions." This in turn laid the foundation for a Hindu nationalist (communalist) interpretation of Indian history.

Van der Veer (1994, 66–67) makes the case that the "tolerance" that is now regarded as a central and long-established characteristic of Hinduism was also an orientalist construction, derived from "the abstraction and universalization of religion that is part of the Western discourse of 'modernity.' " He continues, "This discourse is then brought to bear on Muslim and Hindu populations incorporated in the modern world system. Muslims, the old rivals of the Christian West are labeled 'fanatic' and 'bigoted,' while Hindus are seen in a more positive light as 'tolerant.' At the same time, this labeling explains why Muslims have ruled Hindu India and why Hindus have to be 'protected' by the British. In short, what I want to argue here is that the attribution of 'tolerance' to Hinduism is a product of a specific orientalist history of ideas" (van der Veer 1994, 67).

It was Warren Hastings, the first governor-general of British India, who set in motion the process of codifying Hinduism. Deeply committed to establishing a government based on a "rule of law" that was indigenous to the country but was also compatible with British ideals and colonial needs, Hastings believed that it was his task to recover and systematize this ancient body of "Gentoo laws." To this end, he convened a panel of Brahmin scholars (pandits) to compile a "Code of Gentoo Laws" based on the Hindu shastras. This body of work was translated into English and published in 1776, inaugurating the canonization of brahmanical religious texts as the precepts guiding the everyday behavior of all Hindus. After India came under direct Crown rule in 1858, British interpretations of the *Manusmriti* became the basis for all-India governance of the "Hindu" community. Thus the creation of a monolithic "Hindu community" bound by one set of laws first took place under British colonialism.

Hastings and the other British officials also believed that there was a parallel set of laws that governed the Muslims, derived from the Koran, and known to the *maulavis* (Muslim scholars). William Jones, a scholar and judge appointed to the Crown court in Bengal in 1783, aimed to continue the project begun by Hastings by compiling a "complete digest of Hindu and Mussulman law" (cited in Cohn 1996, 69). As Barbara and Thomas Metcalf (2002, 57) point out, these early British officials thus also initiated the practice of reifying Hindus and Muslims as two cohesive, fundamentally separate communities, each defined by its own textual traditions. Subsequent British policies only further exacerbated the distinction between the two groups. In 1810, the British government in India decided that the state would administer all "Hindu" (or "native") religious institutions, pilgrimage sites, and festivals, a practice that continues to this day (Frykenberg 1997, 238). The religious institutions belonging to other communities were not so affected and remained under the control of committees (whose members were appointed by the colonial government) of the particular groups involved. The first all-India census, conducted in 1872, created the official category "Hindus" by defining them as all people who were not Muslims, Sikhs, Christians, Jains, Jews, or Parsis (Frykenberg 1997, 239), and established that India had a "Hindu majority" and a "Muslim minority." The census also made clear, however, that upper castes, or the "twice-born" communities, only constituted 15 percent of the entire population, less than the percentage of Muslims in the Indian empire (25 percent) and of Untouchable groups (20 percent). This revelation further increased the anxieties of the upper castes and led some reformist leaders to take the first attempts to include Untouchable groups, until then considered to be outside the boundaries of the "pure" Hindu society, within the Hindu fold (Frykenberg 1997, 239).

A variety of Hindu reform movements developed in the nineteenth century in reaction to Christian missionary activity and exposure to Western education and thinking, giving rise to a Hindu revival or renaissance. This Hindu renaissance in turn fed into the development of a Hindu nationalist movement which first emerged in the early decades of the twentieth century. Hindu nationalism resurged again in India from the late 1980s and has led to the politicization of Hinduism and Hindu identity, particularly of "official Hinduism." These developments are discussed in chapter 6.

Popular Hinduism in Contemporary India
Hindu Beliefs

The problem of defining Hinduism and its beliefs and practices has already been referred to. As mentioned at the beginning of the chapter, Hinduism in India consists of an extraordinary array of practices, deities, texts, and schools of thought. Because of this diversity, the nature and character of Hinduism have varied greatly by region, caste, and historical period. Despite these variations, I will try to describe briefly what Hinduism as it is lived and practiced by many Hindus in India looks like.

Hinduism stresses orthopraxis over theological belief. Young Hindus in India learn Hindu rituals and practices from their parents, grandparents, and other elders, and the emphasis is on learning and performing them because they are part of the Hindu tradition, rather than on performing them because they are meaningful. Thus many devout Hindus in India would be hard-pressed to explain why they observe many rituals and practices. Some general ideas and concepts are part of the world (or cosmic) view of most Hindus, however, and undergird many Hindu practices. The concept of dharma or the idea that each individual has a prescribed set of duties or obligations that he or she is required to fulfill, depending on gender, caste background, age, and family status, is one of the central concepts of Hinduism. A related concept is that of karma, the idea that every action has consequences for the individual. Following dharma brings *punya* (merit) and deviations from dharma are *papa*, sin. The balance between punya and papa determines, through the law of karma, how one will fare in this life and how one's soul fares in the cycle of reincarnation: whether as an insect, animal, or human, and if as a human, with what caste and economic status (Weightman 1997, 282). Individuals can also perform meritorious actions such as undertaking austerities, or special worship rituals for their own well-being or that of others. Because being caught in an endless cycle of reincarnation is seen as intolerable, moksha, or liberation from this cycle, and the means to attain this, has been a central preoccupation of most schools of Hindu thought. The *Bhagavad Gita* describes three paths *(marga)* to moksha: by right conduct *(karma-marga)*—the scrupulous and disinterested performance of one's duties irrespective of the rewards or punishments they might occasion, by enlightenment *(jnana-marga)* through meditation and various yoga techniques, or by loving devotion *(bhakti-marga)*, the preferred path for theistic traditions.

Another set of interrelated concepts has to do with hierarchical inequality and its basis. Many scholars have argued that the principle of hierarchical ordering is fundamental to Hindu thought (Dumont 1980; Fuller 1992; Milner 1994). This principle in turn is based on a related set of ideas about the qualities *(gunas)* of nature, about ritual purity and pollution, and about auspiciousness and inauspiciousness. According to Hindu notions, there are three different gunas, or natural qualities, believed to be present in varying degrees in all things: *sattvic,* pure, characterized by light; *rajasic,* energy producing; and *tamasic,* inertia producing, or characterized by darkness. Different castes and communities are believed to have inherent qualities, with the Brahmins or priests being viewed as sattvic, the Kshatriyas or warriors and rulers as rajasic, and the Sudras or the service people as tamasic (Flood 1996, 59). The concept of gunas also extends to a variety of other phenomena, perhaps the most significant of which is food. Thus some types of food, such as milk and dairy products and several vegetables, are believed to be pure or sattvic, giving rise to spirituality; others, like meat, poultry, onions, and garlic, are believed to be rajasic, giving rise to passion and action; and finally, some types of food, such as liquor, are believed to produce laziness (Narayanan 1996, 89). It is for this reason that castes have different dietary regulations. A sattvic diet is prescribed for Brahmins and for widows, who are supposed to cultivate spirituality and avoid passion (Narayanan 1996, 89), while Kshatriyas are permitted to consume rajasic food. Contrary to popular Western impressions, the majority of the people in India are not vegetarian, although most Hindus avoid beef and pork. According to a decade-long survey on the "People of India" conducted by the Anthropological Survey of India, only about 20 percent were vegetarians. The survey found that in many states like West Bengal, Bihar, and Kashmir, even Brahmins were nonvegetarian, eating fish and sometimes chicken (L. K. Jha 1997).

The axis of purity and pollution is superimposed on and reinforces the concept of gunas. Ritual pollution is believed to emanate from a variety of sources, such as bodily emissions and waste (particularly saliva, semen, menstrual blood, feces, urine, and hair and nail clippings); events, such as birth, death, and menstruation; and physical association with those individuals or groups who have either not ritually cleansed themselves from bodily pollution (by a bath or other prescribed ablutions) or who have occupations that bring them into regular contact with sources of pollution. To maintain the purity of the upper castes, the caste system traditionally relegated duties such as barbering, laundering, midwifery, and night-soil removal to low-ranking castes, who were therefore seen as the most polluted. At the other end of the caste structure were the Brahmins, who were viewed as the purest caste. The purity of the upper castes was also preserved by rules of endogamy and commensality and the restrictions on the consumption of food prepared or handled by members of lower castes.

Ideas about auspiciousness and inauspiciousness further complement the concepts mentioned above. Some categories of people are viewed as particularly auspicious or inauspicious. Traditionally, kings have been viewed as auspicious (Milner 1994, 128), as also are wives whose husbands are alive *(sumangalis)* and married goddesses such as Lakshmi. At the other extreme, widows and funeral priests are believed to be inauspicious. In some situations, inauspiciousness can be transferred to individuals belonging to certain types of groups by giving gifts (Raheja 1988). But most commonly the concepts of auspiciousness and inauspiciousness are used to refer to periods of time. Some periods of time are deemed to be inauspicious, particularly to start new ventures, and others are viewed as particularly propitious. Astrology is used to determine what periods are auspicious and inauspicious and this calculation is usually scrupulously followed, particularly for major projects (such as laying the foundations for a building) and rituals (such as marriage). The configuration of planets at the time of birth determines one's horoscope, which in turn is believed to reveal what the person's earthly fortunes will be for the rest of his or her life. Horoscopes are particularly scrutinized before marriages are arranged, to make sure that those of the bride and groom are compatible and that neither the bride nor the groom has a particularly inauspicious fortune.

Another related set of beliefs that are important in Hindu thought are ideas about "heating" and "cooling" and about sexuality. The spiritual power that gods have and that human beings can obtain through extreme asceticism is believed to be "hot." At the same time, uncontrolled heat is seen as being dangerous, and thus heat has to be balanced with "coolness" (Babb 1975, 236). "Cooling rituals" are incorporated into a variety of worship ceremonies, and the opposition between heat and cold is a more general "ordering conception" as well (Babb 1975, 235). For instance, some types of foods are believed to be "heating" (e.g., mangoes and papayas) and others to be "cooling" (e.g., coconuts and limes) and to keep good health, an individual is supposed to consume foods in such a way as to keep the balance between heat and cold (Fuller 1992, 45).

Hindu beliefs about sexuality are connected to ideas about heat and cold. Male power is supposed to be stored in semen and thus sexual asceticism, or the retention of semen, is believed to generate heat. Correspondingly, loss of semen is believed to weaken a man and thus frequent sexual intercourse is considered to be debilitating for men. Women are not so debilitated, however, since they obtain through intercourse the power stored in the semen, thus increasing their own power, or shakti. Uncontrolled female sexuality is therefore considered to be particularly threatening to men.

Although both men and women have their share of shakti (power), women are supposed to embody shakti, or the energizing principle of the universe. For this reason, female sexuality is considered to be particularly powerful but also particularly dangerous, when not suitably controlled. Because of their unreleased sexuality, single goddesses are considered to be very hot. Unreleased female sexuality is also believed to cause rage (which also produces heat), thus making single goddesses even hotter and more capable of destruction. However, when the sexuality of a woman is controlled by marriage and her total devotion to her husband, she is cooled, and thus married goddesses are considered to be benevolent. Through marriage and the transference of control of a woman's sexuality to her husband, shakti can become a positive force (thus sumangalis or married women are considered auspicious). A *pativrata* (devoted wife) can increase her shakti and use it to protect her husband from harm (Wadley 1992, 112–116). Women are therefore considered to be responsible for the well-being of their husbands. It is for this reason that widows are viewed as being particularly inauspicious. There is the suspicion that the death of the husband was the fault of the wife, if only indirectly, either due to the bad karma she inherited from a previous life, or because she did not practice the wifely austerities (the special fasts and rituals described below) that would have ensured his longevity. The woman as mother has a special and honored place in Hindu thought. Hindu goddesses are worshipped as the Divine mother and are loved, feared, and obeyed as powerful protectors.

Hindu Deities and Worship

One of the distinct characteristics of Hinduism is that there is no clear separation between gods and humans and between good and evil. In many contexts, humans are considered divine. Hindu gurus, or living saints, are frequently believed to be manifestations of divinity. In some rituals, Brahmin priests are treated as gods. During the wedding ritual, the bride and groom are worshipped in the same way that deities are worshipped. Hindu gods, far from being unambiguous figures of righteousness, often act like humans and are sometimes immoral, violent, and destructive. The demons, *asuras*, who try to destroy the moral order (dharma) and gain control over the universe, are frequently devotees of Vishnu and Shiva and are often saved by the latter after being defeated in battle (Fuller 1992, 32).

Anthropologists of India have made a distinction between deities of the Great Tradition (the primary Hindu deities of Vishnu, Shiva, and the Goddess, worshipped in some form by Hindus all over India) and those of the Little Tradition (deities that are more local, usually village- or region-based). To some extent, this distinction overlaps with the distinction between upper-caste (Sanskritic) and lower-caste (non-Sanskritic) deities (e.g., see Iliah 1996). In this context, it is important to keep in mind that the vast majority of Hindus in India live in villages (about 70 percent of the Indian population is rural) and that members of lower-caste groups (castes of the rank of Sudra and below) constitute the majority of the Indian population.[9]

There are many differences between the ways the two types of deities are perceived and worshipped (see Fuller 1992). The local deities are believed to be tutelary beings with lesser powers than the primary deities—often having power primarily over that particular locality alone. Some of the local deities are human beings who met an unfortunate death (and who are deified in order to placate their malevolence), or who met a particularly heroic death (heroes who died in battle or women who chose to commit sati by burning themselves on the funeral pyre of their husbands). But precisely because the local deities have more limited powers and some are also ex-humans, they are believed to be more approachable and more understanding of human problems than the higher deities. People are more likely to approach local deities for help with practical problems, particularly those that the deities have power over (for instance, epidemic diseases are often believed to be caused by local goddesses), while approaching higher deities for concerns about moksha or salvation. At the same time, many of the local deities, particularly the goddesses (who at the local level are almost always portrayed alone, without a consort), are also viewed as being particularly quick to anger, and are therefore propitiated with "cooling rituals" in order to ensure that they do no harm, while higher deities are more commonly praised and adored rather than placated. Some of the placatory rituals for local deities include animal sacrifices, while the higher deities accept only vegetarian offerings. In some contexts, however, the local deities are considered to be forms of the higher deities, so there is no absolute distinction between deities belonging to the Great and the Little traditions. Similarly, even upper-caste members of a village approach the local deities to petition them to protect them from harm or to remove some misfortune, so the distinction between upper-caste and lower-caste deities is not a clear one either.

Hinduism accords individuals great latitude in belief. This freedom is exemplified by the concept of *ishtadeva*, the chosen deity. Each Hindu can choose which deity (and which particular incarnation of the deity) he or she considers to be personally inspiring. It is therefore possible for each member of a family to have his or her own primary deity to whom private worship is offered, while at the same time participating in the periodic worship of the family or lineage deity *(kuladevata)* and the village deity *(gramadevata)*. Many Hindus also revere living saints, holy men or women who are considered to be divinely inspired. Each of the six major Hindu philosophical traditions has its own spiritual leader, and the leadership of such schools generally passes from teacher to teacher in an unbroken line of succession over the centuries. In addition, at any particular time, there are numerous charismatic leaders who attract devotees through their special powers or their wisdom and spiritual knowledge. Most of these Hindu saints tend to be celibate ascetics.

Whether at home or at the temple, the primary form of Hindu worship is puja, where the picture or image of the deity is honored with rituals such as the lighting and the waving of oil lamps and incense sticks *(aarti)*, the chanting of sacred texts or the recitation of prayers, ritual bathing or anointing with ghee (clarified butter), and the offering of flowers, fruit, and food. Pujas conducted in temples are more elaborate and will be discussed in more detail in chapter 5. Most practicing Hindus perform domestic worship at a home shrine, which is usually a small space (such as a cabinet shelf or closet, or an entire room) where pictures or images of deities are enshrined. Daily worship is often conducted by one person (often the woman of the house) on behalf of the household, or individually by different family members, but for special occasions the whole family gets together to conduct domestic rituals, sometimes led by the family priest. The drawing of intricate designs (*kolam/rangoli*) with rice flour in front of the house and in front of the home shrine is also part of many people's daily worship ritual (particularly in south India), and this task is usually performed by women.

Most Hindu traditions do not require temple worship, but many Hindus do visit a temple periodically, at least for special occasions. Temples in India are generally dedicated to a single deity, sometimes with secondary shrines dedicated to associated deities. The Indian landscape is dotted with temples and shrines of varying size, from small roadside shrines at the base of a tree, consisting of a few rocks piled on top of each other, to larger structures built with brick and mortar, to the huge temple complexes covering hundreds of acres of land. Hindus go to a temple for the *darshan,* or the visual communion, with the deity; to pray or petition the god or goddess; and to partake of the *prasadha,* or the consecrated food offerings.

Undertaking a pilgrimage to a religious center or shrine is another highly meritorious form of Hindu worship. A variety of regional and national pilgrimage sites in India are dedicated to different concerns and deities. The largest religious gatherings take place at the *melas,* religious fairs, which occur every twelve years at north Indian pilgrimage centers like Allahabad and Haridwar. Hindus also express their devotion and religiosity by celebrating Hindu festivals. As in the case of pilgrimage sites, there are a variety of festivals: some are regional, others are national, some are primarily celebrated by particular castes and sects, and others are primarily celebrated by women. Two of the most important all-India festivals are Navaratri, celebrated for nine nights in September or October (depending on the lunar cycle), and Diwali, the festival of lights, celebrated in October or November. Interestingly, although these festivals are celebrated throughout India, the tradition and mythology underlying the festival vary regionally, as does the manner in which they are celebrated.

Hindu women demonstrate their religiosity and their devotion to their husbands by undertaking periodic *vratas,* votive observances usually characterized by partial fasts, during which they abstain from certain types of food. Unmarried girls fast in order to obtain a good husband, while married women fast to secure the well-being and long life of their husbands. There are also several types of rituals that women perform for the benefit of their husbands and the entire family.

Life-Cycle Rites (Samskaras)

Sanskritic texts prescribe a number of Hindu sacraments, or *samskaras,* to sanctify and mark the major transitions of a person's life. Prenatal rituals are conducted for the safe birth of the child, and sometimes to seek a male child. The exact moment

of birth is noted to draw the horoscope, and after birth, there is a naming ceremony. Other ceremonies follow, marking the child's first eating of solid food, first
tonsure (often at a major temple or religious fair), and first writing. The traditional
ritual that initiates a young boy of the three upper castes into the Hindu fold by
introducing him to Vedic prayers and investing him with the sacred thread is called
the *upanayana*, or initiation. Today this ritual is mainly practiced by Brahmins.
Several south Indian communities also celebrate a girl's first menstrual period,
which is believed to signify a girl's coming of age.

It is considered to be a Hindu's religious duty to marry and have children, and
thus the most important and most elaborately celebrated samskara is that of marriage. Most marriages in India are "arranged" by the parents of the couple who,
with the help of extended family and friends (and today even newspaper and Internet advertisements), find a suitable partner from the same caste, subcaste, linguistic background, and about the same socioeconomic status, who is compatible in
terms of age, education, outlook, and appearance with that of their daughter or
son. In the past, the bride and groom generally only saw and perhaps talked to each
other briefly when the two families met for the first time. Now many families allow
the bride and groom to meet unchaperoned at a public place at least once before
they are asked to decide whether they are agreeable to the marriage.

Such arranged marriages are contrasted with "love" marriages, in which the
couple falls in love with each other and then marries, with or without the approval
and support of their parents. "Love" marriages have traditionally been frowned
upon in Indian culture (e.g., see Derné 1995) for a variety of reasons: the likelihood
that caste, linguistic, and class boundaries might be violated, resulting in an incompatibility between the couple and their families; the fear that the close relationship
between the couple might prevent the man from fulfilling his obligations to his
natal family; and the stigma that such a love marriage confers on the woman and
her family (since women are supposed to be closely guarded and chaperoned until
their marriage to ensure their virginity). Nevertheless, some of these ideas are slowly
changing and "love" marriages are becoming more common among the urban,
educated classes.

Many families go into debt to provide the elaborate feast and the gifts of clothes
and jewelry for close family members and in-laws required to conduct the marriage
ritual appropriately. Families of the bride are particularly burdened, since in most
cases, they have to provide a dowry and bear most of the wedding expenses. There
are many variations in wedding ceremonies by region and caste, but a central ritual
involves the couple's walking seven times (or taking seven steps) around the sacred
fire. In some communities, the elaborate complex of marriage rituals can take up to
a week to complete.

Ritual cremation on a funeral pyre is the final sacrament for Hindus, although
children, pregnant women, sadhus (religious renunciates), and those who have
died of snake bite are buried. Generally the eldest son performs the death rituals
associated with cremation. Death results in a state of pollution for the entire family,
and ritual restrictions are placed on them. These are removed only after a designated

number of days (usually around ten or eleven), and after a ceremony in which food and drink are offered to the spirit of the departed person. Some wealthy families perform ceremonies for the deceased on every new-moon day for a year. The first death anniversary is marked with special rituals.

Everyday Hindu Practice

Hinduism characteristically makes no clear distinction between sacred and secular activities and spheres. Thus Vasudha Narayanan (1998, 129) points out that even "such activities as tree-planting, singing, dancing, medicine, archery, astrology, sculpture, architecture, and building a home might all be considered part of the religious domain." According to Simon Weightman (1997, 286), "few religions have devoted so much attention to ritual as has Hinduism." Hindu manuals and tradition have detailed guidelines on how to perform daily devotions and practically every other activity of daily life.

Thus members of high-caste, orthoprax families are subjected to a variety of prescriptions and proscriptions, which include how to perform the morning ablutions, how to guard the purity of the kitchen and the puja room, the particular type of food that can be cooked for different occasions, the method of cooking, food combinations that are permitted and not permitted, when and how to bathe, how to cut and dispose of hair and nail clippings, and the times of the day, week, and year that are suitable for different activities. In many orthodox south Indian families, menstruating women (who are believed to be polluted) are generally not permitted to enter the kitchen (in nuclear households, the man of the house often does the cooking during this period) or the puja room, and traditionally were not even allowed to have any contact with other members of the household. Rules of inter-caste and interpersonal conduct govern everyday social interaction, from the appropriate distance to be maintained between members of different castes and between unrelated men and women, to the postures, gestures, and forms of address to be used for different categories of people. All of these prescriptions and proscriptions vary by caste and region. Today, however, many Hindus, particularly those of the younger generation living in the Indian metropolises, do not observe most of these strictures.

CHAPTER 3

Transplanting Hinduism in the United States

Hinduism in diaspora rarely manages to institutionalize the diversity and ritualization of Hinduism in India, leading one scholar to remark that "diasporic Hinduism is energetic in its own way but relatively monochromic when compared with the rich colors of religion in India" (Narayanan 2000, 768). Steven Vertovec, in his book on the Hindu diaspora around the world (2000, 21–24), points out that Hinduism has taken different forms in the countries where it has been transplanted, depending on the interaction between the social and cultural characteristics of the particular group of immigrants (their caste, region, and class background) and the characteristics of the receiving society (such as its degree of racial and ethnic diversity and racism). However, his work and that of others among expatriate Hindu communities indicate that common processes are still visible.

Vertovec (2000, 18) argues that Hinduism becomes the basis for ethnic formation and expression for Hindus "in virtually every context outside India." As in the case of the United States, congregationalism, or forms of group worship, increases, with the formation of devotional song (bhajan) and worship (satsang) groups and the tendency for temples to hold worship services over the weekend with people arriving and leaving at set times (Bowen 1987, 18–19; Coward 1998, 784–785; Vertovec 1992). Religious consciousness changes as well, as Hindus come to understand their status as a religious minority in their new homelands (Vertovec 2000, 149). This realization gives rise to attempts to formulate and to formalize Hindu beliefs and practices and also leads to the development of some degree of syncretism or "ecumenicalism" (Williams 1988). An increased awareness of their Hindu identity may also prompt expatriate Hindus to enter the public sphere and to mobilize politically in their new countries (Kelly 1991; Kundnani 2002; Vertovec 1995). The role of women is also altered. According to Vertovec (2000, 17), the literature on Hindu communities around the world indicates that women have been empowered within the expatriate community and function as key agents of religious and cultural transmission, in both the private and the public spheres. Finally, the caste system undergoes some changes. Richard Burghart's (1987a, 12) pithy observation about Hinduism in Great Britain, that "castes have survived, but not the 'system' "—in other words, that while caste identities have been retained by Hindu immigrants, the elaborate systems of interaction and interdependence characteristic of the caste system in India are absent—also seems to hold across the diaspora. We will see that Hinduism in the United States manifests all of these characteristics, but that it has also been uniquely shaped by the American milieu and by the nature of Indian Hindu migration patterns to the United States.

EARLY TEACHERS

Hinduism arrived in the United States long before Hindu immigrants did. Americans encountered the religion in the late eighteenth century, as trade began between India and America. The first significant immigration from India to the United States, however, took place two hundred years later, as around 6,800 Indians, mostly Sikh peasants from Punjab province, arrived in California between 1899 and 1914. In the interim, Americans had learned about Hinduism from travelogues and missionary accounts and from translations of Hindu scriptures, sources that provided the foundation for the love-hate relationship that Americans would develop with the foreign religion (Prothero 2001). The tone of the missionary accounts and travelogues was largely derogatory, while the Unitarians and intellectuals such as Ralph Waldo Emerson and Henry David Thoreau were impressed with the sophistication of Hindu spiritual ideas found in early Hindu texts. From his Walden Pond retreat, Thoreau wrote in 1845, "In the morning, I bathe my intellect in the stupendous and cosmogonal philosophy of the Bhagvat-Geeta ... in comparison with which our modern world and its literature seem puny and trivial" (Krutch 1962, 324–325, cited in Eck 2001, 96). The Transcendentalist movement of the late nineteenth century, inspired by Emerson and Thoreau, embraced Hindu thought, as did the Free Religionists and the Theosophists. But as Steven Prothero points out, all of these Hinduphiles of the nineteenth century, who loved the Hinduism of ancient Hindu texts, "were Hinduphobes when it came to popular Hinduism," since they denounced many of the Hindu rites and practices of ordinary Hindus such as bhakti worship, and the rituals performed by Brahmin priests (Prothero 2002).

Swami Vivekananda, a Western-educated Indian sadhu, was the first Hindu thinker many Americans of the nineteenth century encountered. His powerful oratory at the World Parliament of Religions held in Chicago in 1893 provided an important turning point for Hinduism in the United States. In his speech he emphasized the unity of all religions: "It is the same light coming through different colors ... in the heart of everything the same truth reigns" and called for a universal religion "which would have no place for persecution or intolerance in its polity, and would recognize a divinity in every man or woman" (Eck 2001, 97). Following the parliament, Vivekananda was invited on a speaking tour around the country. In 1894 he founded the first American Hindu organization, the Vedanta Society, in New York, and in 1899 established a branch in San Francisco.

Vivekananda wrote a book on yoga in 1900 that was aimed at an American audience. He died shortly thereafter, however, and the task of establishing yoga in the

United States fell to one of the other Hindu teachers who had followed Vivekananda from India, Swami Paramahansa Yogananda. In his first lecture in the United States in 1920, Yogananda characterized yoga as "a system of scientific methods for reuniting the soul with the Spirit" (Eck 2001, 105). He established the Self-Realization Fellowship in Los Angeles in 1925 to "unite science and religion through realization of the unity of their underlying principles" and to "disseminate among the nations a knowledge of definite scientific techniques for attaining personal experience of God" (cited in Eck 2001, 105). The Self-Realization Fellowship was the most popular and most extensive Hindu organization in the United States until the 1970s. In addition, in the 1960s the mind-body connection that Swami Yogananda had espoused became the basis for another popular movement begun by a Hindu teacher from India, Transcendental Meditation, or TM, introduced by Maharishi Mahesh Yogi in the 1960s. Both Yogananda and the Maharishi downplayed the Hindu basis of yoga and TM and instead promoted them as techniques that had scientifically demonstrable value for everyone, irrespective of religious background.

In 1965 a Hindu teacher arrived in the United States who had an orientation and goals that were different from those of Yogananda and the Maharishi. A. C. Bhaktivedanta, also called Swami Prabhupada, was an elderly immigrant from West Bengal state in India who was inspired by his devotion to Lord Krishna to bring Krishna worship to America. Although he arrived penniless, within five years he was able to establish "Hare Krishna," or the International Society for Krishna Consciousness (ISKCON), with temples in thirty cities around the country. ISKCON emphasized bhakti worship to Lord Krishna through puja, chanting, ecstatic devotional singing, sidewalk evangelism, and an ascetic lifestyle, and emerged as a significant American Hindu movement which persists to the present.

Early Immigrants

Of the 6,800 immigrants from Punjab province in colonial India who arrived in California at the turn of the twentieth century, around 85 percent were Sikhs and another 10–12 percent, Muslim. Despite the fact that people from a Hindu background constituted less than 5 percent of this group, all of them were classified in the United States as "Hindu," the term used to describe all people from India.[1] Alarmed by the increasing popularity of the Vedanta Society in the United States, many American Christians began to denounce Hinduism and Hindu swamis with greater vigor, drawing on the stereotypes provided by the early travelogues and missionary writings. Anti-Hindu sentiments based largely on these negative portrayals resulted in an anti-Indian uprising in Bellingham, Washington, forcing seven hundred Indians to flee into Canada (Prothero 2001). American nativism was codified into law in the Immigration Acts of 1917 and 1924, which restricted, then barred, further immigration from Asia.

The early Punjabi immigrants were largely male, and because of laws curbing Asian immigration and marriage across "racial" lines, most of them married Hispanic women (Leonard 1992). Boundaries between religious groups in Punjab were fluid at the turn of the century and religion was not an important marker of difference. The same was true in the California setting, and there were good relationships between the Sikh immigrants and the Hindu and Muslim immigrants from Punjab. The Sikh temple in Stockton, built in 1915, served as a cultural and social center for the whole Punjabi community. The Sikh temple also played an important political function and was closely associated with the Ghadar, a radical movement originating in Northern California whose mission was the violent overthrow of British rule in India (Leonard 1992).

The children of the Punjabi-Mexican marriages were given Spanish names, spoke Spanish, and adopted Catholicism. Most of the Punjabi men "deliberately de-emphasized" their language, culture, and religion, because they had neither the time nor the ability to convey them (Leonard 1992, 25).[2] Yet despite being brought up in a Mexican American culture, most Punjabi Mexican children identified as "Hindu" or "East Indian." Initially this identification stemmed from the prejudice they faced from Mexican American society, but later, as their fathers' farms flourished, being "Hindu" was a means to distinguish themselves and their families from the largely working-class Mexican American population (Leonard 1992, 131–132). Because "Hindu" was the term then applied in the United States to anyone from the Indian subcontinent (including present-day Pakistan), for the Punjabi Mexicans, "being Hindu" meant identifying with certain values associated with the Punjabi Indian peasant immigrants, who were largely Sikh or Muslim, and had nothing to do with the Hindu religion. According to Karen Leonard (1992, 206), this identification meant being a successful farmer; valuing the ethics of hard work, honesty, and hospitality; taking a general pride in one's Punjabi heritage; enjoying Punjabi American food, society, and politics; and having "a reverence for the 'holy book' from India, whether that was the Granth Sahib [the Sikh text] or the Quran."

The religious cleavages that developed in the subcontinent, giving rise to the partition of India and Pakistan and the independence of the two countries in 1947, brought about changes in the relationships between religious groups among the Punjabi immigrants. Muslim immigrants began to develop separate religious associations and institutions and also to form Pakistani associations (Leonard 1992, 168). The second generation tried to counter these schisms by forming a "Hindustani" club in 1946 for the children of all Punjabis. But the children were proud of the newly independent nations of their fathers. Leonard (1992, 172–173) refers to the selection of "Hindu" (Indian) and "Pakistani" queens in annual contests in the Punjabi Mexican areas of California from the late 1940s.

The Punjabi Mexican second generation was at first enthusiastic about the arrival of new immigrants from South Asia in the 1960s and initially participated in the religious institutions created or revitalized by the latter. Particularly in Northern California, however, where there was a large influx of immigrants, tensions developed between the two groups. The newcomers mocked and challenged the claims of the Punjabi Mexicans to be Hindu (or Indian). The Punjabi Mexicans reacted by distancing themselves from the new immigrants and stressing that they were American as well as Hindu (Leonard 1992).

POST-1965 HINDU IMMIGRATION
Migration Patterns

The second phase of Indian immigration to the United States began after the passage of the Immigration and Naturalization Act of 1965. This immigration was largely family based and brought Indians from all over India and from a variety of religious backgrounds. It is now common to talk about "three waves" of post-1965 Indian immigration to the United States. The first-wave Indians came under the "special skills" provision of the act, and thus were mostly highly educated, fluent English speakers from urban backgrounds, who entered into professional and managerial careers. Education was another primary entry route for a significant proportion of Indian Americans (Nimbark 1980). This explains why Indians became, and remain, among the wealthiest and most educated foreign-born groups in the United States. According to the 1990 census, the median family income of Indians in the United States was $49,309, well above that for non-Hispanic whites, which was $37,630 (Waters and Eschbach 1999, 315); 43.6 percent were employed as either profession-als (mostly doctors and engineers) or managers; and 58.4 percent had at least a bachelor's degree (Shinagawa 1996, 113–119). In the same year, the per capita income in India was $350, and only 48 percent of Indians were even literate, able to read and write their own names (World Bank figures, 1990).

There were fears that the second-wave immigrants, who began arriving in the 1980s, might bring down some of the first wave's high socioeconomic standing. Many of this group were relatives of the first wave immigrants, sponsored under the "family reunification" provision of the 1965 act, and did not have the same edu-cational or professional status as the first wave. In 1996, for instance, of the total 44,859 Indian immigrants admitted, 34,291 were admitted under family sponsorship and only 9,919 in employment-based preferences (Springer 1997). California, which had been among the top destinations for this wave of immigrants, reported that 10.2 percent of the Indian American population and 14 percent of Indian American children (compared with the national average of 9 percent) were living below the poverty line in 1995 (Springer 1995). Beginning in the 1990s, however, there was a 'third wave'—a large influx of computer data programmers (on H-1B visas) and their families (Indians make up the largest single group of H-1B visa holders) to meet the demands of the IT boom in the United States.[3] This group has been tremendously successful, and in late 2001, even after the technology bubble had burst, a Merrill Lynch study estimated that there were around 200,000 Indian American million-aires, many based in Silicon Valley (Srirekha 2003). Another subgroup that has increased its presence in the United States is made up of those on student visas. In 2001 a record 66,836 students came from India to study in the United States, mak-ing India America's leading country of origin for international students (Rajghatta 2002). These two subgroups explain the recent explosion in the numbers of people of Indian ancestry in the United States. According to the 2000 census, individuals of Asian Indian origin in the United States numbered 1,678,765. They were also the fastest-growing community in the country, with a growth rate of 105.9 percent between 1990 and 2000. The 2000 census also showed that this group continued to hold its lead in education and family income despite the second wave of immigration: 41.9 percent of foreign-born Indian men were postgraduates or professional degree holders, compared with only 11 percent among native-born whites. In 2000 the median household income of foreign-born Indians was $68,500, compared with $53,400 for native-born whites (Kibria 2006, 211–212).

The U.S. census does not collect data on religion, and therefore no official figures are available to tell us how many Indian immigrants in the United States are from a Hindu background. It is likely that Hindus in America are a smaller proportion of the population than in India (where they are more than 80 percent), since Indians from Sikh and Christian backgrounds seem to be overrepresented (Min 2003, 29; Williams 1988, 37). National surveys conducted in the late 1990s estimated Hindus to be a little over 1 million, most of whom are believed to be immigrants from India and their children (T. W. Smith 2002, 581–582). Since 1.7 million of the U.S. population identified themselves racially as "Asian Indians" in the 2000 census, Hindus probably constitute around 60 percent of the total Indian American population.[4] Given the elite nature of the migration, we can assume that most Indian Americans are from upper-caste backgrounds. Brahmins seem to be particularly overrepresented. Surveys among Indian Americans conducted in different parts of the country in the 1980s and 1990s indicate that Gujarati speakers (Indians from the state of Gujarat in western India) consisted of the largest group (over 25 percent), followed by Hindi speakers (around 20 percent). South Indians (people from the four states of Tamil Nadu, Kerala, Andhra Pradesh, and Karnataka) constituted around 25 percent (Rangaswamy 2000, 103–104). The relative proportion of south Indians is likely to have increased after the H-1B migration, since globally, the Chennai embassy in south India has been the largest issuer of H-1B visas (*India Post* 1999). Regionally, Indian Americans are the most dispersed immigrant group in the country (Portes and Rumbaut 1996, 40); the largest concentrations are in the New York – New Jersey region, followed by California.

Gender and Migration

Gender ideology has fundamentally shaped the selection of Indians arriving in the United States, and has also had important implications for ethnic formation (see Kurien 1999). Indians who arrived as students in the 1960s and 1970s were overwhelmingly male. Estimates of the proportions of males among Indian students vary from a high of 97 percent in the 1950s and 1960s (Helweg and Helweg 1990, 101) to a low of around 70 percent for the late 1970s (Nimbark 1980, 253). Most of the men came to do graduate work in the sciences or in business-related areas (Nimbark 1980, 260). From the 1980s onward, however, larger numbers of women students arrived, and they were much more diversified in terms of academic disciplines. Many students from India also came to do their undergraduate studies.

Although the proportions of men and women Indian students eventually became more equal, they did not often marry each other. "The men were looking to get married and the women were looking to get married but they rarely connected," said Malini, an Indian graduate student, describing the situation at a university she had attended. She explained that this was because the "Indian men defined the Indian women students in the United States as un-marriageable. They wanted and married brides straight from India." The women, on their part, tended to view many of the Indian men they encountered as "sexist," "traditional," and "boorish" (Kurien 1996). Consequently male and female Indian students generally exhibited very different marriage patterns. Many of the Indian women students married Americans or non-Indians they met in the United States. Many Indian men went home to marry women from the same caste and linguistic background, selected for them by their families (see also DasGupta and Dasgupta 1996, 382). Of course, some number of marriages occurred between Indian men and women who had met in America. In such cases, the couple were frequently from different linguistic and caste backgrounds.

The differences in the marriage patterns of male and female Indian students can be explained by the way in which gender shapes migration (Kurien 1999). Indian gender norms, which emphasize the importance of virginity in women, generally discouraged the migration of young, single women, since the permissive sexual atmosphere in countries such as the United States was viewed as a threat to women's purity. Thus the women who arrived for U.S. graduate study were by definition a very self-selective group, generally hailing from relatively nonconformist families who were willing to go against the prevailing norms. In contrast, middle- and upper-class Indian gender norms have encouraged men to go into professional programs and to migrate to Western countries for education and jobs. Thus men pursuing prestigious professional programs such as engineering, medicine, or business in India and then arriving in the United States for graduate study were more likely to be those who valued conformity, making them, as a group, quite different from the female Indian students in the United States (Kurien 1996).

These differences have played a crucial role in community building and in shaping the nature of the ethnic community and identity that developed in the United States. Men who came here to study and then stayed on, by virtue of their more conformist dispositions and marriages to women from the same linguistic, caste, and religious backgrounds, were more likely to form or join the subcultural Indian community, which is constructed on the basis of common language and religion. Indian women with non-Indian spouses or Indian spouses with a different subcultural background were generally not comfortable (and were frequently not welcomed) in subcultural associations.[5] A significant proportion of the Indian women who arrived as single graduate students and then became immigrants tended to engage in liberal activism in support of feminist and human rights causes (see also DasGupta and Dasgupta 1996, 382) and to form community and friendships on the basis of these shared values rather than on the basis of ascriptive characteristics. In short, those individuals who joined the subcultural community were not representative of all Indian immigrants in the United States, but were likely to be among the more conventional.

Not surprisingly, Indian gender norms also shaped the migration patterns of those Indians who entered the United States as immigrants. A study of Indian American women in Chicago found that all the women who had been married at the time of immigration "came to the United States through marriage, either along with their husbands or later" (Rangaswamy 1996, 426). Most cases of Indian family immigration to the United States tended to be male led, with the man arriving in search of better professional or business opportunities. Sometimes the family arrived along with him. In other cases the man sent for the family after he established himself.[6] Such families also tended to join subcultural Indian American associations. Since it is these groups who largely defined and constructed "Indianness" and "Hinduness" in the United States, this selectivity also affected the nature and content of the Hindu American ethnic identity that was developed.

Transplanting Hinduism: Late 1960s to the Mid-1980s

The first-wave immigrants came in search of an education or better economic prospects and often planned only a temporary stay. In the early years, they were generally preoccupied with building their careers and establishing an economic foothold. Since Hinduism does not require group or even temple worship, Hindu immigrants were able to continue their home-based religious practices and family rituals without much disruption, even after migration. A 1978 Pittsburgh survey (Clothey 1983, 169) indicated that 56.9 percent of Indian respondents maintained a shrine at home, while a mid-1980s survey in Atlanta by John Fenton indicated that 84.7 percent of Hindu Indian homes had such a shrine (Fenton 1988, 69). Home shrines in the United States can consist of a whole room set aside for worship, an elaborate shrine cabinet with images of several deities and other sacred objects, or, more likely, a few pictures or images in a closet or on the kitchen counter. The necessity to guard the shrine from ritual pollution, particularly in the United States, where the home might have visitors who are not familiar with the Hindu rules of pollution and purity, means that it is usually located in a secluded, enclosed space (Mazumdar and Mazumdar 2003, 147).

Fifty-two percent of Hindu immigrants in Fenton's Atlanta survey indicated that they performed some form of individual worship, prayer, or meditation daily and another 19 percent indicated that they did so weekly. Twelve percent said that they did so at least once a month. Only 6.7 percent never engaged in individual worship (Fenton 1988, 50–51). Fenton also found that over one-fifth of his Hindu respondents fasted weekly or at least monthly. Women were more likely to perform individual worship and to fast than men (Fenton 1988). In the 1960s and 1970s, before Hindu Indian temples were established and trained Brahmin priests were available to perform life-cycle rituals at home, such rituals were either postponed and performed in India during a family visit or performed by lay Brahmin men who had some acquaintance with the required rituals and procedures. In this period, some Hindu Indians who missed temple worship and temple celebrations of religious festivals went to local ISKCON temples. Diana Eck (2001, 119) points out that these temples provided a transitional religious public space for Hindu Indians to congregate before they established their own religious institutions. Some Hindu Indians continue to attend these temples today.

The early Indian immigrants made some attempts to seek out and associate with fellow immigrants from India, but scattered settlement and small numbers made such occasions relatively infrequent. At this stage (late 1960s to early 1970s), social groupings tended to be pan-Indian and organized events were largely sociocultural in nature. In areas of the country where there were enough immigrants from a region of India to form a separate organization, linguistic associations such as the Gujarati Samaj and the Tamil Sangam developed to provide immigrants the opportunity to socialize with others who shared their native language, cuisine, and culture. Although ostensibly secular, the dominance of Hindus within them frequently meant that celebrations and programs were conducted in a distinctly Hindu idiom.

The experience of participating in the census of 1970, when there was no appropriate racial category for Indian Americans to check off, mobilized the first national association of Indian Americans, the Association of Indians in America (AIA), formed in 1967 in New York. Through its lobbying, the AIA was able to introduce a new census category, "Asian Indian," for the census of 1980 and was also able to obtain minority status for Indian Americans as "Asians" (Gupta 1999). After the AIA, several other pan-Indian organizations sprang up in the United States. The largest and most widespread of these was the Federation of Indian-American Associations (FIA), which had chapters around the country. Most of them, however, were not too active, only organizing functions to celebrate Indian Independence Day (August 15) and Republic Day (January 26). The schisms endemic to Indian Americans resulted in the frequent formation of splinter groups in the major cities, each claiming to represent the Indian American community. (For example, at one point there were three Indian American organizations in the Los Angeles area, each claiming to be the "real" FIA and even organizing separate Independence Day and Republic Day celebrations; see Potts 2002). An umbrella organization, the National Federation of Indian-American Associations (NFIA), was founded in New York in 1980 to unify and give direction to the regional FIAs.

Home-based religious gatherings were the first centers of group Hindu activity in the United States, with groups getting together to conduct puja, sing bhajans, or to read and discuss portions of the sacred texts. Some groups were ecumenical, including persons from different regions and Hindu traditions. In larger cities, groups based on language of origin and on sectarian affiliation were able to form. These home-based groups provided the nucleus for the larger religious associations and temples that were subsequently established (Williams 1988, 46).

The VHP of America (VHPA) was established in 1970 in New York by four members of the RSS (Lakhihal 2001, 59) and was formally incorporated in 1974. Its first activities were to organize bala vihar programs on the East Coast and to establish a children's bookstore in New Hampshire. Hindu Heritage Youth camps were started in the late seventies (www.vhp-ameria.org/whatvhpa/history.htm). The organization gradually established chapters in cities around the country. The HSS (Hindu Swayamsevak Sangh) was established in New Jersey in 1977 and, like the RSS in India, also started to hold meetings and camps with drills, the chanting of slogans and mantras, and lectures. A related Hindu organization, the Friends of India Society International, was formed at the same time (Lakhihal 2001, 59).

The Hindu Temple Society of North America was formed in New York in 1970 by a group of Hindu immigrants who had been meeting regularly for home-based worship. At around the same time, another home-based worship group, this time in Pittsburgh, also decided to build a temple and affiliated with the Hindu Temple Society. Both the New York and the Pittsburgh groups requested the help of the Shri Venkateswara Temple at Tirupathi in Andhra Pradesh, in south India, the wealthiest temple in India, which as part of its mandate had a scheme to provide "financial aid to temple committees in foreign countries" for the construction or renovation of Hindu temples (Williams 1988, 59). The New York group built a temple to Lord Ganesha (the offspring of Shiva and his consort Parvati) in Flushing, with images of Lord Venkateshwara (a form of Vishnu and the presiding deity of the Tirupathi temple) and other deities, which was dedicated in 1977, and the Pittsburgh group built a temple to Lord Venkateshwara that was dedicated in 1976. In Kauai, Hawaii, the Saiva Siddhanta order established a temple on a 458-acre site in 1973.

Several scholars have pointed out that the construction of temples in the United States began the process of sacralizing the American landscape for Hindus (Clothey 1983; Fenton 1988; Narayanan 1992). Vasudha Narayanan (1999b) notes that priests in these first temples probably started the practice of identifying America as one of the lands in Puranic cosmology at the beginning of their ritual invocations. In 1986, the Sri Venkateshwara temple in Penn Hills, Pittsburgh, issued a cassette of bhajans praising Lord Venkateshwara as abiding in Penn Hills, thus sanctifying America as one of his sacred abodes (Narayanan 1999b). Although these American temples and the later ones that were built tried to adhere closely to the architecture and practices of temples in India, inevitably compromises had to be made in construction, ritual observances, schedules, and interpretations to adapt to the American context (Narayanan 1992; Waghorne 1999), to be discussed in more detail in chapter 5.

Unlike in north India, Hindu temples have played a central role in the religious, economic, and political structure of medieval south Indian kingdoms, and most of the major south Indian temples in India even at the present time were built during the medieval period. Aparna Rayaprol (1997, 28–29) notes that "this difference in the temple cultures of north and south India," combined with "the financial and religious support from Tirupathi," meant that most of the major temples built in the United States, particularly in the 1970s and 1980s, were of the south Indian variety. South Indian Hindus also constitute the majority of the devotees of these temples. Although these American temples attempted to be more ecumenical by including deities from north Indian traditions and by using Sanskrit, there are fundamental differences in architecture, ritual, liturgy, and the religious training of the priests in north Indian and south Indian temples. Consequently, north Indians generally do not feel as comfortable worshipping in them as do south Indians, a source of considerable tension within the Hindu Indian community in several areas in the United States. Frequently the outcome has been that a north Indian group breaks away and builds its own temple.

The Institutionalization of Hinduism:
Mid-1980s to Mid-1990s

As the children of the Hindu immigrants grew older and a permanent return to India grew less and less likely, it became important for parents to develop a more structured means of interacting with co-ethnics, and in the 1980s satsang and bala vihar groups based on region of origin in India began to proliferate among the Hindu Indian community in the United States They represented two different strategies to re-create a Hindu Indian environment on foreign soil. The first, which largely targeted adults, celebrated and reenacted religious practice. The second was directed at teaching the children about the religion. Both options came with their own problems, particularly in the early period, when they were being institutionalized. In the first case, many of the children felt that they were not meaningfully included in the organization. Having a dedicated core of members willing to take on the responsibilities of being the planners and organizers was crucial for the survival of satsang groups. Bala vihars were even more difficult to organize and sustain, since they involved a heavy investment of time and energy by both adults and children. As a much smaller group (compared with a satsang), the bala vihar depended on members' making a commitment to attend most of the monthly meetings. Besides cooking for the dinners and making sure that the children attended regularly and did their homework, parents also had to be willing to share in the responsibility of planning and running the various classes. Many bala vihars disbanded after a few months or years, when the adults and children in the group got too busy. Even if the group was successful in sustaining the bala vihar over a long period, they had to deal with the constant attrition of college-bound children and their parents. Immigrants from non-Hindi- or non-Gujarati-speaking backgrounds, who were interested in transmitting their language, cuisine, and distinctive regional culture to their children but who might not have had the critical mass to sustain a bala vihar, found such problems particularly acute.

In addition to the needs of the children, there were also those of the increasing numbers of retirees, older immigrants who had "made it" (and therefore had more leisure time), and parents of immigrants (brought over under the family reunification provision, often to help with childcare) to consider. Usha Jain (1989, 168–169) notes that religious and philanthropic activities (usually involving collecting money for a cause in India) became increasingly important for the older generation. In addition, such organizations were important to the large numbers of second-wave Indians who began to arrive in the 1980s, because "they provide[d] a renewable continuity with religious organizations and traditions in India" (Williams 1992, 252). Contrary to conventional expectations that the cultural identities and practices of the home country would gradually be abandoned over time, Indians in the United States actually became more community-oriented, more religious, and more "Indianized" as time went on.[7] As the number of Indians in the major metropolitan areas of the country increased, the pan-Indian organizations gave way to more regional and sectarian groups, and thus the first-generation Indians in the United States also became more "parochialized." In areas of the country like New York and New Jersey, where there were large groups of Indian immigrants from a particular region, it was not uncommon for the different castes to form separate organizations. The second generation was simultaneously becoming "Indianized" in the colleges and universities, where there were many pan-Indian organizations—both secular and religious. At home, however, the community with which they identified was the subcultural one, since most family-level interaction was within this group.

Two other milestones during this period were the establishment of a Hindu University of America in Florida and the starting of an ambitious $12 million Encyclopedia of Hinduism project. The VHPA was involved in both these efforts. It began work on the Hindu University of America in 1985, and the university was incorporated in Florida in 1989. Teaching activity began in 1993. By 2000 the university had acquired a permanent campus in Orlando, Florida, and most of the courses offered at the Orlando campus were also available by distance education. At a meeting in 2003, the board members decided to start a course to train priests to run Hindu temples in the United States. The Encyclopedia of Hinduism project was started in 1987 and an eighteen-volume encyclopedia with over ten thousand entries on every aspect of Hinduism, sponsored by the India Heritage Research Foundation (based in Pittsburgh) and prepared out of the offices at the University of South Carolina, is under way.

More temples were built during this period. By the mid-1980s the number of Hindu temples in the United States had increased to over fifty, and Raymond Williams notes that most locations in the United States with more than a hundred families were either building or planning to build a temple (Williams 1988, 56). Some of these temples were built by sectarian groups (groups that follow a particular religious leader or who worship a specific deity). One of the most ambitious of these projects was the Barsana Dham, established in Austin, Texas, in 1990 on a two-hundred-acre site. It attempted to re-create the region of Braj in India where Lord Krishna and his beloved, Radha, are believed to have lived five thousand years ago. All of the important landmarks of Braj were re-created in Barsana Dham (www.isdl.org).

Perhaps the largest and most organized group of sectarian temple builders in the United States has been the Swaminarayan—a neo-Hindu reform Gujarati sect that was founded in the nineteenth century by Sahajanand Swami, believed by his followers to be an incarnation of Vishnu. Among Gujaratis, who form the largest group of migrants from India to the United States and United Kingdom, the largest and fastest-growing subsect is Swaminarayan Hinduism (Williams 2001, 201). Because their chosen method of religious transmission is the mega-festival and the building of large, opulent temples, in the diaspora they often represent the public face of Hinduism to non-Hindus. In the United Kingdom, for instance, the group built a majestic temple complex in Neasden in north London, named one of the seventy wonders of the modern world (Williams 2001, 215), with a permanent exhibition on "Understanding Hinduism" in the basement. Since it opened in 1995 the temple has attracted over 600,000 visitors every year, including the queen and Prince Charles.

In addition to building temple complexes in the United States, the group is planning a large Hindu theme park in New Jersey. In preparation for the latter, the Swaminarayans held a spectacular, forty-acre, thirty-five-million-dollar, month-long Cultural Festival of India in Edison, New Jersey, in 1991 (see Shukla 1997 for a critical assessment). Although the Swaminarayan group emphasizes a Gujarati form of Hinduism, the Cultural Festival projected a more general Vedic Hinduism as the basis of Indian culture and values (Shukla 1997). The group will be discussed in more detail in chapter 5.

The syncretic Hinduism of the Cultural Festival and its Hinducentric vision of India points to another development in the institutionalization of Hinduism in the United States, the development of an ecumenical, pan-Indian Hinduism and a concomitant gradual solidification of the India = Hindu equation. For example, Fenton (1988) outlines the way in which the "India Center" in Atlanta, meant to be a facility for all Indian religious groups to use, was taken over by a group of Hindus who constructed an ecumenical temple inside in the mid-1980s, alienating some Indian religious minorities. Williams (1988, 52) suggests that the ecumenicalism that in the early period was forged out of necessity due to the diversity and small numbers of Hindu immigrants in a region had, by the mid-1980s, "become a conscious strategy to develop a new form of Hinduism among immigrants." As he indicates (1988, 53), the VHPA was a key player in this development. By the mid-1980s, the organization had chapters in twenty-eight states and about seventy-five cities and was also networked informally with Hindu groups, temples, and religious leaders at the national and local levels (Williams 1988, 53). Although the VHP in India also has emphasized ecumenicalism and nationalism (see chapter 6), its message fitted in better in the United States, where the ecumenicalism was occasioned by the diversity within the Hindu American community, the huge expense involved in constructing new temples and centers, and the need to develop a coherent ethnic identity. The India = Hindu equation also conformed well with the American tradition of ethnicizing religion. Recognizing this, the VHPA exhorted Indians abroad to be an example to those in India in the development of ecumenicalism and nationalistic pride. In a resolution passed at the tenth Hindu Conference in New York in 1984, the VHPA urged "all the Hindus of the world—back home and abroad—to act in a broad and nationalistic manner rising above their personal beliefs and creeds, parochial languages, and provincial and sectarian considerations" (cited in Williams 1988, 53). Ecumenicalism and nationalistic pride became central planks of the "official American Hinduism" that began to be increasingly publicized by spokespersons of Hindu American organizations in this period.

From the early 1990s, the Hindu periodical *Hinduism Today*, which claimed its mission as "Affirming the Sanatana Dharma and Recording the History of a Billion Strong Global Religion in Renaissance," played an important role in the institutionalization of Hinduism in the United States and in the development of a global Hinduism. Established in 1979 as a black-and-white newsletter for the worldwide followers (primarily Sri Lankan Hindus) of the Saiva Siddhanta monastic order, based in Hawaii, and its charismatic Anglo-American leader, Satguru Sivaya Subramuniyaswami, the periodical quickly became popular among Hindus in the diaspora as a source of information about Hinduism and Hindus worldwide. Its publishers therefore expanded its circulation and scope and by the 1990s it had become one of the most influential Hindu publications around the globe. The periodical provides answers to frequently asked questions about Hinduism and Hindu practices (as in *Hinduism Today* 1997b, 2000), guidelines on how to be a good Hindu and to raise children according to Hindu precepts (*Hinduism Today* 1997a), articles detailing why Hinduism is "the greatest religion in the world" (February and March/April 2000 issues), and descriptions of the five-day, gift-giving festival in December called Pancha Ganapati that the group developed to provide a Hindu alternative to Christmas (see, for example, the December 1997 and November/December 2001 issues). The magazine began to maintain a comprehensive Web site, and the satguru published several books on Hinduism and organized Hinduism pilgrimages, cruises, and retreats. The monastery also administers a Hindu Heritage Endowment, "a multi-million-dollar trust that maintains permanent sources of income for Hindu efforts worldwide" (www.hinduismtoday.com). *Hinduism Today* has booths at major Hindu and Indian American festivals and conventions around the country, where it gives out tracts summarizing the "nine Hindu beliefs," the "four facts," and the "twenty restraints and practices" that make up "Hinduism's code of conduct." The *Hinduism Today* offices have also frequently been approached by journalists, agencies, and committees for information about Hinduism and the "Hindu position" on various issues and to vet chapters on Hinduism for school textbooks. Today its Hindu Press International is a free daily news summary from a Hindu point of view sent by e-mail to subscribers to the service and posted on its Web site. The organization has become one of the most respected contemporary sources of authority on Hinduism and has played a central role in its propagation and contemporary renaissance. It has also been criticized, however, for its support for the Hindutva movement,[8] for its conservative position on the role of women,[9] and for advocating a strongly Shaivite form of Hinduism despite its mission to represent Hinduism as a whole.

AMERICAN HINDUISM TODAY: FROM THE MID-1990S ON

September 1995 witnessed a phenomenon dubbed the "milk miracle," which demonstrated both the globalized nature of Hinduism and the religious fervor inspired by the Hindu renaissance. For three days, images of the elephant-headed god Ganesha around the world appeared to be drinking the milk offered by devotees. This miracle was first noted in Bombay, but similar accounts of the milk disappearing before the wondering eyes of the devotees were reported from Hindu communities in the United States, Canada, and the United Kingdom.

The doubling of the Indian American population in the 1990s, together with the increase in the numbers of established professionals and retirees with the time and money to devote to religious causes and of second-generation youth searching for identity and community, has resulted in an enormous expansion in the number of Hindu and Indian American associations around the country. For instance, the 1995 directory of the Federation of Hindu Associations listed over thirty such associations for Southern California alone (not all, or even most, satsangs in the region became members of the organization and this number also did not include bala vihars). In addition to organizations based on a region in India, new types of Hindu organizations have been founded, such as the OMkar foundation, whose goal is to provide Hindu prayer and puja services in colleges and universities, and the Network of Hindu Minds (NetOHM), a group in which young professionals can meet and interact. The number of Hindu temples also registered a huge increase. The Harvard Pluralism Project listed 727 Hindu temples and centers in the United States in 2005 (www.pluralism.org). The rise in the numbers of Hindus in the United States has permitted segmentation into regional, caste, and sectarian associations and temples. As the Hindu American community has become established and prosperous, increasingly rare and ancient rituals spread over several days, performed by large contingents of priests brought in from India, are also being performed at these temples and Hindu centers around the country.[10] Hindu saints from India travel the length and breadth of the United States meeting devotees and followers, and as Hindu Americans have remarked, it is often much easier to see and hear such saints in the United States than in India. In 2001 the creation of a "Vedic City" near Fairfield, Iowa, was approved by the state of Iowa. This project was initiated by Maharishi Mahesh Yogi of TM fame, and the city was designed and built to conform to Vedic architectural principles.

Although most of the rules governing intercaste interaction do not apply in the American context, castes, transformed into cultural and social associations, have been thriving, thanks to the multiculturalist emphasis on maintaining one's heritage, the easy access to the Internet, and the availability of quick, inexpensive means of travel. From varna groups such as the Brahmin Samaj of North America (BSNA) to *jati* (subcaste) groups (such as the Telugu Brahmins, Karnataka Brahmins, Leuva Patidars from the Surat, Valsad, and Navsari districts, and Goda Patidars from Goda village in Gujarat), caste associations in the United States organize events in large cities and hold annual conventions around the country with matrimonial meets, fashion shows, and cultural and religious programs. Even Dalit groups have begun to organize and hold conventions.

The "theologizing" effect of immigration (Timothy Smith 1978, 1175) and the desire to transmit Hinduism to its children have meant that the immigrant generation often experiences an increasing interest in reading Hindu texts and in understanding Hindu theology and history. Transnationalism among the Indian American community over the decades has also increased, because of both the Internet and the lower cost of international flights and phone calls. Indian news, movies, and music are also easily accessible, due to the availability of satellite television and the frequent visits of cultural artistes from India. A variety of Indian foods and products, many only available to the very elite in India, have been brought within the reach of the average Indian American. All of this has meant that Hindus in the United States have the resources to be "better" Hindus and Indians than their relatives and friends back home, a fact that they frequently emphasize.

At the same time, the ideology and practice of everyday Hinduism among the immigrant generation have been transformed in the United States in many ways. For instance, in keeping with the American ethos, Hindus in the United States tend to offer more individualistic and cultural explanations for success and failure. Gender and caste ideology are also reinterpreted. Moving somewhat away from an orthoprax tradition, Hinduism in America is becoming more of a theology- and belief-centered religion. Although elderly parents of immigrants may maintain some of the rules of pollution and purity when they visit their children, most of these strictures have been abandoned in the United States. Some groups of Hindu Americans, such as orthodox south Indian Brahmins, devout Swaminarayan members, and those who have adopted some form of neo-Hinduism, eat only vegetarian food, but an increasing number of Hindu Americans in the United States eat meat and even beef (although the latter is usually only outside the home, in fast-food venues and restaurants). Some women do observe weekly fasts, but here again the practice has decreased in the United States. The major domestic and life-cycle rituals are performed, but with several modifications. For instance, for a variety of reasons that will be discussed in chapter 5, many rituals are celebrated in a temple, with priests offering explanations for each aspect of the rite. Most of the village-level deities have not been enshrined in the United States, and thus many of the non-Sanskritic worship practices have been abandoned. Pilgrimages to Hindu temples and centers in the United States and in India are popular among Hindu Americans as a means of reconnecting with their spiritual heritage and transmitting it to their children.

The large influx of software engineers and programmers on H-1B visas from the 1990s has also affected the articulation of a Hindu American identity. Arvind Rajagopal (2000, 482), who met several of these programmers at a Hindu Swayamsevak Sangh (HSS) camp in Northern California, argues that they represent "a different phase of immigration," because they are often from the "hinterland regions" of India, unlike most of the earlier immigrants, who have been from the metropolises. He goes on to say that many of these new immigrants turn to Hindu groups such as the HSS in the United States as a way to counteract the marginalization they experience in their work lives. Besides Hindu camps and events, the Internet has become an important means for this group to re-create community. From around 2000, the Internet became a major site of Hindu American activity, with the formation of hundreds of Internet discussion groups devoted to Indian- or Hindu-related topics and of Internet E-zines like *Sulekha.com* (which bills itself as the "#1 Indian Online Community"), *Outlook.com*, and *Rediff.com*. Software engineers and programmers dominate Indian American Internet forums, discussed in chapter 9. Mathew (2000, 127) notes that "many male Indian professionals surf the Net and converse with other Indian men—talk nostalgia, talk spiritual, and talk India" as a daily "fix" at the end of the day to "cast off the feeling of alienation, that feeling of being ruled, by establishing contact with the mother country each night." The VHPA has been active in developing Hindu Web sites. A VHPA activist whom I met in the summer of 2000 claimed that the organization had 2,600 sites on the Web.

Second-generation Hindu Americans face the difficult task of straddling their parents' culture and that of the wider society, confronting racism, and dealing with the opportunities and pressures of multiculturalism. Hinduism and "Indianness" have seemed to become particularly significant in this process (Maira 2002), with many Hindu American youth either rejecting it strongly or embracing it passionately, and sometimes going from one attitude to the other. Many of the teenagers and college students whom I spoke with described the pain they experienced growing up with "brown skins" in a predominantly white environment (generally, the first generation preferred to avoid talking about race altogether). They said that their eagerness to be accepted had initially led them to turn away from their Indianness and to try to be as much like their white friends as possible. Rejecting their roots, however, only increased their identity crisis and feeling of alienation, since it became obvious to them that no matter what they did, they were not going to be accepted as "just American." The crisis was only resolved when they accepted their heritage and began to learn more about Hinduism and Indian culture, generally through the help of one of the five types of religious organizations described in chapter 1. They told me that over time, they came to see the beauty and value of their heritage and also finally started to feel comfortable with themselves as Hindus and as Indian Americans—Americans with Indian roots. A crisis revolving around racial identity was resolved by turning to religion and religious organizations.

An article by a law student at Yale, Aditi Banerjee (the text of a talk she gave in 2003 at the "Hindu Ideological Empowerment Seminar" held in Chicago), entitled "Hindu-American: Both Sides of the Hyphen," was posted on a number of Indian American Web sites and Internet groups and addresses some of these identity issues. Banerjee (2003) argues that second- and later-generation Indian Americans from a Hindu background should adopt a "Hindu-American" identity as opposed to an Indian American or Asian American identity, because a religious identity is more deep-rooted than ethnicity or even culture. "For example," she states, "while I may go for months without uttering a word of Bengali [her native language] or even without speaking to another Indian, not a day would pass by where I wouldn't pray to Krishna or recite the Gayatri mantra." She also prefers to identify as Hindu American because it is an identity that helps to surmount ethnicization and racialization, since it "looks at the individual rather than broad categories of ethnicity or race; it's an identity that is chosen rather than assigned." She exhorts Hindu American youth to become more educated in Hinduism so that they can come to understand its "faith and philosophy." Becoming so educated will help to separate the essence of the religion from the "social customs and rituals that have come to plague it through the years" and thus enable them to become Hindu in a new American way, as distinct from the Indian way of the immigrant generation. According to Banerjee, becoming Hindu American, embracing "both sides of the hyphen," will help the second generation to overcome the infamous ABCD (American-Born Confused Desis) syndrome and will ensure the survival of Hinduism (Banerjee 2003).[11]

Embracing a Hindu American identity frequently seemed to involve an idealization of India and Hinduism by the second generation, based on the nostalgic constructions of their parents or on their own limited experience of India. On second-generation Internet forums I have seen Indian American youth make sweeping remarks such as, "There is no caste system in India anymore. I just returned from a three week trip to Delhi and I did not see or hear about even one instance of caste discrimination." Another person rejected the argument that poverty was a major problem in India, saying that his own relatives were "fabulously wealthy." Like other American youth, Hindu Americans also demand an intellectual understanding of their religion and tradition, and thus want to know the "meaning" of Hindu practices, chants, and beliefs. The cursory and frequently insulting treatment that India and Hinduism receive in many American school textbooks provides further motivation to learn about Indian history. A trip to India on their own (unaccompanied by parents), to visit relatives, participate in a religious or cultural summer camp, take courses at a university, or, most recently, to do social service on an Indicorps fellowship, has become almost a rite of passage for many second-generation Indian Americans.[12] During these trips they are amazed to find that many youth in India do not know and do not care about their religion or history. "We know more about Hinduism and Indian culture than our cousins in India" is a frequently voiced statement.

CHAPTER 4

"We Are Better Hindus Here"

LOCAL ASSOCIATIONS

It is a pleasant Saturday evening. In a Southern California suburb, a row of expensive cars is parked in front of an upper-middle-class house. Shoes and sandals are arranged neatly outside on the porch. Inside, the furniture has been cleared away from the large living room and sheets spread over the carpet. Arranged against the center of the wall that everyone faces is a makeshift shrine with pictures of various Hindu deities, several of whom are adorned with fresh garlands of flowers. Tall brass oil lamps with flickering flames stand on either side of the shrine. Baskets containing fruit and flowers have been placed in front. A man dressed in traditional south Indian clothes is seated on the floor before the shrine, his wife beside him in a silk sari. Around the couple are seated a group of about fifty people, the men and boys, in casual Western clothes, largely on one side of the room, and the women and girls, dressed in rich and colorful Indian clothes, on the other.

This is the monthly devotional meeting of the Kerala Hindu Organization (KHO), a satsang of Hindu immigrants from Kerala state in south India. The KHO, established in the early 1990s, is an association of fifty to seventy families, including Malayalee Hindus (Hindus whose ancestral language is Malayalam, the language of Kerala) and some Tamil Brahmin families (Brahmins whose ancestral language is Tamil, the language of the adjoining state of Tamil Nadu) who have lived in Kerala for generations and who therefore speak Malayalam in addition to Tamil. Members meet on the second Saturday of the month in different locations (mostly people's houses) around the region for the puja and bhajans. Around forty to sixty people attend each puja. Because the members are scattered over a wide area, except for the "regulars," it is a changing group that attends each meeting, depending on the locality. In addition to the monthly puja, cultural programs are also sponsored several times during the year, when music and dance-dramas are performed by community members or by visiting artistes from Kerala.

The KHO meeting starts with the lay worship leader chanting an invocation (in Sanskrit) to the deities while gently throwing flowers before them, so that by the end of the invocation, there is a fragrant, multicolored mound in front of the shrine. The invocation is followed by the singing of bhajans accompanied by cymbals, played by the leader's wife. Occasionally there is a brief lull, and the leader and his wife call for volunteers to start new bhajans. Different members of the group take turns leading the singing, including one teenage girl. The leader of the bhajan sings a line and the rest of the group repeats it. Fifteen to twenty bhajans are sung, each taking around five minutes.

A few months before my fieldwork with the group ended, a "*Gita* discussion" period was introduced toward the end of the puja, during which two verses from the *Bhagavad Gita* were translated and explained by Mrs. Kala Nayar, followed by a group discussion in English. During one such discussion, a member of the group raised the issue, "If the Pandavas were good, why did they have to suffer and go to war?" More generally he wanted to know why bad things happened to good people and why people should bother to be good if that was the case. Mrs. Nayar's reply was that it could be because of something bad done by the person in a past incarnation. "Good deeds will be rewarded, if not in this life, then at least in the next," she answered firmly. Two of the teenage girls in the group also became involved in the discussion at this point, one pointing out that the Hindu conception of good and evil is more complicated than the Christian one, since "good does not always give place to good." The other elaborated, "Yes, a person may lead a good life and then be rewarded in the next life with a lot of money, but the money may make him arrogant. So he will be punished in the following life." After complaints from the teenagers in the group that they felt alienated from the KHO meetings since they were largely Sanskrit-based and adult oriented, the group was making special efforts to try to involve them through discussions and youth activities. If the participation in the *Gita* sessions was any indication, this effort seemed to be yielding results.

The two-and-a-half-hour worship concludes with further invocations and devotions by the lay priest and a group chant. A potluck vegetarian south Indian meal follows, during which there is a lot of joking and teasing as people catch up on the month's news. Relatives and jobs are inquired after, clothes and jewelry admired, recipes and professional information traded, while those who have recently visited India regale the others with their accounts. Youngsters go off and form their own little groups. In the adult clusters, children are discussed in great detail by the parents—their health, educational progress, extracurricular accomplishments, and in the case of older children, concerns about finding appropriate marriage partners for them.

On a Sunday afternoon in another suburban south Indian household in the same region, a group of twelve Tamil Hindu families gets together for the monthly bala vihar meeting, also led by a lay leader, the father of two of the children in the group. This group has been in existence since 1980, with a changing assortment of families. The bala vihar consists of a three-and-a-half-hour session, divided into several short class periods, each dealing with a specific topic. Children learn bhajans and *slokams* (chants), discuss Hindu philosophy, and are told stories from the Hindu epics. There is also a Tamil language class. The parents (mostly the mothers) are the teachers of the bala vihar.

After singing some bhajans and learning the new one for the month, taught by one of the mothers, there is a discussion (in English) of Hindu philosophy and values and how they can be practiced in everyday life in American society. The first theme is the necessity for each individual to do his or her allotted tasks, however small, to the best of his or her ability for the well-being and smooth functioning of society. Children and parents together discuss the problems involved in maintaining the delicate balance between working toward the good of the whole and achieving individual success. One of the young girls gives an example of this tension: "Like, you know, I may want all my friends to get good grades but my effort is spent in studying to get a good grade for myself." The group nods in agreement. At this point one of the men comes forward to make a further point. He cautions the children that in the work world people are often not given credit for their efforts. "Let me give you an example," he says. "I am a scientist and a common problem that comes up in my field regards who gets to be the first author for publications." He goes on to explain the significance of first authorship and gives examples of when such decisions are not made fairly. He ends by saying, "so you should also be aware of your rights and fight for them."

The leader then moves on and discusses how to cope with disappointment when results fall below one's expectations despite hard work. Here his point is that the children should do their very best and then accept what they get as a result of their work, even if it is a B grade. "Don't care too much about the grade as such," he says. "But how can you not care about grades?" one young girl bursts out. Another teenager tries to explain to her, "Yes, you work really hard but a B somewhere in your transcript prevents you from getting into Harvard and you feel really bad. But sometime later you may realize that the place you did get into was better for you than Harvard." One of the women, a physician, adds, "Not getting the end that you think you deserve is very hard. I used to get very depressed when that happened to me and still do sometimes, but over time I have tried to cultivate a certain detachment. You should try to recognize that your effort is the only thing that you have control over, so do your very best but then stop thinking about it, go out and have a good time to rejuvenate yourself"; she pauses and then adds, "for the next big effort." There is laughter at this. She continues, "But the effect of this attempt to better yourself is that it results in an expanding sphere of influence. Take Gandhi for instance. He was at first only trying to better himself, but soon that started affecting others and finally it resulted in his having a major effect on the whole world."

After a snack break, the group divides into two for the Tamil language class. The junior class focuses on vocabulary while the senior class is taught to appreciate the beauty of classical devotional Tamil poetry. The group reconvenes in the living room for the story session, led by another of the women. The stories are taken from the Hindu epics. Here again the moral of each story is expounded and discussed. One of today's stories has a message about the sanctity of marriage and family, and the evils of extramarital sex. Particular Hindu practices deriving from the stories are explained and the children are encouraged to follow them since they have been "time tested over thousands of years." The eagerly awaited crossword puzzle of the month is given out next. The clues concern Hinduism, Tamil vocabulary, and the history, geography, and culture of India. The bala vihar concludes with the "host family time," when the child of the family which is hosting the bala vihar that month generally makes a presentation. This month the teenage daughter shows the group a home video of a trip the family had made to south India, during which they had made a pilgrimage to several temples, ending with their family temple. She gives an emotional account of the trip and the meaning it had for her, concluding with a beautiful bhajan that she says is the favorite of the deity in their family temple. Several in the group are visibly moved. Finally, there is a lavish potluck meal to end the evening.

THE FIELDWORK

My primary ethnographic study of the KHO was conducted over a period of two years in the 1990s. At the time, I was part of the New Ethnic and Immigrant Congregations Project (NEICP), directed by Stephen Warner. After that period, I sporadically attended events of the organization as long as I was in the region and kept in touch with a few of the members. In addition to attending monthly meetings, I visited the homes of many of the members and conducted semi-structured interviews with thirty-seven members. In the immigrant generation, I focused on eighteen married couples. I interviewed all but one of the wives—either alone or with their husbands, and fourteen of the eighteen husbands. I also interviewed six of the second-generation members. In addition, I talked more informally with many more men, women, and children as I participated in several activities with the members in the group. My own position as a Malayalee immigrant and a professional helped me considerably. However, my Christian background was an initial problem. Delicate situations continued to occur, particularly when I was introduced to new members, since my last name identifies me as a person from a Kerala Christian family.

During my initial meeting with the members of the KHO committee, they told me that they were particularly anxious that I did not perceive or characterize them as "fanatic" Hindus or misrepresent the "spirit" of the organization. They emphasized that they had started the organization with the "best of intentions" and that they had not intended to be "separatist" or to hurt or alienate anyone. Hari Ramanan indicated that the members did not want to be treated "like museum pieces" and that they did not want me to conduct a "Margaret Mead type of study" where they were exoticized. I reassured them as best I could, saying that as an Indian immigrant myself, I had some understanding of the culture and context and could relate to their situation, but I think they were not wholly convinced. My being a young, single woman only increased the unease of members regarding my expertise to do a study of a "sensitive" issue such as religion. At this meeting, the president, Ravi Menon, seemed to want to control the type of information I obtained and my access to the group, telling me that I should turn in my "list of questions" to Meena Ramesh, the secretary of the group, who would answer the ones she knew and consult with the committee to provide answers to the rest. When I told them that I would like to talk to the lay members of the KHO, Menon told me that the secretary would arrange the interviews at her house.

A week after this initial encounter, Stephen Warner, whom the KHO members referred to as my "boss," met with the committee to explain the goal of the study and obtain their permission. As a white, middle-aged, professorial-looking man, Warner radiated an aura of authority and competence that helped to reassure the committee about the nature of the study and my own qualifications. His second visit the following month for a monthly puja assuaged most further concerns of the members, and after that the members were by and large warm, welcoming, and hospitable.

I was introduced to the Tamil bala vihar through Vivek Iyer and his wife, members of the KHO, and attended several of the monthly meetings over a period of a year, also in the 1990s. In addition to the Iyers, the friendship extended to me by another group member—Lakshmi Narayan, a university researcher who could relate to my project—was crucial in helping me enter into the group. I also attended some other public events where group members participated. I talked to first- and second-generation members at the bala vihar, but did not do detailed interviews with them. Although I am a Malayalee by ancestry, I grew up in Tamil Nadu and studied Tamil in school and am therefore familiar with the language and culture. However, as a Christian and non-Tamil single woman, my outsider status was even more conspicuous in the bala vihar setting. Because of this, I was never able to overcome the "outsider" barrier fully and was therefore not able to develop an easy rapport with members of this group.

I chose to study the KHO and the Tamil bala vihar because of my own linguistic and regional background. Since there are distinct social, cultural and historical differences between the northern and southern regions of India, the two south Indian groups in my study have much in common but may not represent north Indian immigrants in some respects. For instance, in general, women in south India are more educated than their northern Indian counterparts. There is also a divergence between Kerala and Tamil Nadu in this regard, with Kerala having higher rates of education in general and female education in particular than Tamil Nadu (and the rest of India).

As I discovered through my subsequent research, however, Brahmins with a Tamilian ancestry (who were in both the KHO and the bala vihar) have been key players in the institutionalization of Hinduism in Southern California and around the country, making them an important group to focus on in a study of American Hinduism. In Southern California, they were the central figures in the establishment and everyday running of the regional temple, the local branch of the VHP, the Chinmaya mission, the HSC chapter, and the unaffiliated Hindu student organization that I studied.

MEMBERSHIP BACKGROUND

Since I only conducted detailed interviews with the members of the KHO, I draw primarily on the information obtained from my interviews with this group.

Although their patterns of migration might be somewhat exceptional, when it comes to the issues raised by migration and settlement in the United States, the concerns of KHO members are fairly typical of those of Indian immigrants who join local associations like the KHO and the bala vihar.

The KHO was a fairly elite group in class and occupational terms, a fact that they repeatedly emphasized to me and, on the two occasions that he met with some of the group, to Stephen Warner. Most members, both male and female, were professionals—mainly doctors, engineers, scientists, and accountants who had been in the United States for twenty to thirty years. Not surprisingly, most of them also hailed from upper-caste and upper-middle- to upper-class backgrounds in Kerala. The largest group belonged to the Nayar regional caste, followed by Tamil Brahmins (mostly those who had grown up in Kerala).

I began the interviews with the immigrant generation by asking the members to describe their family background. The majority of the people whom I interviewed indicated that one or both of their parents had been "religious," conducting daily pujas at home, visiting the local temple regularly, and in the case of women, observing some of the fasts and menstrual taboos. Indira, a woman in her early forties, mentioned that her father (who had doted on her while she was growing up) had spent several hours a day in meditation toward the end of his life. She felt that his spirit was providing her some kind of "coverage" in her everyday life in the United States, since "many times things have had a way of working out for me." Some of those from Brahmin and elite Nayar backgrounds described their families as being "orthodox," by which they meant that they had been strict in observing the rituals and the pollution and purity rules governing their caste. Several mentioned the arduous fasts and dietary codes that their mothers and grandmothers had observed, including avoiding onions and garlic altogether.[1] Only one man explicitly brought up the restrictions on intercaste interaction observed by his family, indicating that he had rebelled against these practices and had ultimately been forced to leave the family home because of his disobedience. Most individuals characterized themselves as having been "religious" or "spiritual" from a fairly young age. Eight of the men, however, indicated that they had become more so over the past decade, either because of a personal crisis or because they had more time to themselves since they had established themselves professionally and their children had left home.

GENDER, MIGRATION, AND SETTLEMENT
Migration Patterns

In the case of fourteen of the eighteen married couples in the KHO whom I interviewed, one or both spouses had come to the United States as graduate students. Typically they arrived with the intention of returning home after their studies, but had found work and stayed on. Not surprisingly, the migration was largely male led. In eleven of the fourteen cases of married couples of the KHO whose migration had taken place through student visas, it was the man who had been the primary visa holder.[2] In most of these cases, the male students had been unmarried when they started graduate studies in the United States. They returned to India to obtain an arranged marriage and then sponsored their wives' immigration.

In the case of the other four couples whom I interviewed, the husbands had come to the United States in search of a job with better professional prospects, and their families had subsequently joined them. Two of these four couples had relatives in the country who had sponsored their visas and helped them to find jobs. Even in such cases, the migration had generally been viewed as temporary, with the families intending to return to India after a few years. Explaining how their plans had changed and they had come to stay on, many interviewees mentioned that their decision had been for the sake of their children, who had quickly "adapted" to American life and had been reluctant to return. The parents had also realized that their daughters and sons would have better education and job opportunities in the United States. Others indicated that they had gotten used to the "standard of living" and all the household conveniences that they were now able to afford. A few of the women told me that they had wanted to stay because they were reluctant to give up the freedom and independence that they found in the United States.

Early Period of Settlement

Although the migration of this group occurred within a patriarchal framework, the settlement process seemed to have changed gender relations toward greater egalitarianism. Two important factors in this change were the social isolation of the family and women's entry into the paid labor force.

The isolation from relatives and friends that migration brings about can be particularly difficult for women who do not work outside the home (Bhutani 1994, 38; Rangaswamy 1996, 426). Many of the women I spoke to described the loneliness and anguish they experienced in their early years of migration. Meena, a woman in her late forties and a member of the KHO, described how desperately unhappy she had been in the first few months. "Arvind [her husband] would go off to work and the children to school and then I would be all by myself in the apartment. I have never been so alone. I did not know anyone around—I had no relatives or friends nearby. I cried a lot during this period but I kept my intense unhappiness from my husband. And when I met other Indians who were smiling and laughing, I would ask them, how can you laugh and smile?"

The isolation is also experienced by Indian men. In a discussion about the initial period of migration, Shankar, a male member of the KHO, mentioned that he and his wife "were so lonely and depressed—it almost drove us out of our minds at times. We looked through the phone book for Indian-sounding names and called them, but many of the Indians we reached were not very friendly."

In India, men and women generally have separate social networks and thus receive most of their social support from members of their own sex. The loss of this social network forces Indian immigrant couples to depend much more on each other for companionship and emotional intimacy than they would have in India. This is particularly the case in the immediate postmigration period, when couples generally have no one else to turn to but each other to process the new experiences they confront.

Ambika told me that one outcome of the difficult early period of migration was that she and her husband developed a closer relationship and "really started talking to each other." Another positive outcome that many women mentioned was the freedom they obtained from the social constraints of in-laws, relatives, and gossipy neighbors. Educated Indian women generally gain more independence and spatial mobility in the United States (see also Rayaprol 1997, 99). As Lakshmi pointed out, "Here you can just get into the car and go where you want to. In India, people don't like women going out alone, so you are always dependent on someone else to take you out." Meena told me that about once a year, she and a few of her female friends would go to a neighboring city, rent a room in a hotel, and spend a weekend sightseeing, relaxing, and talking together, something that would be much less likely to happen in India.

Women's Employment

All of the women in the KHO (except one who was studying at the time of my research, and another who had been a well-known actress in India and had quit acting after her marriage) were working outside the home at the time of my study. All had professional or white-collar positions and worked as doctors (the most common profession), scientists, or accountants, or as employees in banks, computer industries, and government offices. Although almost all of the women had at least a bachelor's degree at the time of their marriage, several would probably not have worked had they stayed in India (see Leonard 1993, 169). A combination of factors was responsible for propelling them into the paid labor force. In addition to the isolation that housewives felt, household chores were less time consuming in America because of the availability of processed food and gadgets and the modification of many of the time-consuming traditional cooking practices, leaving women with more time on their hands. There were also more opportunities for education and more flexibility in the times courses were offered, allowing women to schedule their studies around their household responsibilities by going to school part-time and by attending evening and weekend classes. Even in cases where the husbands had initially resisted, the financial contribution provided by the jobs served to overcome that resistance. In India, family wealth helps individuals launch their married lives and to purchase housing. Foreign exchange restrictions and the low value of the rupee in dollar terms mean that Indian immigrants generally do not have this source of financial support. Thus a second income becomes more necessary in the United States.

The larger proportion of working Indian women in the United States also derives from the redefinition of male and female honor that takes place as a consequence of the combination of social independence and economic need experienced by immigrant families. Several women, including Meena, told me that they had not worked outside the home in India because their husbands had feared that such work would be seen as dishonorable by relatives and friends. Many of these Indian men eventually yielded to their wives' request in the United States, since a wife who worked was much more acceptable and even normative within the Indian American society that now functioned as these husbands' reference group (see also Bhutani 1994, 51).

Vidhya's comment, "Oh, he [her husband] finally said I could work as long as it did not interfere with my household responsibilities," was echoed by many of the women.

All the employed women I spoke to reported that despite the long hours they worked and the problems involved in juggling their household responsibilities and their jobs, their careers gave them a sense of achievement and self-fulfillment. Meena's husband had recently quit his job in a government agency to start his own business at home. When I asked Meena (who had been complaining about her long commute) whether she would also join her husband in the business, she replied quickly, "Oh, no. I need my independence." Indira, who had taken evening classes, completed her CPA degree, and become a successful financial consultant, described the exhilaration she experienced when top company executives called her at home to ask for advice or listened to her deferentially at "high power" meetings. Other studies also refer to the importance Indian American women accord to their careers (Bhutani 1994, 51; Rangaswamy 1996, 426). Only four (of the seventeen) women mentioned any problems with gender or racial discrimination in their jobs, and none felt it was a serious issue. Two women indicated that their "foreignness" was actually an advantage since, in Indira's words, "a hint of an accent adds exoticity and creates interest." According to Indira, it also prevented her male colleagues from categorizing her with other American women. "My male business friends tell me that they find it easier to talk to me than to American women—I am direct and blunt and to the point. I am one of the boys!"

In the context of women's employment, the absence of servants, and the redefinitions of honor, women were often able to get their husbands to help with housework to at least some degree. Kiran, a young Indian woman, told me that she and her husband, Ram, discussed returning to India. She said she had mixed feelings, because she felt that once he was there, the "masculinity thing" would become increasingly important and they would lose some of the companionship they now enjoyed. At this point, Ram entered the room. Turning to him, Kiran said to me, "I asked him whether he would do all this for me [take out the garbage, wash the dishes, help with the groceries] if we were in India." Ram replied, as if on cue, "No, definitely not," and then added, "but there you will have servants to help you." Padma, an officeholder of the KHO, after a discussion of how her relationship with her husband had undergone a transformation after coming to the United States, summed it up, saying, "Now we are almost equal." Other studies of Indian American women support the conclusion that a greater egalitarianism develops in gender relations (Bhutani 1994; Leonard 1993; Rangaswamy 1996; Rayaprol 1997).[3] That men may not be altogether pleased by these developments is indicated by what Shanti, another Malayalee woman in her mid-forties, told me. She mentioned that her husband, who had traveled to India after a space of several years, had remarked rather woefully upon his return that "women there treat their husbands so nicely!"

Men's Employment

Like the women, several of the men had done well in their jobs and most indicated that they had not encountered any significant obstacles in their work lives in the

United States. Five (of the fourteen) referred to problems that they had faced, including being laid off or fired. But only three men referred to racism in the workplace directly, talking about their own experiences or that of a friend. One of them, Shankar, an accountant working for the state government said bitterly, "As immigrants, we have to do 200 percent to get 100 percent credit, whereas people here put in 50 percent and get 100 percent credit." Some of those who faced problems had turned to religion to help them through their difficulties. Gopi, an engineer who had started his own business when he lost his corporate job (and was doing very well), told me that he had started doing daily and weekly pujas after being laid off, "for the comfort and discipline." "Now," he said, "I can't stop." Hari Ramanan, a scientist, confided, "Right now I am going through hell at work. I have a Chinese boss and he does not like me so he treats me badly." Hari said he used yoga to deal with the stress of his work life. He was doing a yoga exercise in which he visualized people—particularly those whom he did not like—as being "full of light." This image helped him be nice and pleasant to his boss, despite the insulting behavior of the latter. He told me that he had done the exercise, thinking of his boss for several weeks, before his contract had been due to expire. "And, sure enough, my boss called me the day before [the contract was to expire] and said that he was extending it for a couple of months. I didn't tell him that I had been manipulating him to do that!"

THE SECOND GENERATION
Raising Children in the United States

The KHO was formed in the early nineties, same years before I started my research on the group. Most families that I interviewed had been in the United States for at least two decades, and a large number had college-age children. Many of the parents talked about the challenges they had faced bringing up their children in the absence of an organization like the KHO. Two of the mothers admitted that in hindsight, they had probably been "overprotective" and too restrictive. Padma told me that she and her husband had never left their children (a son and a daughter) with a babysitter, for fear of what the person might do to them. They had not even left the children alone at home during the day until they were in their late teens. The children had not been permitted to go out alone or to go to a friend's place (unless it was someone in the immediate neighborhood). Padma said that the reason that they had been so strict with their children was because they were "in a strange, new country." They had been one of the earliest Malayalees in the area and their children had also been much older than those of other Indians they knew, so they had no one to consult or model themselves after. Another man mentioned that in order to be close to the university that his daughter was attending, he had found a new job and the family had moved. He would go and pick her up in the evening after her classes, since he did not want her to have to walk through the campus after dark.

In the absence of Hindu organizations like the KHO and the Tamil bala vihar, parents who were knowledgeable about Hinduism tried to educate their children at home by telling them stories from the epics and explaining the meaning of the festivals

they celebrated and the rituals they practiced. One member of the KHO who found
herself unable to answer many of her daughter's questions took her to the ISKCON
temple in the region for their weekend discourses. Parents also tried to take their children to as many concerts and Indian events as possible, so that they could learn about
Indian culture. Families who lived in areas where Indian dance and music classes were
being offered enrolled their children in such classes, in some cases driving two hours
each way to attend them. Several parents talked about the big psychological difference
these classes seemed to make to their children. "They helped Veena and Ambujam
connect with and appreciate their culture," said Prabha Iyer, about her two daughters.
The families also tried to make frequent trips to India so that their children could keep
in touch with their relatives and their Indian background. The Iyers told me that their
two girls had gone to India for two months every summer for well over a decade.
When the girls were young, the parents managed the summer trip by taking turns staying in India with them (each parent had only four weeks of leave a year). One parent
would take the girls to India and the other would bring them back. They did this for
five consecutive summers when the older daughter was between nine and fourteen
years of age. After that the two girls went by themselves. Two families in the KHO had
been part of bala vihars—the Iyers, who had been one of the founding members of
the Tamil bala vihar, and the Ramachandrans, who had been involved with a VHP
bala vihar in the 1980s. Satya Ramachandran indicated that the VHP had been apolitical at the time and that they had dropped out when it became politicized.

Because of the importance of intragroup marriages for Hindus, the choice of a suitable marriage partner for their children loomed as a big concern for parents in the
United States. With the exception of one couple (of the eighteen) in the immigrant
generation, the marriages of all of the other adult members of the KHO whom I interviewed had been arranged by their families following traditional criteria. Both partners
had given their consent to the marriage after a brief meeting with their spouse-to-be.
All of the immigrant parents that I spoke to, however, realized that they could
not expect their children to follow this pattern. They were willing to be much more
flexible about their children's marriages and, within limits, to allow the young couple
more time and opportunity to get to know each other. But they indicated that they
would still strongly prefer that their children marry an Indian Hindu, ideally of the
same linguistic and caste background. Most parents were against marriage to
"Americans" (by which they meant white Americans), since they feared the marriage
"would not last."[4] Many of them, particularly the men, also indicated that they did not
believe in "love" and "romance" as the sole basis for marriage. Krishnan echoed the
opinions of many of the members when he told some white American visitors at a
satsang (friends of the family hosting the meeting that month) that he felt that marriage was "too important to leave to chance" and that the "arranged marriage" system was the best way to build a stable relationship. In discussion with me, Vivek Iyer
elaborated, saying, "Married life is full of compromises and the more the two have
in common, the more successful it will be. Here [in the United States] marriage is
considered to be a union of two individuals. But we believe that marriage is a union
of two families and both families also help to support the marriage." On another

occasion, Ravi Menon, whose daughter had recently become engaged to marry a man in Kerala whom she had been introduced to through relatives (and on whose behalf they were hosting the monthly satsang), said derisively, "It [romance] is good for writing poetry, but we have to look at the practical aspects [of marriage]."

Parents were also very concerned about the professional and financial future of their children, and within the group there was a strong emphasis on professional education. Members felt that medicine, engineering, and law provided the greatest financial security and stability. Hari Ramanan, who had two teenage sons, told me that they often rebelled against his rules and complained that he was too strict with them. He, in contrast, was concerned that "they won't make it in this competitive world unless they work really hard now." In the course of one such discussion, the younger one had apparently retorted, "Dad, I am eighteen—these are the best years of my life!" "What do I do with him?" Hari asked me, half-seriously. "He does not want to plan his day. He feels that things should happen spontaneously. I, on the other hand, want him to be organized so that he uses every hour properly."

Growing Up in the United States

Most of the second-generation members of the KHO talked about how "it is really hard growing up here as both Indian and American." One of the problems was the difference in the expectations of Indian parents compared with their American counterparts. Amit, a young man in his mid-twenties, said that his parents had been very strict with him and had not even let him go to the houses of many of his friends. They had also constantly emphasized the importance of education and had insisted that he come home well in time to do his homework (which they supervised while he was in school). The parents of his friends, in contrast, had given their children a great deal of freedom and "would only ask about their studies when the report card came in." He admitted that he had resented his parents' rules and that there had been periods when there was significant tension at home because of these issues. But in retrospect, Amit said that he was grateful to his parents for being so strict with him, since their rules kept him from neglecting his studies. His good grades had helped him get into a prestigious business program at a local university, while his friends had gone to community colleges. He commented that another big difference between himself and his neighborhood friends was the close relationship that he now had with his parents, something his friends apparently did not have, and envied.

A second problem that most of the second generation mentioned was the racism and ethnocentricism that they faced while growing up. Anand, a young man in his early twenties, told me that he had found the racism in a small town in Northern California, where he had lived as a teenager, hard to handle. He had attempted to overcompensate for it in other ways by trying to be more like everyone else. He told me that his experiences had taught him that "as a person of color you have to be so much better and do so much better to be accepted." The only reason he had survived (and was doing well in college), he said, was his defiant attitude. "If you don't have attitude, man, you are dead." Latha, a teenager who came to the United States at a young age, similarly remembers her early years as being very difficult, because "everything was so different from India." She had been extremely conscious that she looked and spoke differently and said that a few students were mean to her. When she realized that it was because of her background, she had started to hate the fact that she was Indian. The frequent trips the family made to India only made it worse, since she found it difficult to "switch on and switch off" in the two societies that were so different. Latha's negative feelings about herself and her Indian identity only changed in high school. Her family had moved to an area that was more diverse, and she was also able to attend Indian dance and music classes. It was these classes that made her feel that Indian culture and Hinduism were beautiful after all. Meera, a high school student, described how her classmates in her fifth-grade class had taunted her by calling her "Meera Diarrhea" and by asking her if "the red dot on my forehead was a zit." She also mentioned that she used to dread parents' nights, because her mother would come dressed in a sari, wearing that "embarrassing dot." Like Latha, Meera's acceptance and appreciation of her identity came much later, as she started reading "every Hindu epic, story, and legend I could get my hands on" and discovered that there was "so much culture, thousands of years old, to be experienced."

Marriage was of great concern to the second generation, as it was for their parents. But unlike the latter, the children emphasized the importance of romance as the basis of marriage. For instance, although her father had dismissed romance as being only "good for writing poetry," Nitya Menon, the young woman who was engaged to a man from Kerala, described herself as being "totally in love" with her fiancé, Vijay, and indicated that having a romantic relationship with him was important to her. "Growing up here, the importance of romance is instilled in you and I might have felt unfulfilled if I didn't have it." She characterized Vijay as "my soul mate who miraculously dropped right into my arms" and told me that she and Vijay had met a couple of times in Kerala (including taking a trip to a nearby waterfall), discovered that they had a great deal in common, and decided that they were "right for each other" before they had agreed to the match.

Most of the younger generation indicated that although they did not rule out marrying a non-Indian, they would prefer to marry someone from an Indian background and, ideally, from the same subgroup, because it would be "easier to adjust" to such a person (both for themselves but even more so for their families). But except for one young woman (who said that she was "open" on the issue), all indicated that they would not want to marry someone who had grown up in India, because "there is too much difference between someone who is brought up in India and here." Although against such a marriage for himself, Amit, the young man in his mid-twenties, admitted that he knew several Indian American men who had gone back to marry women from India and that he had discussed it with some of his friends who were considering such an arrangement. "They say, then she will be obedient and will look after you. I think that is bizarre." Only one young woman and her brother were sure that they would only marry an Indian American. Sarita, the young woman, indicated, "I have several friends from different backgrounds, but I know that I will only go up to a certain point with them. It might seem like a double standard to distinguish in that way between friends and those I would marry, but that's how it is, I guess." Most of the other youth felt that if "it did not happen" (i.e., they did not find a suitable Indian American partner) and they ended up falling in love with a non-Indian American, they could "work it out" with their parents.

THE KERALA HINDU ORGANIZATION
Formation

In the KHO brochure, the then secretary of the organization, Gopi Nair, offered a poetic explanation of its formation. "Before we established [KHO], many of the true lovers of Kerala heritage and culture were lost in the congested wilderness of Southern California without having any communication with other Kerala members who shared similar interests. Some of them felt lonely in the crowded streets of this faraway land, and hungry and thirsty, in this land of plenty, for company of people who recognized and understood them. They searched everywhere for some familiarity, to prove to their beloved children that the usual bedtime stories of their motherland and her heritage were not some fairy tales but existed in reality."

The founding president and chief initiator of the KHO, Ravi Menon, talking about how the idea of forming an association occurred to him, said, "During that time we used to go occasionally for various [Indian] get-togethers. But it all seemed so superficial. You know the way Americans say, 'How are you,' and rush past without even waiting for your reply. It is a meaningless question. The person doesn't care whether you are ill or have lost your job or if your mother just died. Well, that's the way I felt about those parties." He continued, "The same jokes recycled, the same trivial conversation. And generally the women would be in one room, the men in another, there would be a few people playing cards and the children would be somewhere else. Except for the fact that the different groups were within the four walls of same house there was nothing gained from everyone being together." He hurried to add, "I am not saying such get-togethers are bad. I still go sometimes—it just left me feeling unsatisfied." He paused, and then went on, "I had been thinking about it for a while and I had also talked to some of my other friends. My idea was to develop a support group for Hindu Malayalees. Christians have the church as a support group, Hindus don't have anything." Gopi Nair, another of the original founding members of the group, had made the same point regarding Christian Malayalees to me earlier, using much the same words. The Christian congregational model seemed to be an important influence for this group.

A little later in the conversation, Ravi Menon stated:

I also wanted it to be a group that did some social service. We are all in a good position here, so I wanted us to contribute to support some worthwhile causes in Kerala. Preserving the culture was another goal. And then when our relatives and parents from Kerala came to visit, I wanted them to have a group where they would feel comfortable. These were my long-term goals. But I also had to think of something that would have short-term results and that would hold the group together in a more meaningful way than just a potluck party. That's how I came up with the idea of having a puja and bhajan monthly meeting. So the intention was always that the KHO be much more than just a bhajan group.

To emphasize this, he told me that he had been thinking of organizing a workshop for women in the coming year, open to all but led by the KHO, to impart some basic financial, legal, medical, and childcare knowledge relevant to life here.[5] Referring to Radhika, a woman who had been widowed several years before, he described the difficulty she had experienced in having to deal with all the practical details that her husband had looked after and added, "Some of our group may lose their husbands, and when that happens, they should know how to deal with the many issues that will come up." He also wanted KHO to get involved in planning a retirement home for Indians. "We are all getting older and in ten to twenty years there will be a big need for it. And particularly then, we would prefer to be with others from our own background."

While Ravi Menon, in this conversation, played down the religious aspect, that was also obviously an important reason for the formation of the KHO. "Growing up as Hindus in a Judeo-Christian environment can be difficult. There are so many misconceptions here about Indians and Hindus. People ask us about the cows roaming the streets—they think we are all vegetarians, that India is full of snake charmers. A few of us, not all, feel a sense of being persecuted as non-Christians," Hari Ramanan, an executive member of the group, mentioned during my first meeting with members of the committee. He added that one of the reasons that the KHO was founded was to correct these misconceptions. Priya Ramachandran, another executive member, continued, "We are not fanatics, but being a Hindu organization, we believe very strongly that the Hindu religion and faith should be preserved forever. We believe that Hindu values have a big role to play in the future world and we are all proud of being Hindus."

In addition to the needs of the immigrants, the teaching of Indian culture and values to children was an important reason for the formation of satsangs and the primary reason for the formation of the bala vihars. Indian parents were concerned about the environment in which their children were growing up, and the attitudes and values that the children were picking up from school seemed in many ways completely alien to them and created a frightening feeling that the second generation would become total strangers with whom they could not even communicate. One of the members of the KHO told me about her friend, whose child came home from school one day and asked, "Why don't I have a white mommy like everyone else? I want a white mommy." Another described how her child, when younger, would dissociate herself from anything Indian and would refuse to walk with her father, acting as if she didn't know him, when he wore Indian clothes.

The children in turn had to deal with the difficult issue of negotiating their personal and cultural identity between the values and practices learned at home and those of the American society they faced outside. In the process they raised questions about their own culture and religion to which parents discovered they had no answers. As Sujatha Rajagopal mentioned at my first meeting with the committee members, "It is only when we got here that we realized how little we knew our culture. We wish our mothers and grandmothers were here to answer the questions. Our children and others keep asking us questions about yoga and rebirth, and I find I don't know the answers. This is another reason that we formed the KHO."

In the absence of the residential concentration characteristic of many other immigrant groups, the satsangs and bala vihars of Indian Americans are often the only place at which they interact with other members of the community. It is through their activities that the second generation is socialized into an Indian American identity and meet other young people whom the parents hope will provide a source of support. As Hari Ramanan put it, "You know that children here go in search of their roots. We did not want our children to lose their heritage in a foreign environment and then have to re-create Alex Haley's journey!"

THE TAMIL BALA VIHAR

"What is the most important thing parents should impart to their children ?" Vivek Iyer asked Stephen Warner rhetorically, as the three of us stood outside the prayer hall before a KHO puja. He answered his own question, saying, "Values, those are the most important things—ethical principles of living and values. This is what we should impart to our children when they are young, until they complete high school. If we do this properly, they may have some adjustment difficulties for a semester or so in college, but then they will be set for life." Vivek Iyer was talking about the bala vihar that he is part of and helped to found fourteen years ago (he is a Tamil Brahmin settled in Kerala, so he is a member of both Malayalee and Tamilian organizations). He credits the bala vihar for being vital in imparting a cultural and moral orientation to his two daughters, who were twenty-two and fifteen years of age. He told us that it is important for parents to do this while their children are young, since later they are faced with so many temptations. "This way their time and minds are filled with other things instead of unwanted thoughts," he said.

I was impressed with what the group had been able to accomplish through the monthly meetings. The occasion was clearly one that the children looked forward to, and they seemed to have formed close friendships within the group. Unlike the KHO meetings, the bala vihar provided children with a lot of structured interaction time in which they could talk through many of the issues they were confronting in their everyday lives, particularly their struggles in trying to balance their Indian and American identities. The bala vihar showed the children how this balance could be successfully achieved. Both adults and children sat down together as "an extended family" to discuss the meaning of Hinduism, to explore the ethical and moral dilemmas of day-to-day living in America, and to cultivate an appreciation for the beauty of the Tamil language.

The effect that a bala vihar can have on youngsters was eloquently described by Hema Narayan, one of the members, in a school essay on diversity that won a national prize. Initially, she wrote, she struggled to "fit in" by trying to be just like her classmates and rejecting her Indian identity. But over time, as she began to learn more about the richness of her heritage from her parents and the bala vihar:

> I became more confident and sure of myself. With a wealth of knowledge by my side, I felt strong. I stood up to my classmates and introduced them to my beliefs. To my surprise, they stopped mocking me, and instead, wanted to know more. . . .
> I felt a sense of belonging, but not sameness, as though I were an individual piece adding color to the complete picture. I could fit in but still be different.

Discussing the psychological well-being she experienced after learning about "the uniqueness of my background," Hema goes on to proclaim, "I am no longer ashamed of my dark skin."

ADAPTING HINDUISM

I had been told that KHO was the only organization in the western United States that held a special puja for Lord Aiyappa during the time of the annual Aiyappa pilgrimage in India. I could see that Aiyappa worship was also an important part of the monthly KHO puja, so I asked whether this was because Aiyappa was the most popular deity in Kerala. "No," answered Gopi Nair. "We picked Aiyappa since it was the least controversial choice. He is the one deity that everyone in the group could agree on. Aiyappa worship is a unifying factor in the group since there are Vaishnavaites and Shaivaites and members of different castes." He went on to tell me that Aiyappa was also a "secular" deity since a lot of non-Hindus perform the annual pilgrimage to Sabari Hill. Gopi Nair mentions this in an article on Lord Aiyappa and the pilgrimage he had undertaken with two other KHO members and goes on to say, "What is more important, right in front of the shrine, there is the temple of Vavara, a Muslim, the first lieutenant of the Lord, standing as a permanent monument to the Lord's declaration of the equality of mankind."

I was also curious about how KHO members had learned the bhajans. Most were in Sanskrit and a few were popular in Kerala, but from my conversations I gathered that many of the others were ones that "an average Hindu growing up in Kerala would not know." In fact, I was told that often only the person leading the bhajan knew it. The rest of the group just repeated the bhajan, line by line. I talked to several of the bhajan leaders to ask them how they had learned the songs. Padma Iyer, wife of the lay priest and the primary bhajan leader of the group, said that she made it a point to pick up new bhajans from friends, relatives, and cassette tapes. Kamala Devi told me that she learned them primarily from an older Tamilian woman. Latha, a teenager (who had led a few, including at least one in Hindi), and Ravi Menon, the president, had both learned them at their respective singing classes. Another woman sang two that she had just composed the previous day. It was only during my fieldwork that copies of the bhajans (handwritten by Padma Iyer in English script) were handed out to members before the meeting. Around the middle of my fieldwork, Padma also tried to formalize the sequence of the bhajan singing according to the deities to which they are addressed (using the south Indian practices with which she was familiar). As mentioned earlier, the KHO also instituted a *Gita* discussion period and some youth programs toward the end of my study. The group was thus developing and modifying traditions to fit into the American milieu.

At one of the cultural programs organized by KHO, I spoke to Mr. Ramakrishnan, a person who had initiated many of the bala vihar groups in the region (including the Tamil bala vihar) and his daughter. They were both very involved with the Chinmaya Mission, founded by Swami Chinmayananda.[6] Ramakrishnan told me that they used a book of lectures by Swami Chinmayananda as the bala vihar text and that it was full of matters of everyday relevance. He gave me an example: "For instance, it helps deal with anger. It describes how anger develops and why and gives practical suggestions to deal with it. It also talks about how meditation and yoga help to cope with the daily problems of life." His daughter, who was studying at Stanford University, had started a regular discussion group to discuss the teachings of the swami and how they could be used in their lives. Her goal, she said, was to show students of Indian origin "that our heritage is not a hindrance but a help."

The importance of family relationships and obligations was among the most important lesson that the adults in the bala vihar wanted to teach the children. Undoubtedly this concern was due to the American setting, since the contrast was always implicitly or explicitly with the American family. Here again the aim was to show how Hindu values were important and relevant in the American context. The interpretation given to the story of the pativrata, or "ideal wife," is a good example. The story was about a loving wife who, through her devotion to her husband, was able to amass greater spiritual power than a mendicant who had performed severe austerities for many years. The moral of the story was that earthly duty toward their husbands was more important and fundamental for women than their spiritual obligations and that this devotion alone could procure them supernatural powers. Kalpana Subramanian, the narrator, after concluding triumphantly that therefore, "women actually have a better deal since men do not have this power," hastened to add, "but this is not because women are seen as dumb or passive but precisely because they are capable." She went on to emphasize that this duty was not just one-sided, since men had the obligation to look after their wives and to take care of their needs too. It also did not mean that women should be submissive. She gave several examples from the Hindu epics of loving husbands and assertive women to illustrate her arguments. She concluded: "All these stories were written to show that the family was seen as the fundamental unit of society and to provide rules to keep the family together. If this requires patience and forbearance from the woman, so be it. If the woman is always asking, 'What's in it for me,' the family can never survive." This presentation and interpretation of the story and its moral were considerably different from those traditionally given to the concept of pativrata, according to which the ideal wife is one who worships her husband as God, puts his interest above hers in all situations, and does everything she can to fulfill his every desire. Throughout the narration and explanation, there was much teasing, laughter, and booing along gender lines from the group (both children and adults). In the animated discussion that ensued, several of the older teenage girls seemed to be taking feminist positions—one questioning why it was only women who fasted, and two others presenting feminist interpretations of episodes in the epics.

Although the children graduated from the bala vihar when they completed high school, the parents hoped that they would take with them valuable lessons to help them through college and adulthood. The Tamil bala vihar was going a step further to ensure that the graduates had a concrete reminder of what they learned in the classes by taping the bhajans during the class, "which the children can play in their dorms when they feel homesick," as one mother told me.

Developing an Indian American Community and Identity

Members of the KHO have been able to develop a close-knit community, even though members are scattered over an area with a radius of around 125 miles. Gopi Nair, then the secretary, told me:

> KHO is like an extended family. It helps to alleviate problems—it helps in crisis management, stress management. There are many problems here—job related, domestic. Before KHO I had around four or five people to turn to but now I have around twenty families that I can trust. I have several close friends and we call each other one or two times a week for personal conversation, quite apart from official KHO business. Just talking to others helps so much. The community is small enough to be close-knit. The Kerala Association, on the other hand, is very large. Around four hundred people show up for each function so you won't know most of the people there.

On at least two different occasions, I heard both women and men talk about how they would not have had the type of close friendships that they had in the United States if they had been in India. Over a KHO dinner following the monthly satsang, Kala Ramachandran told her friends about a member of the group who had gone back to India after retirement. Apparently he had told her that he missed them all and that they should not take the kind of friendships they had for granted. It seemed as though both he and his wife were lonely following their return and were regretting their decision to go back.

Gopi continued, "KHO also helps us in practical matters. We have doctors with different specializations from psychiatrists to cardiologists, engineers, accountants, business people, scientists, and attorneys. So, whatever problem comes up, we have an expert who can help us." Earlier, he had told me the story of how he was informed by his office that his immigration papers were not in order (which finally turned out not to be true) a little after getting here. He was harassed by them and ran from attorney to attorney, but they just exploited his gullibility and conned him out of a lot of money. He repeated several times during this narration, "If there had been an organization like KHO, nothing like this would have happened. I did not know the American system and we had no one to turn to for advice or help."

Another time he said, "On the occasions of death, marriage etc., members are there to help with flowers, consolation, and practical details. For instance, Savithri's father died at 4 A.M. in the morning. By 6 A.M. everyone in the community knew about it and many of us went over." I witnessed this community support at an engagement that I attended at which KHO members helped out with the serving and the organization of the function.

Others talked about how beneficial the organization had been for their children. One of the women in the group told me, "Earlier they went through a period when they wanted to have nothing to do with anything Indian. My oldest child (who has a long, traditional name) had Anglicized and shortened his name earlier. Now he insists that his friends call him by his full name. And my other children ask me why I did not give them traditional names!" The effects on the children have sometimes been overstated by the adults, since many teenagers felt that KHO "was an organization for adults." At the same time, all of the teenagers whom I spoke to indicated that the group had helped them indirectly, by putting them in contact with adults and other children from the community. "It made me finally comfortable as an Indian. I realized that there were many other people out there who are like me, who talk like me, and that I am not by myself," elaborated Mohan, one of the teenage boys in the group.

Several of the children in the Tamil bala vihar talked about how much they loved the bala vihar and looked forward to it all month. When I asked Hema what she thought the best thing about it was, she said it was meeting others from the same background. She told me that she was close to the other girls in the bala vihar. Since they had so much in common, the nice thing was that "I don't have to explain things to them." Besides the bala vihar, she generally saw her friends at least one other time in the month, either at a birthday party or a south Indian music concert (there was an active south Indian cultural association in the area that sponsored such events).

While the bala vihar was meant for the children, it was also clear that the adults looked forward to the monthly get-together as much as the youngsters. On one occasion, the family who was hosting the bala vihar invited some parents in the neighborhood who had been part of the group earlier (and had left when their children had gone on to college) for the dinner. After a long discussion of how much they missed the meetings, one of them said, half-seriously, "How about an alumni evening the day before the bala vihar?" Several parents seemed to enjoy learning about Hinduism and Indian culture along with the children. During the pativrata story, for example, I overheard several of the adults animatedly discussing the implications of the story among themselves.

GENDER AND HINDU ASSOCIATIONS

The improvement of women's status during the settlement process is facilitated by the development of associations like the KHO and the Tamil bala vihar, which allows women to strengthen their position in the immigrant community. The friendships formed during the monthly meetings of the KHO and the Tamil bala vihar constituted a support group for women and compensated for the social networks left behind in India. I will narrate three incidents to illustrate this.

Generally women got together in little groups during the potluck dinner that followed the meetings of both associations, to catch up on the month's news. A good part of the time was spent comparing notes on husbands, in-laws, and children. After one KHO meeting, two women were telling the group about how their mothers had impressed upon them, before their marriages, that they should be submissive toward their husband and not contradict him. Devi, known for her outspokenness, laughed as she said, "My mother told me, from now on, you will have no more opinions." The conversation then turned to how to manage or "train" husbands. Devi told us a funny story about an Egyptian friend of hers who sometimes feigned illness in order to get her husband to do more of the work around the house. On one occasion, the friend had climbed up on the window and was helping Devi put up drapes. She told Devi to warn her when her husband returned. On hearing her husband at the door, the woman jumped down and sat on the chair, looking downward meekly. The husband asked Devi if he could help with the drapes, adding, "My wife feels giddy and cannot do such things." Everyone laughed at this story, and the moral Devi drew from it was that women should act helpless right from the beginning, so that the men would do more of the work. Leela added, "Instead, we went out of our way to do things we had never done, to show off to our husbands and impress them, and now they grumble about doing the littlest chore at home." The other women laughed and nodded their heads in agreement.

A husband whom a woman complained about at these sessions was sometimes chided publicly by the rest of her friends. I witnessed one such incident at the Thanksgiving potluck meal organized by the KHO. Malini told the others that her husband, Ramesh, had not wanted to come (since it was a long distance) and had only reluctantly agreed after a lot of persuasion. Apparently the man had continued to grumble during the entire length of the drive. When Ramesh came to pick up his wife at the end of the evening, Malini's friends scolded him for his unwillingness to attend the event and also told him not to complain again on the return drive. Ramesh backed away, muttering about how much "less aggressive, more modest, and more cultivated" Tamil women were (he said he was friendly with a Tamil group). There was an immediate outcry from the Malayalee women (who interestingly only seemed to object to Ramesh's characterization of Tamil women as "more cultivated"), who proceeded to tell him that Tamilians were not "cultivated," since they ostracized women who were divorced or widowed. They mentioned that two such women had turned to KHO and had been taken in as members.

The final incident that I will narrate took place during one of the Tamil bala vihar meetings. During the break, Latha came up to her friends and said she had been "dying" to tell them about a couple she and her husband had had as houseguests. Apparently the wife had done everything for the man, including tying his shoelaces. Latha's friends reacted to this account with amazement, scorn, and amusement. The husbands who were also there said nothing. After the round of exclamations had died down, one of the women said with a laugh, "Well, we have taught our husbands how to do things for themselves and we take pride in the fact that they can now tie their shoelaces on their own!" Obviously this message was also directed at the men standing within earshot.

It was clear that the friendships the men formed during KHO and Tamil bala vihar were important social supports for them as well. In fact, most of the men who attended the Tamil bala vihar went away to another part of the house to talk during the class sessions (which were mostly led by their wives) and only came back for the "story time." However, as a woman, I was not privy to these discussions. On at least two occasions I heard the men claim (to their wives at the end of the evening) that unlike the women, the males did not discuss family matters when they all got together.

Reproducing Status

Timothy Smith (1978, 1168) argues that membership in an ethno-religious group confers a competitive advantage on its members, something that recent scholarship has also corroborated (Zhou and Bankston 1998). As Mary Waters (1999, 5) points out, current research has turned traditional assimilation theory on its head by showing that frequently, "remaining immigrant or ethnic identified eases economic and social incorporation into the United States." Hindu organizations are an important mechanism through which Indian Americans maintain and reproduce their socioeconomic status. I have referred to the comment that Gopi Nair, the KHO secretary, made regarding the benefits of belonging to an organization with such a diverse group of professionals. On another occasion he and a fellow KHO member were talking about a common acquaintance, a Kerala Hindu who had been laid off, and Gopi said, "Ask him to join KHO. It will help him." Besides the psychological benefits, Gopi was referring to the fact that the group, through its professional contacts, might be able to help him obtain a job. Referring to yet another type of "competitive advantage" that groups like KHO could provide, Ravi Menon, then the president, told me that one of his reasons for wanting to have a religio-cultural organization for Malayalee Hindus was because "I noticed that Tamil Brahmins here have a tight-knit community and hold on to their traditions. I felt that their discipline is the reason for their doing so well."

As the examples of the KHO and the Tamil bala vihar demonstrate, being part of such a community helps members create, celebrate, reinforce, and transmit their status and success. Both direct and indirect mechanisms restrict membership to those with similar backgrounds and interests. Members of each organization told me that they did not go out of their way to recruit new members, since it was important that newcomers should be families who would "mix well with us" (in the words of Mr. Rajagopalan, director of the bala vihar), and who would "fit in with the ethos of the group" (as Mrs. Priya Ramachandran, a committee member of KHO, described it). For this reason, new members are carefully selected. Indirect mechanisms, such as the professional, upper-class atmosphere, the religious and cultural orientation of the activities, as well as the discussions regarding children's educational achievements, also seemed to work to push out those who did not "fit in."[7] Satsangs seemed to be largely class based. For instance, in another metropolitan area I did a brief study of a Kerala Hindu association comprising largely middle-class computer programmers and nurses, quite unlike the KHO.

In addition to the material advantages, being part of a successful, professional community also empowers the second generation to "avoid assimilating to the norm" and to choose a trajectory that emphasizes educational achievements over social popularity. Most of the college-going youngsters in both groups were in top educational institutions. University of California–Berkeley seemed to be the favorite choice, but several were also at Stanford, University of California–Los Angeles, Yale, University of California–San Diego, and Harvard. Not only was education strongly emphasized by the professional parents and relatives (who were also willing to shoulder most of the expenses involved, making it easier for the children to spend longer hours at their books), but being part of a group such as the KHO and bala vihar provides both children and parents with the concrete resources and know-how to achieve educational success. Information regarding every step in the process was available within the group and was exchanged over the monthly dinners and the phone. This included advice about which high schools, summer programs, extracurricular activities, and SAT coaching classes had the best record in matters such as placing students in top schools, test preparing and test taking strategies, what to emphasize in personal statements, and how to go about the admission and financial aid process, to give just a few examples. Once in college, there was a sufficiently large number of co-ethnics and friends available to serve as a support group and to provide further information about success strategies and professional opportunities, all of which increased the chances that the teens would continue to do well and end up in good positions.

The nurturing community environment provided by the KHO and the bala vihar also inculcated a strong sense of subcultural affiliation and pride in the children. As mentioned, most of the teenagers who attended the meetings on a regular basis told me that they would prefer to marry a fellow ethnic, since such a person would best be able to relate to their family and their culture. The second generation was still quite young, so it was too early to say whether they would stick with their plans. Since the KHO was a fairly new group, none of the marriages of the second-generation members had been truly influenced by the organization. However, of the eight second-generation marriages that I knew about, three had been arranged by the parents, while the children had taken the initiative in the other cases. Of the five "love" marriages, two were to other Indians (in one case, to a person of the same caste), and one to a fellow South Asian immigrant of Sri Lankan Buddhist background (described to me as someone who had "very similar cultural and religious values" by Mrs. Chandran, the bride's mother). Two marriages had been to white Americans. Whom the second generation marries is a crucial factor in shaping the Indian American community of the future, so these patterns bear watching.

ETHNICITY AND HINDU ASSOCIATIONS

Associations like the KHO and the bala vihar provide members with the institutional structure to forge ethnic communities and to formulate and articulate their identities as Hindu Indian Americans. For members of both groups, being Indian in the United States seemed to mean being affluent, highly educated, intelligent, and hard-working professionals and having "family values" and high-achieving sons and daughters. Those Indians who came to their attention (through the ethnic grapevine or the media) who lacked any of these characteristics were deemed to be exceptions, bringing disgrace to the good name of the community as a whole. Although the members of the Tamil bala vihar were less comfortable with being designated as "elite" (the Narayans, who read an early draft of this chapter, objected to my characterizing them in this manner), like the KHO members they were also well-placed professionals. The two groups also took pride in their subethnic identities as Malayalee Americans and Tamilian Americans, which to them denoted Indians who were more educated and "cultured," and who also accorded a higher status to women than their north Indian counterparts.

Members of both groups also felt that they were able to maintain a balance between Westernization and Indianness, drawing the best from each tradition. In addition to their economic and professional advantages, members primarily emphasized their fluency with American culture, their greater liberalism with respect to intergenerational and gender relations, and the greater openness and awareness that their transnational experience brought when they compared themselves with their Indian counterparts. However, they used the satsang and bala vihar, the close-knit extended families, and the marriages of their children to others within the community as evidence that they were able to do this without losing their inner values or their cultural integrity, which they believed distinguished them not only from the wider American society but also from many Indians in India whom they characterized as "too Westernized."

On several occasions I heard members of the two groups (and many other Indian Americans whom I have encountered) claim that they were "better Hindus here" and "more Indian" than many Indians in India. Both adults and children told me that on their visits back to India, they realized that Indians were abandoning their cultural traditions and becoming more "Westernized." Adults talked about Indian visitors to the United States who had praised them for the satsangs and bala vihars they had developed and who had told them that the expertise many of their children manifested in Indian music and dance was something they rarely saw among the younger generation in India anymore. Other U.S. Hindus mentioned that their relatives in India had remarked that their American-raised children behaved more respectfully and wore more modest clothes than Indian children of the same age. Several of the teenagers said that they knew more about Hinduism and Indian culture than their relatives in India and that they were surprised and shocked at how ignorant Indian youngsters were about their own culture.

Gender and Ethnicity

As Vertovec (2000, 17) points out, it is primarily due to women's activities that the culture and practices of groups are reproduced in diasporic settings. However, women are not just passive conduits of culture. Through their roles as teachers and transmitters of tradition, they also play an important part in redefining ethnic identity. Although both the associations—the KHO and the Tamil bala vihar— were headed by men, women played dominant roles within them. The puja performed as part of the monthly KHO meeting was conducted by a man, Vivek Iyer, an engineer and businessman by profession and the lay priest of the group, but the bhajan singing that occupied most of the evening was primarily led by women. I have also mentioned that it was a woman, Mrs. Kala Nayar, a university professor, who led the *Gita* discussion of the KHO. In the bala vihar, most of the class sessions were taught by women. While one person was designated as the official teacher of each class session, the rest of the parents were encouraged to distribute themselves between the various classes to help the teacher with the task at hand. Most of the women did this, but none of the men except the designated teachers attended the class sessions. The men would generally go off in small groups to different rooms to talk and would only come back at the end when the whole group reconvened.

Because of the dominant role that women played as cultural and religious producers in the KHO but especially in the Tamil bala vihar, they were also able to reinterpret traditional gender images and constructs. Since most of the women who took the lead as teachers in the two organizations were professionals with independent careers and since they were presenting Hinduism and Indian culture to children growing up in America, the interpretations tended to emphasize more egalitarian gender ideologies and relationships. For instance, many of the stories narrated in the Tamil bala vihar by Mrs. Subramanian dealt with philandering men and the punishments they faced. Others dealt with assertive women and the ways in which they were able to influence or direct the course of events. Although the stories were directed primarily at the children, all the adults were generally present at this time, so the import and implications of the message were hardly missed by them. The presentation and interpretation of the story of the pativrata is a good example of the way in which Mrs. Subramanian was able to recast a central concept in Hindu culture to fit the American context. I will give two more examples.

As part of a Father's Day surprise, the older children were practicing a skit written and directed by Mallika Badrinath, a physician and the mother of one of the students, during their language class. They were enacting the bedlam in a Tamil Brahmin household (in India) consisting of a busy professional couple, their three irrepressible children, and their harum-scarum servant. The husband in the skit was loving and solicitous of his wife. On several occasions while directing the boy playing the part of the husband, Dr. Badrinath emphasized to the group of teenagers (and to the other women who were also in the room) what she considered to be appropriate husbandly behavior "which would go a long way in maintaining the harmony of the household." So the boy was directed to be attentive to his "wife"

when she came back tired after a long workday, to tell the children to be considerate of their mother, and to be willing to take the family out to dinner if there was
no food prepared. Thus while improving their language skills, the children who
participated in the skit were exposed to directives on appropriate gender and intergenerational behavior. Since it was to be performed for the men of the group, the
message of the skit was also clearly directed at them.

My final example has to do with the role of women in the production of diasporic culture. Like most other Indian American cultural programs, the annual
Onam cultural program of the KHO was dominated by women.[8] Women and girls
were on stage as singers, dancers, narrators, and comperes. For one Onam (an
important Kerala Hindu festival) function of the KHO, a leading dance teacher in
the region had her students present a series of dances based on the work of a contemporary Kerala poet, Sugathakumari, who has dealt with the position of women
and environmental concerns in her poems. Hindu Indian dance teachers in the
United States are thus able to present unconventional works and to reinterpret conventional dance themes to suit their interests (see also Leonard 1993, 173).

These examples show the more egalitarian interpretation given to gender within
Hinduism and Indian culture in the United States. This development has occurred,
first, because women play a much more crucial role in the United States in defining
and transmitting culture and ethnicity. The nature of the settlement process that
brought about changes in gender relations in turn shapes and modifies traditional
Hindu Indian gender images. Second, these changes are brought about so that
Indian gender concepts fit in with the American context and are then more relevant
to the lives of the first- and second-generation Indian Americans. Rayaprol explains
(1997, 108) that "when immigrants begin to live in a new society and imbibe that
society's values and norms through acculturation, the dominant ideology carried
from their countries of origin undergoes a transformation."

But despite the fact that the women in groups like the KHO and the Tamil bala
vihar play a much more active role in the construction of ethnicity and "Indianness" and can therefore reinterpret gender ideology and practices in their favor, as
a consequence of their position as dependent immigrants they seem to be limited
to operating within a male model of a "patriarchal bargain" (Kandiyoti 1988).
Women's agency within the context of the Indian American religio-cultural associations is largely confined to reinterpreting the conventional patriarchal images of
womanhood in such a way that instead of a one-sided duty imposed on women (as
in the Indian version of pativrata), men are also urged to uphold their share of the
bargain by being responsible and considerate husbands and fathers. Both Mrs.
Subramanian's version of the pativrata story and Dr. Badrinath in her rendering of
appropriate husbandly behavior emphasized men's obligations toward their wives.

However, Hinduism and Indian culture are pluralistic and therefore the patriarchal model of gender is not the only model in India. Besides the conventional
image of the obedient, wifely goddess, there is also another image—that of the
powerful, independent, and aggressive warrior goddess. While the first is the preferred and dominant model, the second model is also respected (DasGupta and

Dasgupta 1996a, 390). DasGupta and Dasgupta argue (1996a) that the second model seems not to have been imported into the United States by Hindu immigrants. Although many of the women in both groups were strong, assertive individuals, I noticed that they took care to make sure that they were not perceived as dominating or "hen pecking" their husbands, and to emphasize that their husband had the ultimate authority in the household. Since a common stereotype within the Indian community (both in India and in the United States) is that Indian girls brought up in the United States are "aggressive" (which is considered to be inappropriate feminine behavior), compared with their Indian raised counterparts, I also heard women constantly emphasizing the demureness, the obedience, and the retiring nature of their daughters. Once I was in the car with several other Indians when a young man (who had been brought up in Hong Kong) was talking about how he had been so put off by Indian American girls because they were "too loud and forward." He said that he would prefer to marry a girl from India because then she would have the "culture." Two women in the car who had teenage daughters objected to this statement, saying that some Indian men felt that way, but that it was wrong to generalize about all Indian American girls. Both talked about their relatives in India who upon visiting them had remarked on how well behaved the girls in the KHO were. One such relative had apparently remarked, "Indian girls here beat Indian girls in India [i.e., are better behaved and more obedient]." Another time, Prabha, whose daughter, Vidhya, had married a white American, described with pride how friends of Vidhya's in-laws had urged her to go and sit in front at an "American" wedding, but Vidhya had modestly refused. Apparently the friends had appreciated Vidhya's self-effacing behavior and had exclaimed, "Oh, I wish my son had married an Indian girl."

CONCLUSION

Developing religious "congregations" as a means of forming an ethnic community and preserving cultural distinctness comes with its own dilemmas and contradictions. The first and second generations have different needs and concerns, and it is difficult to develop an institution that successfully addresses these differences. Mullins (1987, 320–334) has argued that over time ethnic churches become gradually de-ethnicized as a means of adapting to these generational differences (see also Chai 1998). Mullins further argues that if "ethnic closure and support" continue to be the goal of the ethnic churches, their future "is likely to be one of eventual disappearance" as cultural and structural assimilation proceed (1987, 327). How much of this analysis is relevant to the survival of groups such as the KHO and the bala vihars?

It seems fairly clear that Indian languages do not have much chance of surviving beyond the first generation. Particularly because of the English-language fluency of professional Indian immigrants, very little of the ethnic language is retained by their children. Even in the Tamil bala vihar, where Tamil was emphasized and taught, the level of spoken and written language fluency of most children was not high. Moreover, since the rituals and devotional songs are predominantly in Sanskrit, the linguistic distinctiveness of the groups is unlikely to be preserved. For these reasons, together with the development of the "ecumenical Hinduism" noted by Williams, the forging of a pan-Indian American community after a generation or two seems likely. At the same time, however, there is the constant stream of new immigrants from India for whom the support of the linguistic and subcultural community continues to be important. A great deal therefore depends on the future immigration policies of the U.S. government. If immigration is not drastically curbed, the satsangs may become the primary community resource for first-generation immigrants and the satsangs and bala vihars the socializing agency for the second, with third and fourth generations continuing to participate at least occasionally in the cultural and religious programs organized by these groups, particularly if they marry spouses of Indian ancestry.

CHAPTER 5

The Abode of God

TEMPLES

The Hindu temple is the abode of God, and its construction also sacralizes the land on which it is built (Narayanan 1992, 163). Not surprisingly, we see Hindu temple spires rising up all over the United States as the number of Hindus in the country increases. According to the Pluralism Project at Harvard University, in 2005 there were 714 American Hindu temples or centers, with new ones are being built every year. I conducted fieldwork at the Malibu temple in Southern California over a period of a year with some help from a research assistant, Sujatha Ramesh, who was working for the Immigrant Congregations Project of the Center for Religion and Civic Culture at the University of Southern California. This temple interested me because it was first dedicated to a single deity, Lord Venkateshwara, a form of Vishnu worshipped in south India, but over time became "ecumenical" to satisfy the demands of the many Hindu groups in the Los Angeles area. In addition to visiting the temple and attending several of the rituals, my assistant and I also interviewed, either by phone or in person, some of the founding members of the temple, regular attendees of the weekly worship pujas, occasional visitors, and four temple functionaries, a total of sixteen individuals. Other information was obtained from the brochure put out at the time the main temple was consecrated and from additional documents collected from the temple during my visits. Advertisements and articles in local ethnic newspapers also provided reports on temple activities.

This chapter also examines a "sectarian" temple, one belonging to a branch of the Swaminarayan tradition. Although I visited the Swaminarayan temples in Los Angeles and New Jersey, the primary research was conducted at the Swaminarayan temple in Los Angeles as part of the Immigrant Congregations Project by a team of three graduate students, Susan McGhee, Sujatha Ramesh, and Greg Stanzak. Susan McGhee and Sujatha Ramesh were the primary researchers. The research team conducted fieldwork over a period of several months in the late 1990s and early 2000s, during which the researchers attended Sunday services and several other community events, as well as some of the religious education classes for girls. They also interviewed twenty-nine members of the congregation, including men and women from the immigrant generation and second-generation youth. The directors of the Immigrant Congregations Project, Don Miller and Jon Miller of the University of Southern California, graciously allowed me access to the field notes and interview transcripts obtained from this research.

THE MALIBU HINDU TEMPLE

On a balmy spring morning in Southern California, I drive through the winding roads of Malibu canyon to reach the temple. As I turn off the main road and into the parking lot of the temple, the majestic white *gopuram* (towered gateway of the temple) looms against the skyline. It gently tapers upward and is crowned with a characteristic barrel-vaulted roof, topped with several gold finials. The tower is divided into five ascending stories, each intricately ornamented, repeating the same pattern as the story below, in smaller dimensions. The gopuram opens into a courtyard with a walled enclosure, in the middle of which is the shrine to Lord Venkateshwara. The shrine itself is divided into the *garbhagriha* (womb chamber, the sanctum sanctorum), where the deity resides, the *mandapam*, where devotees can receive an audience with Lord Venkateshwara and receive his blessings, and the pillared main hall where visitors congregate for the puja. Within the walled rectangular enclosure are subshrines for several other deities. I had visited the temple on several occasions beginning in the mid-1990s and had always admired its serene beauty. When I began my fieldwork in the early 2000s, however, this serenity and beauty were somewhat marred by the new construction the Hindu Temple Society of Southern California (HTSSC) was undertaking—a temple abutting the Lord Venkateshwara complex, intended as a shrine for Lord Shiva.

It is a Saturday morning and people start to arrive for the weekly 10 A.M. *abishekham* (ritual bath of the deity) and puja. Although most of the men wear Western attire, several of the women are dressed in exquisite silk saris. Many of the devotees bring several gallons of milk and fruit. Others bring Indian sweets. Obeying the sign outside the temple, they leave their footwear outside and go inside the temple enclosure with bare feet. Inside the main hall, people are sitting cross-legged on the floor in two rows in front of the shrine, with a center aisle left clear. A tape of mellifluous devotional chanting plays softly and the smell of incense fills the air. Some people are talking, others are praying, as they wait for the puja to begin.

The Early Stages

The main shrine of the Malibu Hindu temple was consecrated in May 1984 in an elaborate Maha Kumbhabhishekam ceremony, spread over a period of seven days. The rest of the Lord Venkateshwara temple, including the main tower, the auxiliary shrines, a cultural center in the basement, and residences for the priests and manager, were completed over the next few years. In India, although many temples have been built recently, some through the efforts of local communities (Waghorne 2004), most of the major temples were built centuries ago by kings and endowed with revenue-generating properties. Later wealthy donors either embellished existing temples or constructed new ones. Under the British colonial legal system, temples were considered to be public institutions and therefore under the purview of the state, a practice that was continued and expanded in independent India. Today Indian state governments have a Religious and Charitable Endowments department staffed by government employees to manage temples (and the land attached to them), maintain and renovate them, and protect their religious functions.[1] In the United States, in contrast, as Joanne Waghorne (2006) points out, Hindu Indian Americans have to contend with a process of "disestablishment"—a legal separation between church and state. New structures and institutions have had to be developed to obtain financial contributions for the building of U.S. temples, to oversee their construction, and for their upkeep.

The initial impetus for the building of a Hindu temple in India or abroad is often a divine injunction to a devotee through a dream (see Narayanan 1992, 155–157; Waghorne 2004, 26) or a religious medium (Hanson 2001, 352), frequently a deity demanding a home in a particular area. The Malibu temple is no exception. According to one of the founding members of the Malibu temple, the idea of building a temple was first brought up in 1976 when the mother of one of the Indian American residents of Southern California told her daughter that she had a dream that the community should build a Hindu temple in the region. The daughter, Mrs. Padmanabhan, was a former president and active member of the South India Cultural Association (SICA) in Southern California, formed in the early 1970s. Mrs. Padmanabhan consulted with some of the officers of SICA, and at the next SICA function she announced a plan to build a temple in Los Angeles and solicited donations. SICA collected a few hundred dollars that day, beginning the fund-raising for the temple.

At that time construction for one of the first major Hindu temples in the United States, one dedicated to Lord Balaji, or Venkateshwara, had just begun in Pittsburgh with the help of the home temple in Tirupathi, India. Some devotees from Southern California had sent donations for the Pittsburgh temple. The Tirupathi temple, located on Tirumala hill above the town of Tirupathi in present day Andhra Pradesh state in south India, is, as noted earlier, "one of the most popular, richest, and oldest temples in India" (Narayanan 1992, 149), with tens of thousands of visitors every day and a revenue of several billion rupees a year, most of it from offerings made to Lord Balaji by devotees (Krishna 2000, 61). Because of the popularity of Lord Venkateshwara and the support provided to the Pittsburgh temple by the Tirumala Tirupathi Devasthanam (TTD, the administrative board of the Tirupathi temple), Mr. Venkat Kalyanaraman, then the president of SICA, suggested that they build a temple to Lord Balaji, "because ... people from all over India go to Tirupathi, and you know, if we need to have it [a temple] here, we need the participation of the entire community." Although the family deity of the Padmanabhans was the goddess Meenakshi, and Mrs. Padmanabhan's mother had therefore expected the temple to be dedicated to the goddess, Mrs. Padmanabhan apparently had no objection to the building of a temple to Lord Venkateshwara in the Los Angeles region. However, by happy coincidence or by design (I could not determine which), the

Padmanabhans moved shortly thereafter to Houston, where a Meenakshi temple was being planned (this temple was subsequently built and is now a major pilgrimage site for devotees of the goddess).

The original SICA at the time consisted mostly of Tamilians with a few Telugu and Kannada speakers. Members of the original planning group for the temple, realizing that they would have to create an organization to build it, contacted the office-holders of these three south Indian language associations (Tamil, Telugu, and Kannada) in the region, formed a committee, and incorporated as 'the Hindu Temple Society of Southern California' in 1977, with the status of a nonprofit, religious organization. A friend who was going to New York was asked to stop in Pittsburgh and meet with the temple committee there to obtain advice on how to go about the process of building a temple. In Pittsburgh, originally the whole Indian community had been involved in the temple project, but north and south Indians had subsequently split over the choice of the presiding deity for the temple, with the north Indian group choosing to build another temple about four miles away. On the basis of this experience, the Pittsburgh group advised the HTSSC members to start with a "small group of like-minded people," and thus the HTSSC leaders decided to confine themselves to the south Indian community in Los Angeles, although they hoped that once the temple was built, it would be used by the entire Hindu community.

In 1978 the general body of the society met and elected officers for the society. Venkat Kalyanaraman told me with a laugh that the planning group decided to involve people who were substantially well-off, because they needed to raise money to build the temple. A wealthy doctor, who was also a "very dynamic person," was elected as president of the HTSSC. A site selection committee went to work immediately to find a suitable location, and finally a site of 4.5 acres in the Malibu hills was selected. The land was attractive in part because it was hilly like the Tirumala hills where the Tirupathi temple is located, but also because of practical features such as its accessibility by road and the availability of utilities. The site cost $210,000, and a "land group" of thirty families bought the land in 1978 and donated it to the HTSSC the following year. Since the land was located in the prestigious Malibu hills, fairly close to the coast, its value had gone up considerably a year later when the land group had it appraised, so the families were able to take advantage of the tax exemption they obtained from the appreciated value of their donation. I was told that the office-holders of HTSSC had come up with the land-group strategy to purchase the property after a member had explained the financial benefits of the scheme for the donors and had told them that this was a "classic" religious funding arrangement adopted by Christian and Jewish groups in the United States.

Once the land was obtained, the HTSSC needed to acquire the necessary construction permits. Like several other Hindu temples in the United States, the Malibu temple was initially opposed by the local homeowners' association. The HTSSC had to go through a lengthy process and several public hearings before it finally obtained permission to build. Telling me about the various obstacles they had to deal with at each step, Mr. Kalyanaraman concluded, "It was all an act of Providence. We strongly believed that Lord Venkateshwara wanted to have his abode there and that is how we were successful."

The next step was to raise money for the temple construction. HTSSC leaders started out by collecting a membership fee from its members and holding fund-raiser concerts. Very soon, however, they realized that the fund-raisers were not bringing in the money that they needed and also involved an enormous expenditure of time and effort. At this time, the president of the State Bank of India (SBI) branch in New York was transferred to Los Angeles, to become head of the branch there. While in New York, he had loaned money to the Lord Venkateshwara temple at Pittsburgh, and therefore the officers of the HTSSC approached him for a construction loan for the Malibu temple. The SBI president agreed to do this, provided the HTSSC could raise the collateral. Once again, a group of thirty families (including some who had been part of the land group) agreed to pledge securities worth $10,000 each, for a total of $300,000, against which the State Bank of India provided a loan of $620,000 for the temple. The thirty families received interest on their securities.

Constructing the Temple

Since the Hindu temple is a dwelling place for deities in the world of humans (Michell 1988, 62), great care is taken in its construction. Precise mathematical rules laid out in ancient Hindu architectural texts, the Shastras and the Agamas, govern the geometry of the ground plan, the dimensions, shape, and placement of the structure, the proportions of the different parts of the temple, and the size of the *murti* (image). Traditional temple architects known as *sthapathis* follow these architectural texts and design temples in India. All of the major temples in the United States have been designed by well-known Indian sthapathis. The Malibu temple was designed by S. M. Ganapathi, the premier temple architect from Andhra Pradesh state, whose family has been temple architects in south India for eighteen generations (Linda 2001, 389). Later his younger brother, S. M. Muthiah, also a sthapathi, supervised the sculptural work on the main temple. The sculptures were crafted by ten traditional temple *shilpis* (artisans) from Tamil Nadu, disciples of Muthiah. A local Hindu American architect, prepared the plans and architectural drawings to obtain the necessary permits for the construction. Several local Indian American engineers donated their time and expertise in order to make sure that the structure was built to satisfy local building codes (including California seismic requirements).

Many of the older temples in India are constructed out of stone or granite. Since these materials were not easily available in Southern California, the framework for the Malibu temple was built with hollow masonry blocks with horizontal and vertical reinforcements, and covered with plaster. A brick veneer was laid and covered with more cement plaster, on which the figurines and designs were carved. The images of Lord Venkateshwara and his consorts, however, were manufactured in Tirupathi in black granite, according to south Indian tradition and the strict iconographic rules (governing the posture, facial expression, and accoutrements of the murti) laid down in the ancient texts. The murtis were then shipped to the United States. As part of the support provided to the Malibu temple by the TTD, the image of Lord Venkateshwara was donated to the temple free of cost, and the other images were provided at subsidized rates.[2]

The direction the temple faces is another aspect that is specified in the ancient texts. Usually the ground plan is drawn so that the temple is situated on an east-west axis, according to the course of the sun, and ideally the image faces east. But because of the layout of the land, which was located on a slope, the sthapathi felt that it would be best to have the murti of Lord Venkateshwara face the west. Although having a west-facing image was cleared by religious authorities in India, including the Shankaracharya (the head of a Hindu monastic order), one of the directors of the HTSSC objected, citing the precedent of a west-facing Rama temple in Bhadrachalam, south India, which had brought bad luck to its builder, the famous Rama *bhaktha* (devotee) Ramadas. Wanting to "satisfy the community," the board yielded and had the plans redrawn so that the image would face east.

The elephant-headed Lord Ganesha is believed to be the remover of obstacles, so most ventures start with an invocation to this deity. The first construction that took place at the Malibu hills temple was of a shrine to Lord Ganesha, which was completed in 1981 and inaugurated. Once a deity is vivified and installed in a temple by a consecration ritual, daily puja or rituals of worship must be conducted there. Because the HTSSC did not have a priest in the area, volunteers were called on to perform the puja. The Malibu temple brochure (1984) lists forty men who performed the daily and weekly puja from 1981 until 1983, when the temple was able to bring a priest from India. I asked a founding member and one of the volunteers, Mr. Ramamurthy, whether all of the volunteers knew how to do the puja. He replied that many of them did. "In my own house there was puja worship and my dad has taught me and I have learned from our priests. Others may not have learned as much but they have all seen the puja and they can do the puja ... there is one simple thing in our custom—that is, even if you don't know the details of the puja, you have to pray to the deity ... that everybody knows." Mr. Ramamurthy explained that at the ritual's most elemental level, the chanted prayers that accompanied the puja could be just three words, "Om" (the sacred sound), followed by the term "namaha" (which means "I prostrate before you"), and finally the name or the various synonyms for the particular deity being worshipped. He continued, "Whatever Vedic chanting you can do, if you can do, fine. If you don't know, just bathe him, just like a child, bathe him, and dress him and then show camphor—that is called *aarti*—and then offer him flowers, fruit, sweets, whatever offering people have brought."

Becoming Ecumenical

In addition to the consorts of Lord Venkateshwara, the goddesses Padmavathi and Andal, auxiliary shrines to two other manifestations of Vishnu popular among north Indian Hindus—Lord Rama (along with his wife Sita, brother Lakshmana, and loyal simian devotee, Hanuman) and Lord Krishna (with Radha, his consort)—were also part of the original plans, as an attempt to create a temple that would cater to the entire Vaishnava Hindu Indian community in Southern California. Very soon, however, the HTSSC was faced with demands from different constituents for shrines for additional deities. The president of HTSSC was apparently a "great devotee" of the Lord Muruga, and wanted a Murugan temple. Since Lord Muruga is the son of Lord Shiva, the sthapathi who was called to design the temple told the HTSSC, "if you have Murugan, you have to have Shiva too." Local Shaivites, as well, were keen on building a Shiva complex to house Lord Shiva and his associated deities, and thus the HTSSC began to plan a large Shiva temple complex next to the Lord Venkateshwara temple. Although shrines for Vishnu and Shiva temples are generally not located on the same property in India, I was told that being "broad-minded people," the local Hindu community was not opposed to breaking with Indian tradition in this matter. Then a Hindu American leader, who in the 1970s had been instrumental in building the Lord Ganesha temple at Flushing, New York, and who had served as an advisor to the Malibu temple, told HTSSC leaders that he had a vision of the goddess Jyothi emerging from the ocean, and that since the Malibu temple was the only Hindu temple that was near the coast, they should build a Jyothi shrine. Another community of merchants wanted a shrine to their primary deity, the goddess Kannika Parameshwari. All these shrines were built and added to the Malibu temple. At the time of my fieldwork the Kerala Hindu Organization had been collecting money for a shrine to the Lord Aiyappa, which was also in the planning stages. At the twenty-first anniversary celebrations of the temple in May 2005, the board of directors announced that they were planning to build a new Hanuman complex (*India West* 2005).

Religious Rituals

As in India, the puja or worship ceremonies at the temples in the United States are focused on the murtis. There are two types of images of deities: the *mula murti* (immovable image) installed in the temple, which is made of stone, granite, or marble, and the *utsava murti* (festival image), a smaller, lighter image usually made of metal, which is taken out in processions. After the vivification or "breath of life" *(prana)* ceremony, the deities are believed to manifest in their images, meaning that great care has to be taken to honor the murtis and attend to their every need. After the priests undergo the necessary rites of purification, the deities, conceptualized as royal guests, are ceremonially woken up, bathed, dressed, perfumed, and then offered food. Finally, oil lamps are waved before the murti, followed by a candelabrum burning camphor. This is the culmination of the puja, when the priest and the devotees obtain darshan, or visual communion (the eyes of the devotees and the deity meet and the devotees are blessed by the deity's benevolent gaze), offer homage and flowers to the deity, and then take their leave.

The still-burning camphor is then brought out to the devotees in the mandapam, who pass their hands over the flame and then touch their eyes with their fingertips. The devotees also accept the prasadha, consecrated products from the puja: sacred ash and vermillion to put on their foreheads, a spoon of sacred water to drink, and a share of the consecrated food to eat. This puja ritual may be repeated several times during the day, until the deity is put to bed at night. In addition to these daily rituals, there are also weekly rituals, as well as annual festivals and rituals. Thus temples like the one in Malibu, with several deities, each with his or her own festival days and rituals, tend to be very busy. The rituals are performed by priests even without any devotees present, since they are conducted for the benefit of the world as a whole, and not for the individual devotees visiting the temple.

Other types of rituals are performed for the benefit of the devotee. *Archanas* involve the offering of fruit, flowers, or incense to the deity by the priest on behalf of the devotee. *Homams* are pujas involving fire rituals, addressed to a deity of choice, usually for a particular benefit, where products such as ghee, cooked rice, and special sticks are offered to the fire as oblations. Devotees pay a fee to the temple to conduct archanas and homams. Wealthier devotees sponsor all or part of a daily or weekly puja or annual festival conducted by the temple in order to accrue the merit that such sponsorship is believed to obtain. Life-cycle ceremonies may be performed by the priest either in the devotee's home or in the temple. Special pujas, such as the *vahana* (car) puja to inaugurate a new car, are also performed at the temple. Many rituals that are conducted at home in India are conducted in temples in the United States, because of lack of space for invitees at the home or because of restrictions on lighting fires in homes and apartments. Many temples provide calendars for devotees (many are on-line on the temple Web site) listing the festivals, inauspicious times, and auspicious times for each day of the month.

Despite the attempt to adhere to the strict traditional schedule of temple rituals, compromises inevitably have to be made in the American context regarding when the daily, weekly, and special rituals are conducted. For instance, most temples now schedule their major weekly pujas over the weekend for the convenience of the devotees, and thus there is also a greater congregationalization of worship in the United States. In the home temple at Tirupathi, the weekly puja for Lord Venkateshwara is conducted at 3:30 A.M. on Fridays, but at Malibu it was conducted at 10 A.M. on Saturday mornings. (The puja for Lord Shiva was conducted at 9:10 A.M. so that those who wished could attend both ceremonies.) I attended this Saturday puja several times, taking my place among the devotees sitting in front of the Lord Venkateshwara shrine.

Devotees of the Temple

Lord Venkateshwara, or Balaji, is a deity who inspires great personal devotion from his followers and is believed to possess immense spiritual power. In India, devotees have to undertake the long, expensive pilgrimage to the Tirumala hills, sometimes walking the eleven kilometers up to the shrine (which is believed to be more meritorious than taking a car or bus up the hill) to obtain his darshan. The enormous crowds of people thronging the temple every day mean that the typical devotee can only see the Lord for a few seconds before he or she is pushed aside by the priest to make room for the next in the waiting line of pilgrims. Many of the Lord Venkateshwara devotees who came to the Malibu temple on a regular basis told me that they appreciated the easy accessibility to the Lord that they had in Southern California. Contrasting the situation in India, one devotee explained, "I just have to jump into my car, and I am here in an hour. Then I can see the Lord for as long as I want and pray to him." I have often seen men and women standing before the shrine, gazing at Lord Venkateshwara with an expression of great devotion and reverence, their lips moving in silent prayer, sometimes with tears rolling down their faces.

Those Hindus who were used to going to a roadside temple in India every day on their way to or from work, however, complained that in the United States, they could visit a temple much less frequently due to the great distances that they had to drive to reach one. Although some individuals and families attended the weekly puja on a regular basis, many others whom Sujatha and I spoke to came only once a month, or a few times a year. Most devotees we interviewed were not currently part of a bhajan group (a few indicated that they had been members of a bhajan group earlier but had subsequently moved away from that locality), but several members of the Kerala Hindu Organization were regular attendees of the Malibu temple. I was happy to have the opportunity to talk to some of them again (I had completed my research on this satsang a few years earlier). The Ramamurthys, whose home I had visited for my research on the KHO, was one such family. When I reconnected with them, they indicated that they had moved nearby so that they could go to the temple every day after work. Mr. Ramamurthy had been one of the early group involved in the construction of the temple, and it was through him that I was able to make contact with some of the original founders of the temple. Another KHO member, Kannan Nair, told me that he came to the temple on the second Saturday of every month. It was a one-and-a-half-hour drive, but he said it was "worth it." A Shaivite, he told me that circumambulating Shiva's shrine seven times removed the problems that came from bad horoscopes.

Most of the temple visitors that we spoke to said that they visited both the Shiva and the Vishnu shrines when they came to the temple and had no problems doing so. Shaivites seemed to be more likely to do this, however, something that the Vaishnavites themselves admitted. One Vaishnavite woman said that she also visited the Shiva temple, but made it clear that she felt that "Narayana [another name for Lord Venkateshwara] is the ultimate God and other murtis are demi-gods." Several devotees talked about the "peace of mind" that they obtained after attending the weekly puja as the main reason for coming regularly to the shrine. One woman described it as an "adrenalin high." Another said the puja made her feel "like I am in a different world—close to God." Yet another woman told us that she came regularly for the puja since "Balaji always helps me."

Many visitors narrated stories of miracles that the Lord had performed for them or for their friends. One afternoon Sujatha and I were sitting on the steps in front of the temple, talking to the priest, when three members of a family came out from the temple. Seeing the tape recorder, they asked us what we were doing. On learning that we were doing a study of the temple, they asked whether we had faith and whether we believed in miracles. The man then pointed to his wife and told us, "Look at her, she would not be here but for a miracle." He told us that she had gotten a visa the day the priest had told her that she would. The man also indicated that it was his friend who had first told him about the miraculous powers of the deity in the Malibu temple. The friend had been struggling to start a motel business. Finally, he came to the temple three Saturdays in a row to pray to Lord Balaji, and right after that everything worked out and he became very successful.

The priests in the temple also spoke to devotees about the power of the deity and how they could obtain their wishes from him by attending the puja. One weekday, when Sujatha and I went to the temple, the priest who was in attendance asked her if she had children. On learning that she had did not, and had been married for four years, he exclaimed, "Four years and still no children!" He then told her to come on Saturdays for the puja with a gallon of milk. "When you are here," he told her, "focus your mind on whatever you need—if you want your green card, or you want children."

One of the ways ordinary Hindus manifest their fervent devotion to a deity is by giving generously to the *hundi* (collection box) usually placed in front of the shrine. Monetary donations are given by devotees as part of a vow, to redeem a pledge, or as a thank offering for being particularly blessed by good fortune. The Tirupathi temple in south India is so wealthy because grateful devotees give generously, and "cars, diamonds, and approximately 20 kg of gold (from various pieces of jewelry dropped in the hundi) are collected every month" (Narayanan 1992, 150). Mr. Ramamurthy talked about how the money pours into the Malibu temple and that people give without any hesitation, "as if they are indebted to God." He gave one example of a person he knew. "You know, one of the members of our temple, he went to Las Vegas and hit a jackpot of 250,000 dollars. The very first thing he did was, from Las Vegas, he called our temple, and he told the manager, I am so and so, I want to donate 25,000 dollars to the temple. The moment he hit the jackpot! And he did it [made the donation]!"

I was told that there were some Anglo-Americans in the area who were members of the HTSSC. Since I was interested in the perspective of a non-Indian Hindu worshipper, I was eager to meet at least one of them. The wife of the head priest of the Lord Venkateshwara temple was the first to tell me about a man, Mr. Will, who was a good friend of the head priest of the Venkateshwara temple, Mr. Bhattar. I talked to Mr. Will at a coffee shop in Southern California. Will told me that he had begun to be interested in meditation as a teenager. In the 1970s, like many other Americans, he got involved with Maharishi's Transcendental Meditation. He was also interested in Hindu astrology, or Jyotish, and started reading about Hinduism at that point, but "the religion really came to life only after I got close to Bhattar." He had been going to the Malibu temple for ten years, ever since he had moved to the area. But for the first few years, he didn't really talk to anyone while he was at the temple. He would go a couple of times a month, and would often be a sponsor at the pujas. He would repeat the Sanskrit chants after the priests, "mangling it horribly, but they didn't care. They were just happy that I was interested. And that is the greatness of the culture—this generosity of spirit and welcoming nature, unlike many other cultures that are more closed." He said that he was always made to feel welcome, both by the priests and by the other worshippers. There was no feeling of "this is an Indian place; what was I doing there." He continued, "We Westerners are part of the Judeo-Christian tradition. So in the Catholic tradition, *this* is what it is, in the Baptist tradition, *this* is what it is, but in Hinduism, it is, what do you want it to be." He went on to talk about the difference between the Judeo-Christian framework, "where the question always asked is 'what do you believe.' But that word implies that there can be doubt. Bhattar, on the other hand, just takes it for granted." He said he found this orientation powerful and refreshing.

Will spoke about being part of a group of about thirty people who had been sponsoring a homam every month for the past one and a half years (only five to fifteen people actually showed up for each ceremony). He said that they needed a group because the homam was expensive. Will predicted that there would be more temples built in the United States over time, because the Jyotish tradition was catching on among Anglo-Americans. "So, when people realize that there is going to be a difficult time ahead of them, they say, so what can I do about it. And the only thing you can do are the archanas and the homams. And to do them, you need a deity and a temple."

Temple Administration

Although the Hindu temple in the United States does not come under the direct purview of the government (unlike in India), the state indirectly shapes the organization of temple affairs by laying out and enforcing the framework within which the Hindu temple exists as a legal and corporate entity in the United States and by its judicial interventions into temple disputes (see Kurien 2006b). In India, temples are not just religious institutions but are also important symbolic and economic spaces. As Franklin Presler (1987, 42) points out, "temples in all their dimensions are arenas where people pursue strategies designed to protect, enhance, or stabilize social position or rank." Scholars who study Hindu temples in India either past or present emphasize the concept of *maryada,* or honor, as being central in understanding the symbolic importance of the temple. Maryada refers to rights of precedence in obtaining prasadha, in being able to hold special rituals, in conducting ceremonies, and in being a trustee of the temple. Temples also have important material resources that can be controlled by those who participate in the decision-making process. There may be special family or caste groups that have traditionally received a "share" in the symbolic and material resources of particular temples. Wealthy donors to the temple (who often hail from such family or caste groups) are accorded special rights to temple honors and are often involved in the running of the temple as trustees or advisors. Thus the Indian government and courts recognize a category of symbolic and material rights of "custom and usage" that regulate how resources in the temples are to be allocated. Temple trustee selection in India, for example, is organized in a manner very different from that of the United States. Two categories of temple trustees are recognized in India: hereditary trustees, who obtain their position by membership in a family or group recognized as having special ownership rights in the temple, such as a descendant of the family that originally built the temple, and nonhereditary trustees, who are government appointees and are appointed to office for a specific period of time.[3] Except in the case of temples that have been built recently by urban middle- and upper-class neighborhood groups, trustees in India are not elected to their position.

Although there are some continuities between the situation of the Hindu temple in India and the one in the United States, distinct features of the American environment are also evident. The Hindu temple in the United States is founded as an American corporation and a nonprofit organization, and therefore it is subject to several rules and restrictions. Temples have to have, for example, a "general body" and a "board of directors." Thus they have to develop "membership lists," and the members of the temple in turn hold elections to choose members of the board of directors, neither of which is a traditional Indian practice. These requirements in turn lead to disputes over who is a "member" of a temple, who is a "Hindu," and the position of wealthy donors of the temple.[4] Disputes are exacerbated by the fact that rules of "custom and usage" governing symbolic and material temple transactions that are applicable in India are not recognized in the United States. At the same time, in the American context, where immigrants, particularly nonwhites, are stripped of many of the traditional sources of status, temple honors become an even more fiercely guarded prize. Rights of precedence and control over trusteeship become the battleground for a status struggle within the American Hindu community. Even though democratic elections of trustees are not a traditional practice in India, the temple "membership" in the United States may desire a more democratic system of trustee selection, or individuals interested in becoming trustees may use that issue to force the incumbent trustees out of office. In the past decade, major legal conflicts have taken place in American temples across the country over these issues.[5]

The Malibu temple was one of the first in the United States to get embroiled in a nasty and drawn-out legal battle, primarily between the founding members and trustees, and a later group who had been in control of the temple since 1992. The financial criterion for temple membership became the main point of contention. Each group also accused the other of financial mismanagement, secrecy, running the Hindu Temple Society of Southern California as a "private trust," and not holding democratic elections. The conflict was played out publicly, with both sides taking out advertisements in the local Indian American newspapers. Periodically during my visits to the temple, I would see, posted on the notice board and available as handouts for visitors, letters from the attorney representing the board of trustees, stating the trustees' position and disputing the position of their challengers. It was a difficult time for the temple, and none of those involved wanted to talk about the dispute except off the record. Several of the devotees whom we interviewed spoke negatively about the impact the temple politics had had on worshippers, with some arguing that because of the actions of the current board, the temple no longer had any sense of community. Other devotees were critical about the special privileges that the trustees received. A similar legal conflict over the criteria for membership and trusteeship erupted a few years later at the Flushing temple in New York and was covered in detail by several newspapers (see Kurien 2006b).

The Temple Priests

Temples in India employ a large number of paid workers. Arjun Appadurai (1981, 48) indicates that a medium-sized Vaishnava temple in Madras city employed approximately 76 functionaries, including 2 priests, 12 priest assistants, roughly 30 reciters of sacred texts, 10 clerical staff, and 22 "inner" and "outer" staff (inner staff included cooks, those in charge of the clothes and jewels of the deities, and the sandal-paste

maker; the outer staff included musicians, torchbearers, sweepers, washermen, gar-
deners, and the elephant mahout). American temples have far fewer paid workers, and
instead volunteers play an important role. At the time of the study, the Malibu temple
had a longtime office manager, a man who had worked in an administrative position
on the Hindu Endowment Board in Tamil Nadu for twenty-three years before immigrating to the United States. His wife and sons ran the temple kitchen. The temple also
employed six priests, three for the Balaji temple and three for the Shiva complex.

Of the six priests employed by the Malibu temple, five were from Tamilian backgrounds and one was Telugu. The priests were paid a salary, and the temple even
regulated how much they were paid when they went to private houses to perform
pujas (in India, temples do not regulate the income priests obtain from sources
outside the temple). Sujatha and I interviewed the chief priest of the Balaji temple,
Mr. Bhattar, together, and Sujatha later interviewed two of the priests who worked
in the Shiva temple. The interviews with the priests were conducted mostly in
Tamil. All three priests hailed from families where priesthood was the traditional
occupation for the men. Bhattar told us that his father and grandfather had been
temple priests, but that his father had not been keen on his son's following in his
footsteps, since priests were paid so little. He, Bhattar, had been adamant, however,
and at the age of eight entered a well-known training school for priests in Srirangam,
Tamil Nadu, which taught the Vedas (the Yajur Veda tradition) and the Agamas. He
studied there for twelve years, learning the temple rituals, how to conduct major
festivals, and all the details of temple priesthood. One of the Shaivite priests had
similarly enrolled in a famous Shaivite religious school in Kanchipuram in Tamil
Nadu; the second had enrolled in a Vedic school but had also studied with his father
for ten years. In India, priests for whom the profession is a traditional one often
learn their trade informally by studying and working with their fathers. But over
the past few decades, specialized religious schooling for temple priests has become
increasingly common and even a requirement for employment at the major south
Indian temples (Fuller 2003). After their religious schooling, the graduates appren-
tice with a senior priest for a few years. Mr. Bhattar told us that he became a full-
fledged temple priest only after his marriage, since there were some rituals that
unmarried priests were forbidden to perform (see Fuller 1984, 30–31).

The status and role of Hindu temple priests in the United States are affected in
many ways by the American context. Visa rules regulate how priests can arrive in the
country, what their relationship should be to the temple that employs them, and how
long they can stay until a temple sponsors them for a green card.[6] The ecumenism of
major Hindu American temples means that priests who specialize in particular theological traditions (such as Shaivism or Vaishnavism) may have to be willing to officiate in temples belonging to opposing traditions. Although the Malibu temple hired
priests trained to officiate in south Indian Vaishavite traditions for the Balaji temple
and in Shaivite traditions for the Shiva temple, there was still a shortage of priests and
priest assistants. Each group of priests sometimes had to assist in conducting rituals
at the other temple, particularly during special festival days. To do so required learning new rituals and chants. Because the temple catered to a pan-Indian clientele,
priests also had to learn new pujas, including some from north Indian traditions, and

had to learn the differences in the rituals and approach between the north Indian tradition and the south Indian one with which they were familiar.

In India, life-cycle ceremonies are conducted by a different category of priests, and funeral rituals are conducted by a third group. In the United States temple priests are often expected to perform all these ceremonies, particularly the domestic rites and life-cycle rituals, and Mr. Bhattar and the other priests had to learn them after beginning their work at the Malibu temple. (Mr. Bhattar indicated that he did not perform funeral rituals, but that one or two of the other priests at the temple did.) Priests also had to learn to drive, in order to be able to go to private homes to conduct these ceremonies. Finally, unlike in the Indian context, Hindu priests in the United States must often be able to "explain" the rituals they perform to the audience, particularly to second-generation American members and non-Hindus. Mr. Bhattar told us that he had improved his English-speaking skills in order to answer all the questions put to him by American devotees. For all of these reasons, the priests we interviewed stressed that the demands on Hindu priests in the United States were much greater than in India and that consequently they had to do much more work in their new country.

In India, priests, particularly those working in the larger temples, generally do not develop a personal relationship with temple worshippers and often are not very polite or helpful to devotees (see Fuller 1984, 132). In the United States, in contrast, priests are usually courteous and friendly (several of the devotees remarked on this) and sometimes even act as counselors and advisors to some of the regular temple visitors (see also Rayaprol 1997, 102). Mr. Bhattar talked to us about counseling or advising several such individuals, and a few of the regulars we interviewed mentioned turning to him for guidance regarding the appropriate rituals to be performed for different occasions. Other visitors, however, said that they did not need to consult the priests, since their families in India kept them informed about upcoming auspicious and inauspicious days as well as the different festivals and how to observe them.

Many of the strict regulations regarding the maintenance of purity and pollution in the temple have to be relaxed in the American context where, following the rules of a nonprofit organization, the temple and its shrines have to be open to all—Hindus and non-Hindus alike[7]—and where people often do not observe the rules of purity. A little before we started our interview with Mr. Bhattar, an Anglo-American man outside the temple had engaged him in a conversation and had shaken his hand at the end. In speaking about the differences between temples in India and in the United States, Mr. Bhattar told us that in India people had a more reverential attitude, "but here people just come and go. Women come to the temple even when they are menstruating. And that man, for instance [the white man, apparently a stranger, who had been talking to him]—who knows where he has been before coming here. And he touched me, so that is why I did not want to go inside the temple but decided to sit outside [on the steps] to talk to you."

The Ecumenical Temple and the Formation of a Hindu American Community

In a study of the Pittsburgh temple, Aparna Rayaprol (1997, 101) focuses on the transformation of the temple from a place of worship to a community that becomes "almost a substitute for the large extended family gathering." She argues that because of the greater participation of women in the administration and services of the temple at Pittsburgh when compared with typical temples in India, the public institution of the temple was transformed as it incorporated values of the private sphere. Through the "kinwork" of women, regular visitors and participants at the temple were knit into a surrogate extended family and the temple became a "second home" for such people (Rayaprol 1997, 102). Women also played a larger role at the Malibu temple than they would have in a traditional temple in India. For instance, a woman performed the cashier's function at the Sri Venkateshwara temple, receiving money from devotees requesting archanas and giving them receipts. Karen Leonard (1997, 113) notes that women used to sit at the reception table in the temple, handing out pamphlets and explaining Hindu beliefs and rituals to casual visitors (this practice seemed to have been discontinued by the time I began my fieldwork). At the time of my research, however, I did not feel that a sense of community prevailed at the temple, even among the regular visitors. In fact, although some individuals and families came regularly, there seemed to be very little interaction among them. Mrs. Venkatachari, a woman who had been coming to the temple at least once a week since its construction, told me wistfully that in the early period, women used to be "really" involved, always had volunteered in the kitchen, and would sometimes spend the whole day at the temple. After the new trustees took office and the legal conflict had erupted, she felt that everything had changed, since "they did not want volunteers at the temple anymore." Mrs. Venkatachari indicated that very few regulars were left at the temple. Most of the devotees who came to the weekly pujas were recent H-1B immigrants or people she had never seen before. Unlike many other major Hindu temples around the country, the Malibu temple did not have a library or hold any regular Hinduism classes for children.

Even Rayaprol (1997) admits, however, that the "community" that was created by women at Pittsburgh was one that was predominantly south Indian. Although many temples around the country have been able to overcome the deep schism between Vaishnavite and Shaivite theological traditions by constructing shrines to both deities within the same temple, few temples have been able to bridge the divide between north and south Indian traditions. This division has also been noted in Canada (Sekhar 2001) and in Australia (Bilimoria 2001, 26). North and south Indian temple traditions are fundamentally different in terms of building styles, rituals, worship customs, language, and chants, so worshippers from one tradition often do not feel at home in temples belonging to the other tradition. Despite the Malibu temple's attempts to be pan-Indian, its worshippers were predominantly south Indian. Several north Indian temples were subsequently built in the Los Angeles area to meet the needs of this group of Hindus.

THE BOCHASANWASI AKSHAR PURUSHOTTAM SANSTHA TEMPLE

The Bochasanwasi Akshar Purushottam Sanstha (BAPS) is a Vaishnava *sanstha* (subsect) from the state of Gujarat organized around a guru, or charismatic leader. According to the BAPS Web site, the group has a million followers around the world (www.swaminarayan.org, retrieved July 23, 2005). Although they constitute only about 5 percent of the population of Gujarat, or about a third of the Swaminarayan sect in the state (Williams 2001, 68), they probably make up a much larger proportion of Swaminarayan followers overseas, because the BAPS is the fastest-growing branch of this tradition outside India. According to Raymond Williams (1988, 177), one-third of the adherents of the BAPS whom he surveyed indicated that they had turned to the religion after their arrival in the United States. Despite this increase in membership, however, BAPS followers still make up only a small percentage of Hindus in the diaspora. Yet they often become the public face of Hinduism, particularly in the West, and are one of the most studied groups within American Hinduism (Hanson 2001; Kim 2000; Moffat 2000; Rudert 2004; Williams 1988, 2001).[8] The anthropologist Michael Moffat, who conducted a study of the group in New Jersey, describes the BAPS as "the most effective south Asian religious group ... in the organized practice of overseas Hinduism" (Moffat 2000). Being a diasporic community also seems to have revitalized the members' religious faith: in Raymond Williams's survey, over 80 percent indicated that they had become more active in religious affairs after emigrating to the United States (Williams 1988, 177).

Some of the biggest and most ornate temples outside India have been built by this group, largely through volunteer labor contributed by its devotees. Their temple in Neasden, London which cost £12 million, was declared by the Guinness World Records to be the largest Hindu temple outside India (2000 edition, cited on www.swaminarayan.org). A similar temple was built in Nairobi, Kenya. In the United States, intricately carved limestone and marble temples built from the ground up, with domes or spires over the central shrines called *shikarabadda mandirs*, were built in Houston and Chicago and inaugurated just two weeks apart in 2004 by their guru, Pramukh Swami. The group also had 38 smaller temples (*hari mandirs*, or buildings converted into temples) across the United States in 2005. In chapter 3, I mentioned the month-long Cultural Festival of India that the group organized in New Jersey in 1991.

Although the BAPS claims that it practices "the purest form of Hindu religion" (www.swaminarayan.org retrieved June 7, 2006), it is an atypical Hindu group in many ways, and its unusual aspects have to be factored into explanations of its phenomenal success. Unlike most traditional Hindu groups, the Swaminarayan *sampradaya* (religious tradition) has a founder, Sahajanand Swami (1781–1830), whom devotees worship as Lord Swaminarayan, a manifestation of Purushottam, or God. Their current spiritual leader, Pramukh Swami, is believed to be his contemporary spiritual successor and as such, a manifest form of divinity. The BAPS acknowledges the authority of the Vedas, but it has its own sacred scriptures—primarily the *Vachanamrut*, the compilation of the sermons of Lord Swaminarayan, and the *Shikshapatri*, the code of conduct for Swaminarayan followers written by Lord Swaminarayan. The *Swamini Vato*, excerpts from the spiritual talks of Lord Swaminarayan's closest follower, Gunatitanand Swami, whom the BAPS reveres as Lord Swaminarayan's chosen successor, is also sometimes included as part of the BAPS scriptural canon. The group also has its own *sadhus* (male spiritual ascetics)—over seven hundred of them in 2005 according to the BAPS Web site—who go through several years of rigorous education and training in the theological schools run by the subsect. The sadhus live in *ashrams* (monasteries) attached to the major BAPS temples and play an important role in the propagation and practice of the religion.

Temple worship is not central to most guru-centered traditions, but it is at the center of the BAPS practice. Its Sunday assembly, or *sabha,* is quite different from the weekly *abishekham* (ritual bathing of the deity) worship at the Malibu temple, since it is explicitly congregational, including the group singing of *kirtans* (religious songs), sermons or discourses by laymen and saints (usually on some aspect of the life of Lord Swaminarayan), and often a video presentation of supreme leader Pramukh Swami's current activities. Because of the group's congregational nature, members refer to it as a satsang, and to themselves as *satsangis* (members of the satsang). The actual puja is only the final part of this weekly service and is followed by a community meal. While parents are in the sabha, children attend formal religious educational classes in the temple, organized by age and gender. Temples also hold religious education classes for adults.

In addition to being involved in temple activities, BAPS members are expected to observe certain religious practices at home, which include performing a puja and aarti to the murtis of Lord Swaminarayan and the guru lineage every morning, singing kirtans and reading the Swaminarayan scriptures, and ritually offering food items to God before each meal time. But the most important requirement is the evening *ghar sabha,* or family assembly, where all the family members sit together, pray, sing kirtans, and share the events of the day. BAPS members are encouraged to spend at least half an hour a day together as a family, and the maxim "A family that prays together and dines together stays together" was frequently uttered by members at the Los Angeles temple. Besides being strict vegetarians, BAPS members are required to avoid onions and garlic and to fast at least two days of each lunar month (although many fast more often). Celibacy outside marriage and chastity within marriage are also strongly emphasized. Members are expected to tithe one-tenth or one-twentieth of their income to the temple.

The strict gender separation in the temple during religious and social activities is the most striking feature of BAPS Hindu practice. Since the sadhus are not supposed to look at women, talk to them, or even address them in a public discourse, the women in the group go to great lengths to make sure that they are never, even accidentally, in the line of vision of any of the sadhus. Usually women sit either on one side of the temple or at the back behind the men, and the sadhus officiating at the puja or offering the sermon keep their eyes trained on the men. Men and women and boys and girls have their own separate educational and activity groups in the temple. The women and girls in the group are not permitted to speak in front of a group of men or even before a mixed congregation, and thus only men and boys are present in front or on stage during any group event. Women and girls have separate activities and festivals, where they have opportunities to address a female audience and perform on stage. Women are also not allowed in the temple while they are menstruating.

The BAPS has a highly centralized administrative structure, with Pramukh Swami being the paramount head as well as the ultimate administrative and spiritual authority. He plays an active role in decision making for the whole sanstha, not just at the organizational level but for individual devotees as well. BAPS members send him e-mails and letters to ask for advice regarding personal decisions about career choices, marriage partners, and new business ventures or talk to him in person (men and boys) about these issues when they meet him.[9] Over half of the BAPS members in the United States whom Raymond Williams (1988, 177) surveyed indicated having communicated personally with Pramukh Swami. A clearly organized and hierarchical chain of command in the sanstha is evident, with a few selected sadhus below Pramukh Swami, followed by lay leaders (male trustees), who in turn are organized into a hierarchy based on their recognized commitment to the group. The world headquarters of the group is in Gujarat and from there Pramukh Swami, his team of sadhus, and the trustees provide guidance to all BAPS temples and centers around the world. This leadership group defines the religious teachings to be taught in the temples. Most of the BAPS books, pamphlets, audio and video tapes, and CD-Roms come from there. All the icons and images in BAPS temples in different countries are also sent from Gujarat. Beneath the central committee of trustees at the world headquarters is a central executive committee, comprising parallel male and female subcommittees to look after male and female affairs within each country or region (Kim 2000, 81). The United States headquarters is located in New Jersey. Within each mandir or center, devotees are divided into subgroups based on age and gender, each with its own volunteer leaders. Each mandir also has coordinators for various aspects of the temple, such as administration, finance, audiovisual equipment, security, building, and housekeeping (Kim 2000, 82–83). Perhaps because Pramukh Swami is the ultimate authority in the group and a clear chain of command exists below him, the BAPS has been able to avoid the type of public conflicts and court cases that have paralyzed many other temples in the United States. The members of the sanstha themselves attribute their success to their centralized management structure. As one member explained, "We have to have this structure because of people's egos—if we didn't, everyone would be going off and doing their own thing and the sanstha would not have achieved what it has" (Kim 2000, 84). The same basic hierarchy of leaders, executive members, and temple coordinators exists throughout the diaspora, and this structure allows members, particularly the local leaders, to feel part of the larger international body.

The BAPS is a truly transnational organization. BAPS groups in different countries are connected not just to the headquarters in Gujarat but also to one another. Members living in various parts of the world meet at the major BAPS festivals held in India and in other countries. When Pramukh Swami decides that a new shikarabadda mandir should be built in a particular country, money for the temple is solicited from members throughout the diaspora. When that temple is inaugurated, visitors and donors from all over the world attend the ceremonies. A member of the BAPS temple in Los Angeles elaborated, "When the London temple opened up, many from L.A. paid their respects at the inauguration. So we get to meet all these people and representatives from all over. In August, we will be inaugurating a temple in Nairobi, Kenya. There will be at least 60–70 people from L.A. that will attend this function in Nairobi." He continued, "Close connections are maintained so that if members of the temple have to go to Nairobi, for example, they will be able to stay in the home of one of the temple members. Hospitality is an important aspect of this temple. There is a close kinship amongst these congregations. It is like one big family. The spiritual leader is our father and everyone else are the children within the family." The transnationalism of the BAPS allows members around the globe to take pride in the majestic temples in London, Nairobi, Houston, and Chicago, even if they do not have a shikharabadda mandir in their vicinity.

As Williams points out (2001, 176–177), one of the distinct characteristics of Swaminarayan theology is the emphasis on the celebration of mega-festivals. Williams (2001, 178) describes these festivals as being like American state fairs, with amusement rides, entertainment, food, and exhibitions—but one for which the primary purpose is religious transmission. The Cultural Festival of India, held in New Jersey in 1991 by the BAPS, was preceded by three earlier mega-festivals—two in Gujarat and one in London. Several more festivals were subsequently conducted by the BAPS in India. Such festivals are a means of spreading the Swaminarayan message to a large number of people. They also have an important effect on the volunteers who work to make them happen, providing them with leadership training and enhancing their faith and understanding of their religion. Williams (2001, 177) indicates that in a personal interview, Pramukh Swami attributed the rapid growth of the BAPS in the recent period to the success of such festivals, which began in the early 1980s. The development of large Hindu theme parks is part of the same theology. The biggest pilgrimage center for the BAPS is the Akshardham in Gujarat. In addition to the Hindu theme park, the center has exhibits on Indian culture, Hinduism, and the Swaminarayan tradition, all using the latest multimedia technology to communicate (Williams 2001, 122). In November 2005, a second Akshardham was inaugurated in India's capital, New Delhi. The use of the latest and most sophisticated technology is another characteristic of the BAPS. Most of the larger temples use multimedia images, particularly for the large festivals, projected on large screens so that all members of the audience have a clear view of the stage. The BAPS Web site is elaborate and frequently updated.

Origins

The Swaminarayan sect was founded in Gujarat in 1801 by Sahajanand Swami during a period of terrible natural disasters (famines and an earthquake) and great social and political turmoil. Williams (2001, 31) describes Sahajanand Swami as being the first of the neo-Hindu reformers. Sahajanand Swami propagated a religion with strict codes of conduct for both sadhus and householders. He enforced a rigid discipline on sadhus and forbade them to have any contact with women or money and to eschew violence. In contrast to ascetics in other Hindu traditions who focused on their personal salvation and were cut off from society, Sahajanand Swami insisted that his ascetics live within society and engage in manual labor for social welfare projects (digging wells, constructing reservoirs, building and repairing roads, temples, and homes, and helping with famine relief operations). Swaminarayan sadhus were also sent as preachers to villages.

Swaminarayan householders were expected to practice *ahimsa* (nonviolence). Sahajanand Swami was against animal sacrifices for rituals, and all Swaminarayan followers were required to become vegetarians. Like Jains, they were even prohibited from killing insects and bugs. In addition they were to give up consumption of alcohol, tobacco, and other intoxicants. Sahajanand Swami also attacked violence against women, so the infanticide of female children and the immolation of widows were strongly forbidden. Women at that time were often abused by predatory men (including sadhus belonging to some traditions) and also subjugated by them, and thus the separation of women and men during temple services and the creation of separate institutions for women were practices designed for their protection. Sahajanand Swami propagated a religion with puritanical ethical teachings, particularly regarding sexual morality for both men and women and regarding financial dealings (he emphasized strict accounting and forbade the taking of bribes). During this period the British gained control of Gujarat, which until then had been in the hands of warring kings, and imposed some order and political stability on the region. British officials were impressed with the social reforms Sahajanand Swami was able to accomplish and gave him some support in his efforts. This stability and support enabled the new religious movement to flourish, and "the 'Pax Britannica' and the 'Pax Swaminaraya' complemented each other" (Williams 2001, 32).

Before his death, Sahajanand Swami divided his followers into two territorial dioceses in Vadtal and Ahmedabad and appointed two of his nephews as heads of each diocese. The issue of succession has proved to be a divisive one, with the formation of breakaway subsects from the Vadtal and Ahmedabad dioceses after the death of Sahajanand Swami. The BAPS was founded in 1907, when one of the members of the Vadtal diocese, Shastri Maharaj, left to form his own group over differences with the leaders of that diocese. Over time, several other subsects have developed within the Swaminarayan tradition (see Williams 2001). The largest group of Swaminarayan devotees are Patels. Originally a group of farming and landowning castes, many of them turned to business activities in the nineteenth century, became upwardly mobile, and subsequently adopted the surname "Patel," originally an honorific title in Gujarati (Moffat 2000).

The Swaminarayan tradition became transnational, with major emigrations from Gujarat to East Africa, in the early twentieth century, followed by an exodus to Britain from the middle of the century. The immigration to the United States began after the passage of the Immigration Act of 1965. In 1970 Dr. K. C. Patel, a chemistry instructor at Brooklyn College, New York, was commissioned by Yogiji Maharaj, then the guru of the BAPS, to organize and establish the Swaminarayan religion in the United States. Yogiji Maharaj gave him the names of twenty-eight followers around the country, mostly students, and also sent four sadhus to tour the country. The visits of the sadhus helped to energize BAPS followers, and in several cities, small satsang groups started gathering every Sunday in the homes of devotees. The BAPS (then known as BSS) was established as a nonprofit organization in the United States in 1971, with Patel as the president. In the same year, he purchased a property in Flushing, New York, as headquarters of the organization and in 1974 he purchased a site for a temple, also in Flushing. A few months later, Pramukh Swami, who had been installed as the guru of the organization after the death of Yogiji Maharaj in 1971, made a trip to the United States, along with several sadhus, to install images of deities in the Flushing temple. The group also traveled to other cities in the United States to meet followers and establish satsang groups. Pramukh Swami visited again in 1977.

The Los Angeles Temple

In 1980 Pramukh Swami made his third trip to the United States and spent a week in Los Angeles. During his visit, Swami met with the devotees in the area and told them that they should start Sunday sabha meetings in the homes of devotees and should also establish a hari mandir in the area. Alka Patel, a member of the temple, described how her husband, a member of the Vadtal group of the Swaminarayan, attended the meeting and was very impressed by Pramukh Swami, whom he had not met before. Before leaving, Pramukh Swami apparently called her husband and entrusted him with the responsibility of being in charge of the Sunday sabhas, this despite the fact that the Swami had only just met him. This story is a common one—men speak about the intense experience of meeting Pramukh Swami for the first time and of being entrusted with a major responsibility, which they then go on to perform diligently. In 1981 BAPS members in Southern California, with the help of the contributions of members of the sanstha in other parts of the country, purchased a building on two and a half acres of land, which was then converted into a temple (Williams 1988, 168). The temple was dedicated by one of the BAPS swamis in 1982, and Pramukh Swami installed the deities in the temple during his visit in 1984.

As a congregational group, the temple plays a different religious role for the BAPS than for the more traditional Hindu worshippers already discussed. Besides being the house of God, the Swaminarayan temple is also the space where the religious community meets to learn about their scriptures and their Lord, hear about the activities of their guru, and perform the public rituals that are central to their faith. Thus the focus is more on the development of the community and finding a building to hold the large programs that they are famous for, rather than on constructing traditional temples to house the deities. After meeting in houses and rented halls and becoming large enough financially to acquire a temple, the community tries to find a big building with a lot of open space (such as a warehouse or an ice rink), to purchase and renovate quickly. Once the temple has been acquired, the emphasis is on the activities that are conducted within the temple rather than on decorating the structure. Elaborate shikharabadda mandirs built from the ground up based on the *shastras* are only undertaken after the community has grown numerically and can financially bear the burden of raising the millions of dollars that are required for such a structure.

At the time of my study, the Los Angeles BAPS temple was a hari mandir, a large, plain, single-story building without windows. Most of the inside consisted of open space with mats on the floor. Four small buildings at the back of the temple served as classrooms for the children—two for girls and two for boys. There were separate kitchens for men and for women. As in other Swaminarayan temples, the dominant murti in the center of the temple was that of Lord Swaminarayan, with a smaller image of his faithful disciple Gunatitanand Swami by his side. There were pictures of members of the guru lineage in the shrine (Pramukh Swami is the fifth spiritual successor of Sahajanand Swami) and murtis of Lord Krishna and his consort, Radha. (Swaminarayan temples may have murtis of Hindu deities, including those from the Shaivite tradition.) The temple had a resident Brahmin priest. He was married, and his wife was also very involved with temple work. The temple had three sadhus, or sants (saints), who wore saffron-colored robes and lived on the grounds.

As a congregational sect organized around a central figure, Pramukh Swami, the Swaminarayan temple is able to create community and to provide for the transmission of religion to adults and children in a much more systematic way than can the more traditional temples. On weekends, the Southern California temple was a hive of activity. On Sundays, the formal sabha began at 4:00 P.M. and was mostly conducted in Gujarati. Since the second generation was typically not fluent in the language, separate religious classes were held for them in English while the sabha was going on. (Gujarati language classes for children were held before the sabha and the religious classes began.) The classes ended in time for the children to attend the aarti, or the worship service at the end of the sabha. About three hundred to six hundred members attended the weekly sabha. A sabha was held on Saturdays as well, with discourses, aarti, and dinner, but more people attended on Sundays. At *samaiyos* (sacred festival celebrations), sometimes spread over several days, a larger group of individuals attended (usually over a thousand), including those who lived several hours away.

Besides the sabhas and samaiyos, the temple organized several other programs: language classes in Gujarati and Sanskrit, classes for traditional dance and traditional instrumental music, and even tutoring for the SAT. The temple also conducted workshops on Hindu heritage and Hindu rituals. Occasional seminars were geared toward explaining the immigration process, including how to obtain passports or visas, and programs were set up to help new arrivals find jobs and homes. Mrs. Jyothi Patel, a member of the temple, indicated that whenever BAPS members from India were preparing to move to the Los Angeles region, they would contact the temple first. The temple then made arrangements to find them a temporary home within the congregation and to provide them with financial and emotional support during the settling-in process. The larger American BAPS group organized annual conventions and family seminars, summer camps by region, and youth tours to India (separate tours for boys and girls) for selected youth from all over the United States, and various Los Angeles members participated in these activities.

Since the BAPS describes itself as a socio-spiritual organization, social welfare projects are an important part of its mission. Most of these projects, which include hospitals, healthcare centers, environmental activities, and disaster relief operations, are in India. However, every temple has some local social service activities that it organizes. Thus in addition to all the classes for devotees, the Los Angeles temple organized social welfare programs open to everyone: blood drives, health camps, and health seminars. Temple leaders also hoped to set up a permanent free medical clinic in the area. At Thanksgiving, members of the temple had started a tradition of distributing fruit baskets to the entire neighborhood. Temple members also helped during the 1991 Los Angeles riots: volunteers organized some of the clean-up operations and also set up medical camps. During the 1995 earthquake, volunteers went from home to home in the affected region with food, water, baby formula, and other items. Engineers from the temple also went around on a Saturday and Sunday to inspect homes to see if they had structural damage.

At the time of our research, members of the temple were planning to build a shikharabadda mandir in the region, since Pramukh Swami had designated Los Angeles as a site for such a mandir and had commissioned the congregation to begin its fund-raising campaign. The campaign was led by a financier, Samir Mehta, based in New York, who became a Swaminarayan in 1997 after a meeting with Pramukh Swami. He was awestruck by Pramukh Swami's charisma and deeply honored when the Swami requested his help in raising money to build a shikharbadda temple in Los Angeles at their very first meeting. Ever since, he had taken a leadership role in the fund-raising efforts. A 45-person fund-raising committee had been organized in the temple, which included women. Some of the women on the committee were being sent to Chicago for a conference, led by an expert on endowment management and philanthropy, to learn the principles of fund-raising for charitable causes. The conference attendees would then return and train other women in the congregation. The congregation had been organizing a variety of fund-raising programs, such as launching a catering service for birthdays and other events. The youth were also involved in some fund-raisers, such as a walk-a-thon and bake sales, "so that they will feel part of the temple that we are going to build."

Male Devotees

In the United States, laymen play a central role in Swaminarayan temples. They organize and conduct weekly sabhas and other functions, perform some of the rituals, give the lectures, lead the singing, and take care of the administrative duties, all tasks that would be performed by religious specialists or retired laymen in India. Lay leadership is a coveted honor, since it provides an avenue for gaining prestige and honor, within the Gujarati American community (Williams 1988, 172–173). Participating in temple activities also enables male devotees to develop strong friendships with other men in the group. Sometimes they also form close ties with BAPS members in other regions of the United States or even in other parts of the world when they meet during BAPS events. This kind of networking often helps them professionally as well.

But perhaps the most valued part of their involvement with the BAPS is the close communication and contact male devotees are able to have with the sadhus and with Pramukh Swami during the latter's visits to the United States or during the visits of the devotees to Gujarat. Some devotees even travel with Pramukh Swami for short periods of time to gain access to him. Male devotees also have access to the sadhus through phone calls and letters, which are promptly answered. Many men spoke about the thrill of meeting and talking to Pramukh Swami or the other sants and the way in which these meetings transformed their lives or brought them to the religion. Sanjay Patel was a young man in his thirties who had been converted to the BAPS group some years earlier. He said that in the period before becoming a member himself, he would bring his wife, who was a BAPS member, to the temple periodically and wait in the car for her to be finished with the sabha. At that time he was an alcoholic and was also a meat eater. All this had changed after a meeting with Pramukh Swami in 1990, when Sanjay was in his late twenties. "When I met him also I was drunk, and I don't know what he did ... his power or whatever ... that was my last of eating meat, drinking. Everything changed 100 percent." Sanjay mentioned that his doctor was surprised that he did not have symptoms of alcohol withdrawal when he gave up drinking so suddenly. He went on to describe his meeting with Pramukh Swami as a "born-again" experience, saying that when Pramukh Swami blessed him, all his sins were washed away.

Female Devotees

A question that has puzzled many scholars (Moffat 2000; Rudert 2004) who have studied the BAPS is what women get from their involvement in the group, given how gender segregated the temple is and the numerous restrictions placed on female devotees. The justifications for the segregation usually provided by members are variously that Lord Swaminarayan instituted the practice to protect and emancipate women from the control of men by creating women's own organizations and even their own temples (these are in India); that it prevents the rise of sexual temptations in the congregations and "allows us to focus on God and worship"; and finally that women are stronger spiritually and therefore that men need more help from the sants and from Pramukh Swami (Kim 2000; Williams 2001, 168).

Drawing on Swaminarayan research, Sujatha Ramesh (2000) notes that many immigrant women in the congregation viewed the religion as "feminist," while contrasting it to "Western feminism." According to Ramesh, unlike Western feminists, BAPS women "do not seek a joint platform with men, as such a step is considered unnecessary and potentially problematic. Instead, they seek a separate, exclusive platform for women where they have a voice to express their opinions, [and] develop [their] skills" (Ramesh 2000, 14). This point of view was illustrated by Banu Dalal, a woman who said that she was drawn to the religion because of its "feminist outlook." She went on to explain to Sujatha:

> Even though when you look at it outwardly, it seems like this religion is putting women behind or considering women as second-grade citizens, when you get into the religion and get involved, you realize that we are not that behind. We are actually way forward ... Looking at the women's wing as such, we cannot talk to the saints, we cannot go near them and so we don't have any one-to-one touch

with any of the saints and Pramukh Swami Maharaj ... That way, when some people look at it they say, Well, okay, this is a very backward religion, but the ladies' wing as a whole for this entire religion, I am counting India and USA, we have our own magazine that is written by ladies, and it is being published by ladies, the editor, everybody involved are all ladies. There is no other religion in the world that has ladies printing, doing their own magazines. We have our own celebrations of certain big festivals during the year here in USA. During the year, we do four festivals by ourselves. We take care of everything starting from organizing, deciding the program, all the participants are ladies, the audience is ladies only. PR system is being handled by ladies, the audiovisual is being handled by ladies. The press release is being handled by ladies, marketing is handled by ladies. The men are not involved in anything except when we need something heavy moved. Then we ask them. They have to do it before we start our program. Once we start our program, they are not allowed to come in unless there is an emergency, then we go and ask them and then only the number of people that we want can come in there. Otherwise the whole program is organized and run by ladies. This is [at the] ... local level. At [the] national level, we have our own meeting, own national coordinators, they guide us throughout the year, they help us out. When you look at the international level, whenever we have big celebrations in India and when we had the cultural festival in New Jersey, the ladies wing did everything on their own with about 4,000 women volunteers. The sants gave us direction, but the final decision was ours. During that time, we even had seminars on religion in your life, child rearing, how to handle your teenage kids, how religion is affecting them, how peer pressure is affecting them.

The women spoke eloquently about the many benefits they obtained from the religion and especially from Pramukh Swami. One woman told Sujatha that her involvement in *seva* (service) activities was a way of "paying back the obligation," adding that Pramukh Swami gave so much to his devotees that they in turn felt like passing that on. "My purpose is to achieve ultimate salvation and my Guru is the only means to attain it," another explained. Radha talked about how Bapa (father), or Pramukh Swami, saw to it that women's spiritual needs were met in some manner or the other and that even though they could usually not obtain darshan directly from him, women got his darshan "in their sleep, in their dreams, in their homes." Tarini, a woman who had gotten in Pramukh Swami's way by accident (she was not a BAPS follower at the time, but her husband was a devotee), described the powerful darshan she experienced during the chance encounter. "He stood over there and gave me eye-to-eye contact and I was just spellbound. I was just looking at him, I didn't speak a word. I didn't say a word. Almost for two minutes he looked eye and eye into my eyes and he made my soul go blank ... After this incident, slowly I started going into the sanstha ... without a question in my life I just ... I didn't even argue with my husband because in my mother's house it was completely different ... a different deity, a different caste, a different community, a different worship, everything. And then, slowly, I merged into it."

In addition to the great love and reverence that women had for Pramukh Swami and the personal connection they felt with him, they obtained other spiritual and social benefits from being part of the BAPS group. For instance, Roma spoke of the vast Swaminarayan literature that was available to devotees and the ways in which it had answered many of her questions as she began reading more and more. Another woman said that her involvement in the temple gave her "this real satisfaction, inner peace. I feel I have done something positive. I feel very fulfilled because anything I do at the mandir, I haven't done it for myself. I haven't really done it for anybody else either. I have done it for God. It doesn't matter who it benefits, you know, and it becomes my seva. That gives me the most, the utmost satisfaction and peace." Sarla and Anita talked about problems they had in their marriages and with their in-laws and how their faith had taught them tolerance, humility, and to take things calmly instead of being "all uptight and upset." Sarla mentioned that she had stopped being affected "by people's cruelty" toward her; Anita said that her friends at the temple had been a source of support, since they could "appreciate the problems I am having in all areas. If I was having problems with my mother-in-law, or need to get things off my chest, I wouldn't hesitate to call my friends who attend the temple. I can confide in them and know that it will not be spread around. I trust them." Mona had been childless for many years after her marriage and said that she became pregnant after some BAPS sadhus had visited her home and had given her holy water from a temple in India, with instructions to drink it every morning. She considered her son a divine blessing and said that she would be very happy if he chose to become a sant one day so that he could serve God.

All of these voices were from immigrant women in the congregation. But how did young women who were brought up in the United States feel about the position of women in the BAPS? The second-generation women and girls who were interviewed for this project generally accepted the gender segregation in the temple. Various ten- and eleven-year-old girls explained to Sujatha that if the monks interacted with the girls, "they will think only about women, they will think about marriage, you know, and if they fall in love they will forget about their devotion to God … if they look at us, they have to fast for three days." Another said, "If the family was all sitting in one area they will start talking about family problems and getting in fights. With the girls and boys, they could get into girlfriend and boyfriend, you know, then all this love stuff will happen." Girls who had joined the sanstha when they were older, however, talked about how it had been difficult to accept the gender segregation rules initially, even while they had understood why they were in place. Some of the girls also expressed resentment about the elaborate process they had to go through before they could get a reply to their questions from the sants or Pramukh Swami. They had to be dependent on male members in the congregation to pass on their message and it had to go through so many lay leaders that it often took a long time for them to receive a response.

Sujatha sat in on a few class sessions for young women in their early twenties held at the temple from 4 to 7 P.M. on Sundays. Her observations provide a glimpse into the concerns and viewpoints of some second-generation Swaminarayan women in the temple, as well as some of the differences between the perspectives of the first and second generations. The class had seven students and two teachers, and the session began with a prayer and bhajan. The temple was organizing an important celebration to honor Pramukh Swami the following month, and the women, as was the custom, were going to attend the main function on Sunday but were also going to have a separate women-only samaiyo the previous day. The first part of the class time was spent in discussing what kind of presentation the young women in the class were going to make for the samaiyo. Apparently the men in the temple had told the teachers what they thought the class should do (projects linking together the scriptures with the life of Bapa). The young women, who wanted to speak about women's issues at the samaiyo, protested these "orders" coming from the men and asked why the male members interfered when they were not even going to be attending the women's samaiyo. Although the teachers sympathized with the girls, they were firm that the presentations had to relate women's issues with the Swaminarayan tradition and Pramukh Swami. Ultimately the group decided that the young women would talk about famous female devotees in the Swaminarayan tradition. The speeches for the samaiyo were to be in Gujarati, but they were going to be transliterated into English so that the young women could read them. Sujatha notes that throughout the discussion, "both the teachers spoke mostly in Gujarati that was spiced with an occasional English word or sentence," but the girls in the class "only spoke in English." They seemed to understand what the teachers were saying but could not or did not want to speak in Gujarati.

After more informal chatting and discussion about the different events that were going on in the temple and about a few temple personalities, they turned to the main part of the class—a discussion about the significance and rituals to be performed at an important upcoming religious festival. One of the young women who recently had had an arranged marriage complained that her mother-in-law had been upset with her because she had not followed all the traditional customs fully. This remark led the class to burst into an animated discussion about FOB (Fresh Off the Boat—i.e., recent immigrants) mothers-in-law and how demanding they were. The teachers were troubled and tried to share their own personal examples about how they listened to their mothers-in-law even when they were unreasonable, but the girls were not persuaded; instead they hoped that their in-laws would simply stay in India and not bother them. They were also concerned that a husband could have an FOB attitude and create trouble. This discussion sparked an animated conversation about arranged marriages and marriages outside the community. Although the girls gave examples of Indians they knew who had married non-Gujaratis and had had successful marriages, the teachers were much more pessimistic and told the girls that such marriages were stressful for everyone. Another young woman talked about how she would never be happy marrying a traditional man from India. One of the teachers sympathized, but told her that "it is the duty of the woman to always give in more and try to fit in." The topic of Indian men and marriage came up again the next time that Sujatha attended the same class. This time apparently the students became quite outspoken about Indian men and described them as selfish and easily threatened by a woman's success. The teacher tried to tell them that most men were good, and that there was nothing wrong in accepting that a woman should be a step below the man. According to her, a wife who was more educated or who earned more than her husband emasculated him. Since the girls were not convinced, she concluded by saying that these things (relative levels of education and income) became trivial if there was true love and commitment between the couple.

Many second-generation women experience difficulty accepting traditional Indian gender norms and expectations regarding the role of women in marriage. Differences between first- and second-generation members on these and other issues often lead to a lack of communication or the breakdown of communication between parents and children as the latter grow older. Recognizing this, the Swaminarayan sanstha provided a space where teenagers and young adults could have discussions about matters of concern with sympathetic members of the older generation as a group, instead of as individuals. From the point of view of the parents, such class discussions helped reinforce their values and goals and improved family relationships (see Radha's comments on this issue below). At the same time, the very real differences between the outlook of the two generations seen in the above vignette may bring about changes in the relationships between men and women in the sanstha in the long run.

Children

Children were introduced to the religion from infancy and usually started to attend the religious education classes from the time they were quite young. The classes were in English, but the teachers encouraged the use of Gujarati and spoke in Gujarati whenever possible while offering English translations. There were also separate Gujarati language classes. Classes followed a standardized syllabus that came from the national headquarters, which also created the exams. Notes about what happened in each class were compiled and given to students who were absent and also sent to the head office. Teachers went through a training session in April, where they were taught how to communicate effectively with children, how to tell stories to them, and how to teach them to resist peer pressure. The typical class for the children consisted primarily of formal religious teaching, but also included time for informal discussions about issues that children had to confront in their everyday lives. Teachers used several strategies, including games, competitions, and quizzes, to make the classes interesting, particularly for younger children. Because the classes were small, each was usually a close-knit group and children often confided in the teachers. The youth classes also helped to provide the students social support during times of personal crises. A class of ten- to eleven-year-old girls to whom Sujatha and Susan spoke talked about how much they enjoyed coming to the temple on Sundays and attending the classes. They came at around 2 P.M. and stayed until 8:30 or even later on some Sundays. None of the girls wanted to go home even then, because "it is so fun here" and "because you see your friends once a week." All mentioned that their closest friends were from the temple, although they had lots of friends in school.

The sants played an important role in immigrant congregations. Since they were generally young, well-educated second-generation Indian Americans who were also wellversed in the religion and mores, they served as an important bridge between first- and second-generation members. They were frequently called on to intervene to help resolve conflicts. One devotee pointed out that often parents found it difficult to communicate with their American-born children because of the differences between the Indian and American cultures. "On the other hand, the saints … are able to communicate much better. They understand the pressure much better … the kids trust the saints, and tell them lots of things." Girls could not talk directly with the saints, but could write notes and pass them on.

Both parents and children credited the temple with being an important social and moral force for second-generation youth. Arpit, a young man who had grown up in the temple, said, "Without this temple, I don't know where I would be in life. It has helped me guide my life in a straight path. I learned how to set goals and how to pursue them. If I had not been involved in the temple, I may have been on the streets!" He went on to speak about how he was able to avoid the alcohol and drugs that were a big part of the lives of many of the other students in his college. Another young man echoed this sentiment:

> I attribute a lot of what I am because of this involvement in terms of my ethics, morality, and living a good life away from alcohol and drugs. They start "hammering" it on us at a very young age, not in a bad way, but just to help us lead a good, pure, clean, and healthy life. And I feel grateful for that, because I do have friends that have such bad habits that I do not desire. Some of them do not have very promising futures. I feel sad for them, because they are wasting their lives away just because they don't have religion in their lives.

The boys also appreciated the opportunities the temple provided for leadership and public speaking. Suraj emphasized that these opportunities had helped him in his college classes. "Presentations and singing are events that help our self-esteem. I was always afraid of being in front of a large crowd, but through these events, I have learned to conquer my fears."

Parents felt that participating in the temple helped children not to "get involved with the U.S. culture" but to be "within our own culture and religion." For instance, one woman pointed out, "this is an open-sex society, and here we are, we believe in virginity till your first night after the wedding, but they [the children] have managed it very well. The teachers have helped, the saints, they help a lot. Saints are not only talking to kids but they are talking to parents about it. They are telling us how to be better parents." Radha mentioned that she did not

> have to sit down with my daughters and give them "lectures" because both of them have grown up in the satsang. So right from childhood, they have this moral value that was instilled in them not only by me and my husband but it was by the saints and the religion itself. They also have friends in the same religion and so I don't think I ever had to really sit down with either of my daughters and

tell them that alcohol is bad for you or that you should not be doing drugs. So when they go out, I am with peace of mind. I know where they are and I know they will not be pulled into something just by peer pressure. So, not having to give lectures keeps the relationship more open because they don't feel that I am lecturing them all the time.

Most of the youth, both male and female, who were interviewed indicated that they would like to marry a Swaminarayan member, and that they wanted their children to be part of the sanstha. Most also seemed to be open to having an arranged marriage. An important benefit of being part of the BAPS was that neither boys nor girls had difficulty obtaining alliances within the sanstha. One man pointed out, "This sanstha is a great network system, here, New Jersey, Africa, everywhere ... we have contacts and we can arrange marriages." The attachment of many of the youth to the temple and to having arranged marriages within the sanstha seems to augur well for the continuation of the group. One young man noted that temple leaders "emphasize that we, the youth, are the future, so I guess that being drilled into our heads, we have to move up and take the initiative." The main issue that the BAPS will have to face in the long term is the centrality of the Gujarati language to the tradition. The adults repeatedly mentioned that the second generation did not know Gujarati well (something that was borne out by our visits to the classes) and that at best, they could only speak in simple, conversational Gujarati (very different from the Gujarati used in the Swaminarayan scriptures and the sabha discourses). At present Gujarati language is central to the religious services and discourses, and the second-generation members only come in at the end, for the puja. Clearly this pattern is not viable if the group is looking to the American-born youth to "move up" and start taking over the running of the weekly sabhas. Because lay members play such an important part in the group and the sabha, this issue will need to be resolved in the near future.

CONCLUSION

We have looked at two different types of temples. The Malibu temple represents the more typical American model, built as the abode of a primary deity following the guidelines laid down in the shastras, but subsequently becoming more ecumenical and congregational because of the need for social and financial support from local Hindus. As is also typical, the role of the temple priests was also different from that in India. The conflict that was taking place at the time of the study meant that the temple had become less community oriented and also offered fewer services such as the Hinduism or Sanskrit classes that most other Hindu American temples conducted. The conflict itself, however, was not unusual, as temples face the many challenges posed by U.S. rules governing the formation and management of American nonprofit corporations and are forced to transform the way they are organized (see Kurien 2006b).

The BAPS temple is primarily a congregational home, so there is less emphasis on constructing an "authentic" temple before temple worship begins. Thus the

Swaminarayan leadership's strategy for fund raising and temple building is different from that of the HTSSC. We have seen how the BAPS was able to create a tight-knit spiritual and social community for the men, women, and children of the group and that the temple also functioned as a satsang and a bala vihar. The centralized transnational organization of the BAPS has been effective both in administration and in mobilizing resources. The close personal tie with Pramukh Swami that members feel leads many talented individuals to volunteer their time and effort to construct the massive ornate temples and to organize and run the mega-festivals that are a distinctive feature of the sect. How the language issue will be resolved will be an important determinant in shaping the character and long-term viability of the group in the United States and in other diasporic contexts.

PART II

Official Hinduism

CHAPTER 6

Forging an Official Hinduism in India

HINDU UMBRELLA ORGANIZATIONS

Given the great diversity in the theology and practice of Hinduism, both in India and in the United States, who speaks for Hinduism? Who are the public representatives of Hinduism and what are they saying about the religion and its adherents? All religious communities draw boundaries between themselves and the members of other religions. How do the spokespersons of Hinduism do this? As we will see, defining what Hinduism and Hindus are about has become particularly salient today both in India and in the Hindu diaspora.

A variety of spokespersons for Hinduism are present in the United States. Many Hindu Americans are called upon to define, articulate, or defend Hindu beliefs and practices to their non-Hindu colleagues, classmates, or friends at one time or another. Parents, teachers at bala vihars, and those who make presentations about Hinduism to student groups perform a similar task for Hindu youth growing up in the United States. On a more formal level, members of temple boards and temple public relations committees often represent Hinduism at interfaith public events, but such participation is not the central task of temples or of temple board members. There are other groups whose primary goal is to represent Hinduism and Hindus in the United States, they will be the focus of part II.

I have already mentioned the absence of any traditional pan-Hindu ecclesiastical structure or central religious authority. Temple priests are trained primarily in temple rituals and are therefore not viewed as experts in Hindu theology. Religious authority in Hinduism is typically sect based. Some sects, like the Swaminarayan, are organized around a lineage of spiritual leaders. Other traditions revere the Shankaracharyas, or the heads of monastic orders, that are tied to particular Hindu philosophical schools. Newer religious movements spring up around charismatic male or female renunciative saint-teachers. Two recent changes in the contemporary period, however, are notable. First, the formation of the Vishwa Hindu Parishad in the 1960s gave rise to an initial attempt to create a non-sectarian Hinduism and a central authority structure. Subsequently other leaders and organizations have taken this task forward, resulting today in a variety of organizations and spokespersons claiming to represent Hindus and Hinduism. Second, the central spokespersons of Hinduism today, particularly in the United States, are typically not traditional ascetic religious leaders or teachers but instead are educated lay Hindus (almost always men) who use their accomplishments in the professional and business world to legitimize their religious authority within the Hindu community (see Waghorne 2004, 181, 237).

In part I we saw how the institutionalization of Hinduism in the United States led to the development of new types of transnational connections with India. Members of satsang groups went looking for audiotapes of bhajans to introduce to their groups; others obtained pictures and statues of deities to install in their prayer rooms. Teachers at bala vihars turned to traditional sources on Indian history and Hinduism to expound on in their classes. Temples like the one at Malibu and the Swaminarayan temple in Los Angeles forged connections with established temples in India to obtain the traditional architects, priests, icons, and other materials needed to establish Hinduism in the United States. In part II we will look at the forging of a different type of transnationalism, as Hindu organizations in the United States turn to Hindu nationalist groups and ideologies in India to formulate a unified and "official" American Hinduism. These ideologies were first articulated during the colonial period by Hindu reformers and Hindu nationalists in the early twentieth century. This chapter traces the development of Hindu nationalism in India under colonial rule and its resuscitation over the past few decades.

THE DEVELOPMENT OF HINDU NATIONALISM IN INDIA
Hindu Reform Movements

Hindu nationalism has its roots in the Hindu reform and renaissance movements that emerged in the late colonial period. Although the Hindu reform movements that developed differed, they also had many commonalities. First, these movements drew on Orientalist constructions regarding both the universal religious core contained in the Vedic corpus and the greatness of ancient Hindu society and its subsequent decline, particularly under Muslim rule (Hansen 1999, 34). Thus all reform efforts, in different ways, attempted to restore Hinduism to its pristine Vedic foundations. Second, they attempted to reformulate the theology and practice of Hinduism on a rationalist Western model. Thus they criticized icon worship, excessive ritualism, and customs such as sati and child marriage, and emphasized the importance of having an educated, scientific understanding and appreciation for Hindu texts and doctrines. Third, most of them emphasized that Hinduism, unlike the Semitic religions, was characterized by pacifism and tolerance.[1] The syncretic, intellectual, outward-looking religion promoted by these reform movements has been termed "modern" Hinduism.

Brahmo Samaj. The earliest of such reform movements was the Brahmo Samaj, founded in Calcutta (Bengal) in 1828 by Raja Ram Mohan Roy (1772–1833). Roy came from a traditional Bengali Brahmin family and had an extensive education before embarking on a career in the East India Company (which he left in 1814, to devote himself full time to religious and social reform). He had learned Arabic, Persian, Sanskrit, Hebrew, and Greek in addition to English and had been exposed to the philosophy of the *Upanishads* and the Sufi tradition as well as Christian Unitarianism and Deism. On the basis of this study he came to the conclusion that all religions have the same central truth. He espoused a return to the teachings of the *Upanishads* and a form of deistic monotheism: a belief and worship of the "Eternal, Unsearchable and Immutable Being who is the Author and Preserver of the Universe," and a rejection of later accretions to Hinduism.[2] The Brahmo Samaj instituted a form of congregational worship on the Christian model, meeting regularly for religious services where passages from the *Upanishads* were read, sermons delivered, and hymns (some composed by Roy) sung. Roy was also an ardent social reformer who was vehemently opposed to the practice of sati (as a youth he had witnessed a favorite sister-in-law being forced onto the funeral pyre of her husband, and this incident had left a deep impression on him). The banning of the practice by the British government in 1829 was at least partly due to Roy's campaign. Splits in the Brahmo Samaj after Roy's death weakened the movement.

Arya Samaj. The Arya Samaj was founded in Bombay in 1875 by Swami Dayananda Saraswati (1824–1883), a Gujarati Brahmin who was influenced by the Brahmo Samaj. When he was twenty-one, Dayananda left home to become a *sannyasin* (a world-renouncing ascetic). After several years as an itinerant preacher, he returned to western India to found his organization. Swami Dayananda believed that the Vedas contained revealed wisdom and manifested the eternal law, or Sanatana Dharma. Daniel Gold (1991, 543) notes that in so doing, Dayananda reformulated the diffuse idea of Vedic authority in which traditional Hindus believed into a closed scriptural canon more akin to those of the Christian and Islamic traditions. Swami Dayananda went even further. He asserted that the Vedic revelation not only was the "highest ever received by humankind" but contained all scientific discoveries known to modern society (Gold 1994, 544). The kings of Aryavartha (his name for ancient India) "ruled over all the earth and taught the wisdom of the country to all. Through their great knowledge, the ancient Indians were able to produce the extraordinary weapons of war described in the epics. . . . After the great war described in the Mahabharata, however, all this knowledge was lost. . . . The Swami's mission was to restore Aryavartha to its ancient glory" (Gold 1994, 545, based on chapter 11 of *The Light of Truth*). Some Hinducentric scholars today also argue that the Vedas contain all knowledge known to sciences.

Unlike the Brahmos (members of the Brahmo Samaj), Swami Dayananda emphasized the older Vedic hymns and paid less attention to the Upanishads. He believed that all the other secondary scriptures, such as the epics and Puranas, should be abandoned (though he did accept the teachings of the Dharma Shastras such as the *Manusmriti*). Swami Dayananda also espoused the simplification of the traditional life-cycle rituals practiced by Hindus and sought the revival of old Vedic rites for occasions such as marriage. Swami Dayananda's interpretation of the caste system is also one that many contemporary Hindu Americans espouse, namely that the varna scheme was based on individual differences in ability, character, and accomplishments. In the Punjab, the Arya Samaj was able to reconvert to Hinduism many low-caste converts to Islam and Christianity through a *shuddi* (purification) ceremony that transformed them not only into Hindus but also into members of the upper castes (Flood 1996, 256).

Unlike the Brahmo Samaj, which had affirmed the equality of all religions, the Arya Samaj was fiercely critical of Christianity and Islam. Christian and Islamic doctrines were examined and mocked in the last two chapters of Swami Dayananda's book *The Light of Truth* and contrasted with the doctrines of the Vedic religion that were expounded in the first part of the book. The Arya Samaj was also critical of Buddhism and Jainism and even other Hindu groups, which came under attack in *The Light of Truth*. Thus although the movement was strongly nationalistic, and its ideology was central in the subsequent development of Hindu nationalism, Christophe Jaffrelot (1996) points out that in the nineteenth century, the nationalism of the Arya Samaj was not a "Hindu" nationalism in the sense that we know it now, since the members preferred to distinguish themselves as "Aryas" practicing a pure Vedic religion, in comparison with the other Hindu groups around them. In fact, the leaders of the Arya Samaj called on their members to identify themselves as "Aryas" and not Hindus in the 1891 census (Jaffrelot 1996, 17).

Paramahamsa Ramakrishna and Swami Vivekananda. Paramahamsa Ramakrishna (1836–1886) was a Bengali Hindu mystic who declared the unity of all religions and claimed to have visions of Hindu deities but also of Jesus and Allah. His best-known disciple was Swami Vivekananda (1863–1902), who became a sannyasin after Ramakrishna's death. As we saw in chapter 3, Swami Vivekananda emphasized the truth of all religions, and also stressed the importance of religious tolerance in his 1893 addresses at the World Parliament of Religions in Chicago. In his subsequent lecture tour of the United States, he went on to develop several of his ideas further. Swami Vivekananda is credited with being the first to bring modern Hinduism to the United States and also with being the first to successfully promote Hinduism as a world religion.

Probably since Swami Vivekananda developed his ideas in the context of his engagement with the West, and particularly with the United States, several of those ideas have been pivotal to the official Hinduism that is being developed in America. First, however, it is important to understand how the American context affected the swami. Swami Vivekananda's visit to the United States and particularly the experience of how negatively India was viewed in the popular press there led to a transformation in his message. From a reformer who had embarked on his foreign journey to raise money to finance social uplift programs in India, he became in the United States, Carl Jackson (1994, 33) argues, a fierce defender of many of the same practices (such as the caste system and the position of women in India) that he had earlier condemned. Jackson (1994, 34) continues, "When he conceded that abuses existed, he argued that 1) they were not central to Hinduism; 2) they had been introduced by foreign conquerors; 3) they represented conceptions and practices that had once served a positive function; or 4) they were badly misinterpreted by Western critics" (see also Sil 1997). He also repeatedly emphasized the superiority of Hindu civilization when compared with that of the West. For instance, in a lecture in Brooklyn in 1895 entitled "India's Gift to the World," Swami Vivekananda described India as the "earliest cradle of ethics, arts, sciences, and literature," arguing that it had "exerted a great influence on Christianity, as the very teachings of Christ could be traced back to those of Buddha, whose ideas were spread in the Middle East through missionaries of the Emperor Asoka." After giving numerous examples of Indian inventions and contributions in a variety of areas, he concluded, "So great in fact was the superiority of India in every respect, that it drew to her borders the hungry cohorts of Europe, and thereby indirectly brought about the discovery of America" (Vivekananda 1895). Many of these same arguments are made by Hindu Americans today.

Swami Vivekananda received a tremendous reception upon his return to India and was invited to give lectures throughout the country. In clear, simple terms, these lectures, compiled into a book, *Lectures from Columbo to Almora*, outline his Vedantic philosophy and his interpretation of Hinduism as a scientific, pluralistic religion based on the revealed wisdom of the Vedas, one that Hindus should take great pride in and not be apologetic about. The swami also founded the Ramakrishna Mission in India, which emphasized the importance of education, social reform, and social service. Schools, colleges, and hospitals run by the Ramakrishna Mission were established throughout the country. Vivekananda's powerful oratory and inspirational message uplifted the morale of Hindus. His ideas became popular among the English-educated middle and upper classes in India and were central in the development of a "modern Hindu self-understanding" (Flood 1996, 257). Many of these were later appropriated by the Hindu nationalist movement; organizations like the RSS, for example, now claim to be the "embodiment of Vivekananda's teachings" (Singhal 2004).

Swami Vivekananda expounded the Vedantic idea that "God is within, that Divinity resides within all things" (Vivekananda n.d., 7). All human beings are therefore united in this Oneness, and Vivekananda argued that this understanding should promote love and harmony and should also be the basis for ethics and morality. Disagreeing with the Christian idea that all humans are sinners, Vivekananda instead preached that all human beings were Children of God and therefore holy beings whose objective was to achieve union with God. He also promoted the idea that Hindus had based their existence on the idea (found in the *Rig Veda*) that "God is one, the sages call him variously." In "The Mission of Vedanta," he proclaimed, "We live that grand truth in every vein, and our country has become the glorious land of religious toleration. It is here [India] and here alone that they build temples and churches for the religions which have come with the object of condemning our own religion" (Vivekananda n.d., 5). The idea that God is one also explained the plurality of deities worshipped by Hindus, he argued, emphasizing that Hinduism was not a polytheistic religion, since the numerous deities were just different names for the same Infinite Reality. (He also stressed that the images of the deities were only symbols on which to hang spiritual ideas, and that Hindus should therefore not be characterized as idol worshippers.) The belief in the Oneness of God and the universe led to the idea of the universality of all religions, which Vivekananda claimed would be very important for the future of mankind. "The world is waiting for this grand idea of universal toleration" from India, he said (Vivekananda n.d., 5).

At the World Parliament of Religions, Swami Vivekananda ended his lecture on Hinduism by calling for a universal religion, "which will have no location in place or time; which will be infinite like the God it will preach, and whose sun will shine upon the followers of Krishna and of Christ ... which will not be Brahminic or Buddhistic, Christian, or Mohammedan, but the sum total of all these and still have infinite space for development. .... It will be a religion which will have no place for persecution or intolerance ..., which will recognize divinity in every man and woman." He gave credit to the United States for organizing the World Parliament and of thus "marching at the vanguard of civilization with the flag of harmony" (Vivekananda 1893b). In his final address at the parliament, he cautioned that this universal religion would not come "by the triumph of any one of the religions and the destruction of the others" (Vivekananda 1893c). But in his lectures in India upon his return from the United States, he argued that "it is Vedanta, and Vedanta alone that can become the universal religion of man, and ... no other is fitted for the role" (Vivekananda n.d., 3). He went on to state that Hinduism was the only universal religion, because "excepting our own, almost all the other great religions in the world are inevitably connected with the life or lives of one or more of their founders. All their theories, their teachings, their doctrines, and their ethics are built around the life of a personal founder, from whom they get their sanction, their authority, and their power; and strangely enough, upon the historicity of the founder's life is built as it were, all the fabric of such religions. If there is one blow dealt to the historicity of that life, as has been the case in modern times with the lives of all the so-called founders of religion ... if that rock of historicity, as they pretend to call it, is shaken and shattered, the whole building tumbles down, broken absolutely, never to regain its lost status" (Vivekananda n.d., 3). Hinduism, in contrast, was built not on historical characters but on principles, and was an "accumulated treasury of spiritual laws" discovered by sages. Its validity thus did not depend on the historicity of sages, prophets, or incarnations "just as the law of gravitation existed before its discovery, and would exist if all humanity forgot it" (Vivekananda 1893b). He also emphasized that "of all the scriptures in the world, it [the Vedas] is the one scripture the teachings of which is in entire harmony with the results that have been attained by ... modern scientific investigations" (Vivekananda 1897).

Vivekananda was one of the earliest to propagate the dichotomy of the spiritual East and the materialistic West (Flood 1996, 258), believing that "India's gift to the world is the light spiritual." He argued that it was therefore the obligation of Indians to "start the wave which is going to spiritualize the material civilization of the world" (Vivekananda 1897). He went on to say that it had been foretold by the German philosopher Arthur Schopenhauer that Indian ideas would produce a "revolution in thought more extensive and more powerful than that which was witnessed by the Renaissance of Greek literature. Today his predictions are coming to pass" (Vivekananda 1897). We will see that each of these arguments has been incorporated into the official Hinduism promoted by American Hindu leaders.

Gandhi. Mohandas Karamchand Gandhi (1869–1948) was born in Gujarat into a devout Vaishnava merchant caste, with close ties with Jainism (one of the important sources of his belief in nonviolence). He studied law in London, where he encountered and was influenced by Theosophy, a European movement that looked to the East for its spiritual wisdom, as well as the writings of pacifists like Leo Tolstoy and John Ruskin. As a lawyer he went to South Africa, where he lived for twenty-one years. It was there that he first developed his political philosophy of *ahimsa* (nonviolence) and *satyagraha* (truth-force), a nonviolent, moral, and ethical struggle to bring about social change. He returned to India in 1915 and joined the nationalist movement. For Gandhi, true independence would involve not only a liberation from British rule but a thoroughgoing transformation of Indian society, a rejection of the materialism and industrialism which he identified with the West, and a return to a simple, self-sufficient village life. As part of this social transformation, Gandhi worked to uplift the status of the Untouchables, whom he called Harijans (children of God). He did not, however, repudiate the traditional varna structure, but merely wanted to transform it to ameliorate the situation of the Untouchables, a position that did not sit well with Dalit leaders like Ambedkar, who eventually converted to Buddhism.

Although Gandhi consciously tried to be pluralist, quoting from the Bible, the Koran, and the *Upanishads* and promoting the notion of "equal respect for all faiths" (Hansen 1999, 45), his idiom was unmistakably Hindu and upper caste. For instance, he described himself as an orthodox Hindu who believed that Hinduism was a universal religion, accepting all paths to God. He also described his ideal society as a Rama Rajya (kingdom of Rama), where the love and protection of the mother cow would be the central binding force. His emphasis on the importance of asceticism, vegetarianism, and sexual abstinence, and his chosen clothing of loin cloth and shawl, similarly drew on the Hindu renounciate (sannyasin) tradition. The conservative and strongly Hindu character of his nationalism ended up alienating Indian Muslims, and his stress on nonviolence antagonized militant Hindu nationalists, including Nathuram Godse, a member of the Hindu Mahasabha and a former member of the militant Hindu organization RSS, who assassinated him. At his trial Godse declared, "I firmly believed that the teachings of absolute ahimsa as advocated by Gandhiji would ultimately result in the emasculation of the Hindu community and thus make the community incapable of resisting the aggression or inroads of other communities, especially the Muslims" (quoted in van der Veer 1994, 96).

The Rise of Hindu Nationalism

The rise of Hindu nationalism can be first seen in some of the literature that was part of the Hindu renaissance. Several vernacular writers in the nineteenth century tried to mobilize and unify Hindus by recalling the glory of premedieval India. The central theme of this literature was the destruction of Hinduism and of Hindu society under Muslim rule, which was seen as a "chronicle of rape and abduction of Hindu women, the slaughter of sacred cows, and the defilement of temples" (Hasan 1996, 200).[3] Not surprisingly, such writing alienated Indian Muslims, for whom the Mughal rule represented the apogee of Muslim culture and glory in India. In 1893 the first of a series of "cow protection," or anti–cow slaughter, movements, in which Hindus would try to rescue cows from Muslim slaughterhouses, led to the outbreak of Hindu–Muslim riots around Patna, in eastern India. These cow protection movements sharpened tensions between the two communities.

The next stage in the development of Hindu nationalism came with the transformation of the Arya Samaj. We have seen that in the nineteenth century, the Arya Samajists had declared themselves "Arya" and not "Hindu." But by the first decade of the twentieth century, Arya Samajists had established the Hindu Sabha (council) in 1909, and in the 1911 census, they declared themselves to be "Hindus" and not "Aryas." Quoting an Arya Samaj leader, Lal Chand, to make his point, Jaffrelot (1996, 18) argues that Hindu feelings of vulnerability vis-à-vis Indian Muslims were responsible for this shift. In 1909 Lal Chand argued, "Mohammedans have Constantinople behind their back, not to speak of other Mohammedan independent States . . . British statesmen, therefore, not only desire to conciliate Muslim opinion, but are seriously nervous lest they should give any offense to it" (quoted in Jaffrelot 1996, 18).

Savarkar and Hindutva. The mobilization of Indian Muslims through the Khilafat movement, which began in 1919 in opposition to British policies toward Turkey and the Ottoman Sultan, roused the anxieties of Hindus (particularly since the Muslim mobilization and militancy were occasionally turned against them), and eventually led to the explicit codification of Hindu nationalism in the 1920s. The book *Hindutva*, written by Vinayak Damodar Savarkar (1883–1966) in 1922 while in prison and published in 1923, was central in achieving this codification. Savarkar was a Maharastrian Brahmin who was inspired by the Italian revolutionary Giuseppe Mazzini and had formed a secret society, Abhinav Bharat (Modern India), in 1904, probably modeled on Mazzini's Young Italy organization (Jaffrelot 1996, 26). Savarkar was arrested and sent to prison several times by the British on charges of sedition and anti-British activities. During a four-year stay in Britain from 1906 to 1910, he studied Mazzini's writings, translated them into Marathi, and sent the compilation back to India to be published. The idea of an organicist nationalism, based on primordial ethnic and racial substance (rather than the English notion of a nation based on a social contract), which was prevalent particularly in Italy and Germany in the early decades of the twentieth century, was an important influence on Savarkar and also on Golwalkar, the second leader of the RSS (P. Ahmed 2001, 15).

In *Hindutva*, Savarkar tried to settle the question of who exactly was a Hindu. He argued that the term "Hindu" or "Hindustan" (land of the Hindus) must have been an indigenous word for the territory between the Himalayas and the sea, and that it was "so perfectly designed by the fingers of nature as a geographical unit" (Savarkar [1923] 1969, 32) that the Aryans who settled in this land at the dawn of history and intermingled with the non-Aryans to form the Hindu race were one single nation from antiquity. Hindus were thus the original inhabitants of this territory and "all Hindus claim to have in their veins the blood of the mighty race incorporated with and descended from the Vedic fathers" (Savarkar [1923] 1969, 85). A further tie was the common culture shared by Hindus, which he defined as "Sanskriti," saying "suggestive as it is of that language, Sanskrit, which has been the chosen means of expression and preservation of that culture" (Savarkar [1923] 1969, 92).

The subcontinent was also a holy land, which had nurtured many religions, including, besides Hinduism, Buddhism, Jainism, and Sikhism. An additional attribute of Hindus was therefore that they regard India as their holy land. Although Indian Jains, Buddhists, and Sikhs were thus included in his definition of a Hindu, Indian Muslims and Christians were excluded, because "their holyland is far off in Arabia and Palestine. Their mythology and Godmen, ideas and heroes are not the children of this soil" (Savarkar [1923] 1969, 113). In this way Savarkar arrived at his condensed and much-quoted definition of a Hindu: "A person who looks upon the land that extends from the Indus to the sea as his Fatherland and his Holyland."[4] Hindus, as the rightful heirs of this land, he argued, should reject any dominance from foreign elements like Muslims and Christians. They had resisted many such invaders in the past, and should continue to do so whenever the Hindu Nation was threatened.

The significance of Sarvarkar's effort to find a precise definition of a Hindu can be seen in the statement made by the publisher in the preface to the fourth edition of the book, published in 1949. "The definition acted as does some scientific discovery of a new truth in re-shaping and re-coordinating all current Thought and Action. . . . At its touch arose an organic order where a chaos of castes and creeds rule. The definition provided a broad basic foundation on which a consolidated and mighty Hindu Nation could take a secure stand" (p. vi, quoted in Pandey 1993, 249). Although the claim was undoubtedly hyperbolic, the importance of the book for the development of Hindu nationalism is clear. Savarkar's historical writings, focusing on the threats faced and successfully overcome by Hindus, were also influential in the rise of the Hindu nationalist movement, especially his last work, *Six Glorious Epochs of Indian History* (first published in 1963), dealing primarily with the period of Muslim rule. In this work, the themes of constant Hindu resistance against Muslim control and of the abductions and rapes of Hindu women, which would become central to Hindu nationalist historiography, were emphasized. Savarkar later went on to become the president of the Hindu Mahasabha (Grand Council) from 1937 to 1942.

The Formation of the RSS. Savarkar's ideas so impressed Keshav Baliram Hedgewar, another Brahmin from Maharashtra who had been involved in national politics but had who been frustrated by Gandhi's principles of ahimsa and satyagraha, that he went on to form the Rashtriya Swayamsevak Sangh (RSS, the National Volunteer Corps) in 1925. Hedgewar's inspiration was Shivaji, a seventeenth-century Maharastrian Hindu king who successfully led a revolt against the Mughals, and his goal was to develop a committed and disciplined cadre of young men *(swayamsevaks)* to serve the cause of Hindu unity and defense. The swayamsevaks were organized into *shakhas* (local branches) that met regularly for paramilitary drills, religious and ideological instruction, and social service. They wore a uniform of khaki shorts, similar to that of the British police. Despite the martial tone of the movement, however, Hedgewar was adamant that the RSS should be a nonpolitical organization and even refused to allow it to participate in the anti-British nationalist movement, a decision that alienated many of its supporters, particularly those in the Hindu Mahasabha, and led to the two organizations' severing their links (Frykenberg 1997, 242).

After Hedgewar's death in 1940, yet another Hindu nationalist from a Maharastrian Brahmin background, Madhav Sadashiv Golwalkar, took over as the leader of the RSS. In his book *We, or Our Nationhood Defined*, published in 1939, Golwalkar argued (in contrast to Savarkar) that Hindus did not come to this land from elsewhere, "but are indigenous children of the soil always, from times immemorial" (Golwalkar 1939, 8) and that this racial factor was "by far the most important ingredient of a nation" (ibid., 23). The concept of indigenousness subsequently became central to the Hindu nationalist platform. Golwalkar (ibid., 32) compared the arousal of the Hindu racial spirit to that of the Italian and German *Volkgeist* and then went on to say, "to keep up the purity of the Race and its culture, Germany shocked the world by her purging the country of the semitic Races—the Jews. Race pride at its highest has been manifested here. Germany has also shown how well nigh impossible it is for Races and cultures, having differences going to the root, to be assimilated into one united whole, a good lesson for us in Hindustan to learn and profit by" (ibid., 35). Golwalkar argued, "The non-Hindu peoples in Hindustan must adopt the Hindu culture and language, must learn to respect and hold in reverence Hindu religion, must entertain no idea but glorification of the Hindu race and culture ... in a word, they must cease to be foreigners, or must stay in this country wholly subordinated to the Hindu nation, claiming nothing, deserving no privileges, far less any preferential treatment, not even citizenship rights" (ibid., 55–56). Both Sarvarkar and Golwalkar refer to Nazism and Hitler approvingly (see P. Ahmed, 2001), a fact that is constantly emphasized by those opposed to Hindu nationalism. Gold (1994, 566), however, points out that these references were made before the "full horror of Nazi persecution" was known and that this aspect of their platform was abandoned or at least suppressed subsequently. It was Golwalkar who first articulated the anti-Communist platform of Hindu nationalism, which has become a centerpiece of the movement today. In his book *Bunch of Thoughts*, published in the mid-1960s, he indicated that the three internal threats facing the Hindu nation were (1) "The Muslims," (2) "The Christians," and (3) "The Communists" (Pandey 1993b, 251).

The increasing communalization of Hindus and Muslims resulted in the separation of Urdu and Hindi, which had historically been "two modes of writing the same language, Hindustani" (Hansen 1999, 73). From around the middle of the nineteenth century, the Urdu language came to be associated with Muslims, and Hindi with Hindus, and both languages became more differentiated by the development of distinct scripts, vocabularies, and literary traditions. The rise of Hindu nationalism also led to the development of a Dravidian (the term for the people and languages indigenous to south India) movement. Reacting to the Aryan and north

Indian focus of Orientalists and Hindu nationalists, and the often concomitant denigration of Dravidian culture (for example, in the Aryan invasion theory), a neo-
Shaivist movement emerged among the non-Brahmin castes in south India from
around the 1880s. The leaders of this movement argued that "it was not the Dravidians who corrupted a pristine Hinduism ... on the contrary, it was Brahmanism and
Aryanism that had debased the original Tamil religion" (Ramaswamy 1997, 29–30).
They believed that it was the Dravidian religion that was indigenous, not just in the
south but also in the north, and that it was not Sanskrit but Tamil that was the "world's
original, divine language" (Bryant 2001, 50). In this version of history, the Aryans
were the barbaric invaders who had colonized the sophisticated Tamilian culture, and
therefore, "most of what is ignorantly called Aryan philosophy, Aryan Civilization is
literally Dravidian or Tamilian at bottom" (Sundaran Pillai, quoted in Bryant 2001,
50). This neo-Shaivism led eventually to a full-blown Dravidian, anti-Brahmin (and
later anti-Hindi) movement in Tamil Nadu.

Toward Independence and Partition. The Indian National Congress was formed in
1885 and subsequently went on to play a central role in the Indian independence
movement. Mohammed Ali Jinnah, the pivotal figure behind the creation of Pakistan, was a successful Muslim barrister who had entered politics as part of the Congress, but joined the Muslim League in 1913 and became its president in 1936. The
reforms and promise of power held out by the British Montagu-Chelmsford
Reforms implemented in 1921 whetted the political ambition of Hindu and Muslim
leaders, who increasingly began to mobilize their followers by using a religious platform, and the conflict between the two groups turned more and more violent and
deadly. The hostilities between the Congress and the Muslim League intensified
when the Congress, in its 1928 session, bowed to pressure from Hindu nationalists
and refused to yield to Jinnah's demand for a guaranteed minority representation
for Muslims in return for a unified platform against the British. Adding insult to
injury, the emboldened Hindu nationalists then demanded that Congress support a
program to "reconvert" non-Hindus back to Hinduism (Stein 1998, 316), leading Jinnah and his supporters to abandon their alliance with the Congress.

The first demand for a separate Muslim nation was launched by a group of Muslim students at Cambridge University in 1933 (Metcalf and Metcalf 2002, 204), but
they were not taken seriously. Jinnah himself ignored them, arguing instead for a
secular nationalism with special protections and representation for Muslims.
Although he criticized the Congress leaders for alienating Muslims through their
"Hindu" policies (Hasan 1997, 58), Jinnah was still open to cooperation with them
to achieve this goal. The outbreak of World War II in 1939, however, brought a decisive change in the position and platform of the Muslim League.

At the outbreak of the war, the British government declared unilaterally that India
had entered the war against Hitler's Germany on Britain's side. Angered at this high-
handed treatment, the Congress refused to cooperate. The British government therefore turned to the Muslim League for support. By this time, relations between the
Congress and the Muslim League had further deteriorated because of the Congress's

refusal to entertain the idea of entering into a coalition with the Muslim League and insistence that the League dissolve and its members join the Congress (Metcalf and Metcalf 2002, 194). At this juncture Jinnah, taking advantage of his strategic bargaining position vis-à-vis the British, demanded that the League be treated on par with the Congress and floated the idea of an independent nation for Indian Muslims in his 1940 presidential address to the League. At that time most Muslims were opposed to the idea of a separate nation (Hasan 1997; Metcalf and Metcalf 2002, 205). But Jinnah, through his impassioned appeals to the Muslim intelligentsia, his exploitation of economic schisms and vulnerabilities among Muslim landlords and businessmen, and the use of Islamic holy men to persuade the Muslim peasants, was successful in mobilizing support for Pakistan from a significant group of Indian Muslims by 1946. The Congress also exploited Britain's wartime vulnerability to demand independence in return for supporting the war effort, and the country moved toward partition and violence on an unprecedented scale.

Partition in 1947 resulted in the creation of over 10 million refugees in the northwestern region alone, with around 5 million Hindus and Sikhs from the Pakistan area moving into India and around 5.5 million Muslims from India moving in the opposite direction. Many of the trains carrying refugees were ambushed and arrived at their destination carrying hundreds of corpses, which in turn led to further retaliatory violence. The death toll in northwestern India as a result of the post-Partition riots is estimated to have been between several hundred thousand and a million (Metcalf and Metcalf 2002, 218–219).

THE POSTCOLONIAL PERIOD

Jawaharlal Nehru, a secular Congress leader with socialist leanings, became the first prime minister of independent India and remained in that office until his death in 1964. The first two decades of Indian independence were crucially shaped by his ideology and commitments. Under his leadership, India became a secular democracy, pledged to the promotion of a "socialist pattern of society." Nehru's determined secularism pitted him against right-wing Hindu groups, and he waged a constant battle with them in the first few years of independence.[5] By the early 1950s Nehru had succeeded in relegating such groups to the margins of the political system. Hindu nationalists were also forced to adopt a more moderate public face in these decades as secularism, which in the Indian context meant that the state recognized and sustained all Indian religions without favoring any (rather than the separation of church and state as in the United States), was accepted as normative and as official state policy.

Nehru institutionalized several policies that roused the resentment of Hindu groups. The difference in Nehru's treatment of Hindus and Muslims regarding their personal laws was one example. The Hindu Code Bill was intended to consolidate the heterogeneous personal laws of the Hindus into a uniform civil code. No such action was taken for the Muslims, who continued to be governed by their personal laws. Particularly in the aftermath of the violence of Partition, Nehru wanted to reassure the

Muslims who had remained in India. His biographer explains that Nehru felt strongly that "there should be no impression of the Hindu majority forcing anything, however justified, on the Muslim minority."[6] Although Hindu groups were able to pressure Nehru into modifying the bill (into three more specialized bills governing marriage, adoption, and inheritance, respectively, which were less far-reaching in scope than the original bill), they were not successful in their attempts to maintain the Hindu personal laws or in getting a uniform civil code imposed on all religious groups. This decision of Nehru's subsequently gave rise to the Hindu nationalist charge of "pseudo-secularism" and pandering to Muslims. Nehru's goal of a "socialist pattern of society" was also strongly opposed by right-wing Hindu groups like the Jana Sangh and by wealthy farmers, and thus was watered down and resulted only in the implementation of very moderate land reforms, some community development schemes, and a planned economy with sequential five-year plans for India's development. The new constitution also outlawed untouchability and established a system of "reservations" (affirmative action) in the legislature for the former Untouchables and tribal groups, which were listed on a special schedule in the constitution and hence called "Scheduled Castes and Tribes" (SCs and STs). Subsequently the reservations were expanded to include preferential access to administrative services and educational institutions, and to encompass a wider range of lower castes (termed "Other Backward Classes" or OBCs). These provisions again aroused the resentment of Hindu groups like the RSS, which were dominated by higher-caste members.

The Resurgence of Hindu Nationalism

Christophe Jaffrelot (1996, 75) points out that the violence of Partition made people receptive to Hindu nationalism and that the membership of the RSS soared from around 76,000 in 1943 to around 600,000 by early 1948. The popularity of the organization in the immediate post-Independence period was due largely to the assistance it offered to Hindu refugees fleeing from Pakistan. In 1951 the Hindu Mahasabha officially proclaimed its goal of "establishing a Hindu state" in India so that "Hindu cultural life [would] receive official recognition" through the state patronage of Hindu festivals and the teaching of Sanskrit in schools. The party also called for the annulment of Partition and the restoration of a united India—Akhand Bharat—if necessary, by force (Jaffrelot 1996, 107–108). In an interview, the president of the organization, N. B. Khare, declared that Muslims in India "would be considered as second class citizens" and that they "should not be permitted any part in the political life of the country" (cited in Jaffrelot 1996, 108). By this time, however, the organization was so weakened and marginalized that it had support in only a few pockets of the country. The Hindu Mahasabha was soon eclipsed by the Jana Sangh, an all-India Hindu party established in 1951 by some members of the RSS. In 1977 the Jana Sangh joined with the Janata Party, formed by a coalition of individuals and parties opposed to the Congress prime minister Indira Gandhi, the daughter of Nehru.

The Bharatiya Janata Party. The Bharatiya Janata Party (BJP, the Indian People's Party) was formed in 1980 by a group of former Jana Sangh members, including

Atal Bihari Vajpayee and Lal Krishnan Advani (both of whom had originally been in the RSS), after the collapse of the Janata Party coalition. Vajpayee became the president and Advani, the vice-president and later the general secretary, of the party. In order to distance itself from the unsuccessful Jana Sangh, the BJP adopted a secularist, multicultural platform, for instance describing India as a "unique, multi-hued synthesis of the cultural contributions made over centuries by different people and religions" (cited in Jaffrelot 1996, 317) in its election manifesto of 1984. The communalization of politics and the decline of secularism that began with Indira Gandhi and that continued under the leadership of her son, Rajiv Gandhi, however, created space for the reemergence of Hindu nationalism, initiated by another Hindu organization, the Vishwa Hindu Parishad. This Hindu nationalism was subsequently capitalized on by the BJP, and the party became a key player on the national stage.

The Vishwa Hindu Parishad. The Vishwa Hindu Parishad (VHP, World Hindu Council) was founded in 1964 by Swami Chinmayananda of the Chinmaya Mission and by S. S. Apte of the RSS. As a religious group, it was not bound by the restrictions placed on the Jana Sangh, a political party, and it became the central promoter of Hinduism and Hindu unity in following decades. It also played an important role in educating and mobilizing the Hindu diaspora around the world. As Peter van der Veer points out, the group's universal and global scope was highlighted by the definition of Hindu that it adopted: "The term 'Hindu' embraces all people who believe in, respect or follow the eternal values of life—ethical and spiritual—that have evolved in Bharat [another name for India]."[7]

An important reason underlying the group's formation was the threat that Hindus seemed to feel from Islam and Christianity, and the resulting need to "compete" with these religions by adopting some of their central characteristics, a strategy that Jaffrelot (1996) describes as stigmatizing and emulating the threatening "Other." S. S. Apte, the VHP co-founder, explained the basis for the organization as follows: "The declared object of Christianity is to turn the whole world into Christendom—as that of Islam is to make it 'Pak.' Besides these two dogmatic and proselytising religions, there has arisen a third religion, communism. . . . The world has been divided into Christian, Islamic and Communist, and all these three consider the Hindu society as a very fine rich food on which to feast and fatten themselves. It is therefore necessary in this age of competition and conflict to think of, and organize, the Hindu world to save itself from the evil eyes of all the three."[8] The organization justified its attempt to bring about a greater uniformity of beliefs and practices by again pointing to Christianity and Islam: "Christians and Muslims are generally found observing, strictly and scrupulously, some religious rules of conduct. . . . The Parishad happily arrived at a 'code of conduct' which would be agreeable to all the sects and creeds."[9]

By 1979 a threefold minimum code was formulated: (1) that all Hindus should venerate the sun every morning and evening; (2) that the symbol "Om" be used regularly by Hindus to represent their Hindu faith; and (3) that every Hindu must keep a copy of the *Bhagavad Gita* in the house, since it "is the sacred book of the

Hindus irrespective of various *sampradayas* [sects] which contains the essence of Hindu Philosophy and way of life."[10] Although this code of conduct was subsequently abandoned, it was significant since it was the first attempt to develop a unified, nonsectarian Hinduism. Other ideas, such as the emphasis on proselytism and the attempt to make temples places where Hindu doctrines and ideas were disseminated, were also foreign to Hinduism, as was the very attempt to create a central authority and organization. Swami Chinmayananda admitted, "I know that religious organization is against the very principle of Hinduism, but we have to move with the time. We seem to have entered today, all over the world . . . into an age of organization. Therefore in the spiritual field . . . if religion wants to serve the society, it also has to get organized."[11] In 1982 the VHP formed a Hindu ecclesiastical body of spiritual leaders from different sects of Hinduism, whose task was to "direct and guide the religious ceremonies, morals and ethics of Hindu society."[12] This Sadhu Sansad (Sadhu Parliament) expanded into a Dharma Sansad (Parliament of the Hindu Religion) in 1984 and met periodically to debate the central problems facing Hindu society.

The VHP participated in the 1966 cow protection movement (Jaffrelot 1996, 193), and in the 1970s it focused on missionary work among tribals and Untouchables and on building up its overseas constituency (van der Veer 1994, 132). It was only in the 1980s that the VHP emerged as a Hindu nationalist organization, assuming leadership of the Ram Janmabhumi (birthplace of Ram) movement. Van der Veer (1994, 136) argues that since then the VHP has been trying to "formulate a modern Hinduism that can serve as the basis of a Hindu nation."

The Ram Janmabhumi movement. The town of Ayodhya in north India is believed by Hindus to be the birthplace of Lord Ram, one of the incarnations of Vishnu. The town is also the site of the Babri Masjid, a mosque commissioned in 1528 by Babur, the first Mughal ruler. From the mid-nineteenth century on, a movement alleging that the mosque had been built on the site of a Ram temple commemorating the exact place of his birth had developed, and in 1949 an image of Lord Ram mysteriously appeared inside the mosque. Following clashes between Hindus and Muslims, the government had closed the mosque but had permitted the image to remain. In 1984 the first VHP Dharma Sansad called for the "liberation" of Ram's birthplace and a few months later established a militant wing, the Bajrang Dal, to accomplish its goal (Jaffrelot 1996, 363).

From early 1987, a serialized version of the *Ramayana* was shown every Sunday morning on the state-controlled national television. The success of the *Ramayana* serial resulted in the televising of a serialized version of the *Mahabharata* in the following year. Television encouraged the homogenization of the epics, which had always had many regional variants. Even more important, the serials popularized the stories of the epics and their central characters (who had not been central to the Hinduism of many groups) and thus contributed to the creation of a pan-Indian Hinduism that would be crucial to the success of the Hindu nationalist movement (Rajagopal 2001).

The RSS abandoned its nonpolitical platform in the late 1980s, beginning with the centenary celebrations of the birth of its founder, K. B. Hedgewar, in 1989 (Rajagopal 2000, 480). In the same year the VHP's Dharma Sansad pledged to work for the "Hinduisation of public life" by electing pro-Hindu politicians and the building of the Ram temple. Later that year the VHP began a series of Ram Shila Pujas (pujas to sacralize the bricks for the Lord Ram) around the country to raise the money and acquire the sanctified bricks to build the temple, and also organized processions to bring the sacred bricks to Ayodhya. By this time the VHP and its affiliates had become well established in the United States, and according to Arvind Rajagopal (2000, 474), groups in thirty-one American cities organized Ram Shila Pujans and sent bricks to Ayodhya, thus contributing substantially to the financial support of the campaign.[13]

During the Ram Shila Pujans, prerecorded audiocassettes with Hindu nationalist songs and messages were played. Among the most violent of such prerecorded messages were those of the two well-known female Hindu leaders—Sadhvi (female sadhu) Rithambara, who proclaimed, "The blood of foreigners, of traitors who do not pay tribute to the ancestors, will flow,"[14] and Uma Bharati, who declared that "when ten Bajrangdalis [members of the Bajrang Dal] will sit on the chest of every Ali [i.e., Muslim], then only will one know that this country belongs to Lord Ram."[15] In 1990 the VHP set up a temporary building next to the Ram Janmabhumi site, which contained a model of the proposed Ram temple and posters describing the supposed history of the area. VHP propaganda included the claim that Hindus had fought as many as seventy-seven wars (seventy-five against the Mughals and two against the British) to prevent the demolition of the temple and the construction of the mosque or to subsequently liberate the site.[16] Other posters contained exhortations to Hindus to rise up and "wipe out these tyrants [a reference to Muslims] from the world and become world-conquerors" and urged that "it is the religious duty of every Hindu to slaughter those who slaughter cows" (Pandey 1993a, 15–16).

On December 6, 1992, a crowd of Hindu activists was able to climb on top of the ancient Babri mosque and demolish it, despite efforts of the Congress government at the center to prevent such an eventuality. Although the BJP, which was in power in the state, claimed that the demolition was a spontaneous act by the crowd, much evidence indicated that it was meticulously planned and orchestrated by Hindu nationalist Sangh Parivar leaders (e.g., see Jaffrelot 1996, 455). Communal riots followed, and several thousands, mostly Muslims, were killed.

The Rise of the BJP

The demolition of the Babri mosque, a watershed event in the history of the Hindu nationalist movement, propelled the BJP and its Sangh Parivar affiliates into the limelight. The BJP was able to take advantage of the power vacuum at the center created by the decline of the Congress Party to continue to gain seats in the Indian parliament and finally came to power at the head of a coalition government in 1998 and again in fresh elections in 1999. It stayed in power until 2004, when it was defeated in elections and another coalition government, this time headed by the Congress, came to power.

The rise of the BJP was marked by violence against Muslims and, by the end of the decade, when the issue of "conversions" had again become an emotional rallying point, against missionaries and recent converts (mostly lower caste or tribal) to Christianity. The state of Gujarat, where there was a long-standing BJP government, was particularly prone to communal unrest. The worst such episode in the post-1992 period took place in early 2002. In February of that year, a crowd of Muslims allegedly halted a train carrying Hindu pilgrims and activists, returning from Ayodhya in Godhra, Gujarat, and set fire to some carriages. (Since then, some investigations suggest that the fire in the carriages was ignited from inside the train, probably as a result of a cooking accident.) Fifty-nine people, mostly women and children, were burnt to death. In what several independent investigators have characterized as an organized, state-sponsored retaliation, Hindu mobs in Gujarat targeted Muslims, and around one thousand people, mostly Muslims, were killed, and several thousands more were injured or rendered homeless. Several hundred women were raped (and often subsequently burnt) in the attacks. According to Tanika Sarkar (2002), VHP leaflets that were signed by the state general secretary and openly circulating in Gujarat at the time claimed, "We will kill Muslims the way we destroyed Babri mosque" and that "We have widened the tight vaginas of the bibis [Muslim women]."[17] After the violence had been brought under control, Muslims were warned by members of the VHP that if they wanted to return to their villages, they should "do so as a subject, not an equal" and that they should learn to "live like a minority" (Waldman 2002). In January 2003 the BJP achieved a landslide electoral victory in Gujarat. Overjoyed by the outcome of the elections, the VHP leader Pravin Togadia vowed that the "experiment of the Hindutva lab" (referring to the pogrom against Muslims in the state) that had been successfully concluded in Gujarat would be repeated throughout the country. He also pledged that India would be converted into a "Hindu Rashtra [country]" in two years (*Hindustan Times* 2002; *Rediff.com* 2002).

It is now well understood that a significant degree of the financial support for the Hindutva movement in India comes from the United States (see Anderson 1998, 73; Mathew 2000; Mathew and Prashad 2000, 529–530; Rajagopal 2000, 474). This support appears to have been crucial, both in bringing the BJP to power in India in 1998 and in implementing many of its central policies. In a public acknowledgment of the support the BJP received from NRIs (Non-Resident Indians), particularly in the United States, the party presented a budget in June 1998 that had several special provisions for members of the Indian diaspora willing to invest dollars in the country, including a Person of Indian Origin (PIO) card, costing $1,000 and valid for twenty years (after protests, the price of the card was reduced to $310 and the validity period was shortened to fifteen years), entitling the holder to several benefits such as visa-free visits to India; and economic, financial and educational benefits, such as the right to own and dispose of property in India, the ability to open bank accounts in India on par with rupee accounts maintained by resident Indians, and the inclusion of PIO children under NRI quotas in educational institutions, including medical and engineering colleges.[18] The government also raised the limit on shareholding for NRIs in Indian companies, and launched new funds to obtain NRI dollars with competitive rates of interest.

Shortly after taking over the reins of leadership in the country, the BJP also embarked on a nuclearization program that culminated in the now historic nuclear explosions of May 1998. American Hindu groups like the FHA had long been advocating nuclearization for India (Singh 1996a, 1997b, A26) Although initial support for the nuclear program quickly evaporated in India in the wake of the explosions in Pakistan and the increasing prices that resulted from international sanctions (both of which led to protests around the country), the BJP government's actions dramatically increased its popularity among Indian Americans. Groups like the Federation of Hindu Associations (FHA) and its Hindu nationalist allies were jubilant at the explosions. A statement signed by the Overseas Friends of the BJP and other Hindu organizations asserted, "The vast majority of Indian Americans who comprise one of the most educated groups in the US, and the 900 million people of India, have given their overwhelming support to India's testing" (cited in Rajagopal 2000, 486). My survey of Indian American newspapers and Websites indicated that the statement was not too far off the mark regarding the response of Indian Americans, since large sections of even relatively apolitical Hindu Indian Americans seemed to come out strongly in support of the Indian government's actions with jingoistic assertions of nationalistic pride and fervor.

The BJP wasted no time in harnessing the enthusiastic response to its nuclear program by Indian Americans. (In fact, the party's confidence in going ahead with the program despite the certainty of sanctions was based on its confidence that it could count on the support of the overseas Indian community to offset the sanctions' effects.) Calling on the NRIs to "stand up for India at this critical hour" (*India West* 1998), the Indian government launched a Resurgent India Bond to enable NRIs to help the Indian government tide over international sanctions. The response to the scheme was so positive that the government far exceeded its target of $2 billion, achieving a total of $4.6 billion by the time of the close of the issue at the end of August 1998 (Nanda 1999, A1). And because of its large Hindu Indian American business constituency in the United States and India, the BJP hastily abandoned its nativist *swadeshi* platform and came out strongly in support of economic liberalization.

Hindu Indian American organizations also pressed the BJP government for representation in the Indian parliament. Under such pressure, the prime minister announced that a separate department would be created within the External Affairs ministry to act as a link with NRIs (*India Journal* 1999a) and to deal with their concerns. This department, the Non Resident Indians' Division, set up a High Level Committee in September 2000 to travel to countries around the world and study the Indian diaspora. Its goal was to develop a comprehensive database of "achievers, entrepreneurs, experts and eminent people in every field from amongst the NRI's and PIO's." The committee also planned to develop a database that would list the top fifty companies run by the NRIs-PIOs in each country. In addition, the committee formed subgroups to study topics of particular relevance to NRIs and PIOs (Singhvi 2000). The committee submitted its report and recommendations to the Indian government in January 2002. On its recommendation, the granting of dual citizenship to people of Indian origin living in "certain countries" (the United States, the United Kingdom, Canada, Australia, New Zealand, and Singapore) was announced with great fanfare at the first government-organized convention of the Indian diaspora, held in New Delhi in January of 2003.

HINDU INDIANS AND HINDU NATIONALISM

Following the rise of the contemporary Hindutva movement, critics argued that the movement, though claiming to represent all Hindus, was actually an upper-caste project, since it was supported primarily by the upper castes and since proponents of Hindutva were opposed to reservations for the lower castes. Over time, Hindutva groups have become acutely conscious of the need to gain the support of the lower castes (who constitute the majority of the population) and, while not yielding on the reservation issue, have started speaking out against caste discrimination and wooing lower castes with special programs. A particularly vexing issue for Hindu nationalists is the religious status of tribal Indians and Dalits. As mentioned, several prominent Dalit leaders in India have argued that they do not consider themselves to be Hindu, both because in traditional Hinduism, Untouchables and tribals were regarded as falling outside caste Hindu society and because their religious practices are very different from those of the upper castes, whose Hinduism has been decreed normative by Hindutva (see Iliah 1996). Lower castes in India have also become increasingly mobilized and militant, and caste clashes between lower and upper castes throughout the country occurred in the late 1990s. Because the idea of India's being a Hindu-majority country (the basis of the Hindu nationalist movement) collapses if lower castes and tribals are not included in the Hindu category, these two groups have become a special focus for Hindu nationalists. It is also for this reason that missionary activities of Christians and Muslims among these two groups have been perceived as a major threat. The success of the reconversion activities of the Sangh Parivar among tribals and lower castes was attested to by the fact that many of the perpetrators of violence against Muslims in the 2002 Gujarat pogrom were members of these two groups.

Several scholars have noted the ways in which Hindu nationalist organizations have managed to erase the "boundaries between home and the world, private and public spaces, religion and politics . . . [and thus] transform and reinscribe the public Hindu cause as a deeply felt and experienced private wrong" among ordinary Hindus (Geetha and Jayanthi 1995, 246–247) over the past decade and a half.[19] The Sangh Parivar has been able to accomplish this erasure by organizing religious processions (yatras) across India and by its presence at major festivals, in music and dance associations, and in bhajan groups and other lay Hindu organizations. Although most Hindus recoil from the violence that communalism produces, many Hindutva ideas have thus now become so part of the everyday thinking of average Hindus that they are perceived as common sense. The communalization of Hindu women through the highly sexualized Hindutva discourse that portrays Hindu women as the victims of Muslim aggression and simultaneously as the guardians and protectors of Hindu tradition has also been noted.[20] In short, the Sangh Parivar has been successful in intertwining political Hinduism and popular Hinduism.

CONCLUSION

Colonialism and the exposure to Western education and thinking gave rise to the first attempts to formulate a unified, universal, textually based, intellectual Hinduism on par with Christianity and Islam. The Hindu reformers and Hindu nationalist leaders also repudiated most of the rituals, practices, and beliefs that were central to popular Hinduism. In many cases this reformulated religion was then used to argue for the distinctiveness and superiority of Hinduism. We have also seen that with the development of the Hindutva movement in India, political Hinduism became official Hinduism. For Hindutva proponents and hence for official Hinduism, the Vedic age (conventionally dated between 1500 and 1000 B.C.E. but dated at least as early as 3000 B.C.E. by Hindutva supporters) represents the essence of the Indian culture. Hindutva-vadis therefore view Indian culture and civilization as Hindu, whose true nature and glory was sullied by the invasions of Muslims and the British and the postcolonial domination of "pseudo-secular" Indians who actively discriminated against Hindus (by instituting affirmative action programs for minority religions and lower castes). According to the Hindutva perspective, these historical wrongs can only be righted by a state that is openly and unashamedly Hindu. Hindus are defined as those for whom India is homeland and holy land. Thus the definition includes groups like the Sikhs, Buddhists, and Jains, whose religions originated in India (although these groups themselves frequently resist this classification), but excludes Indian Muslims and Christians, who are often described as "foreigners," despite the fact that both groups are made up almost entirely of indigenous members and both Islam and Christianity have existed in India for well over 1,200 years. Under a Hindu state, these two groups would be allowed to remain in the country, but Hindu nationalists make it clear that their existence would be at the pleasure of the Hindus, on the terms of the Hindus. The need for Hindu nationalism and Hindu self-assertion is justified by the argument, dismissed by most analysts, that Hindus will soon be reduced to a minority in India because of the proselytizing activities of Muslim and Christian missionaries and the higher fertility rates of Indian Muslims.

Not all of the Hindutva platform is so explicitly political. As the term Hindutva or Hinduness implies, the movement is multistranded. It also stresses the greatness of Hinduism and Hindu culture, the importance of Hindu unity, and the need to defend Hinduism and Hindus against discrimination, defamation, and the pressure to convert to other religions. All of these strands are related to the central Hindu nationalist perspective, but they can each be unbundled and selectively disseminated and absorbed. The multifaceted nature of Hindutva is the source of its power and appeal, enabling the movement to recruit even apolitical supporters.

The concept of "indigenousness"—that Hindus are the only autochthonous group in India and that Hinduism is the sole and authentic manifestation of Indian culture and values—is the cornerstone of the Hindu nationalist movement. As we have seen, however, the central components of modern Hinduism, such as its definition, its claim of distinctiveness and superiority when compared with other religions, as well as the relationship between Hindu people and the Indian nation, have all been strongly shaped by Western influences, specifically the encounter with colonial scholars, administrators, and missionaries and with Italian and German nationalism. The major Hindu leaders—Ram Mohan Roy, Dayananda Saraswati, Vivekananda, Sarvarkar, Golwalker, Gandhi, and Chinmayananda—first developed their ideas while outside the country or in interaction with Westerners and Orientalism. As mentioned, Jaffrelot (1993) characterizes this strategy as being one of stigmatizing but simultaneously imitating "threatening Others," in this case Christianity and Islam. A similar strategy has been adopted by Hindus in the United States.

CHAPTER 7

Forging an Official Hinduism in the United States

HINDU AMERICAN UMBRELLA ORGANIZATIONS

We have seen that official Hinduism in contemporary India is articulated and represented by umbrella Hindu groups that are part of the Sangh Parivar. Although many other Hindu groups exist in India, most are sectarian, regional groups that do not have the pan-Hindu platform or the resources of the Sangh Parivar affiliates. Since the Sangh Parivar developed in the context of Hindu nationalism, this is the official Hinduism that it promotes. Official Hinduism in the United States is articulated by Sangh Parivar affiliates as well, but also by a variety of independent Hindu umbrella organizations. This chapter examines the rise and development of Sangh Parivar and independent Hindu umbrella organizations in the United States. We will also examine the ways in which the platform of some organizations, such as the VHPA (World Hindu Council of America) changed beginning in the late 1980s with the development of a Hindu renaissance movement in the United States and in other Hindu communities around the world, paralleling the resurgence of the Hindu nationalist movement in India. As part of this global Hindu renaissance, Hindu nationalist ideas have been resuscitated and modified by contemporary Hindu leaders and ideologues. Hindus in the United States have played an important part in this transnational Hindutva mobilization.

The multiculturalist context of the United States has provided some of the impetus for the rise of Hindu nationalism among Hindu Americans. Several scholars have argued that multiculturalist policies, despite their intended goal of facilitating the integration of immigrants and winning their loyalty, seem to often do the reverse, strengthening immigrant attachment to the ancestral homeland and giving rise to diasporic nationalism. Yossi Shain (1999), who asserts that multiculturalism "ties U.S. identity to international politics and transnational movements" (xiv), argues that this linkage occurs because "ethnic involvement in U.S. foreign affairs may be seen as an important vehicle through which disenfranchised groups may win an entry ticket into American society and politics" (x). Other scholars refer to the resources and space for the institutionalization of ethnic and religious organizations provided by multiculturalism (Faist 2000, 214), the marginalization and stigmatization experienced by immigrants that feed into the identity politics of multiculturalism (Anderson 1998, 74; Mathew and Prashad 2000; Rajagopal 2000), and the contemporary postnational and globalized context that exacerbates such politics by promoting "translocal solidarities" and "cross-border mobilizations" (Appadurai 1996, 166).

Although these arguments provide insight into why multiculturalist policies often lead to greater homeland loyalty and involvement, they do not entirely explain the phenomenon. An important but generally neglected issue is the role that immigrant religion tends to play in this process. Not surprisingly, immigrant religion and religious institutions are directly involved in the endorsement and sponsorship of religious nationalism in immigrants' home countries (Bhatt 1997; Dusenbery 1995; Ghamari-Tabrizi 2001; Kelley 1993, 83; Tatla 1999). But immigrant religion has often played an important indirect role in supporting homeland politics even when the nationalism that is being supported is ostensibly secular. For instance, in the United States, immigrant mobilization around homeland issues has taken place through the use of religious organizations and religious symbols in the case of the anti-Castro movement of Cuban Catholics (Tweed 1997), the homeland-oriented activism of groups like Dominican and Polish Catholics (Bernstein 1992; Jacobson 1995, 38; Levitt 2001, 136), Armenian and Greek Orthodox church members (Dekmejian and Themelis 1997), Sri Lankan Tamil separatists, Kashmiri Hindus and Muslims, Mexican, Irish, Arab, Israeli, Sinhalese, and Croat immigrants (Appadurai 1996, 158–177; Bhatt 1997; Bernstein 1992), and even Chinese and Korean Christian Americans who redefine their ethnic identity to be congruent with their Christian beliefs and practices (Chai 2001; Yang 1999). In all of these cases the imbrication of religion has deeply affected and complicated the direction and nature of immigrant political mobilization.

Arjun Appadurai (1996) and Benedict Anderson (1998) make clear that incendiary ethnic nationalism is not unique to Hindu Americans. In fact, Anderson (1998, 73–74) maintains that U.S. diasporas seem to support reactionary, antidemocratic forces more often than progressive ones. He therefore takes a somber view of "long-distance nationalism," describing it as a "menacing portent for the future" since it "creates a serious politics that is at the same time radically unaccountable" (74). Although Yossi Shain (1999) recognizes that U.S. diasporas are often "critical players in defining the national identity and political ethos of their homelands" (8), he sees this role as positive, because he believes that U.S. diasporas generally support progressive politics by "marketing the American creed [of capitalism, secularism and democracy] abroad." But because a variety of forces determine the direction and effectiveness of immigrant nationalism and its impact on host and home societies, such as the majority or minority status of the group in either the homeland or in the host country (see Kurien 2000, 2001), the nature of the host country state and its politics, and the nature of the home country state and its politics, mono-causal explanations or normative discussions regarding whether transnational political practices are "good" or "bad" are best avoided (see also Østergaard-Nielsen 2001b, 21).

MULTICULTURALISM AND THE POLITICS OF RECOGNITION

The ethnic resurgence of the contemporary period has given rise to a burgeoning literature on the socially constructed aspects of ethnicity (Nagel 1994, 1995; Olzak 1992; Roosens 1989), which emphasizes that ethnicity is not the immutable, pri-mordial essence that it appears to be, but instead is fluid, amorphous, and con-stantly being reinvented. Critics point out, however, that most formulations of multiculturalism seem unaware of this insight and instead operate with an essen-tialized conception of ethnicity, according membership and participation in the societal "mosaic" to individuals as members of hermetic groups, groups which are expected to manifest homogeneous, "authentic" cultures that their members know, practice, and are proud of (Caglar 1997; Heller 1996, 28; Modood 1998, 378–379; Stratton and Ang 1998a, 38; Vertovec 2001). This view of multiculturalism leads to several contradictory processes.

The need to have a distinctive, coherent heritage to "celebrate" puts pressure on members of ethnic groups to be ethnic in certain formulaic ways, including con-structing a monocultural homeland in order to be part of a multicultural society. Most ethnic groups celebrate their ethnicity in similar ways, but since recognition claims are based on the supposed uniqueness of the group's culture, they tend to emphasize group differentiation (Fraser 1997, 25). The distinction between ethnic pride and ethnic chauvinism is often blurred, and thus the cultural eulogization demanded by multiculturalism can sometimes shade into ethnic jingoism. Yet another contradiction is that at the same time that multiculturalism legitimizes having "ethnic pride," it also legitimizes a rhetoric of "victimization." Mitch Berbrier (2002) discusses the ways in which victimization rhetoric has made a minority status desirable today, since it lays the blame "for the problems of minority groups upon the dominant culture" (555).[1] Finally, ethnic groups face a delicate balancing act in order to both maintain their distinctiveness and accommodate to American norms and practices. If they remain too separate, they face hostility and repression; if they assimilate too much, they may lose their identity as an ethnic group (Mauss 1994, 4–7).

To make sure that mobilization over homeland concerns is not seen as politically threatening, ethnic groups often resort to two types of strategies—they may mobilize as a pan-ethnic coalition based broadly on continent of origin, such as "Asian," "Latino," "African" or "black," or "European" or "white," or they may mobilize as a pan-ethnic coalition based on religious affiliation. Often these two types of coali-tions overlap. In the United States, as we have seen, religion frequently comes to define and sustain immigrant ethnic life. As de facto ethnic organizations, different religious groups tend to develop definitions of nationality from their own perspective, resulting in variations in the construction of homeland culture and identity along religious lines (Kurien 2001b; Min 1992; Yang 1999).

Migration, Marginality, and Émigré Nationalism

Two other factors—the "migration dynamic" (the psycho-social consequences of migration) and the experience of racism and marginality—strengthen homeland affiliation and religious involvement, feeding into the politics of recognition of multiculturalism.

The process of migration by itself can often give rise to immigrant nationalism, even when the official policy of the host society is assimilation. First, the personal, cultural, and social dislocation caused by migration often strengthens immigrant nostalgia for home, which feeds into nationalist romanticism (Appadurai 1996; van der Veer 1995, 7). Second, relocation to a different context frees people from many of the social, cultural, and mental constraints they faced at home and forces the imagining and articulation of personal and group identity in a new way (Appadurai 1996; Eikelman and Piscatori 1990, xi). Immigrants thus often embrace wider identifications than at home (Park 1921, 495; van der Veer 1995, 7).

Immigrants also manifest a stronger attachment to the homeland when they experience a hostile reception in the receiving country. Studies have shown that encountering hostility tends to trigger a process of "reactive ethnicization" (Portes 1999, 465–466), whereby home country culture and traditions are reaffirmed and acquire a heightened significance as a self-defense mechanism against discrimination (Basch, Glick Schiller, and Szanton Blanc 1994; Juergensmeyer 1979, 1988; Østergaard-Nielsen 2001a, 263). The experience of racism and marginalization can also push immigrants toward religion and religious institutions, since emphasizing a religious identity can be one way to avoid being identified on the basis of race (Busto 1996; Rajagopal 1995). Religious institutions also help immigrants cope with marginalization by providing fellowship, social services, and leadership positions to compensate for the downward mobility many of them experience (Ebaugh and Chafetz 2000; Min 1992).

Multiculturalism, Immigrant Religion, and Diasporic Nationalism

Multiculturalism thus provides the impetus, legitimacy, and space for the development of ethnic mobilization around home-country culture and interests, challenging the traditional "container" model of the nation-state by setting the stage for transnationalism and a diversity of attachments (Vertovec 2001). Because religious organizations are often the preferred means for immigrants to develop and maintain ethnic identities, much of this group formation and mobilization is accomplished by using religious organizations and symbols. The process of migration and the experience of marginalization intensify the emotional attachment to the homeland and increase the importance of religion and religious institutions. This combination of forces tends to lead to the development of an expatriate nationalism that attempts to rewrite the past, reconstruct the present, and reshape the future of the homeland in ways that are congruent with the religious identity of the group. Globalization has strengthened ethnic nationalism by increasing the scale and scope of ethnic groups, whose development and mobilization across national boundaries are aided both by large-scale international migration and by the accessibility of electronic media. The presence of wealthy expatriate communities around the world, along with the ease and speed of global financial transfers, allows groups to mobilize and move resources quickly in support of their causes.

In the Hindu American case, a conjunction of factors—Hindus' being a majority in their homeland but a racial and religious minority in the United States, their perception that the American administration has long manifested a pro-Pakistan tilt (Lal 1999, 144–145), anti-Islamic sentiment in the United States, the history of Hindu nationalism as a reaction to Western colonialism and racism, its recent resurgence in India and the encouragement of diasporic Hindu nationalism by the BJP government between 1998 and 2004—have all helped shape the group's mobilization and impact. Hindu American groups use a variety of transnational connections and resources to obtain recognition and validation within American society. They draw on a model-minority discourse, celebrating the achievements of Hindu culture and Hindu Indian Americans. Simultaneously, they also use an oppressed-minority discourse, highlighting a history of victimization and the need for recompense and self-determination. Although these two discourses seem contradictory, they are interlinked and are both rooted in the Hindutva ideology.

THE RISE OF THE HINDUTVA MOVEMENT IN THE UNITED STATES

Despite the development of Hindu nationalism within a section of the Hindu American community by the mid- to late 1980s, the Hindutva voice was at first overpowered by secularists (see Bacon 1996, 32). For instance, the emphasis on Hindu solidarity used in the first press statement of the Hindu Federation of America (HFA), an organization founded in 1985 by a small group of Hindus in the San Francisco Bay Area, was denounced by several organizations, including the VHPA. Dr Mahesh Mehta, general secretary of the VHPA, expressed concern about the very concept of Hindu solidarity, arguing that "when we speak of Hindu Solidarity, we are speaking of taking a stand, even antagonizing, if necessary, powerful forces such as Christianity." Criticizing the HFA, Rajen Anand, the president of the NFIA, said, "Our organization promotes the culture and integrity of the Asian-Indians rather than of just one religion. Anything even remotely divisive of India's society we condemn." He went on, "You cannot promote India unless you also promote secularism, because India is built on secularism, just like the U.S." (*Hinduism Today* 1985, 1–2).

By the early 1990s, however, Hindu nationalism was on the ascendancy in the United States. As we have seen, Hindu groups from around the country participated in the Ram movement and contributed money and sanctified bricks to build the temple at Ayodhya. The demolition of the Babri mosque on December 6, 1992, energized American Hindu nationalist groups and encouraged them to publicize their efforts to a greater extent. The VHPA started to emphasize openly the need for Hindu unity and also became more militant and more overtly political. In 1993 the organization held a conference in Washington, D.C., labeled "Global Vision 2000," to celebrate the centenary of Vivekananda's famous speech to the World Parliament of Religions, attended by over five thousand Indian Americans. Attendees included Uma Bharati, the fiery Hindu nationalist leader from India, as one of the most popular speakers at the conference (*Hinduism Today* 1993). In her speech, Bharati denounced those Hindus who did not support Hindu militancy: "To those of you who say you are ashamed to be Hindus, we want to tell you: we are ashamed of you. After December 6, the tiger has been let out of the cage." When she shouted, "Say it with pride, 'we are Hindu,'" the enthusiastic crowd roared in reply, "We are Hindu, we are Hindu" (Rajagopal 2000, 238). The BJP president, Murli Manohar Joshi, emphasized the same theme at the conference, declaring to a cheering audience that the day of the Babri mosque demolition was the "most memorable day" of his life, one that had inaugurated a "new phase of Indian history" (ibid.). In a 1994 speech commemorating the Hindu militants who had been killed in the Ram Janmabhumi movement, the president of the VHPA, Yash Pal Lakra, made the link between the establishment of a Hindu nationalist state in India and the status of Hindus abroad, arguing that until a strong nationalist party came to power in India and brought the country international recognition, Indians abroad would not get the respect they deserved. Hindus in the United States, he said, should therefore support the BJP in India (cited in Rajagopal 2001, 239).

It is significant that the central essay on the BJP's philosophy, entitled "Hindutva: The Great Nationalist Ideology," on the organization's Web site (www.bjp. org/history/htvintro-mm.html, retrieved September 4, 2001) was written by Mihir Meghani, a second-generation Indian American, a former leader in the Hindu Student Council, and an activist in the VHPA and the HSS.[2] Meghani has since become a prominent American Hindu leader, and his essay provides a better understanding of what Hindutva means to its Hindu American supporters and the significance of the demolition of the mosque to the contemporary Hindu renaissance. Meghani begins his essay with the statement that: "In the history of the world, the Hindu awakening of the late twentieth century will go down as one of the most monumental events. . . . This movement, Hindutva, is changing the very foundations of Bharat [India] and Hindu society the world over" (1). He chronicles the "proud history of tolerance for other faiths" of Hindu society, as well as all the abuses that the "tolerant" Hindus had to undergo beginning with the "Islamic invasions" and later "the greatest abuse of Hindu tolerance" by Muslims: the demand for Pakistan. Meghani turns to the "minority gifts" that Muslims have enjoyed in postcolonial India: their personal laws, the special status given to Kashmir state, "and other rights that are even unheard of in the bastion of democracy and freedom, the United States of America" (1). He continues with a critique of the "pseudo-secular" leaders of the Congress Party, whom he accuses of having denigrated Hindus and Hinduism in the postcolonial period, forgetting that "it was the Hindu psyche that believed in secularism" (because Hindus are tolerant and pluralistic) and that Hindu ideas had been appreciated by Western intellectuals in a variety of disciplines (2). He then goes on to outline the development of Hindu nationalism.

According to Meghani, Hindus began to get angry at the way their treasured traditions were being denigrated by the Congress leaders and thus rose up to demand a "true secularism" where the government would not favor any religion. Meghani describes the Hindutva movement as being modeled on the ethnic nationalistic movements of countries around the world, but particularly Israel: "Hindutva awakened the Hindus to the new world order where nations represented the aspirations of people united in history, culture, philosophy, and heroes. Hindutva successfully took the Indian idol of Israel and made Hindus realize that their India could be just as great and could do the same for them also" (2). Meghani draws a parallel between the Hindu experience and that of Jews, African Americans, and colonized groups, arguing that as for these groups, freedom for Hindus meant that the Holocaust inflicted on them by Muslims and the racial discrimination and economic imperialism inflicted by the British should be condemned and also that their own heroes, epics, and culture should be respected.

He then links the Ram temple and the freedom of Hindus: "The humble and fair demand for RamaJanmabhoomi could have resulted in a freedom for India, freedom from the intellectual slavery that so dominated India. This freedom would have meant that all Indians regardless of religion, language, caste, sex, or color would openly show respect for the person that from ancient times was considered the greatest hero to people of Hindusthan [India] (3)." After outlining the way this demand was thwarted by "vested interests," Meghani concludes,

> The destruction of the structure at Ayodhya was the release of the history that Indians had not fully come to terms with. Thousands of years of anger and shame, so diligently bottled up by these same [vested] interests, was released when the first piece of the so-called Babri Masjid was torn down.
>
> It is a fundamental concept of Hindu Dharma that has won: righteousness. Truth won when Hindus, realizing that Truth could not be won through political or legal means, took the law into their own hands. . . . The future of Bharat is set. Hindutva is here to stay. It is up to the Muslims whether they will be included in the new nationalistic spirit of Bharat.

Meghani adds, however, that the establishment of Hindutva would not mean that India would become a "Hindu theocracy" but that the "guiding principles" of the country will be based on "two of the great teachings of the Vedas . . . TRUTH IS ONE, SAGES CALL IT BY MANY NAMES—and—THE WHOLE UNIVERSE IS ONE FAMILY." (4, emphasis in original).

As we shall see, the argument that only Hindus are "truly secular," the attempt to link the contemporary Hindutva movement in India with the struggles of Jews and African Americans, drawing parallels between the Hindu holocaust and the Jewish Holocaust and between Hindu nationalism and Jewish Zionism, the emphasis on Hindu intellectual contributions in several fields, and finally the paradoxical argument that the destruction of the Babri mosque was necessary to pave the way for the institutionalization of Hindu values of tolerance and pluralism, all go on to become central in the discourse of official American Hinduism.

The Federation of Hindu Associations was formed in Southern California in early 1993 in the wake of the demolition of the mosque, which the activists claimed inspired them. For the FHA, the destruction of the mosque symbolized the fact that the Hindus, who had suffered injustices for so long, had finally decided to assert themselves. Group members saw the event as the beginning of a new era, one in which Hindus were going to be in power. An FHA publication summarizes their feelings: "On December 6th of 1992 when the Babri structure was demolished in Ayodhya to restore the history and rebuild the Ram *mandir* [temple], an awakening of [the] Hindu soul took place to turn the direction of glorious Hinduism and make all of us so proud" (FHA 1995a, 76). The FHA was one of the first Hindu umbrella organizations to be based in the United States (earlier Hindu American groups had been branches of organizations based in India). I collected data on this organization over a period of six years (1995–2000) through in-depth interviews with leaders and members, and participation in some of their meetings.[3] In addition, I monitored their activities between 1995 and 2003 through an examination of their own publications in newspapers, magazines, and newsletters, and the accounts of their activities given in Indian American newspapers. The FHA's influence seemed to wane after 2000, when other Hindu American groups appeared on the national scene. In 2003 the organization compiled a book entitled "How to Present Hinduism to Younger Generation [*sic*]," which was advertised as well as discussed and praised in some Indian American newspapers on the West Coast, but except for this book and a few occasional letters to the editor in these papers, the group has not seemed to be very active since 2000.

The FHA was the first expatriate Hindu organization to reach out publicly to the Indian citizenry. In January 1993, describing themselves as "Concerned NRI's [Non-Resident Indians] of Southern California," they issued a full-page advertisement in all editions of the *Indian Express,* a widely read English-language paper in India, urging their "brothers and sisters in India" to work toward making India a Hindu country (personal interview and McKean 1996, 319). FHA leaders claim that they received hundreds of enthusiastic and supportive letters from Hindus in different regions and of different socioeconomic backgrounds. The organization launched its major activities in Southern California in 1995 and within a few years emerged as a powerful force within the Indian American community, both locally and nationally, and was very successful in recruiting supporters and influencing community affairs. Although the organization was based in Southern California, its leadership had close ties with like-minded individuals and organizations around the country. Since the VHPA, as a nonprofit religious organization, could not support an overtly political platform, the founding goal of the FHA was to unify Hindu Americans to "specifically pursue Hindu political interests."[4] In its first few years of operation, the FHA therefore did not register as a religious organization and thus gain tax-exempt status, since this would have meant that like the VHPA, they would not have been able to promote an openly political agenda. But under pressure from donors, who sought tax advantages, they registered themselves in 1997. Yet their platform did not substantially change. The activists were mostly wealthy, middle-aged, upper-caste, north Indian businessmen with established businesses, which were often managed by wives or relatives. Their economic security gave them the leisure and the resources to pursue their Hindu nationalist activities.

In the late 1990s the FHA sponsored visits of Hindutva leaders from India to Southern California and claimed to have significant influence over such leaders and the Indian politicians who supported Hindu nationalism. Earlier in the group's existence, one or two of the most extremist of such individuals had been given the annual "Hindu of the Year" award by the organization. The FHA leadership propagated their ideas by organizing and speaking at religious celebrations at which the message of Hindutva was promoted and through their copious writings and frequent full-page advertisements in Indian American newspapers. In the mid- to late 1990s they organized an annual open-air celebration in Southern California for Diwali, a major Hindu festival, which reportedly drew several thousands of attendees every year.[5]

FHA's vision of what a Hindu rashtra will look like was presented in an article written by Prithvi Raj Singh (1996b, A28–29), president of FHA, in the *India Post* entitled, "Can 'Hindutva' Be Indian Nationalism?" His view of a Hindu rashtra (country) was somewhat different from that of Meghani's, in that the argument that Hindutva promotes true secularism was abandoned. For instance, while Hindu groups were to be given full "freedom of thought and action" in a Hindutva state, Singh indicated that "Hindutva culture will enforce restriction[s] on some portions of other religions like Islam or Christianity" such as the right to preach that their deity is the only God. The Hindutva state would also "not allow anyone to convert any child to any faith, until the child becomes a[n] . . . adult." Another restriction was that "outside resources of money and power cannot be used to erect . . . Mosques or Missionary churches" (1996b, A29). Although Singh stated that "local people and [the] local population of Muslims will be exempt from any mistreatment for atrocities committed by their invading forefathers in the past," his caveat that "injustices committed by those invaders, like destruction of Hindu temples or forceful conversions shall be corrected" was ominous. Singh added that marriage and divorce procedures would be standardized (rather than, as now, governed by the "Personal Laws" of each religion) and that the Islamic call to prayer from minarets of mosques would not be allowed "as it disturbs the basic rights of non-believers of Islam." (He did not mention prayers and music broadcast from temple loudspeakers.) Singh concluded, "Thus Hindutva culture will be a blessing to the soul-less society of Western style governments. Without imposing religious teachings and directions, the culture will bring religious values into public life" (1996b, A29).

The FHA has tried to influence American foreign policy by assiduously wooing politicians in an attempt to communicate FHA ideas regarding Indian society and politics. FHA leaders told me that they had explained to a congresswoman in Southern California, Loretta Sanchez, that it was the Indian Muslims "with their four wives and ten children" who were responsible for the population problem in India (interview, June 18, 1997). Openly anti-Muslim, the leadership called in one instance for Muslims in India to be moved to Pakistan, "since history has shown that Hindus and Muslims cannot coexist" (K. Patel 1998). As part of its anti-Muslim agenda, the FHA also allied itself with certain Jewish and Christian groups. In the summer of 1997 the FHA "gladly took part" in a conference on the "impact of Islamization on international relations and human rights" in Washington, D.C. (Bhatia 1997, A5). Organized by what leaders described as a "coalition against Islam" (interview, June 18, 1997), the FHA "along with Jewish representatives and more than 100 delegates from around the world . . . discussed how the population of minorities gets reduced by Islamic beliefs and Hadith practices" (Bhatia 1997).

Although the FHA was a dominant force in Southern California in the 1990s, many Hindus in the region were not interested in or were opposed to the group's political agenda. Such disapproval was evident even in some organizations that were members of the FHA. FHA activists themselves mentioned that they had faced opposition from some temples and individuals. In a letter to *India West*, an Indian American weekly, several faculty and graduate students, mostly from Southern California universities, protested FHA's decision to confer Hindu of the Year awards to two individuals in India whose statements were believed to have incited violence against Muslims, saying: "Most of us are Hindus; nor are all of us 'secularists' and we most emphatically repudiate the attempt of the FHA to speak for us and to speak for 'Hindus.' It is curious that self-styled Hindus here appear to know better the meaning of 'Hinduism' than do most Hindus in India" (Lal et al. 1995, A5).

The Internet became a major site for Hindu nationalist propaganda and mobilization from the early 1990s. The Hindu Student Council leadership took the initiative, developing electronic bulletin boards and Hindu Web sites through its Global Hindu Electronic Network, GHEN (Mathew 2000, 113–114; Rai 1995). The Hindu nationalist message also began to be carried by several Indian American newspapers, such as the *India Times*, based in Washington, D.C. (Waghorne 1999, 106–107), and the *News India Times*, based in New York City (Mathew 2000, 126). In the mid-1990s the California news weekly, *India Post*, launched in 1994 by Romesh Japra (one of the leaders of the Bay Area–based Hindu Federation of America), gained prominence and a wide readership through its strident promotion of Hindu nationalist views, ultimately becoming a high-circulation national newspaper on this plank.[6] Even fairly liberal papers such as *India Abroad*, *India West*, and *India Tribune* frequently carried Hindutva opinion pieces, advertisements, and letters.

The coming to power of the BJP in India in 1998 gave the Hindutva cause more legitimacy within Hindu circles, both in India and in the United States, and Hindu umbrella organizations in the United States used Hinduism to unify and politically mobilize Hindu Americans. Narain Kataria, a member of both the Hindu Swayamsevak Singh (HSS, the American branch of the RSS) and the Overseas Friends of the BJP (OFBJP) in New York, noted proudly in an interview, "We are witnessing a great awakening among the Hindu society" (Lakhihal 2001, 59). Similarly, the president of the VHPA, Jyothish Parekh, indicated that "we were earlier hesitant to call ourselves as Hindus . . . now we proudly say we are Hindus" (ibid.). This "wave of proudly identifying oneself as Hindu" was dubbed the "Hindu Renaissance in the U.S." by another Hindu leader, Mukund Mody, founder of the OFBJP, and Sangh Parivar organizations and affiliates in the United States registered a "phenomenal growth" in this period (ibid.). In 1999 a senior member of the HSS told sociologist Arvind Rajagopal that there were over 150 branches in the tri-state area of New York, New Jersey, and Connecticut, with between fifteen and twenty members attending each weekly meeting (Rajagopal 2000, 480).

The India = Hindu equation was further tightened as even ostensibly secular organizations like the Federation of Indian Associations came to be dominated by Hindutva activists. In 1998 the FIA allowed the VHPA to march in the India Day Parade in New York for the first time, something that it had previously not permitted. Other Indian American groups like the Friends of India Society (FISI), the Indian American Intellectuals Forum (based in New York), and the India Development Center (based in Atlanta) were founded by Sangh Parivar activists. Mathew (2000, 126) comments that "the India = Hindu equation [also] stands out" in many of the India studies chairs and programs that were established with the support of the community in universities around the country after 1995. The solidification of the India = Hindu equation also meant that Hindutva sympathizers and activists demonstrated considerable hostility toward the South Asian studies programs and centers that existed in several universities and toward attempts by academics and secularists to develop a South Asian American identity, as we shall see in chapter 9.

Hindu community leaders have long sought to emulate the model of Jewish Americans. American Jews, as a highly successful group that is integrated into mainstream American society while maintaining its religious and cultural distinctiveness, close community ties, and connections with the home country, are viewed as a group that has been able to "fit in" while remaining different. This is the route to success that Hindu Americans also want to adopt in their quest to stake a position in American society. Thus the FHA stressed the need for Hindu Americans to "establish a Hindu defense council like the Jewish defense council [a reference to the Jewish Defense League]" (FHA n.d. b), and Hindu Student Council leaders in Southern California urged members to network with each other and with members of other Hindu organizations by pointing out that "the Jews have been successful because they are really networked."

Following the pattern of American Jews, one of the first types of organizations that Hindu Americans formed that were explicitly oriented toward the wider American society were antidefamation groups. In 1997 the VHPA formed the American Hindus against Defamation, which had as its goal the aggressive defense of Hinduism against defamation, commercialization, and misuse. The organization has been involved in several successful protest campaigns against the use of Hindu deities, icons, and texts by American businesses and the entertainment industry. The success of AHAD was followed by the formation of several other antidefamation groups around the country, including the Hindu International Council against Defamation (HICAD), based in New Jersey, and the Internet-based India Cause (www.indiacause.com).

Many Hindu American leaders also refer to a Hindu "holocaust" (perpetrated mostly by Muslim invaders), which is described as "unparalleled in history, bigger than the holocaust of the Jews by Nazis."[7] There have been calls to build "Hindu

Holocaust Museums" to document and keep alive the memory of these historical atrocities. The argument made is that as in the Jewish case, the constant reminder of the Hindu holocaust would help to unite Hindus and would also secure them the recognition and respect of the international community.[8] This argument is also used to emphasize the need for Hindus to have a religious homeland like Israel.

In 1998 the VHPA convened a Dharma Sansad, a parliament of Hindu swamis and community leaders, to address the concerns faced by Hindus in the United States. This event was followed by a Dharma Prasaar Yaatra in 1999, which the organization's Web site describes as a "unique event . . . in which eminent Sadhus from Bharat [India] made a sweeping 10 day tour of 10 major cities in USA giving spiritual guidance to over 15,000 people." In 2000, the VHPA organized an event in conjunction with the United Nations World Peace Summit, where "108 eminent Sadhus from Bharat and many other learned scholars participated in spiritual discussions at the UN followed by lecture tours across the country" (www.vhp-america.org). A Hindu Leaders Forum was launched in 2001, "to provide a unified global voice for the Hindu community on world issues." In its mission statement, the forum notes that "as a non-hierarchical religious tradition, representing a variety of views, Hinduism has not historically addressed the global community with a singular voice. However, with the growth in the Hindu population around the world, there is increased opportunity to promote greater understanding and expression of the messages of nonviolence and human unity that are the core or cardinal principles of the ancient Hindu tradition" (www.hindunet.org/vdpy/hlforum.htm, retrieved August 12, 2003). The forum organized a Vishwa Dharma Prasaar Yaatra, a massive global tour by Hindu sadhus that covered forty-seven cities in thirty-eight countries in 2001. In the United States, the arrival of the Yaatra coincided with a survey commissioned by the forum (conducted by the Opinion Research Corporation, based in Princeton, New Jersey, in 2001) to gauge the level of awareness among Americans regarding Hinduism. The survey found that over 95 percent of Americans had little or no knowledge of Hinduism and that 71 percent had no contact with a Hindu of Indian origin. Fifty-nine percent indicated that they had no interest in learning more about the religion. Although members of the Hindu Leaders Forum were not surprised at the limited knowledge of Americans about their faith, they were concerned that most Americans were not even interested in learning more about it (Srirekha 2001).

One of the major Seva (social service) projects that VHPA launched in the 1990s was Ekal Vidyalaya, which seeks to provide small one-teacher schools for children in tribal areas of India, continuing the organization's focus on tribal groups (earlier targeted with the Vanvasi Seva and the Support-a-Child programs). Critics have charged, however, that the goal of the schools has actually been to "Hinduise" the tribals and to spread hatred against Indian minorities (Sabrang Communications 2002). In the 1990s the VHPA was also able to raise millions of dollars through its tribal charities causes. Biju Mathew (2000, 123), who analyzed the funding received by the VHPA in this period, argues that by the group's own documentation, $2.6 million of the money that was legally transferred to India for these causes did not actually get to the tribal charities. He points out that the money that was transferred illegally as well as that donated through corporate matching gift programs and the United Way probably far exceeded this amount (Mathew 2000, 123–125).

Another central activity of the VHPA in the late 1990s was the further development of Hindu Web sites. A VHPA activist I met in California in the summer of 2000 claimed that the organization had 2,600 Web sites on the Internet. Many of these sites are strongly, even militantly, Hindu nationalist. The largest is the previously mentioned Global Hindu Electronic Network, run by the Hindu Student Council under the auspices of the VHPA (Mathew and Prashad 2000, 526). Its strongly Hindutva orientation is evident in its discussion forum and its history and culture sections. In addition to the GHEN, and the 1,003 Hindu Web sites that it provides links to, there are hundreds of other Hindutva sites on the Internet, each with links to several dozen others. Besides the Web sites of Hindutva organizations such as the BJP, the RSS, and the HSS, there are also Web sites such as the Hindutva Defenders Army (www.hinduweb.org), which claims to be a "network of proud Hindu fundamentalists working to defend Sanatana Dharma and promote Hindutva philosophy. Down with the Christians, Muslas [Muslims] and Pseudo-Seculars who have tried to take over and ruin our Bharat for so long!"; and the "Nation of Hindutva (www. geocities. com/CapitolHill/Lobby/9089/), with several essays, including some critical of Christians, and links to several hundred related sites. Other similar sites include "Our Mission Hindu Nation" (http://home. 123india.com/hinduswaraj), again with links to dozens of other sites (including anti-Islam sites); Web magazines such as *Sword of Truth* (www.swordoftruth.com) and the *Organizer* (put out by the RSS, www.organizer.org); "resource centers," such as Hindu Vivek Kendra (www.hvk.org), which monitors scholarship critical of Hindutva; and Voice of India, now Voice of Dharma (www.voi.org), defined as the "real essence of Hindu Intelligentsia." The Hindutva perspective dominated Hindu and Indian American Web sites and Internet discussion groups I monitored, where anti-Islamic, anti-Christian, anti-Western, and antisecular bigotry seemed to be the norm (see also Lal 1999). Some of the individuals writing on these sites have even called for the total expulsion of Muslims and Christians from India[9] or the "nuking" of Pakistan.[10] Those critical of the Hindutva perspective have generally been mocked, denounced, silenced, or forced to leave. At the same time, it must be noted that these active participants made up less than 5 percent of the total membership of all of the discussion groups I followed. Most members never took part in the discussions. The anonymity, lack of censorship, wide dissemination, and relatively easy access of the Internet make it an ideal tool for extremist propaganda, particularly for groups like Indian Americans, many of whom have computer access.

Two Hindu American organizations received some negative publicity in the mainstream American press in the early 2000s: the New York–based Hindu Unity, the equivalent of the militant Bajrang Dal in India, and the India Development and Relief Fund, a Maryland-based charity supported by Sangh Parivar organizations. Hindu Unity advertised on its Web site that it was "determined to get Muslims and Christians out of Bharat by whatever means possible. Peaceful methods and appeasement have not worked. Total war is the only solution left." It also had a "Hit List" (subsequently changed to Black List after the organization was briefly taken off the Internet due to its extremism), which included writers, politicians, and academics who had been critical of Hindutva, and prominent figures such as the pope and Pervez Musharraf, president of Pakistan (www.hinduunity.org, retrieved June 4, 2001). In June 2001 the organization was profiled by the *New York Times* for its alliance with the Jewish extremist Kahane group on the basis of their common anti-Muslim bond (Murphy 2001).

The India Development Relief Fund (IDRF), founded in 1988 and registered as a tax-exempt organization in 1989 by an RSS supporter, Vinod Prakash, received a tremendous boost in its financial contributions in the late 1990s. According to its Web site, the fund was able to raise $10 million between its inception and 2002, more than 90 percent of which was raised after 1997 (www.idrf.org, retrieved August 8, 2003). In November 2002 the charity came under attack by a group of leftist Indian American social activists and academics, who mobilized a "Stop Funding Hate Campaign," charging that the organization had been diverting some of the millions of dollars earmarked for nonreligious humanitarian causes to the support of extremist groups in India, such as those behind the Gujarat violence (Sabrang Communications 2002).[11] The organizers of the campaign were successful in getting software corporations like Cisco and Oracle to stop their matching contributions to the IDRF and also in obtaining the endorsement of over three hundred academics in the United States. According to some accounts, in 2003, the U.S. government investigated the charges as well (Padmanabhan and Bhasi 2003; Rajghatta 2003). The attack galvanized several Hindu groups in the United States to come out strongly in defense of the IDRF, and the criticism actually increased the contributions to the charity (Padmanabhan and Bhasi 2003). Several passionate rebuttals to the Stop Funding Hate report in a variety of Indian American newspapers, e-zines such as *Sulekha.com*, Web sites, and Internet discussion groups were followed in March 2003 by a counter-report, *A Factual Response to the Hate Attack on the India Development and Relief Fund (IDRF)* (www.letindiadevelop.org). The six authors called themselves Friends of India (FoI) and included Indian American academics, software engineers, and a freelance writer. A few were members of an Internet discussion group, IndDiaspora, and some of the initial discussions of the Stop Funding Hate report took place there (Haniffa 2003; Verma 2003). Despite the fact that the IDRF was registered as a nonprofit, nonpolitical, nonreligious charity organization in the United States, its links with Hindutva groups like the RSS were apparently undeniable, so in addition to the IDRF itself, the FoI defended Hindutva and the RSS as well. Arguing that one of the "guiding grand narratives" of the anti-IDRF report was Marxism, the FoI maintained that in contrast, they were adopting a "postmodernist" approach in that they were defining Hindutva from the perspective of Hindus and Hindutva supporters. They went on to describe Hindutva as a "way of life":

> It is a proactive ideology based in the belief that Hindus must build community solidarity, inculcate individual and collective pride, and advance cultural and civilizational renaissance among Hindus. For some other supporters of Hindutva,

it is a contemporary Hindu movement trying to make a particular historical identity a central element of its image. Hindutva is also a framework for maintaining an identity within societies where Hindus are small minorities, like in the U.S. None of these narratives, however, make Hindutva a fundamentalist or an extremist movement. (www.letindiadevelop.org/thereport/introduction.html)

Denying that the RSS was a violent organization, the FoI instead described it as "the world's largest NGO, . . . often first on the scene of a crisis and the last to leave. RSS workers are a class apart in their tenacious commitment to public service and getting the job done, and in their non- partisan approach to providing help" (www. letindiadevelop.org/thereport/synopsis.html). The authors claimed that the IDRF was similarly nonpartisan, "serving economically and socially disadvantaged people irrespective of caste and religion" (ibid.). This view was contradicted by a journalist sympathetic to the Hindutva cause who stated, on the basis of an interview with the founder couple of the charity, Vinod and Sarala Prakash, "It is true that they are RSS affiliated and that they give first priority to Hindus afflicted by riots/cyclone/ poverty. So what? We find nothing to say that [sic] Saudi Arabia only funds Muslim refugees in Bosnia, Palestine or Chechnya. Is it not time to call a spade a spade?" (Gautier 2003).

A key characteristic of the RSS, regular meetings with paramilitary drills and ideological training, was transplanted to the United States as well. Besides the regular meetings, the HSS, and other American Hindu groups have also held regular summer camps. Arvind Rajagopal (2000, 480–484) has written about attending such a camp in 1997 in Northern California, organized by the HSS. Participants were divided into groups by age and sex, with the daily activities consisting of "general assemblies and collective exercises, including salutes to the bicornuate saffron flag, games and martial arts, lectures and prayer, and mealtimes" (Rajagopal 2000, 482). During the martial arts exercises with sticks for his group, Rajagopal indicates that they were taught "how to strike an opponent on the head" (ibid., 483). The lectures included spiritual discourses but also talks about Hindu nationalist history.

Jessica Falcone, who attended a Hindu summer camp run by the VHPA and the HSS in Washington, D.C., in 2002, similarly describes the camp as "four days of intensive education in political, religious, and cultural aspects of Hindutva ideology" (2004, 5), accomplished through "military drills punctuated with loud nationalist chants" (ibid., 6). She continues that the camp included "a treasure hunt for children with pictures of Osama Bin Laden, a Moghul emperor, Hitler, and the Pakistani President Pervez Musharraf as the four 'demons' that were the arrow targets during the hunt, and sessions [for older participants] on how to fight the 'Muslim and Christian onslaught' in India, 'How to be an Assertive Hindu' and the 'Importance of Marriage within the Hindu Community' " (ibid.). The Gujarat riots, which were under way at the time, were supported as a "righteous defense" of Hinduism at a meeting during the camp, and a speech from Swami Vivekananda, calling for Hindu unity and a willingness to die for the cause of Hinduism, was read at the meeting (Falcone 2005). There were also violent games, apparently designed to "toughen up overly 'soft' Hindu American kids" (ibid., 1). In one game, for instance, teenagers had to throw *lathis* (wooden truncheons) at running members of the opposite team; Falcone received a painful bruise on her back after getting hit on the backbone by a lathi during the game (ibid.).

The Formation of Indic Organizations

The reconsideration and revision of Indian history have been an important part of the contemporary Hindu renaissance movement. Many Hindu groups that are interested in challenging the academic portrayal of their religion and culture have been increasingly mobilizing under an "Indic" identity. The term "Indic" refers to religious groups, cultures, and traditions that are "indigenous" to India—and thus theoretically includes groups such as Jains, Buddhists, and Sikhs, but in practice usually refers to Hindus. The term was originally used in linguistics and Indology to refer both to the linguistic group from which Sanskrit and several other Indian languages originated and to early Indian texts, but recently has been reappropriated and redefined by Hindus in the United States and United Kingdom as an academic term to denote the philosophy, science, culture, and spirituality of Vedic India. Even more broadly, it is employed to signify a cultural—some would even argue a civilizational—identity with "deep roots" in India.[12] The first major Indic studies organization to be established in the United States was the Dharam Hinduja Indic Research Center (DHIRC), formed in 1994 in the religion department at Columbia University. A similar institute at Cambridge University in the United Kingdom was set up a year later. Both were sponsored by the Hindujas, a prominent and wealthy Indian business family. The DHIRC at Columbia came under a great deal of criticism both within the university and from outside, with leftist critics charging that the term "Indic" was manufactured to disguise a Hindutva agenda under the garb of academic respectability (Mathew 2000, 126; Visweswaran and Mir, 1999/2000, 102–103). These attacks and disagreements between DHIRC faculty and the Hinduja Foundation finally led to the closing of the center in 2000 (the Cambridge University center closed in 2004). The next Indic studies organization established in the United States was the Educational Council of Indic Traditions (ECIT), which was founded in 2000 (along with an associated Indictraditions Internet discussion group) under the auspices of the Infinity Foundation, based in New Jersey. The Infinity Foundation was formed in 1995 by the wealthy Indian American entrepreneur Rajiv Malhotra, who, after a career in the software, computer, and telecom industries had taken an early retirement to pursue philanthropic and educational activities. As Indic studies gradually became the main focus of the Infinity Foundation, the ECIT was disbanded (the Indictraditions group was also closed down later, in the summer of 2003). The Infinity Foundation has since become the most prominent and active Indic studies organization in the United States.

When the ECIT was founded, its mission was described in the following way: "This Council . . . will be involved in the process of conducting independent research to a) document the contributions by India to world civilization and to b) ascertain the degree to which Indic traditions and their contributions are

accurately and adequately portrayed in contemporary American society. Prelimi-
nary findings indicate that Indic traditions, which include Hinduism, Buddhism,
Sikhism and Jainism have been and continue to be misrepresented, stereotyped, or
pigeon-holed both in academic institutions and by the mass media." The mission
statement made clear that the term "Indic" excluded religions that had been
"imported" into India, such as Islam and Christianity, and although the term "Indic
traditions" was defined to include Buddhism, Sikhism, and Jainism, in practice, the
focus of the foundation has largely on Hindu traditions and culture. The Infinity
Foundation took a leadership role in the sponsorship of Hinducentric revisionist
scholarship, which will be discussed further in chapter 9. Several other Indic organizations followed, such as the Center for Indic Studies at the University of Massachusetts at Dartmouth, the Foundation for Indic Philosophy and Culture at the
Claremont Colleges in California, and the Indic Culture and Traditions Seminars
(ICATS) in Houston, all of which focused on the study and promotion of "Indic traditions," primarily the religious, philosophical, and scientific traditions of ancient
India. Leaders from these organizations often explicitly compare and contrast Indic
traditions with "Abrahamic traditions," that is, Judaism, Christianity, and Islam.

Although these American Indic groups do not officially endorse Hindutva (for
instance, Rajiv Malhotra explicitly criticizes the movement and distances himself
from it), some overlap between the ideologies (and the rhetoric) of supporters of both
types of organizations is evident. In some instances, there has been a direct relationship between Hindutva supporters and Indic studies. Several of the invited speakers
at the July 2002 International Conference on India's Contributions and Influence in
the World, for example, organized by the Center for Indic Studies at Dartmouth,
were prominent Hindutva leaders and supporters.[13]

Another foundation, established about the same time as the ECIT with somewhat overlapping goals, was the Vedic Foundation, affiliated with the Barsana Dham
temple in Austin, Texas. Arguing that Indian history and Hindu religion were being
misrepresented in the books "written by renowned scholars and university textbooks," the foundation sought to educate people about "authentic Hinduism." To this
end, the spiritual leader and founder of the Barsana Dham, Swami Prakashanand
Saraswati, published an eight-hundred-page tome in 1999, a reference book to
Indian history, religion, and civilization entitled *The True History and Religion of
India.* The Web site of the foundation indicates that the book "substantiates and
describes the uninterrupted history of our existing Bharitya civilization that goes
back to 1,972 million years," and provides a summary of the central Hindu scriptures
and a "complete review of Sanatan Dharm and the universal path of God as revealed
by God himself" (www.thevedicfoundation.org). The site lists the laudatory comments the book has received from prominent Hindu academics and leaders in the
United States and India, and the book also won an award at the World Religious
Parliament in New Delhi (organized by the VHP in 1999). A simplified and abridged
version of this book for college students, entitled *Amazing Facts about Hinduism,*
was released at the Global Dharma Conference in 2003. Another organization, the
Bharatvani Institute, was established in the United States in 2000, with the aim of

"providing an ideological defense of Hindu religion and culture through a series of publications" (www.bharatvani.org). Major Hindutva publications (books and articles) are provided on its Web site along with scathing critiques of "South Asian" or secularist writings.

Dharma as an Organizing Principle

Other Hindu groups that are interested in emphasizing the distinctiveness of Hinduism and contrasting it with Abrahamic religions have been mobilizing under a "Dharma" umbrella. The Hindu Student Council, which had been holding annual national conferences, camps, regional conferences, and festivals (such as the Freedom Festival in 1997, to commemorate the fiftieth anniversary of Indian independence), began a focus on dharma and the applications of dharmic principles to various aspects of life in 2001 as a starting point for the Global Dharma conference that the group was going to sponsor in 2003. During 2001–2002 local chapters held discussions on these topics, and in the spring of 2003 the organization sponsored a "Dharma van," an exhibition on dharma that traveled to most of the HSC chapters around the country.

The Global Dharma Conference was held in Edison, New Jersey, in June 2003, bringing together about two thousand attendees from around the country and dozens of speakers from around the world. This conference was organized by the largely second-generation members of the HSC and was supported by the Dharma Association of North America (DANAM), an organization formed in 2002 with the goals of undertaking "the recovery, reclamation, and reconstitution of Hindu Dharma for the contemporary global era" and of "providing bridges between, and networks among, the practicing Hindu Dharma scholars and the Diaspora Hindu community in North America" (www.danam-web.org/missionpage.htm, retrieved November 4, 2003). The conference and the speeches were apolitical, but Hindutva ideas and agendas were not far from the surface. The goal of the conference was to distinguish between dharma, defined as the "natural law of Truth and its universal and eternal principles," and "religion" or belief-oriented traditions such as Christianity and Islam that relied on a savior or a prophet to "reveal" the truth, a differentiation that was made by Swami Vivekananda. On that basis a sharp distinction was drawn between Hinduism, which was portrayed as a positive, scientific, and rational complete system (including "religion, yoga, and mysticism, philosophy, arts, science and culture as part of a single reality"), and Christianity and Islam, which were criticized implicitly and sometimes explicitly for being simplistic and dogmatic and for instigating violence. The pluralistic slogan "truth is one, sages call it by different names" was transmuted into the conventional Hindutva argument that while "all religions of the world have some aspect of this [Sanatana Dharma] spiritual tradition . . . [n]either it means that religion and spirituality are the same nor it means that all religions are same [sic]. All water can be [the] same, but all water may not be fit to drink!" (Banerjee 2003). Hindus were depicted as the only group that held "the key to peace and progress in the world of tomorrow. We the people of Dharmic traditions, will not only contribute towards the minimization of conflicts but will also give the light to the world, leading it toward the recognition of one global human culture where unity in diversity will be the keynote" (ibid.). The absence of any Islamic representative on the interfaith panel, which otherwise included all the major religious traditions, was also conspicuous.

The most notable feature of the conference, however, was the presence of Hindutva leaders as presenters and presiders at the various sessions. The two chief guests for the conference were prominent Hindutva leaders: former BJP president and then current minister of human resource development Murli Manohar Joshi and Swami Dayananda Saraswati of the Arsha Vidya Gurukulam (a residential center for Hindu learning located in Pennsylvania). Murli Manohar Joshi had publicly celebrated the destruction of the mosque in Ayodhya, and Swami Dayananda Saraswati similarly spoke in strong support of the Ram Janmabhoomi movement and the demand to construct temples where mosques currently stand in Mathura and Kashi (interview with T. R. Jawahar, www.newstodaynet.com/swami/0107ss1.htm). Although the Hindu Student Council claims to be independent of the VHPA, VHPA members were quite visible at the conference; members of the VHPA and the HSS conducted most of the sessions except for those at which members of Hindu student groups made presentations. HSC conference organizers also publicly acknowledged them as being "very instrumental in organizing the conference," and Sangh Parivar leaders were eulogized and honored. A variety of Hindutva books and tracts were on display at various booths, including the militant fifteen-page tract "Why Hindu Reaction to Godhra" by Gaurang Vaishnav, general secretary of the VHPA, describing the killing of Muslims in the post-Godhra riots in Gujarat as the justified punishment by death of those described as Aattayis in Hindu scripture ("one who plunders, takes away other's women folk, rapes or sets fire to others' property," 4) and the reaction of a Hindu society "that has given up hope of any justice from the politicians or the courts" (2).

The legitimization of the Hindutva discourse in the United States has enabled some individuals to use aggressive Hinduness as a means to obtain status within the Hindu American community and to enter into mainstream American politics as representatives of all Indian Americans. The control that Hindu groups have been able to gain over Indian American politics can be seen in the comment of Narayan D. Keshavan, a special assistant to Congressman Gary L. Ackerman (one of the former co-chairs of the Congressional Caucus on India and Indian Americans), who told the *India Post* journalist Prashanth Lakihal that "there are scores of congressmen and dozens of senators who clearly equate the growing Indian American political influence to the 'Hindu Lobby'—very much akin to the famed 'Jewish Lobby' " (Lakihal 2001, 59). The Hindu = Indian equation can be seen in the campaign, waged by some sections of the Hindu American community, against fellow ethnic Bobby Jindal, who was running as a candidate for the governor of Louisiana in 2003. Many Hindu Americans were unhappy that Bobby Jindal, who was born into a Hindu family, had converted to Christianity as a teenager in the United States. Jindal's conversion and possible motives (including the allegation that he had done so only in order to enter American politics) were discussed in detail by several Indian American Internet groups. These issues were also articulated publicly by Beloo Mehra, one of the authors of the pro-IDRF report, in an article on *Sulekha.com*. Mehra asks "why [Jindal] felt his native Hindu faith to be insufficient as a means to worship God" (2003, 2) and also questions whether as a Christian convert, Jindal could represent Indian Americans. "Hindu political representation in the United States largely gets channeled through Indian-American forums," Mehra argues, and then goes on to say that "it is important to examine how well Bobby Jindal's candidature represents these interests" (ibid.). Mehra made no comment on whether it was appropriate for the interests of some Hindu Americans to be represented as those of Indian Americans as a whole.

The Hindu American Foundation was formed in the summer of 2004 in Fremont, California. The organization describes itself as a "human rights group whose purpose is to provide a voice for the 2 million strong Hindu American community." Its Web site (www.hinduamericanfoundation.org) indicates that the group "interacts with and educates government, media, think tanks, academia and public fora about Hinduism and issues of concern to Hindus locally and globally." It also describes its members as "promoting the Hindu and American ideals of understanding, tolerance and pluralism." Although the organization indicates that it is not affiliated with any religious or political organizations or entities, its president, Mihir Meghani, has been an active member of the VHPA and the HSS (see Rao et al. 2003, 2) and, as mentioned earlier, is the author of the essay entitled "Hindutva: The Great Nationalist Ideology" on the BJP Web site.

In the same summer (2004), the BJP lost the national elections in India and had to take its place in the opposition. Analysts argued that the party had spent too much time emphasizing the glory of India (a central campaign slogan was "India Shining"), neglecting the basic needs of the masses. Hindutva supporters, however, argued that the party lost not because voters rejected Hindutva but because the BJP had not gone far enough in implementing the ideology. This theme was sounded by Ram Madhav, the national spokesperson of the RSS, who visited the United States in October 2004, "to present its position . . . [and] clear misconceptions" (Ludden 2004). As part of his tour, Ram Madhav had contacted several universities, asking if they would be interested in hosting him. Some institutions, such as the University of Pennsylvania and Johns Hopkins, did invite him to make a presentation, although many academics at these institutions protested. Writing about Ram Madhav's presentation at Johns Hopkins, Itty Abraham and Samip Mallick describe it as focused on "the rate of reproduction of South Asia's Muslims and their threat to democratic and peace loving India" (Abraham and Mallick 2004, 1). They also describe how Madhav came with a large group of supporters—seven senior RSS members from the larger D.C. area and another twenty-five to thirty RSS members. According to the authors, the RSS members immediately began a campaign of intimidation by tearing up the protest fliers handed out by anti-RSS activists, threatening them with "arrest, deportation, and more," and trying to find out details about the backgrounds of the activists. Abraham and Mallick also note that the RSS activists interrupted questions with loud, angry comments, wrote

down the names of questioners, copied the names on the sign-in sheet, and video-
taped the entire meeting (ibid., 2).

CONCLUSION

We have seen that practically all Hindu American umbrella organizations, even those
who do not officially endorse Hindutva, have adopted some aspects of the Hindu
nationalist ideology. In fact, scholars like Vinay Lal (1999, 149) have argued that
despite being a minority, "the Hindutva-vadis have gained ascendancy" among Hindu
Indian Americans and that consequently the Hindutva ideology has obtained more
support and less opposition among Hindus in the United States than in India (see
also Mathew 2000; Mathew and Prashad 2000; Rajagopal 1995). This idea is difficult to document with any certainty, both because of the lack of hard data and
because Hindu nationalism in both the United States and India is a constantly
growing and changing entity.

I have argued that ironically, multiculturalism often seems to exacerbate, rather
than weaken, diasporic nationalism. In the case of Hindu Indian Americans, spokespersons articulate two seemingly contradictory discourses. On the one hand, they promote themselves as "patriotic Americans" and espouse a "genteel multiculturalism"
(Rajagopal 2001, 267), emphasizing the tolerance and pluralism of Hinduism as
well as its contribution to American society and to solving global problems. On the
other hand, they also use the discourse of multiculturalism to promote a militant
Hindutva movement, replete with diatribes against Muslims, Christians, and secular Hindus in India and the United States. Even more paradoxically, in the name
of their rights as a global minority, American supporters of Hindutva demand a
Hindu state in India which would deny Indian minority groups many of the basic
rights that Hindu Indians enjoy in the United States, and that make their activism
possible.

Although the two faces of American Hinduism—genteel multiculturalism and
militant Hindu nationalism—appear to be very different, they are interlinked. The
two self-presentations grow out of the contradictions of being part of a professionally successful but racialized minority group in contemporary multicultural America.
Both are strategies to obtain recognition and validation within American society—
one drawing on a model-minority discourse, the other drawing on an oppressed-
minority discourse. As Berbrier (2002) points out, both of these discourses are
encouraged by multiculturalism. Multiculturalism enjoins individuals to "celebrate" and be "proud" of their ethnic heritage. But in aiming to correct racial and
ethnic injustices, multiculturalism also legitimizes an ethnic victimization discourse.
The Hindutva platform intertwines these two types of discourse.

Although the Hindu nationalism of many Hindu American leaders and
umbrella groups is usually regarded as being a "reflection of homeland politics,"
I argue that it is also "made in America" as a situational response to the realities they
confront in the United States (Portes and Rumbaut 2001, 284). As several American
Hindutva supporters themselves point out, the Hindu nationalism that they now

embrace is something they "converted" to in America, not something they brought with them from India. In Internet groups and letters to the editor in Indian American newspapers I monitored, several people mentioned that they had to come to the United States to overcome the "pseudo-secularism" that they had been conditioned to in India and become "real Hindus." One e-mail message by an Indian American to an Internet discussion group is typical. After saying that the Muslims had brought the 2002 pogrom in Gujarat on themselves, the writer continued, that India's "only solution" was to make Indian Muslims renounce Islam as much as possible. But the writer questioned if this renunciation could ever be achieved if there were so many Hindus behaving in "this crazy liberal way," concluding that being born outside or spending time outside India was necessary in order to give up the "self-righteous liberal attitude" that people seemed to acquire there. The American Hindutva platform has many similarities with the platform of Hindutva groups in India, but it also has several emphases deriving from the American context that are not central in India. The parallels drawn between Hindus and Jews and between Hindus and African Americans, the FHA's linking of their anti-Muslim platform with that of conservative Jewish and Christian groups, and the development of antidefamation groups are specific to the United States. The emphasis on postmodernism and the denouncement of Marxism by the FoI also fits better in the American context than in the Indian, where Marxist parties are often in power in states like Kerala and West Bengal and also have some representation in parliament.

The Hindutva movement first emerged as a reaction to the experience of Western colonialism. It is not surprising, therefore, that the "Hinduism under siege" message, and its emphasis on the need for Hindu pride and assertiveness, is particularly attractive to Hindus in the United States who experience racism and marginality as minorities, a point that Hindutva supporters themselves make (Rao et al. 2003, 2). In the United States, Hindutva has become an important magnet around which Indians from a Hindu background can cluster in their effort to obtain recognition and resources as American ethnics. An important concern of Indian Americans has been their relative invisibility within American society, which is due to their ambiguous racial status, the American identification of the term "Indian" with Native Americans and the term "Asian" with East Asians, and finally, the perception that successive U.S. administrations have followed a pro-Pakistan policy and paid relatively little attention to India (Lal 1999, 144–145). The central goal of Hindutva groups has thus been the improvement of the image of Hinduism and of India within American society, as will be discussed further in chapter 9.

How can we reconcile the existence of "genteel multiculturalism" with the militant nationalism of many of the same organizations and leaders? Although it is tempting to believe that we can separate the two aspects of American Hinduism as discourses employed by different groups, or as discourses used strategically by the same group of leaders for different audiences (external versus internal), my argument is that the militant nationalism that many Hindu American leaders exhibit can only be understood if we see it as integrally intertwined with the multiculturalism that many of the same individuals profess. The interrelationship between the two sides can be seen by the fact that both pluralist and ethno-nationalist discourses are frequently used simultaneously at Indian American gatherings and discussion groups. We have seen that Mihir Meghani argues that the destruction of the Babri mosque in India is necessary to institutionalize religious tolerance in India. I saw this argument frequently repeated by Indian Americans on Internet discussion groups. The vituperative diatribes against Islam and Christianity that appear on the discussion groups, moreover, generally seek to make the point that both those religions are "closed" and "intolerant," in contrast to Hinduism, which is tolerant and pluralistic. Because the two discourses are interlinked, it is not a coincidence that there are many similarities between the multiculturalist Hindu and the Hindu nationalist discourses. The tolerance, antiquity, and sophistication of Hinduism that the multiculturalist discourse emphasizes draw heavily on Hindu nationalist constructions. It is these very qualities of Vedic Hinduism that are used to justify the Hindutva demand for a Hindu state in contemporary India, so that Hinduism can once again be restored to its former glory. Furthermore, both discourses draw on the Jewish American model, with the multiculturalist discourse drawing parallels between Jewish success in the United States and that of Indian Americans, and the Hindu nationalist discourse comparing the Jewish Holocaust and the holocaust of Hindus in India, using the latter to justify the need for a religious homeland like Israel.

CHAPTER 8

Re-visioning Indian History

INTERNET HINDUISM

Ethnic groups try to construct themselves as natural, ancient, and unchanging sociocultural units that individual members owe loyalty to and have an obligation to uphold. The invoking of an idealized and generally sacralized past has thus been central in attempts to create a new or redefined ethnic identity (see, e.g., Marty and Appleby 1991, 835). History becomes the anchor that grounds conceptions of a primordial peoplehood and an authentic culture. The resuscitation of ancient grievances also justifies current negative treatment of other groups. History therefore is seen as much more than an academic matter—it becomes central in defining the "essence" of a culture, in legitimizing current policies, and in providing a blueprint for the future.

Thus one consequence of the Hindu nationalist movement has been the development of "history wars" between proponents of rival versions of Indian history (Darymple 2005). Hindu American scholars have played a significant part in these battles over history, because they are often cited as experts by Hindutva supporters and politicians (see Habib 2001, 15–17). In India, these history wars have resulted in political rallies, mob riots, and a even a threat by the then BJP prime minister, Atal Bihari Vajpayee, warning "all foreign scholars that they must not play with our national pride" (cited in Darymple 2005, 3)[1]. Successive political administrations in India have also attempted radical revisions of school textbooks. In the United States many Hindu leaders have launched organized campaigns against scholars and textbooks that contain what are characterized as "anti-Hindu" points of view. A central plank of official Hinduism in the United States consists of articulating and disseminating an alternative version of Indian history from that accepted by most professional historians.

The revisionist history of Hindu nationalists has focused on two primary issues. First, they argue that Hinduism is the indigenous religion of India and is several thousand years older than conventional historical accounts have acknowledged, making it the oldest culture known to mankind. Hindutva scholars therefore claim that India is the "cradle of civilization" and the homeland of the Aryans, the group from which Europeans are believed to have descended (see Feuerstein, Kak, and Frawley

1995; Rajaram and Frawley 1995). Many Hindus also claim that Hinduism is the original religion (which at one time existed in most major regions of the world) from which all other religions subsequently developed (e.g., Knapp 2000). Hinducentric scholars also dwell on the sophistication of the Vedic culture. The second issue that Hindu scholars have focused on is a reexamination of the period of Muslim domination in India. Here the goal is to show that many of the negative features of Hinduism (such as the change in the position of women from the Vedic period) came about as a result of Muslim invasions and that the period of Muslim domination was far more brutal than conventionally acknowledged. According to this perspective, it was due to the "tolerance" of Hinduism and the lack of unity of Hindus that the "genocide" of Hindus by Muslims and the subsequent colonization of the country by the British took place.

THE TEXTBOOK CONTROVERSY IN INDIA

From the mid-1980s, as the BJP rose to power in states around India, they began to issue new textbooks that presented the Hindu nationalist version of history. Soon after taking office in 1998, the BJP's minister of human resource development, Murli Manohar Joshi, began appointing scholars sympathetic to the BJP's view of history to key national academic bodies such as the Indian Council of Historical Research (ICHR), the Indian Council of Social Science Research (ICSSR), the Indian Institute of Advanced Studies, the National Council of Educational Research and Training (NCERT), and the University Grants Commission. The hostility of the Hinducentric scholars and their supporters was directed particularly against the leftist school of historians who had dominated the Indian historical scene in the postcolonial period. Calling them anti-Hindu and antinational and branding their work as "intellectual terrorism unleashed by the left" and "more dangerous than cross border terrorism," Murli Manohar Joshi's first task was to purge the educational bodies of such scholars and to remove or "revise" the books written by them.[2]

In 2000, the BJP-appointed president of the ICHR recalled two volumes of the "Towards Freedom" series, which were already in production (with Oxford University Press), edited by two distinguished leftist Indian historians. The new director of the NCERT attempted to delete passages in school history textbooks, proclaiming that the earlier versions were biased and furthered a "narrow political agenda."[3] There was also an attempt to introduce courses on "Vedic Mathematics," "Vedic Astronomy," and "Vedic Astrology" in Indian universities around the country. The BJP defended itself against charges of "saffronizing" or "Talibanizing" school education by arguing that it was merely revising textbooks to correct errors and to reflect the true cultural heritage and values of India.[4] After the new Congress-led government came into power in the summer of 2004, one of its first actions was to fire J. S. Rajput, the man who had supervised the preparation of textbooks under the BJP government, and to embark on a process of "de-saffronization."

In subsequent sections, I will discuss the interpretation of Indian history of Hinducentric revisionists (many of whom are based in the United States), on the one hand, and that of most professional academic scholars, on the other. The Hinducentric reinterpretations of Indian history have been mainly propagated through the Internet, while the accounts of historians are contained in scholarly books and articles. I use the term "Hinducentric" instead of Hindutva, because the term "Hindutva" has come to denote the espousal of a particular type of political standpoint that is not accepted by all those engaged in the revisionist enterprise. By "professional academic scholars" I mean those who have research degrees (typically a Ph.D.) in areas directly relevant to the study of Indian history, who hold academic jobs in reputable universities, colleges, or research centers around the world in their areas of specialty, and whose publications are largely directed toward other scholars in the area (i.e., articles in academic journals or books published by academic presses). The two categories of Hinducentric revisionists and professional academic scholars are not always mutually exclusive, of course, and overlaps will be noted below. Most professional historians dismiss the revisionist attempts of Hinducentric scholars as "pseudo-history" (since these accounts are usually not substantiated using the standard evidentiary canons of academia), and thus usually do not engage with these accounts, even to rebut them. This public silence on the part of most historians, however, has helped Hinducentric ideas to gain greater credibility within the Hindu American community.

THE ARYAN MIGRATION—WAS IT INWARD OR OUTWARD?

The Aryan Migration Theory (AMT)

The Aryan invasion theory first developed by Müller, as we saw in chapter 2, has become the central issue in the struggle between Hinducentric revisionists and professional academic scholars. Subsequent archeological, linguistic, and textual evidence refined many of the propositions of Müller's theory, and the idea that the Aryan entry into India was sudden, large-scale, and violent (an "invasion") was abandoned several decades ago. It is now thought that a more gradual movement of small elite groups into India from Central Asia (although where exactly the original "Indo-European" homeland was is still a matter of dispute) took place, with a resulting linguistic and cultural diffusion from them to the native population (see Bryant 2001; Witzel 2001). The Indo-Aryan groups are believed to have been largely nomadic cattle-herders (raising horses, cows, sheep, and goats), who used horse-drawn chariots in sport and warfare and worshipped the gods of nature with elaborate rituals. The Rig Veda (the earliest documents of the Indo-Aryans) is now generally dated between 1200 and 1500 B.C.E. Most professional academics around the world in a wide range of disciplines (historians, Indologists, linguists, archeologists) whose research has a bearing on the issue support some version of an Aryan migration theory into India.[5] However, they take pains to emphasize the distinction that Müller had tried to make between linguistic and racial groups, pointing out that by Aryan, they mean "Indo-Aryan–speaking people" and not an Aryan "race."

The scholars point to evidence from a range of sources to support the theory of an Aryan migration into India and to date the Rig Veda: textual (from the Vedas and the Iranian text, the *Avesta*), linguistic, and archeological (Bryant 2001; Witzel 2001). This evidence includes: (1) the striking linguistic, cultural, and economic similarities between the material in the Iranian Zoroastrian text, the *Avesta*, and the Vedas and the fact that the old Persian of the *Avesta* appears to be older than the Sanskrit of the Vedas;[6] (2) the presence of loan words in Sanskrit for flora and fauna native to the northwest of India and for most agricultural terms;[7] (3) the familiarity of the Aryans with the horse, which was known to the undivided (premigratory) Indo-Europeans in the steppes as early as 4000 B.C.E. but (on the basis of archeological evidence) was not present in India until around 1700 B.C.E.; (4) the reference to the use of iron in some of the later Vedic texts (the Brahmanas), which is seen in India only about 1200 B.C.E. at the earliest. The events referred to took place over five thousand years ago, however, and the evidence for the Aryan migration theory (AMT) is thus sketchy and far from conclusive, something that the Hinducentric revisionists emphasize.

The Out of India Theory (OIT)

Müller has become a favorite target of attack for contemporary Hinducentric individuals, who accuse him of being a "missionary bigot" (in the words of an author of one Internet article).[8] He is also blamed for creating the Aryan/Dravidian divide in India. The "Out of India" theorists argue that the Aryans were autochthonous to India and that a branch of this group subsequently migrated from the Punjab in northern India to Iran and to Europe. Some supporters of this theory therefore claim that the Vedic culture is the source of world civilization (Feuerstein, Kak, and Frawley 1995; Knapp 2000; Rajaram and Frawley 1995). The *Rig Veda* is dated to 2500 B.C.E. (Bryant 2001, 238) or even 5000–4000 B.C.E. (according to Kak 1994 and Misra 1992, cited in Witzel 2001, 22), and the later Vedic texts (such as the Brahmanas) are dated to about 1900 B.C.E. (Kak 1994). Although there are some professional academics among this group, including Western archeologists such as Jim Shaffer, leading Indian archeologists such as B. B. Lal and S. R. Rao, and an Indian linguist, S. S. Misra, by and large the best-known contemporary exponents of this school of thought today are self-styled scholars who include Shrikant Talageri, K. D. Sethna, and P. N. Oak (all based in India), David Frawley (based in the United States), and Indian or Indian American computer scientists such as N. S. Rajaram, S. Kalyanaraman, and Subhash Kak (a professor of engineering at Louisiana State University).[9] The Belgian scholar Koenraad Elst is the one exception in this group in that he has a research degree (Ph.D.) in an area relevant to the topic (linguistics and the Aryan debate). An independent scholar, he has written fifteen or so books, almost all published by the Hindutva publishing house, the Voice of India.

Like the AMT scholars, the OIT supporters marshal an array of sources to support their arguments. While they largely ignore or dismiss the linguistic data (claiming that linguistics is not a "science"), they point to archeological and textual evidence to make their case. Most important to this group is (1) the archeological evidence that shows considerable continuity in the material culture of the northwestern portion of India from around 7000 B.C.E. without any evidence of the intrusion of a new culture during this period, and (2) a variety of textual evidence from the Vedas. The textual evidence includes the following: that (a) there is no evidence or memory of any large-scale migration into India in the *Rig Veda*; (b) the river Saraswati is described as a mighty river in the *Rig Veda* while the later Brahmana texts refer to its disappearing underground in the desert (this evidence, together with contemporary satellite photographs and geological data that they claim indicate that the Saraswati dried up around 1900–1500 B.C.E., is used to argue that the *Rig Veda* must have been composed well before 1500 B.C.E.); and (c) the *Rig Veda* refers to astronomical events taking place as early as 2500 B.C.E. or even 4500 B.C.E., according to some scholars. (See the discussion in Bryant 2001, 251–266.) Finally, the OIT scholars argue that much of the evidence the AMT scholars use to argue for an *immigration* into India from Central Asia (in other words, evidence of linguistic and cultural similarities) can just as well be reinterpreted to support the *emigration* of a branch of Aryans out of India. Many of these claims have been challenged by AMT scholars (see Witzel 2001 and Bryant 2001 for summaries of these rebuttals).

A related issue that plays an important role in the AMT versus OIT debates concerns the identity of the civilization first excavated in 1921–1922 on the banks of the river Indus and called the Indus Valley civilization (IVC). The excavations revealed a sophisticated urban civilization, with cities planned with meticulous detail and uniformity. A distinctive feature of the civilization was its elaborate bathing, drainage, and sewerage systems. Subsequent excavations demonstrated that this civilization had existed over a vast area of around 750,000 square miles (covering most of present-day Pakistan and some of the areas in northwestern India), had started developing as early as 7000–6000 B.C.E., reached its peak around 2500–2000 B.C.E., started declining by 1900 B.C.E., and had faded away by 1500 B.C.E. (Flood 1996, 24–25). It is also clear that the people of the IVC had conducted a flourishing maritime trade with countries on the African coast and the Persian Gulf (S. R. Rao 1991, 15). Unfortunately, however, the identity of the civilization has not been conclusively established, because the Indus Valley script, found inscribed on seals and copper plates, remains undeciphered.

The Indus Valley Civilization: Dravidian or Aryan?
A Dravidian Civilization

According to the AMT scholars, the Aryan migration into India took place after the Indus Valley civilization had declined, and thus they argue that the IVC was a non-Aryan and pre-Aryan civilization. As evidence, they point to the fact that the *Rig Veda* does not show any familiarity with the IVC towns, with the staple foods of the IVC (wheat and rice), or with the Indus script. Nor does the IVC seem to be familiar with the horse or with the use of iron, both of which were known to the Aryans. Many AMT scholars therefore believe that the IVC was probably a Dravidian civilization. Some scholars, such as Asko Parpola (1994), have made attempts to decipher the script on this basis. Those positing a Dravidian affiliation for the IVC interpret the figure of an ithyphallic figure in a yogalike posture, with what appears to be three faces, surrounded by animals, found in several seals, as a prototype of the god Shiva, and the female figurines as a prototype of the later Hindu goddesses. Both of these deities are taken as being Dravidian deities who were later integrated into the Vedic pantheon (Bryant 2001, 162–163).

A Vedic or Post-Vedic Civilization

Several of the OIT scholars, such as S. R. Rao and Subrash Kak, however, argue that the IVC was a Vedic civilization, and they have tried to show the similarities between Sanskrit and the IVC script, and between Vedic culture and the culture of the IVC. The fire altars found at the IVC are cited as further proof that the IVC was a Vedic civilization (since such fire altars were a central part of the religious practices of the Aryans). These scholars identify the three-headed figure in a seated position variously as the god Agni or the god Indra (both of whom are featured in the *Rig Veda*) or even as Shiva (who in this case is viewed as an Aryan deity). Some passages in the *Rig Veda* referring to large thousand-pillared houses of the gods are taken by the autochthonists as referring to the Indus Valley cities (these passages are interpreted by AMT scholars as poetic hyperbole). The OIT supporters seized upon the discovery of what appear to be horse bones among some IVC sites as proof that the horse was known to the people of the Indus Valley and that it was therefore an Aryan civilization. AMT supporters argue that the bones actually belong to the domestic ass, not the horse.[10]

In a book entitled *The Deciphered Indus Script* (2000), N. S. Rajaram and his collaborator, N. Jha, declared that they had successfully decoded the Indus script, proved that it was late Vedic Sanskrit, and had in addition located a seal from the Indus Valley that had a picture of a horse on it, the first of its kind. But both the decipherment attempts and the picture were subsequently shown to be incorrect, with the picture of a horse being nothing but a computer-enhanced and artist-embellished image of a broken unicorn bull seal (Witzel and Farmer, 2000).

Both the AMT scholars and the OIT scholars trade insults and accuse each other of manipulating the evidence to support their own respective political interests. The AMT scholars argue that the eagerness of the OIT scholars to establish that the Aryans were autochthonous to India is due to their support for Hindu nationalism (a central tenet of which is the indigenous origin and development of the Hindu people and the Hindu religion), and their need to establish that Indian Muslims are alien invaders. The OIT supporters point to the colonial and missionary biases in much of the early scholarship on Hinduism and accuse contemporary Western AMT scholars of continuing the same Eurocentric and neocolonial agenda. OIT scholars dub Indian supporters of the AMT as (godless) Marxists (since it is the largely leftist school of historians in India that has championed the theory) who have a need to denigrate Hinduism and make India into a nation of immigrants, where no group can claim cultural hegemony and which can only be governed by a secular, pluralist state (see Bryant 2001, 280).

THE VEDIC PERIOD

In a series of books and articles and on Internet Web sites, Indian American scientists, mostly engineers (all of whom are also OIT supporters), have been arguing that the

Vedas enshrine knowledge of advanced scientific, mathematical, and astronomical concepts. Subhash Kak, for instance, claims that the Vedas provide evidence to show that the seers who composed them had estimated the distance between the sun and the earth (108 solar diameters), between the moon and the earth (108 lunar diameters), and possibly even the speed of light (Feuerstein, Kak, and Frawley 1995, 205; Kak 2001). Kak also argues that he has detected a sophisticated astronomical code in the design of Vedic altars (Kak 1994) and in the organization of the material in the *Rig Veda* (Kak 1993).[11] Another author, Raja Ram Mohan Roy (for whom Kak writes an enthusiastic foreword and David Frawley a laudatory blurb), goes further and indicates that the frequently abstruse verses of the Vedas are due to the fact that the Vedic sages had discovered the complex nature of reality and coded it in the form of the Vedas (1999, xii), and that therefore, the *Rig Veda* is really a "book of particle physics and cosmology" (Roy 1999, xiii). Roy argues that the Vedic sages, besides discovering electricity and magnetism, the accurate analysis of the atom, and the creation and annihilation of matter and antimatter, also knew about quark confinement, bosons and fermions, and gamma-ray bursts (Roy 1999). Other scholars point to evidence in the Vedas that the Hindu ancients were familiar with airplanes and were aware of atomic energy and even the atom bomb.[12]

Kak and others cite the work of Abraham Seidenberg, an American historian of science, to prove the mathematical sophistication of the Vedic people. Seidenberg argued (1983, 106) that it was "certain that knowledge of Pythagoras' Theorem was known to the Satapatha Brahmana, which mentions calculations connected with the *purusa* bird altar, and to the Taittiriya Samhita, which showed similar geometrical awareness." Because these texts are dated long before the development of geometry in Greece, and also show an awareness of aspects of the theorem not discussed by the Babylonians (who preceded the Greeks in this knowledge), Seidenberg concludes that either "Old Babylonia got the theorem of Pythagoras from India or that Old Babylonia and India got it from a third source" (Seidenberg 1983, 121). The Indian American scholars also draw on the work of Georges Ifrah (2000), who argues that the base ten decimal system of calculation appears first in the Vedas and developed subsequently in India (pp. 399–409) and that the numeral zero was also invented in India (pp. 417–419).[13]

Indian American Web sites like www.atributetohinduism.com further point out that various ideas enshrined in the Vedas have been recently validated by the Western scientific community. The cyclical theory of the universe propounded in the Vedas, for example, is beginning to have many supporters among contemporary American scientists. Authors such as Kak also argue that the Vedas had a sophisticated theory of consciousness and of the relationship between the mind and the body (as testified, for instance, in the theory underlying the science of yoga), which parallel modern quantum mechanics and neuroscience.[14]

What was Vedic society like? Because the Vedic period has been characterized as representing the ideal Hindu society, this issue becomes important in contemporary debates. The debates revolve primarily around the nature of the caste system and the status of women in the Vedic period, and these will be discussed in a later section. A third issue that has recently become controversial is concerns whether beef was eaten by the Vedic people. References in the Vedas make it clear that beef was served on some ritual occasions (when, for instance, cattle were sacrificed) or as a special honor for important guests,[15] findings that were established by a variety of scholars several decades ago.[16] The issue was brought to the forefront by the attempt by the BJP government to expunge passages that refer to beef eating from school textbooks in India, and the publication of a book by the historian D. N. Jha documenting beef eating in ancient India (Jha 2001). The book prompted court cases against the author by petitioners who argued that it was "opposed to the religious sentiments and fundamentals of Jainism, Buddhism and Hinduism" (*Hindu* 2001). The book was subsequently banned in India.[17] The topic of beef eating during the Vedic period was extensively debated by Hindu Indian American Internet groups and in publications between 2000 and 2002. Some refused to believe that beef had been eaten in ancient India; others accused the author of publishing his book solely to embarrass contemporary orthodox Hindus, for whom beef eating is taboo.

Are the Epics Historical?

Although traditionally many devout Hindus believe in the historical veracity of the *Ramayana* and the *Mahabharata,* some do not. Certainly the importance of the epics within Hinduism does not rest on whether or not the events described in them actually took place. The historicity of the epics, however, has recently become an issue. The destruction of the Babri Masjid mosque in Ayodhya by Hindu nationalists stemmed from their belief that it had been built over a temple that marked the spot where the god Rama, whose story is told in the *Ramayana,* was born. Satellite pictures taken by NASA that reveal a submerged land-bridge between Sri Lanka and India's southern tip are taken by many Hindus as evidence of the historicity of the *Ramayana,* since the epic refers to Rama's building such a bridge to rescue Sita from the clutches of her abductor, the Sri Lankan king Ravana. The recent discovery of an underwater settlement in western Gujarat has also aroused interest because it is believed to be the city of Dwarka, founded by Lord Krishna (S. R. Rao 1999). According to legend, on his deathbed Lord Krishna asked his followers to leave the city, so that the sea could engulf it. In addition, Indian American Internet discussion groups, Websites, and e-zines frequently feature articles discussing astronomical evidence (descriptions of celestial conjunctions in ancient texts are compared with modern studies reconstructing the ancient skies), the lists of kings in the Puranas, and other Hindu texts to date the Mahabharata war and the events that took place in the *Ramayana* (e.g., Kak 2003; Prasad 2003; www.newdharma.org/royal_ chron.htm).

Medieval and Early Modern, or Muslim Period?

The periodization of Indian history has also become controversial, with Hindu revisionists challenging the accounts of professional historians. Controversy even exists over how the post–fifth-century period should be designated. Contemporary historians designate it as the medieval period (600 to around 1500), followed by the early modern period (1500 to around 1850). Hindu revisionists follow earlier British colonial practice and label the period from 711, when the first Arab invasions into India began, to around 1725, when the Mughal empire disintegrated, as the "Muslim" period. But the central controversy has to do with the characterization of this period.

In a series of books (mostly published by the Voice of India) and in Internet articles, Hinducentric scholars like Koenraad Elst, Sita Ram Goel, François Gautier, and Arun Shourie accuse the mainly leftist group of professional Indian historians of whitewashing the history of this period or of "negationism" (Elst 1992) to fit in with their Marxist agenda.[18] The Hinducentric scholars argue that the entire history of this "Muslim" period is characterized by the bloodthirsty massacres of tens of millions of Hindus, the destruction of thousands of Hindu temples and centers of Hindu learning, the rape and abduction of Hindu women, and forced conversions, all due to the Islamic zeal of the invaders. Others, like self-styled historian P. N. Oak (1969), have claimed that the Taj Mahal and many of the other major architectural monuments attributed to the Mughals were actually earlier Hindu constructions, misappropriated by the Muslims. Several Hindu revisionists also believe that Hindus began practices such as child-marriage, sati, and the purdah during the Muslim period, as a result of fears that Hindu women would be abducted by marauding Muslims.

Leftist Indian historians may have downplayed the negative aspects of Muslim conquest and rule in India in the interest of forging and maintaining communal harmony in the post-Independence period (see Lorenzen 1999, 646). Their overall evaluation of the period in question, however, does not differ substantially from the characterizations of their non-Marxist and non-Indian counterparts.[19] There is general agreement that the term "Muslim period" is a misnomer, since (a) this ignores the experience of the south, where Muslim rule was not established; (b) there were several non-Muslim kingdoms in this period even in the north; and (c) there was an efflorescence of Hinduism at this time. Scholars also point out that no single generalization about the Muslim rulers is possible, because there were many of them and they followed a variety of policies, from the pillaging incursions of Mahmud of Ghazni, to the pluralism of Akbar, to the Islamic zeal of Aurangazeb.

Undoubtedly several bloody wars occurred during this period. Historians emphasize, however, that bloody wars were characteristic of the medieval period in several parts of the world (including Europe) and that they were generally a by-product of conquest and territorial expansion rather than a result of a deliberate policy of religious cleansing. Thus the Mughal rulers were as apt to fight against rebellious Muslim warlords as against Hindu kings. Historians further argue that although many temples were looted and razed, the numbers have been vastly exaggerated by Hindutva writers, who often rely on the hyperbolic accounts of court chroniclers, and that there were economic and political reasons for targeting temples (the temples often contained a great deal of wealth and were also a symbol of the monarch) in addition to the purely religious motivations. They point out, for instance, that staunch Muslim emperors like Aurangazeb endowed temples even as he destroyed others, and that Hindu kings were also known to have looted Hindu and Jain temples. In some cases, Muslim sultans and emperors did use material from the earlier destroyed monuments to build their own structures, but historians do not seem to give any credence to the claim that buildings like the Red Fort and the Taj Mahal were simply taken over by the Mughal emperors. There is also agreement that there is no evidence of large-scale forced conversions and that the majority of those who did convert did so voluntarily for a variety of religious, economic, or political reasons. Finally, all writers agree that a greater or lesser degree of Hindu–Muslim cultural and even religious syncreticism (a concept that is anathema to Hindutva supporters) developed over the course of this period.

Professional scholars do differ on the question of whether or not Hindus were a self-conscious religious community, in opposition to a Muslim "Other," at this time. Several scholars, including Robert Frykenberg (1989) and Heinrich von Stietencron (1989) and Indian historians like Romila Thapar (1989, 2000b), maintain that this self-consciousness and confrontation only developed in the late colonial period, as a result of British policies. This view is contested by others (see Lorenzen 1999, 630). Lorenzen (1999) reviews this debate and argues that this process had actually begun "through the rivalry between Muslims and Hindus in the period between 1200–1500" (631). We have also seen that a demarcation between Hindu sects and Buddhism and Jainism had developed much earlier, indicating that there was some awareness among Hindus of being part of a common tradition well before the advent of Muslim rule in India.

The Colonial Period

Colonialism had a tremendous impact on India—economically, socially and culturally, and politically. This period of Indian history has been the focus of much research by professional scholars, and most of these details are beyond the scope of this chapter. In chapter 2, I discussed the role of colonial scholars and administrators in the shaping of contemporary Hinduism. In this section, I will provide a brief overview of some of the colonial influences that Hindu American Websites and discussion groups emphasize. The impact of colonialism on the caste system and on the position of women in India will be discussed in the next two sections.

Colonialism led to a drain of wealth out of India into Europe. Some Hindu American leaders are interested in trying to obtain estimates of how much wealth drained out of in current dollar terms, to argue that the roots of contemporary Indian poverty and underdevelopment can be traced back to the colonial period.[20] Indian industries which in the precolonial period had produced a wide range of goods of high quality (textiles and metalwares being among the leading products) were closed down, and from at least the middle of the nineteenth century India became primarily a supplier of raw material for British industries and a market for its industrial goods (Stein 1998). The revenue system put in place by the British disinherited peasants of their customary rights to the land in many parts of the country, created a class of wealthy landowners with absolute property rights in those areas, and also extracted very high taxes. A combination of these and several other factors led to a series of terrible famines during the eighteenth and nineteenth centuries that devastated the countryside and killed tens of millions.

The educational policy put into place by the British has come under the most attack by contemporary Hindu nationalists, both in India and in the United States. It was enshrined in the famous Macaulay "Minute on Indian Education of 1835." Lord Thomas Macaulay, who was appointed to India in 1834 to assist in the codification of Indian law, asserted in his "Minute," "I have no knowledge of either Sanscrit [sic] or Arabic. But . . . I have read translations of the most celebrated Arabic and Sanscrit works. I have conversed with men distinguished in the Eastern tongues . . . [and] I have never found one among them who would deny that a single shelf of a good European library was worth the whole native literature of India and Arabia." He turns then to his central argument. "We must at present do our best to form a class who may be interpreters between us and the million whom we govern; a class of persons Indian in blood and colour, but English in taste, in opinions, in morals and in intellect" (cited in Stein 1998, 265–266). This class was to be formed by means of education in the arts and sciences of Europe, with classes conducted in English.

Macaulay's "Minute" was decisive in shaping the Indian educational system in the subsequent period, and consequently also in affecting the course of Indian colonial and postcolonial history. The alienating effects that this education has had on the Indian, particularly the Hindu, psyche is constantly pointed out by contemporary Hindu American leaders, who argue that the neglect of Sanskrit and Indian classics (religious, philosophical, scientific, and literary) in the higher educational system of contemporary India is a holdover of this policy. The term "Macaulayite" and, to a lesser extent, the terms "brown sahib" and "brown memsahib" have become popular terms of opprobrium used by Hinducentric individuals to disparage anyone of Indian origin who adopts what they perceive to be a "Eurocentric" point of view.[21]

Internet discussion groups also frequently refer to the internalization of racial and cultural inferiority by Indians as a consequence of colonialism, as well as the continuing "colonizer mentality" of many Westerners and Western scholars. The physical brutality of colonialism and its co-opting of Indian sepoys (soldiers) as agents of carnage is another theme. A common example is the Jallianwala Bagh massacre of 1919. On April 13 of that year, a crowd of several thousand men, women, and children gathered at Jallianwala Bagh, in Amritsar, Punjab, it is believed, to celebrate Baisakhi, a popular spring festival. At that time anticolonial civil unrest was beginning to spread across north India, and since there had been trouble in Amritsar just three days before, all meetings and demonstrations had been prohibited. On hearing about the assembly, Brigadier-General Dyer marched into the Bagh with a force of Indian and Gurkha (Nepali) sepoys, blocked the main entrance, and without any provocation or warning, ordered his troops to fire straight into the crowd. Over 1,650 rounds were fired, and then the troops were ordered to turn around and leave. Hundreds were killed and over 1,200 men, women and children were seriously wounded (Keay 2000, 475–476). General Dyer was never punished for his actions. On the contrary, he was commended and rewarded in England.

PARTITION AND THE POSTCOLONIAL PERIOD

The Hinducentric version of history puts the blame for the partition of India on Mohammed Ali Jinnah for floating the demand for Pakistan, on Indian Muslims for supporting his demand, and on Gandhi for pandering to Muslims. As we have seen, however, the sequence of events leading up to Partition was more complex. British policies created and reified cleavages between Hindus and Muslims, and the rise of Hindu nationalism from the late nineteenth century with its negative characterization of the Mughal period and of Muslims in general undoubtedly played an important part in arousing Muslim anxieties. The Hinduisation of the independence movement, and the refusal of the Congress to acknowledge the Muslim League or its demands for minority representation for Muslims, all further contributed to the development of a Muslim separatist movement. The institutionalization of secularism under Prime Minister Nehru in the immediate post-Independence period and the introduction of affirmative action provisions for minority religious groups and lower castes angered many upper-caste Hindus. The management of Hindu temples in India by Religious and Charitable Endowments departments of state governments has increasingly become another source of resentment for many Hindu leaders, since the religious institutions of minority groups are not so governed. Hinducentric scholars and activists cite all of these as examples of "pseudo-secularism" (since government rules are not applied equally to all religious groups) and the anti-Hindu bias of the postcolonial Indian state.

THE INDIAN CASTE SYSTEM

For most Americans, the caste system, seen as a rigid, oppressive structure, constitutes the defining feature of Hinduism and Indian society. Hindu Americans have a variety of responses to counter this negative view. Some argue that the caste system was never religiously sanctioned by Hinduism and thus was not central to Hindu practice (e.g., see *India Post* 1995). Others make the case that the flexible employment system of caste became fossilized and oppressive after thousands of years (at around 600 B.C.E.), giving rise to Buddhist and Jaina reform movements. Still others argue that the caste system is central to ancient Hinduism, but that it was originally based on individual attributes and was a voluntarily chosen group that functioned like an extended family or kinship system, providing a social security structure for its members. This system then became rigid only much later, as a consequence of colonial policies. There is some truth in all these assertions, but the reality tends to be more complex.

"The Hymn of Man" in the *Rig Veda* (10.90) provides us with the first description of the fourfold varna system. It describes how the gods create the world by dismembering and sacrificing the primeval man, Purusha. The different parts of the cosmos and society are formed from his body. The Brahmins came from his mouth, the warriors (Kshatriyas) from his arms, the common people (Vaishyas) from his thighs, and the servants (Sudras) from his feet. Even in this early period, therefore, we can see that the hierarchical ordering of the four classes was sacralized and was also related to purity and pollution associated with the body (an idea that was to become central in the practice of Hinduism), with the head, the highest part being the purest and the feet, the lowest part, the most polluted.[22] Later Vedic texts described the varna system in more detail. The highest three classes were described as "twice-born," because their male members went through an initiation ceremony that made them full members of the society and eligible for marriage. The varna classes were divided into smaller endogamous, occupational groups called *jati* (literally, birth group). It is these groups that are generally described as "castes" in the Indian context. The four varnas are little more than the larger Procrustean framework that the local jatis are sometimes, but not always, fitted into. Thus only varna is described in the Vedas, not caste (jati), and this is one reason that Hindus argue that the caste system was not religiously sanctioned. The varna system does appear to have been fairly flexible in the Vedic period. But there are indications that even in the first millennium B.C.E. there were some groups (such as leather workers and those dealing with the disposal of human excrement) who were ranked lower than the Sudras and designated as "untouchable," since their occupations were considered to be deeply polluting (Flood 1996, 61; Stein 1998, 57).

Lord Krishna's statement in the *Gita* (4:13), "The four orders of men arose from me, in justice to their natures and their works," is often cited by contemporary Hindu Americans to argue that the varna system was originally based on occupation and personal qualities, rather than birth. Hindu Americans also argue that the caste system has no scriptural sanction because caste strictures such as those of Manu are found only in the secondary smriti texts and not in the primary Vedic, or sruti, texts. Normative texts like the *Laws of Manu* also give us no real indication of the extent to which these codes were actually followed in practice.

By the period of classical Hinduism (500 B.C.E. to 500 C.E.), the position of the Sudras had declined. According to the law books of this period, a Sudra had few legal rights. He had to eat the remnants of his master's food, wear his cast-off clothing, and use his old furniture. Sudras could not hear or recite the Vedas, and their lives were valued at very little; a Brahmin who killed a Sudra only had to perform the same penance as for killing a cat or dog. Other sources make clear, however, that at least some groups of Sudras were able to engage in commerce (forbidden by law) and also to become free peasants and even kings (Basham 1967, 145), so perhaps the restrictions were not always implemented. The legal position of the Untouchable, not surprisingly, was far worse than that of the Sudra. According to the law books, the *candala* (the lowest of the untouchable castes) had to eat his food from broken vessels and had to wear the clothes of the corpses he cremated (ibid., 146). The fifth-century Chinese pilgrim Fa-hsien mentions that the Candala were forced to announce their arrival in the town by the means of wooden clappers, so that higher-caste members would not accidentally come into contact with them (cited in Flood 1996, 61).

Some of the earliest references to jatis occur in the dharma texts of the period of classical Hinduism. The proliferation of jatis is seen as a result of the cross-breeding of varnas. *Anuloma* (with the grain) unions, where the husband's varna is higher than that of the wife's (the anthropological hypergamy), are tolerated, but *pratiloma* (against the grain) unions, where the wife's varna is higher than the husband's (hypogamy), are strongly condemned. In fact, the candala group is described as having originated from the union of Sudra men and Brahmin women (Hiltebeitel 1987, 345). It appears that endogamy was becoming the ideal, even if not the practice, in this period as can be seen by the fact that the great abomination of the dharma texts is the mixing of castes, believed to result in social disorder. The *Gita* mentions this fear as well (see 1:40).

Along with many contemporary Hindus, professional scholars argue that it is important to acknowledge the positive contributions of caste to Indian society—that it was the caste system that provided stability, identity, and continuity to local Indian communities through the long millennia of conquests and regime changes. Scholars have also pointed out that the caste system was much more dynamic than is commonly acknowledged. In the medieval period, several martial groups were able to claim Rajput or Kshatriya status by adopting titles and enlisting the support of Brahmin scribes and ritual experts, who were in turn richly rewarded through gifts of land (Stein 1998, 115). Dirks (2001) and Bayly (1989), among others, argue that in the precolonial period, the caste system was organized around local political structures; these scholars emphasize the role of medieval kings in "creating" castes by conferring differential honors and privileges to the various groups under their control. The corollary to this is that downward mobility was as likely as the movement upward. Stein (1998, 115) points out that those who became landless also became untouchable, and that the number of households considered to belong to the "Untouchable" category increased during the medieval age, as previously forest-dwelling and pastoral people were deprived of their livelihood with the spread of cultivation.

In a series of articles (e.g., 1989, 1992) and a 2001 book, *Castes of Mind: Colonialism and the Making of Modern India,* the anthropologist Nicholas Dirks has argued that caste, as we know it today, is a product of British colonialism (see also Inden 1990). In Dirks's words, it is "not in fact some unchanged survival of ancient India, not some single system that reflects a core civilizational value, not a basic expression of Indian tradition. Rather, . . . [it] is a modern phenomenon, . . . specifically, the product of an historical encounter between India and Western colonial rule." Dirks is not arguing that caste did not exist in the precolonial period, and he provides several examples of the prevalence of some kind of caste order in medieval times. But he points out that some variation was evident in the descriptions of caste provided by European travelers during this period and even by the officers of the early colonial state, and that it often only merited a passing reference in such accounts. In Dirks's view,

> Caste . . . was just one category among many others, one way of organizing and representing identity. Moreover, caste was not a single category or even a single logic of categorization, even for Brahmans, who were the primary beneficiaries of the caste idea. Regional, village, or residential communities, kinship groups, factional parties, chiefly contingents, political affiliations, and so on could both

supersede caste as a rubric for identity and reconstitute the ways caste was organized. Within localities, or kingdoms, groups could rise or fall (and in the process become more or less castelike), depending on the fortunes of particular kings, chiefs, warriors, or headmen, even as kings could routinely readjust the social order by royal decree. (2001, 13)

It was only later, under direct crown rule, that caste became reformulated, standardized, and reified as the central defining character of Hindu society. Dirks (2001) argues that this was primarily a consequence of the administrative needs of the colonial state. Colonialists tried to develop a method to generate uniform social data for the whole country by surveying, classifying, and cataloguing its populace through censuses, ethnographic studies, and anthropometric measurements. This knowledge then led to the formulation of legal codes along caste lines, as well as the consolidation of theories about the martial nature of some castes, and the criminal nature of others. The publication of Dirks's book was heralded by Hindu Internet groups and is cited by Hindu American intellectuals, though he is often interpreted to mean that before the advent of the British, caste was nonoppressive and was based on personal abilities and occupation (with the latter presumably being freely chosen on the basis of the former).

THE POSITION OF WOMEN

The position of women in India and in Hinduism is another issue that is generally perceived negatively by most Americans. Here again, Hindu Americans have formulated a response to counter this characterization. They argue that Hinduism gave women and men the same rights and that gender equality and respect for women were therefore integral parts of the Hindu tradition. To support their arguments, they point out that the Hindu pantheon includes several powerful goddesses. They also insist that women were held in great esteem in ancient Hindu India. Many of them claim that it was the Muslim conquest of India that was responsible for the subsequent decline in the status of women. The actual historical data seem to suggest more variation and complexity.

The Vedic Period

The Hindu American Web site www.atributetohinduism.com states, "In ancient India, women occupied a very important position, in fact a superior position to men." This and similar statements are common on Hindu Internet sites and are also frequently repeated by Hindus. The status of women in the early Vedic period indeed appears to have been higher than it became in subsequent centuries. Women were educated, and were also instructed in the religious texts. The Vedas refer to female seers, and some of the hymns in the Vedas were composed by women. There are also references to women philosophers engaging in theological debates with male sages. No restrictions were made on the movement of women, and they had some freedom in selecting their mate. They could even choose to remain unmarried. Although there was some prevalence of polygamy among wealthy families and royalty, monogamy was the norm. The participation of the wife in the sacrificial ritual was a requirement. Widows could remarry. In general, property was passed down to male heirs, but in the absence of sons, daughters could inherit the family property (Altekar 1959; Stein 1998, 57–58). But despite these rights, the society was still male dominated.

The Period of Classical Hinduism (500 B.C.E. to 500 C.E.)

By around 100 C.E. the age of marriage for women had gone down considerably and prepubertal marriages were regarded as the ideal. By about 200 C.E. prepubertal marriage may have become a fairly common practice, at least among Brahmin castes (Altekar 1959, 56–58). *Manu* approves of child-marriage for girls and considers an eight-year-old girl suitable for a man of twenty-four. The reasons for this change are not clear. It could be linked with the concern about miscegenation, since women were considered to be highly libidinous (Altekar 1959, 320–321; Basham 1967, 168). As the marriage age went down, the education of girls suffered and they were gradually excluded from Vedic studies and even many of the Vedic sacrifices. The initiation ceremony *(upanayana)* for the twice-born castes was also abandoned for women (Altekar 1959, 347–348). According to *Manu* (II:67) and other dharma texts of the period of classical Hinduism, in the case of women, the nuptial ceremony was the equivalent of the initiation ceremony. In the same passage, Manu goes on to state that serving the husband was equivalent to residence in the house of the teacher (i.e., education) and that the daily performance of a woman's household duties was the same as the daily performance of Vedic rituals.

The texts indicate that the giving of a dowry (even if only a token amount) was known and approved of by this time. According to *Manu*, the most prestigious form of marriage was that of "a duly dowered girl to a man of the same class," arranged by the parents and solemnized by an elaborate and expensive Rig Vedic ceremony (Manu III:27).The remarriage of widows was not endorsed. Instead widows were exhorted to remain chaste and encouraged to spend the rest of their days performing austere penances. Although there are stray references to wives' choosing to immolate themselves in the funeral pyre of their husbands in the texts of this period, it was not a recommended practice, and many authors strongly forbade it. No restriction was imposed on widowers' marrying again; in fact, remarriage was recommended. While monogamy was the ideal, men were permitted to take an additional wife, but generally only if the first wife failed to produce a male heir after a period of several years. References to polygamy among the wealthy classes are numerous and indicate that men of the upper classes were not so constrained in their ability to contract additional marriages (Altekar 1959). Purdah, or the hiding of women from the gaze of male strangers (through seclusion and/or the use of a veil), was not common in the general society, but appears to have been practiced by some royal and upper-class families, though not strictly enforced in this period (500 B.C.E. to 500 C.E.). However, there were restrictions on the freedom of movement of upper-class women (Altekar 1959, 168–179; Basham 1967, 180–182).

In general, the attitude of *Manu* and the other texts of this period is ambiguous with respect to women. On the one hand, we have passages from *Manu* such as the following:

> In childhood, a female must be subject to her father, in youth to her husband, when her lord is dead to her sons, a woman must never be independent. (V:148)

> Though destitute of virtue, or seeking pleasure [elsewhere] or devoid of good qualities, [yet] a husband must be constantly worshiped as a god by a faithful wife. . . . if a wife obeys her husband, she will for that [reason alone] be exalted in heaven.

> A faithful wife, who desires to dwell [after death] with her husband, must never do anything that might displease him. (V:154–156)

On the other hand, elsewhere *Manu* stresses the importance of honoring women and keeping them happy, as in the following passage that is often quoted by Hindu Americans: "Where women are honored, there the gods are pleased; but where they are not honored, no sacred rite yields rewards" (3:56). The figure of the pativrata, or the dutiful, devoted wife, develops during this period in the epics and the Puranas. The texts have passages in her praise and she is accorded great powers. "The sanctity of gods, sages and holy places is all centered in her. The world is sanctified by her existence, and there is no sin that would not evaporate by her mere presence" (Altekar 1959, 99, citing the *Brahmavaivarta-Purana*, 35, 119, and 127).

The Medieval Period

The institution of purdah became more widespread during the medieval (or Mughal) period. Scholars, however, believe purdah was adopted not out of fear of Muslims, but because the custom was considered prestigious (see Altekar 1959, 358), as can be seen by the fact that it was also practiced in Tamilian south India (which did not come under the Muslims) by some Brahmin and royal groups (Dirks 2001, 73). In the medieval period, prepubertal marriages were not only encouraged, but exhorted by the smriti writers and became more widespread. Akbar, the enlightened Mughal ruler, apparently tried to discourage the practice (Altekar 1959, 61, citing the *Ain-i-Akbari*, 277), to little avail. According to Altekar (1959, 61), "Eight or 9 was the usual marriage age of girls at the advent of the British rule."

Similarly, widow remarriage became uncommon during this time. The practice of sati gained in popularity among the warrior classes. According to Altekar (1959, 126–127), the custom began to be strongly advocated by a variety of smriti writers from about 700 C.E. (i.e., before the establishment of Muslim rule) and became more frequent in north India, particularly in Kashmir. It gradually became well established among the ruling Rajput families in north India and then spread to other groups. For instance, the Brahmin and royal groups in south India that secluded their women also had strictures on widow remarriage and practiced sati (Dirks 2001, 73). It is important to emphasize, however, that the proportion of widows who became satis even at this time is only thought to be around 2 percent (Altekar 1959, 132). Here again, Mughal emperors like Humayun and Akbar discouraged the practice and Akbar appointed inspectors to ensure that the widow ascended the pyre voluntarily (Altekar 1959, 132–133). Hindu Americans who argue that sati was introduced in the Mughal period tend to confuse the practice with *jauhar,* practiced by royal women belonging to some Rajput groups in medieval times. Jauhar refers to the mass suicide (usually by self-immolation) of Rajput queens when their castle was besieged by an invading Muslim (Turko-Afghan or Mughal) army, putatively to prevent molestation, captivity, or forced conversion.

The Colonial Period (1750–1947)

The "women's question" loomed large in the debates about social reform during the colonial period, and several laws aimed at ameliorating the position of women advocated or supported by Indian reformers were passed. These measures included the outlawing of sati in 1829, the Widow's Remarriage Act of 1856, the banning of female infanticide in 1870, and the raising of the age of consent (for sexual intercourse) from ten to twelve for girls in 1891.[23] At the same time, however, colonial policies had the unintended consequence of reformulating patriarchy in such a way as further to disempower and oppress women.

Bristling against the colonial attacks on Hinduism and Indian culture, and alarmed by the economic insecurity created by colonial policies, conservative Indian leaders (and even some who had taken earlier taken a reformist position) began to be suspicious of British policies and Western values from around the last two decades of the nineteenth century. In Bengal in northeastern India, one of the earliest areas of India to come under British colonial rule, one result of such suspicions was an extremist nationalism in which the figure of the pure Hindu woman became a central icon. Hindu revivalists in Bengal thus fiercely opposed the social reform laws aimed at women on the grounds that the crown jewels of the Hindu culture and the basis of its superiority over the Western were the chastity and self-abnegation of its women, molded and disciplined from infancy by the Shastras. Infant marriage, sexual intercourse upon menarche, the exhortation to absolute fidelity toward the husband, austere widowhood, and sati were all justified as part of this Hindu discipline (Sarkar 2001, 143).

The proposal to increase the age of consent from ten to twelve was opposed by the following argument:

> It is the injunction of the Hindu shastras that married girls must cohabit with their husbands on the first appearance of their menses and all Hindus must implicitly obey the injunction. And he is not a true Hindu who does not obey it. . . . If one girl in a lakh [100,000] or even a crore [1,000,000,000] menstruates before the age of twelve it must be admitted that by raising the age of consent the ruler will be interfering with the religion of the Hindus. But everyone knows that hundreds of girls menstruate before the age of twelve. And garbhas [wombs] of hundreds of girls will be tainted and impure. And the thousands of children who will be born of those impure garbhas will become impure and lose their rights to offer "pindas" [ancestral offerings].[24]

Female satis (women who committed sati) were eulogized by Bankimchandra Chattopadya, the author of the *Vande Mataram*, which has become the anthem of contemporary Hindu nationalists, as regenerators of the nation.[25] "I can see the funeral pyre burning, the chaste wife sitting at the heart of the blazing flames, clasping the feet of her husband lovingly to her breasts. . . . Her face is joyful. . . . When I think that only some time back our women could die like this, then new hope rises up in me, then I have faith that we, too, have the seeds of greatness within us. Women of Bengal: You are the true jewels of this country." [26]

Eventually, interaction between Hindu nationalists, reformers, and the colonialists created a new model of middle- and upper-class female domesticity.[27] Barbara and Thomas Metcalf (2002, 146) summarize: "In that ideal, women were meant to be educated, and 'respectable' according to the models of behavior set out by government and missionary example; but, in dramatic contrast to these models, they were meant also to be upholders of their sacred religious traditions. In addition, they were conceived of as bulwarks protecting what was seen as the 'uncolonized' space of the home against an outside world dominated by colonial values. In Bengal, that woman was the *grihalakshmi*, or goddess of the home." In Kerala in south India, several communities, such as the Nayars and the Ezhavas, which had traditionally been matrilineal and matrilocal (and occasionally polyandrous), with loosely structured marriage systems, "reformed" and outlawed many of their marriage and inheritance patterns, under pressure from colonialists and missionaries who considered such practices to be immoral.

The impact of colonial policies on women in rural areas of colonial Punjab in northwestern India has been studied by Veena Oldenburg (2002).[28] She argues that colonial policies were indirectly responsible for an escalation of dowry and marriage expenses as well as an increase in violence and abuse against women. Colonial land policies created individual, male property rights and also transformed land into a commodity that was divisible and alienable. Thus women, as well as a host of men who worked on the land, lost their customary rights to the produce of the land (see also Sangari and Vaid 1990). In addition, land taxes were fixed for two to three decades at a time (as opposed to the earlier annual assessments by the native rulers of the region, which had allowed for some flexibility in bad years). This combination meant that peasants sold or mortgaged their land during lean years and gradually became mired in debt and impoverished. The creation of male property rights and the opportunities in the army for men of the area (who were designated as a "martial race") increased the preference for male children and was responsible for the rise in female infanticide. Peasant impoverishment often led to increasing drunkenness and domestic violence (Oldenburg 2002). It also led to a reformulation of the dowry, which was now often demanded and used to redeem land debts.

Until around 1870, Oldenburg argues that dowry consisted of voluntary gifts (a bridal trousseau) given by the family of the bride for her use and pleasure, and also as recourse in an emergency. These gifts were comfortably within a family's means and were usually accumulated gradually by the bride's immediate relatives and extended kin. However, the commodification of land, together with the increased circulation of cash and consumer goods, meant that all of these became part of the dowry. In the codification of customary law by the British through the use of male informants, women lost control over their dowry, which became defined as a payment from "bride givers" to "bride takers." The transformation from "gift" to "payment" also resulted in the dowry's being vulnerable to demands from the groom's family (Oldenburg 2002).

Because the land tenure system, colonial policies, and marriage patterns varied in different regions of India, it is not clear to what extent Oldenburg's argument can be taken to apply to all of India. But Oldenburg's book, with its provocative title *Dowry Murders: The Imperial Origins of a Cultural Crime* (2002), is triumphantly cited by Hindu Americans as evidence that the dowry and dowry deaths (murder of brides who don't bring the demanded dowry)[29] that have been so sensationalized by the American media were a product of British colonialism and not an outcome of a misogynist Hindu culture. In the final section of the book, Oldenburg makes the argument, based on her work with a women's center in Delhi dealing with domestic violence, that present-day "dowry deaths" are often not about dowry at all but are about other reasons (personal or sexual incompatibility, extramarital relationships, or alcoholism), which are only couched in the language of dowry because of the Indian law specifically targeting dowry murder. She concludes that dowry murders should be taken as a general case of violence against women, and that viewed in this light, the rate of wife murders in Delhi is actually lower than in New York City. This argument has been enthusiastically adopted by Hindu Americans and frequently repeated on Hindu American discussion forums.

CONCLUSION

The details of the Hinducentric view of history outlined are posted on Hindu American Web sites, published in Indian American newspapers and magazines, discussed passionately and frequently on Internet discussion groups, and promoted at Hindu conferences and many other public events in the United States and India. The Hindu Net Web site, for example, features articles on Kalyanaraman's work on the Out of India theory and an article on the "Myth of the Aryan Invasion" by David Frawley. It also has a section entitled "Islamic Era: The Dark Ages," with articles on the Hindu genocide, the "true story" of the Taj Mahal, and one called "The Magnitude of Muslim Atrocities" (www.hindunet.org/hindu_history, retrieved December 1, 2005). The main Web site of the Hindu Student Council has carried an article entitled "Hinduism Timeline, The Demise of the Aryan Racial/Invasion Theory" and a Powerpoint presentation, "Biases against Hinduism in Academia"(www.hscnet.org, retrieved September 7, 2005). The Web site of the Infinity Foundation has several essays which "Revisit" Indian history. Conferences, including these organized by Hindu American groups such as the World Association for Vedic Studies and the Annual Human Empowerment Conference frequently feature panels and scholars on various contested topics on Indian history.[30]

Hindu umbrella organizations also propagate the Hinducentric perspective on Indian history. The FHA, through publications, newspaper articles, and full-page advertisements between 1995 and 2000, argued that the true Vedic Hindu "essence" was besmirched by successive foreign invasions and could only be restored by a Hindu state. The FHA's characterization of the caste system and the position of women in the Vedic period will be discussed in the next chapter. The interpretation of the Muslim period was central to the historical constructions of the FHA. In an advertisement for a Hindu center that the FHA wanted to build in Southern California, the group declared that they viewed the Muslim period as "a prolonged national struggle [by Hindu kings] against foreign Islamic imperialism and not the conquest of India" (FHA 1997a), indicating that from the FHA perspective, Islamic control over India was attempted but never really accomplished and that therefore the Islamic rulers played no role in creating modern Indian society or culture. A memorandum the FHA presented to the Indian ambassador to the United States stated the organization's position on the nature of the Islamic period even more explicitly: "The FHA feels that the government of India fails in her duties to teach the factual history of the past invaders, by not telling our generations that invaders from Islamic blocs destroyed our culture, people and their temples. Instead, these ruthless barbarians are depicted and praised as kings of cultural achievements" (FHA 1997b, C20).

A major FHA grievance concerns the Partition. Members emphasize that while India was partitioned on the basis of religion to create Pakistan, an Islamic state, no Hindu state was given to the Hindus. "Where is the country for the Hindus?" the FHA cries (the existence of the Hindu country of Nepal is ignored by the FHA and other Hindu nationalist groups) and this issue had become central to its platform (FHA 1995a, 117; n.d.b., 2). The FHA was further aggrieved that after demanding an Islamic state, most of the Muslims stayed in India and were now demanding a secular state and special concessions from the government (FHA 1995a, 117). The FHA has viewed the post-Independence period as one dominated by "pseudo-seculars" who have been "pampering" minorities and engaging in "Hindu bashing." According to the FHA, Hinduism was discriminated against because it was "a compassionate and tolerant religion" (ibid., 80), and, the group argued, it was time to construct a more assertive Hinduism.

CHAPTER 9

Challenging American Pluralism

HINDU AMERICANS IN THE PUBLIC SPHERE

Although the Hindu nationalist side of American Hinduism is often hidden, expressed in internal communications and events directed at the Hindu Indian community in the United States and around the world, it also has a "public face" that is shown to the wider American public. Mobilizing to defend a beleaguered Hindu identity has become an important way for Indians from a Hindu background to counter their relative invisibility within American society and to obtain recognition and resources as American ethnics, as we have seen (Kurien 2004; Lal 1999; Mathew and Prashad 2000; Rajagopal 1995). For some years now, these Indian Americans have been organizing on the basis of a pan-Hindu, or "Indic," identity to protest the Eurocentric bias of many American institutions. Such groups have focused their attention on a variety of targets, including the misrepresentations or negative portrayals of Hinduism and of India within the American media and the wider society; the commercialization and misuse of Hindu deities, icons, and texts by the music, entertainment, and advertisement industries; and the lack of attention to Hinduism and Hindu American issues by the U.S. government. After the events of September 11, 2001, this public discourse shifted to some extent, but did not cease. In addition, Hindu Americans have increasingly mobilized against what is for them an important and emotional issue: the portrayal of Hindu and Indian culture within American academia.

Hindu American leaders position their challenges to American pluralism within a dynamic, multicultural model of national identity, arguing that the United States needs to redefine itself to take account of the large and growing group of non-European, non-Christian citizens who are now a significant part of the population. This conception of nationhood is very different from that of scholars like Huntington (2004), who view the essence of American identity as defined by its Protestant, Anglocentric origins. But although Hindu American groups advocate a multicultural model of nationhood for the United States, their challenge to Eurocentrism is grounded in an essentialist, unicultural, valorized model of Indianness that is in many respects the mirror image of what they seek to critique, since they emphasize

revisionist versions of Hinduism and of Indian history that glorify "Indic" traditions as the original source for much of world civilization. By falling into the mirror-
image trap, these Hindu American leaders end up undermining many of their own
arguments for the importance of pluralism.

Not all of the Indian American leaders who are at the forefront of this campaign
can be described as Hindutva supporters, but many share at least some of the assump-
tions of the movement, and the two efforts are therefore related. Hindu American
leaders harness the passions roused by the Hindutva mobilization to obtain support
for their cause, and their presentation of the disrespectful treatment accorded to Hinduism by the American media, entertainment industry, politicians, and by teachers in
schools and colleges further feeds into the grievances of those already galvanized by
the Hindutva movement.

Celebrating Hinduism and Hindu Americans

In their public presentations to the Indian American community and to the wider
American society, Hindu American spokespersons deploy certain standard themes
to characterize Hinduism. These themes are carefully chosen to fit into a contemporary, politically correct, pluralist American discourse. For instance, in keeping
with the multiculturalist emphasis on "tolerance" (Berbrier 1998), Hindu American
leaders describe Hinduism as the only world religion that is truly tolerant and pluralistic (in contrast to religions in the "Abrahamic" tradition). The *Rig Veda* verse
(1.164.46), "truth is one, sages call it by different names" is constantly reiterated to
underscore this claim. According to the Federation of Hindu Associations, Hinduism is the most suitable religion for the twenty-first century, because the modern pluralistic world "requires all religions to affirm [the] truth of other traditions
to ensure tranquility" (Singh 1997a) and only Hinduism fits the bill. The FHA's mission is therefore to safeguard Hinduism "for our children, for the world" (Singh,
interview, February 9, 1997). When Hindu American leaders refer to Hinduism as
Sanatana Dharma (eternal faith), they are emphasizing that it is the most ancient
and universalistic of all religions.

The content and meaning of a Hindu American identity are articulated by the
Hindu umbrella organizations described in chapter 7, whose leaders describe Hindu
Indian Americans as the proud descendants of the world's oldest living civilization
and religion. They counter the negative American image of Hinduism as primitive
by arguing that contrary to U.S. stereotypes, Hinduism is actually very sophisticated
and scientific. Many examples are provided, such as the Hindu conception of the
history of the universe as billions of years old and ancient Indian knowledge of astronomy, mathematics, metallurgy, and physics.

Hindu Americans are characterized as a group that has been able to maintain
the balance between materialism and spirituality in successfully adapting to
American life and drawing the best from it without losing their inner values and
cultural integrity. The model-minority label is used explicitly by group leaders,
who attribute the success of Indians in the United States to their Hindu religious

and cultural heritage, arguing that it gives them a special aptitude for science and math and makes them adaptable, hard working, and family oriented. Community spokespersons indicate that all of these qualities, together with their professional expertise (particularly in the fields of computers, medicine, and engineering) and affluence, mean that Hindu Indian Americans are a group that has an important leadership role to play in twenty-first-century America.

Antidefamation

Antidefamation issues became central to Hindu American umbrella groups beginning in the late 1990s. I have mentioned the formation of the American Hinduism against Defamation by the VHPA in 1997 and the subsequent formation of other antidefamation groups around the country, such as the Hindu International Council against Defamation and India Cause. The AHAD has been involved in successful protest campaigns, for example, against the "Om" perfume of the Gap, a CD cover of Sony's that featured a distorted image of a Hindu deity, a Simpsons program on Fox TV that caricatured the Hindu god Ganesha, a *Xena* episode in which Lord Krishna was a character, the use of a verse of the *Bhagavad Gita* as background music during an orgy scene in the film *Eyes Wide Shut*, and a shoe company and a company making toilet seats which had both used pictures of Hindu deities on their products. In all of these cases, AHAD and other Hindu groups were successful in getting the company to withdraw or modify the offending product or show. Portrayals of Hindus and of India in the American news media have also become a special target of antidefamation groups, who have contacted television networks and program hosts and newspaper and magazine editors to express their concern regarding what is perceived to be biased coverage.

Antiproselytization

From about the year 2000, in interfaith and human rights forums around the country, Hindu American leaders also started taking a public stand against the right of Christian missionaries to proselytize in India, arguing that such proselytization violates the rights of members of nonproselytizing religions to practice their religions without harassment (Sharma 2000/2001), that conversions are often carried out unethically through the use of fraud, deception, and material inducements, that the negative stereotypes of Hinduism promoted by the missionaries exacerbate communal tensions (Malhotra 2000b), and finally that proselytization is an act of cultural violence because converts are often asked to give up many of their traditional religious and cultural practices.

Challenging Misrepresentations of Hinduism in American Society

Several other Hindu leaders around the country have spoken up against what they feel are fundamental misrepresentations of Hinduism within the wider society. These efforts focus on three central issues that Americans have generally tended to view negatively: Hindu conceptions of the divine, the nature of the caste system, and the position of women in Hindu society.

Many American Hindu spokespersons object to the characterization of their religion as "polytheistic" and "idol worshipping." They point out that although the Hindu pantheon consists of an array of deities, many Hindus believe that all of these deities are different forms manifested by one Supreme Being. They argue that most Hindus have a primary deity that they worship, and that some traditions (such as Vaishnavism) only acknowledge the existence of that primary deity. For all of these reasons, they have claimed that Hinduism is in reality a monotheistic religion. Others maintain that neither Western conception ("monotheism" or "polytheism") is suitable to describe Hindu notions of the divine. Similarly, most American Hindu leaders find the English term "idol" offensive, since it has the negative connotation that the worshipper considers the graven image to be divine. They prefer the term "icon" or "image" and argue that these images only represent the idea of the divine and provide the worshipper with a tangible mental focus.

Hindu organizations like the FHA contest the notion that caste stratification is a by-product of Hinduism by maintaining that the caste system "was never integrally connected with the inner spirit of Hindu religion" and that "there is no religious sanction to the practice of [a] caste system of any kind in the primary Hindu scriptures" (*India Post* 1995, A6). Leaders also point to the absence of immutable birth-based caste groups in the *Rig Veda* and Lord Krishna's statement in the *Bhagavad Gita* (4:13), mentioned earlier, to make the argument that the varna system that is described in Hindu scriptures as based on occupation and individual qualities, not birth. Spokespersons also emphasize that manuals like the *Laws of Manu*, where caste prescriptions and proscriptions are stressed, are not part of the sruti or the primary scriptural corpus of Hindus.

I have argued that women play an important part in religio-cultural associations that operate at the community level and can therefore shape the construction of gender and of ethnicity and identity within such associations. Their position as ethnic architects in that context is informal, however, because their influence is largely confined to the household and community. It is the leaders of pan-Indian ethnic organizations, both religious and secular, who have the formal and officially recognized task of codifying and communicating what Indian culture and Indian religion stand for (see also Bhattarcharjee 1992, 23). They speak at large public functions, and their speeches and publications are carried by both ethnic and nonethnic media and thus obtain wide circulation. The umbrella Indian organizations are dominated by upper-class, upper-caste males, and these characteristics go a long way in shaping the content of the ethnicity that they present (Bhattacharjee 1992; DasGupta and Dasgupta 1996). Faced with the pressures of racism and assimilation, Hindu Americans strive to perfect a model-minority image of themselves and their culture. We have seen the way in which an idealized Indian womanhood became a central icon in the development of the Hindu reaction to colonialism and Westernization. In a similar way, class and gender become central elements in constructing the essence of Indianness in the United States. The figure of the chaste, nurturing, and self-sacrificing Indian woman becomes the linchpin of the family values and work ethic that Indian Americans deem as being responsible for their professional success (see also Bhattacharjee 1992; DasGupta and Dasgupta 1996). In this construction, it is the unconditional faithfulness, the homemaking and child-rearing talents, and the uncomplaining and self-sacrificing nature of Indian women that allow men to invest all their energy in their professional careers, work long hours, and become successful. Acutely sensitive to the negative perception among Americans of the status of Indian women, the ethnic architects also emphasize that Hindu culture treats women with honor and respect and that Hindu culture is gender egalitarian. The large proportion of Indian American women professionals is cited as proof of this assertion.

This idealization of Indian womanhood and gender relations is one of the central indicators within the American Hindu discourse used to signify that Hindu Indian culture presents the ideal middle ground between "Western" culture (which is criticized for its high divorce rates and "promiscuous" sexual relations), on the one hand, and "Islamic" culture (criticized for polygamy and the repression of women), on the other. The FHA characterizes Hindu culture as placing a "high premium on character and chastity in marriage. One-wife-one-husband is the banner of Hinduism." The association goes on to argue that in terms of "religious, cultural, social, and individual aspects, a woman has the same rights as man in Hindu society. 'Where women are honored, gods are pleased' declare Hindu scriptures. Hindus have elevated women to the level of Divinity. Only Hindus worship God in the form of [the] Divine Mother" (FHA 1995a, 6). Thus they claim that a Hindu rashtra is necessary to rescue Indian Muslim women from the oppression they now have to experience under the Muslim Personal Law.

The centrality of gender to the construction of ancient Hindu India is made clear by the FHA in a page entitled "Proud to Be a Hindu Woman," which argues that in "no nation of antiquity were women held in so much esteem as amongst the Hindus. The position of women thus supplies a good test of the civilization of the great Hindus" (FHA 1995a, 48). The umbrella group claims, as do many other Hindu American leaders and Hindutva ideologues, that it was the Muslim conquest of India that was responsible for the subsequent decline in the status of women. The restrictive image of womanhood in the Hindutva discourse is echoed in the FHA's characterization of Hindu women. The first sentence of the section titled "Proud to be a Hindu Woman" describes Hindu women as the embodiment of "patience, . . . virtue, love, life, self-control" and as "chaste" and "giving" (FHA 1995a, 48).

Seeking Acknowledgment of Hinduism as an American Religion

Other umbrella groups have focused on getting Hinduism publicly acknowledged as an American religion at the national level. In September 2000, despite some opposition from conservative Christians, Indian American lobby groups succeeded in having a Hindu priest open a session of Congress (at which the Indian prime minister addressed a joint session of the House and Senate) for the first time, something that was reported with great pride in Indian American newspapers and on Web sites. The second indication that Hindu Americans were being recognized by Washington came a month later, when President Bill Clinton issued a proclamation from the White House wishing Indian Americans a Happy Diwali (an important Hindu festival). In return for contributions from Silicon Valley to the Democratic Party for the 2000 elections, Indian American computer professionals had requested that the festival be officially recognized by the White House. The Indian American paper the *India Post* reported that Indian Americans were jubilant when Clinton issued the greeting, since this "is a symbolic gesture that speaks volumes to the fact that Indian culture is accepted as part of America's overall fabric" (Krishnakumar and Prashanth 2000, 22). Recently there have been attempts to get a Diwali stamp approved and issued.

The terrorist attacks on the United States of September 11, 2001, brought about a shift in the patterns of activism of Hindu American groups. In the days following 9/11 a number of interfaith services were organized in different parts of the country. These services, typically conducted by Protestant ministers, Catholic priests, and Jewish rabbis, also for the first time included Muslim clerics. Muslim spokespersons traveled around the country, emphasizing that they were part of the same tradition as Christians and Jews, and proclaimed that "we worship the same God as you do." Their lobbying appeared to yield immediate results, most visibly in the attempt to enlarge the American "Judeo-Christian" sacred canopy into an "Abrahamic" one that included Muslims.

The need to include Muslims, frequently termed "the fastest growing religious group in the United States," within the fabric of American religions had been recognized several years earlier by the Clinton administration. But it was only in the wake of 9/11 that this initiative bore fruit, with the term "Abrahamic" entering public discourse (see Prothero 2001). Several newspapers and magazines carried reports on this development. Hindu Americans, however, viewed such a reconfiguration with alarm, fearing that it would further marginalize non-Abrahamic religions like Hinduism.

The Hindu umbrella organization HICAD and several hundred individual Hindus sent a petition to President George W. Bush, emphasizing that Hindus were a numerically and professionally significant part of the United States and were model citizens who needed to be included within "America's pluralistic and multicultural traditions." The petition also protested the exclusion of Hindus from the national prayer service organized in the wake of the events of 9/11.

Many of the themes mentioned earlier are found in the petition, such as a reference to Hindu monotheism (worship to the "One Almighty God") and being a religion that is over "8,000 years old," an emphasis on the exemplary intergenerational and gender relations among Hindus ("We are a family oriented people with low divorce rates . . . we save for our children's education and support our elders and extended families") and repeated stress on the tolerance and pluralism of Hindus (descriptions of Hinduism as "peace-loving," upholding "non-violence, pluralism and respect" as central tenets). The petition also subtly drew attention to the difference between Hinduism and Islam (by pointing out that Hindus "never threaten violence against our host country" and that there was "no world-wide Hindu network of terrorists"). This emphasis on the distinction between Hinduism and

Islam became prominent in the post-9/11 public statements of many of the self-styled representatives of American Hindus.

The previously tolerant, pluralistic tone of the public voice of Hindu Americans changed overnight with the terrorist attacks of September 11, 2001. Suddenly the militantly anti-Islamic, Hinducentric side, which had been previously hidden from public view, began to emerge. Many Hindu Indian Americans bombarded their politicians and the media with anti-Pakistani and anti-Islamic propaganda, filled with quotes from the Koran, and also called in to radio and television talk shows to criticize Islam. (One Internet group circulated "talking points" for Hindu Americans to use while calling in to such shows.) Others spoke up at town meetings to condemn the treatment of minorities in Muslim countries and to challenge the positive portrayals of Islam by Muslim speakers. Some Hindu Americans also sent e-mails and letters to "South Asian" groups to press a point that they had been making all along, asserting that India had nothing in common with Islamic countries like Pakistan and Bangladesh and should therefore not be lumped together with them. Groups such as the Global Organization of Persons of Indian Origin (GOPIO) were also criticized for trying to create a pan-Indian platform that included both "Indic" and "non-Indic" members. Members of one Internet discussion group sent letters to the president of the American Academy of Religion (AAR), Vasudha Narayanan, demanding that the organization sponsor panels on Islamic fascism and on "Jihad: God as Weapon of Mass Destruction" at its upcoming annual meeting. Such gestures, they claimed, would serve to counterbalance the organization's excessive focus on Hindu fascism. Another member of the same group documented the alleged contempt for Hinduism and Hindus by Hinduism scholars by culling the Internet archives of the Religions in South Asia list-serv (RISA-L) and of the Society for Hindu-Christian studies. This putative evidence was then sent to the president of the AAR as well as to several Internet discussion groups.

In the weeks immediately following 9/11, Rajiv Malhotra of the Infinity Foundation was invited to several universities to speak about the unfolding events from a Hindu perspective. In his talks at the American University and at Princeton University, he took the offensive against Islam, criticizing its leadership of "duplicity" for projecting a face of peace and tolerance in the United States while promoting fundamentalism at home. In light of the September 11th backlash in the United States, "a lot of Hindus suddenly have started realizing they better stand up and differentiate themselves from Muslims or Arabs," the journalist Sarah Wildman (2001) quotes Malhotra as saying. In a presentation entitled "The Gita's Perspective on the War against Terrorism" at the American University, Malhotra rejected an antiwar stance and made the argument that the *Bhagavad Gita* supported "dharmic," or just, wars to combat global evil, provided that they were not merely in self-interest and were carried out ethically, without colluding with evil. (Many other Hindu Americans argued that Hindus should drop the emphasis on *ahimsa,* or nonviolence.) Malhotra thus publicly articulated a Hindu argument supporting the war in Afghanistan and against U.S. alliances with Pakistan or Saudi Arabia in its fight against the Taliban.[1]

Hindu Americans were also more willing to mobilize in support of Indian and Hindu causes in the post-9/11 period. A petition charging CNN with pro-Pakistan and anti-Indian bias (on the basis of an article by Rajiv Malhotra published on *Sulekha.com* alleging the same) obtained 55,000 signatures. Such an outpouring of support compelled CNN executives to meet with representatives of the Indian community in Atlanta during February 2002.[2] Several Hindu American groups also protested the planned February 2002 screening of two films critical of Hindu nationalism by the American Museum of Natural History in New York as part of its exhibit "Meeting God, Elements of Hindu Devotion."[3] A petition (again sponsored by the HICAD) to the authorities at the museum bore an introduction similar to the Bush petition, pointing out that there were a large number of Hindus in the United States, and that they were a visible and very productive American community. It then went on to argue that it was inappropriate for the museum to screen the films: "As an analogy, please consider if it would be appropriate to stage a documentary on Osama bin Laden and the destruction of the World Trade Center in an exhibit on the elements of Islamic devotion; or a documentary on slavery, colonialism, Christian crusades, white supremacy, Holocaust, Auswitcz [*sic*], or killings of native Americans, in an exhibit on the Elements of Christian Devotion."[4]

The showing of the films was initially canceled, allegedly because of the threat of violence. Later, when the films were shown at a different venue, a large number of aggrieved Hindus reportedly turned out. Later in 2002, at the showing of another film critical of Hindu nationalism (this time at Barnard College at Columbia University), Hindu protesters apparently grew so unruly that the police had to be called in and the organizers of the showing were whisked away in a van under police protection.[5]

Since its formation in 2004, the Hindu American Foundation has projected itself as the public voice of Hindu Americans. In 2004–2005, the organization held events to educate legislators about "issues of concern to Hindu Americans," such as the abuses to Hindus in Kashmir, Bangladesh, and Pakistan, and domestic issues such as "prayer-in-schools and ten commandments displays in public places."[6] I have mentioned the HAF's participation in the legal challenge to the Ten Commandments monument in Texas on the ground that the state-sponsored display violated the rights of non–Judeo-Christian religions whose conceptions of the divine were different. We have also seen that the president of the HAF, Mihir Meghani, argued in an article on Hindutva that a Ram temple in Ayodhya was necessary, because all Indians ought to show respect to the Lord Ram. The contradiction between the rights of minorities in India and the rights demanded for Hindus in the United States was not addressed by Meghani. In addition to the Ten Commandments issue, the organization participated in a legal campaign in support of the New York Hindu Temple's federal court case against the injunction to hold elections for temple trustees. The HAF also introduced a brochure prepared for U.S. public officials that summarized the principles of Hinduism and its "inherent values of tolerance, pluralism and peace." Additionally, HAF leaders met with leaders of the American Jewish Committee in San Francisco, and the American Israel Public Affairs Committee in Washington, D.C., to stress the common issues faced by

Jews and Hindus. In the meeting in San Francisco held in October 2004, Mihir Meghani noted the "declining number of Hindus in India owing to growth rate and dubious methods of conversion to other faiths" and compared it to the demographic decline faced by Jews in Israel. He also spoke about "the shared risks they face from neighbors with long histories of terrorism."[7]

CHALLENGING AMERICAN ACADEMIA

As children grow up in the United States, immigrant parents find to their dismay that many of their offspring absorb the negative messages about Hinduism and India from the wider society and turn away from their culture and traditions. Indian American Internet groups feature frequent discussions about insensitive, ignorant, Eurocentric teachers and classmates and the pain they cause Indian American students. A letter from a fourteen-year-old Indian American schoolgirl from Houston that appeared in many Indian-American newspapers, Web sites, and Internet groups, poignantly describes the way "every day, young *desi* [Indian] children and teenagers are unreasonably tormented [in American schools] because of our perceived background." The writer continues, "The school textbooks are half the cause. The average American doesn't know squat about India, and with the help of poorly researched textbooks, they learn nonsense" (Trisha Pasricha, cited in Malhotra 2003b, 43; see also Rosser 2001). Second-generation Indian Americans have been entering American high schools and colleges in large numbers over the past few years, making the surveillance and shaping of the presentation of Hinduism and Indian history in American school textbooks and within academia a central and emotional issue for some sections of the Hindu American community. The activities of "Indic" organizations whose central agenda has been to challenge the academic portrayal of Hinduism, particularly the Infinity Foundation, express this concern.

Scholars who are viewed as being critical of any aspect of Hinduism, India, or Hindutva conceptions of history have come under attack. These attacks have not just been directed against Euro-American scholars. In fact, leaders of the movement such as Rajiv Malhotra make clear that the "insider–outsider" distinction that they make is based not on skin color or ethnicity but on "practice": in other words, between individuals (including non-Indians) whom they define as Hindu practitioners and those (including scholars from Hindu backgrounds) whom they define as non-Hindus or "pseudo"-Hindus (Malhotra 2002b, 8). Some of the harshest criticisms of the movement have been leveled at Indian American scholars who have been characterized as being stooges of the Western academy.

In chapter 7, I referred to the founding of the Infinity Foundation, an organization promoting Indic studies. This foundation, and particularly its president, Rajiv Malhotra, has played a central role in the mobilization against anti-Hindu biases in American academia. Except for a year (2000–2001) when David Gray, who holds a religious studies Ph.D. from Columbia University, was appointed as the executive director of the ECIT, the foundation has functioned without any full-time workers with the exception of Rajiv Malhotra himself. All the members of the volunteer advisory board are described on the foundation Web site as being "Indian American entrepreneurs."[8] Most work in the software industry and none are academics. Although also not an academic, Rajiv Malhotra has been an influential figure within Indic studies in the United States. He was a prominent speaker at an international conference held at the Center for Indic Studies at the University of Massachusetts at Dartmouth in July 2002 and was a board member of the Foundation for Indic Philosophy and Culture at the Claremont Colleges in California. Since 2000 Malhotra has succeeded in building up a large constituency of support from sections of the Hindu American community, primarily through his writings on Hindu and Indian American Internet discussion groups and e-zines like *Sulekha.com, Rediff.com,* and *Outlookindia.com.*

Many of the Hindu activists in the United States are computer scientists, and like them, Rajiv Malhotra approaches his critique of American academia with a belief in the superiority of the sciences and a contempt for the humanities, its methods, and its scholars (who are frequently described as being individuals who turned to the humanities when they could not get into a science field; see Malhotra 2001b:13). He also uses his background in the business sector (another background common to many Hindu American activists) to argue for the need for a "business model of religion," saying that Hinduism needs to adopt the model of other religions, like Christianity, which are run like a business. He believes that Hinduism should assess its market position and strategic direction, and then engage in better advertising and brand management practices to sell its products, increase market share, and deal with competitors (Malhotra 2001b, 2002a).

Through his indefatigable effort and dedication, shrewd use of resources, and the mobilization of Hindu American supporters, Malhotra has become an influential, though often controversial, voice within the academy (in the United States, and also in the United Kingdom and India) in a very short period of time. The Infinity Foundation has provided small grants to many of the major universities in the country to support a variety of programs, such as a visiting professorship in Indic Studies (Harvard University), yoga and Hindi classes (Rutgers University), research on and the teaching of nondualist philosophies (University of Hawaii), a Global Renaissance Institute and a Center for Buddhist Studies (Columbia University), a program in religion and science (University of California, Santa Barbara), an endowment for the Center for Advanced Study of India (University of Pennsylvania), and lectures at the Center for Consciousness Studies (University of Arizona). The foundation also provided some funding to the Association for Asian Studies for a special journal issue of *Education about Asia* (Winter 2001), on the topic of "Teaching Indic Traditions." In addition, the foundation is sponsoring, as documented on its Web site, several book projects on ancient Indian contributions to science, mathematics, technology, psychology, and music; a multivolume Encyclopedia of Indian Philosophy; and research projects on topics such as the U.S. media bias in reporting on India, the position of Indian women, and American attitudes toward Indic traditions; as well as several seminars and conferences in India and the United States on Vedanta, yoga, India's contributions to the world, and India's traditional knowledge systems. The Web site also hosts articles and essays on topics ranging from religion, science, and technology in ancient India, to the controversies over Indian history, to contemporary Hinduism studies and the contributions and applications of Hinduism to the world today.

In the spring and summer of 2005, the foundation developed several new initiatives. In February an e-mail that was widely circulated on the Internet to Indian American discussion groups called for grant proposals (apparently funded by donations raised by Hindu Americans around the country) to "study Hinduphobia as a sociological topic." Specifically, the grant, which promised up to $50,000 a year for an initial period of eighteen months for a candidate with a Ph.D. in a relevant discipline, was to "research the social, political, cultural, and economic contexts which help shape the works of US academics who specialize in Hinduism, and others who write on the subject and distribute knowledge and information in contemporary US society." This description was followed by detailed suggestions on how the candidate might proceed with the research. Another call for proposals went out to educational institutions in August 2005 (I received it through Syracuse University), seeking academics "to do research or develop educational materials, whose objective would be to improve the authenticity of portrayal of Indic traditions in the educational system." The announcement added that the initiative was "in response to growing concern over inaccurate and damaging 'Orientalist' portrayals of India and India's cultural legacy." The announcement added a list of specific projects in which the foundation was particularly interested. In June 2005 the foundation announced the appointment of a director of India Activities, to, among other duties, coordinate between project leaders in India and the United States, promote Infinity's scholars as public intellectuals in India, and lead a new Infinity initiative on documentary film production. Malhotra's initiatives have received some support from a variety of academics in the United States and in other countries. But I am aware that his frequently distorted presentation of arguments and his abrasive personal attacks against scholars who do not share his viewpoints have alienated many others, even those who were initially sympathetic to some of his goals.

Four major critiques against the American academy are mounted by Hindu American leaders like Rajiv Malhotra. First and most broadly, Hindu American leaders charge that American academia is dominated by a Eurocentric perspective that views Western culture as being the font of world civilization and refuses to acknowledge the contributions of non-Western societies such as India to European culture and technology. Second, they maintain that the academic study of religion in the United States has been based on the model of the "Abrahamic" traditions and that this model is not applicable to religions such as Hinduism. Related to this critique of Abrahamic religions is their condemnation of the study and presentation of Hinduism by American scholars. Hindu American leaders maintain that unlike the academic study of Abrahamic religions, Western scholars of Hinduism like to focus on the sensationalist, negative attributes of the religion and present it in a demeaning way that shows a lack of respect for the sentiments of the practitioners of the religion. Finally, Hindu American leaders denounce South Asian studies programs in the United States for creating a false identity and unity between India and the more Muslim countries in the South Asian region like Pakistan and Bangladesh, and for undermining India by focusing on its internal cleavages and problems. In each of these four areas, Hindu American leaders are working to introduce and popularize a Hindu (or Indic) perspective as a corrective to the biases they perceive as being entrenched in the academy.

Challenging Eurocentrism

The Infinity Foundation has taken a leadership role in the sponsorship of scholarship on important tenets of the Hinducentric perspective—that civilization developed on the banks of the river Saraswati in northwestern India around five thousand years ago and from there spread to the rest of the world, that the Vedas enshrine knowledge of advanced scientific, mathematical, and astronomical concepts, encrypted in code form, and that the effects of the Muslim invasions of India were debilitating. For instance, its Web site hosts an essay entitled "The Myth of Aryan Invasions of India," by M. Lal Goel, and a "Sourcebook on Indic Contributions in Math and Science," edited by Subhash Kak. One of the first major Indic studies projects that Rajiv Malhotra commissioned, completed in 2001, was the compilation of a database of passages to document the destructive nature of the Muslim (Arab, Persian, and Turkish) invasions of India, based on the accounts of the royal historians who had accompanied the invaders (archived at the foundation Web site under "Resources for the Study of Indian History").

Rajiv Malhotra has also been at the forefront of the Hindu American effort to challenge the Eurocentrism of the academy. In a coauthored article, he and David Gray (then the executive director of the ECIT) write:

> Traditional accounts of the development of Western thought tend to emphasize its continuity. Modern philosophy and science we are told, go back in an unbroken lineage to the ancient Greeks. . . . This narrative, like all myths, is remarkably resilient. It also has what we might call a dark subtext; as a product of cultural chauvinism, it has served to downplay or gloss over the very real contributions of non-European civilizations to European thought and technology.

The authors go on to argue that many of the foundational concepts of Western mathematics, such as "Arabic" numerals and the decimal system, were borrowed from India by Arabs and then picked up by the Greeks and Romans. They also point out that many leading Western intellectuals—thinkers such as Emerson and Thoreau, philosophers like Arthur Schopenhauer, psychologists Carl Jung and Ken Wilber, poets like Goethe, Walt Whitman, W. B. Yeats, and T. S. Eliot, and physicists like Erwin Schrödinger—were all influenced by Indian writing and literature, but that these Indic contributions to Western thought have been obscured by the Eurocentrism of the academy (Malhotra and Gray 2001).

In July 2002 Rajiv Malhotra and Robert Thurman, a professor in the religious studies department at Columbia University specializing in the study of Tibetan Buddhism, organized a colloquium, "Completing the Global Renaissance: The Indic

Contributions," in New York, bringing together prominent scholars of Hinduism and Buddhism. This conference was a follow-up to a Global Renaissance Institute that they had established at Columbia University in 2000. In their mission statement to the conference, Malhotra and Thurman echo a theme articulated by Swami Vivekananda (who in turn drew on some of the ideas of Schopenhauer—see chapter 6) and argue that the Renaissance was European and incomplete, because it was based primarily on knowledge from the physical, or "Outer," sciences, where the contributions of non-Western sources had been denied. Insisting that knowledge based on the "spiritual or Inner sciences" (philosophy, psychology, epistemology, linguistics) is equally important, they go on to write, "We believe that the mother lode of these inner sciences is to be found within the matrix of Indian civilization, loosely associated with the numerous Hindu, Buddhist, and Jain subcultures that thrived throughout that most populous and wealthy subcontinental part of Eurasia for thousands of years, until foreign conquerors impoverished it almost beyond recognition" (Malhotra and Thurman 2002, 4). Malhotra and Thurman contend that what the world needs is a "second renaissance," this time a "more holistic and truly global" one, and that this can be achieved by incorporating the "Indic traditions," those of both the Outer and the Inner Sciences, into Western thought. The conference was therefore organized to critique Eurocentricism and the negative stereotypes of Indic traditions, to consider measures to counteract them, to provide a deeper appreciation for the contributions of the Indic traditions, and finally to develop strategies to showcase these traditions as being "highly valuable to the rebalancing and furthering of contemporary science in the global context" (ibid., 5–6).

One of Malhotra's central arguments has been his "U-turn" theory, which he discusses often in his writings and which has been picked up by many of his supporters. According to this theory, the West has repeatedly appropriated and then denied Indic contributions and has been able to mobilize Indian American "sepoys" (like the Indian police who served the British in colonial India) and *becharis* (whom he describes as "women who overdo the 'I have been abused' roles . . . in exchange for a benefit" [Malhotra 2002b, 9]) to focus on the negative aspects of the tradition.

Malhotra argues that for a variety of reasons, most of the scholarship on Indic traditions has to date been conducted by "outsiders" and that "no other major world religion has such a low percentage of insiders as does Hinduism, in its academic study today" (Malhotra 2002b, 8). He is also a fierce critic of anthropologists and their methods, arguing that they set themselves up as the authority to interpret non-Western cultures and traditions and do not allow the "natives" to challenge them or to talk back. The domination of Indic studies by Westerners, he maintains, has led to Western academic and media biases against the tradition. Furthermore it has meant that the many contributions the tradition makes in the areas of psychology, linguistics, postmodernism, political and social theory, eco-vegetarianism, feminism, religious studies, and philosophy have been neglected or overlooked. He therefore calls for a "Satyagraha [Gandhi's term for nonviolent protest or agitation] against the establishment, a review of the ethics of the academic treatment of India's civilization" (ibid., 10), and also argues for the need to have more "insider," or practitioner, scholars. Malhotra maintains that all this is necessary to revise history to focus on India's achievements and the "true historical causes of India's problems" today (ibid., 26) and to learn from Indic traditions. He feels that such revisionism is also important to promote multiculturalism in the United States, to prepare American children for globalization, and to address the needs of Indian Americans (ibid., 30).

Critiquing Abrahamic Traditions

Hindu American Internet groups and Web sites often feature discussions to make the case that the term "religion" does not apply to Hinduism, since Hinduism is a "way of life." As mentioned, some Hindus prefer to use the term Sanatana Dharma (eternal, universal dharma), or Hindu dharma, to refer to the panoply of their beliefs and practices. We have also seen that Hindu Americans frequently compare and contrast Hinduism or Dharma with the Abrahamic traditions (particularly Islam and Christianity), arguing that unlike these religions, which make exclusive claims to the truth and are therefore intolerant, Hinduism is tolerant and pluralistic.

Some Hindu Indian scholars based in the West, such as S. N. Balagangadhara in Belgium and Arvind Sharma in Canada, have elaborated on the distinction between Indic and Abrahamic traditions. In a book published in 1994, Balagangadhara argued, following Wilfred Cantwell Smith (1962), that the concept of religion as a "belief" system that is accepted as "true" and is validated by textual tradition is derived from Christianity and was subsequently adopted by Jews and Muslims. Thus it is a concept that "cuts across the three Semitic religions" (Balagangadhara 1994, 322). He maintains that Hinduism is not a religion in that sense, since it does not provide a single authoritative belief system, scripture, or adjudicatory body. Arvind Sharma has made similar arguments in his own work (e.g., see Sharma 2002). Both Balagangadhara (1994) and Sharma (2002) go on to point out that such a definition of the concept of religion has wider implications. Balagangadhara argues that it can shape the nature of science, in that it constrains the types of questions and theories that can be formulated (Balagangadhara 1994), while Sharma (2002) focuses on its implications for defining the nature of secularism and religious freedom. Sharma (2000/2001) has argued against the right to proselytize, saying that the right is based on a "Western" conception of religion, which sees religions as mutually exclusive. Balagangadhara introduced himself on one of the Indian American Internet discussion groups in 2002, and his work subsequently generated considerable interest and enthusiasm among members. Arvind Sharma is also well known to Indian American Internet participants; he has occasionally joined in Internet discussions and has contributed Internet articles about Hinduism to the Indictraditions group (many of these are archived at the Infinity Foundation Web site).

The events of September 11, 2001, led to a shift in the discourse about Abrahamic traditions within Indian American discussion groups with anti-Abrahamism resulting in a growing antimonotheistic mood. We have seen that earlier many Hindus had taken offense to any description of Hinduism as "polytheistic." In the post-9/11 period, however, Hindus began to take pride in polytheism, arguing that monotheism led to triumphalism, proselytization, and violence against other faith communities. This mood was very much in evidence at the Dharma conference discussed in the last chapter.

Many of the Hindu arguments against Abrahamic traditions were brought together by Malhotra (2003a) in an article in the e-zine *Sulekha.com* which he circulated to several religious studies scholars and which also formed the basis for several of his presentations at academic venues. Entitled "Problematizing God's Interventions in History," the article is a critique of Abrahamic traditions "on scientific and ethical grounds" (ibid., 1). Malhotra argues that Abrahamic traditions and Indic traditions are based on "two different, and often competing ways of arriving at spiritual truth," with the Abrahamic traditions relying on historical narratives (about "holy" events), and the Indic traditions relying on *adhyatma-vidhya* (inner "science" or esoteric processes). He goes on to write:

> The former's premise is that human limitations are inherently insurmountable without divine intervention. The latter's premise is that humans have infinite potential. These, in turn, correspond to the view of man being essentially evil, and hence in need of being salvaged by God's agency, versus the view of man being essentially . . . the Supreme Being in limited form, with the built-in capacity to achieve self-realization. . . .
>
> The Abrahamic means of bridging the gap emphasizes a top-down, God-initiated intervention in human history. This intervention is via a prophet, who is also God's son in the case of Christianity. . . . [U]nless such an intervention is taken literally and its message is implemented, man is doomed to remain in darkness. . . . On the other hand, the Indic traditions claim an endless stream of enlightened living spiritual masters, each said to have realized the ultimate truth while alive on this earth, and hence, able to teach this truth to others. Unlike in the case of Indic traditions, the great teachers of Abrahamic traditions are not living models of embodied enlightenment for the student. Instead, Abrahamic teachers proclaim the truth based on historical texts. The consequences of these divergent systems are enormous and are at the heart of Indic-Abrahamic distinctions. (ibid., 3)

Malhotra maintains that the Abrahamic traditions are less scientific, since they are based on unique historical events in which adherents believe, not because there is any compelling empirical evidence to substantiate the beliefs, but because the historical narrative has been passed down through the generations by the faith community. In contrast, the Indic traditions are not dependent on the histories of the saints who contributed to them, just as the laws of nature are not contingent upon the validity of the histories of the scientists who discovered them. He claims that although Abrahamic religions are now busy trying to "repackage their Grand Narratives in science-compliant ways" (ibid., 14), they have difficulty in harmoniously merging scientific and religious explanations of the origins of the cosmos, and the natural laws. (See Edelmann 2004 for a critique of this argument.) However, "Indic traditions have no such problem to begin with, because within Indic theistic traditions, Saguna Brahman [the Supreme Being] acts through his Shakti (the kinetic/intelligent power), which is innate and immanent within the physical universe.

No fracture of natural law is necessary for Brahman to act in Indic systems"
(Malhotra 2003a, 14).

On ethical grounds, Malhotra argues that "non-negotiable Grand Narratives of
History" lead to conflict, because they promote triumphalism and the belief "that
there is only One True History. Monotheism turns into My-theism, the belief that
only one's own conception of theism is valid, and that all others must be falsified
and demonized. Religious institutions get obsessed to defend, control and enforce
their Grand Narrative of History" (Malhotra 2003a, 16). In contrast, not being
"handcuffed to history," Indic traditions, even those dealing with the past, are "pli-
able and fluid . . . with no compulsion to find 'one true canon'" (ibid., 14). Again
Malhotra argues that since Indic traditions accept multiple manifestations of the
Supreme Being, they are inherently pluralistic. All these arguments are based on
Swami Vivekananda's ideas.

Leaders at the Global Dharma Conference of June 2003, as we have seen,
assented that Hinduism was the one universal and eternal religion, and that all religions were not the same. This argument was subsequently emphasized by Rajiv
Malhotra (2004f) and Frank Morales (2005), a Euro-Hindu convert. Thus Hindu
American leaders seem to be returning to the hierarchical relativism that van der
Veer (1996, 258) has suggested was the original basis for the formulation of Hindu
tolerance and pluralism. Discussions on Internet groups and the article by Morales
make clear that the impetus behind this change in the interpretation of pluralism
was the conversion of some second-generation American Hindus to other religions. As Morales (2005) explains in his article, American Hindu parents frequently
approach him after his lectures to ask for advice. "The oft-repeated story," he says,
"goes somewhat like this":

> We raised our son/daughter to be a good Hindu. We took them to the temple for
> important holidays. We even sent him/her to a Hindu camp for a weekend when
> they were 13. Now at the age of 23, our child has left Hinduism and converted to
> the *(fill the blank)* religion. When we ask how could they have left the religion of
> their family, the answer that they throw back in our face is: "but mama/dada, you
> always taught us that all religions are the same, and that it doesn't really matter
> how a person worships God. So what does it matter if we've followed your advice
> and switched to another religion?" (Morales 2005, 2)

Morales argues that the idea that all religions are the same, or "radical universal-
ism", was not part of "traditional Hinduism" but was a "liberal Christian inspired
'reformism'" that neo-Hindu leaders such as Ram Mohan Roy, and even Swami
Vivekananda to some extent, incorporated into their syncretistic presentations of
Hinduism. Traditional Hindu leaders, in contrast, had made clear distinctions
between those traditions that were Hindu (which accepted the authority of the
Vedas) and those that did not (including Buddhism and Jainism). As an example
Morales cites Manu's (XII:95) statement, "All those traditions and all those disrep-
utable systems of philosophy that are not based in the Veda produce no positive
result after death; for they are declared to be found on darkness." He also points out

that radical universalism has several internal contradictions and also promotes "an intolerant tolerance," since it would "deny any non–Radical Universalist religion the very basis of their existence." Morales concludes that to "ensure that our youth remain committed to Hinduism as a meaningful path, . . . we must abandon Radical Universalism. . . . Let us instead look them in their eyes, and teach them the uniquely precious, the beautifully endearing, and the philosophically profound truths of our tradition. . . . Let us teach them Sanatana Dharma, the eternal way of Truth" (ibid., 28). A Dharma Summit in August 2005, a gathering of "almost 450 Hindu leaders, gurus, and intellectuals" at Rutgers University, apparently endorsed these ideas. The leaders asserted "the importance of referring to our religion as 'Sanatana Dharma' . . . [and] the rejection of Radical Universalism" (Ravu 2005).

Critiquing Hinduism Studies

The most volatile issue in the controversy over the alleged Eurocentric bias within American academia has undoubtedly been the portrayal of Hinduism and Hindu deities by American religious studies scholars. Western scholars writing on Hinduism and Hindu nationalism had come under attack from Hindu American leaders since the 1990s with the rise in the Hindutva movement. The year 2000, however, was a watershed in terms of Hindu American activism targeted at academia. Over the course of that year, several dozen Hindu and Indian American Internet discussion groups were formed, some of them, like Indictraditions and IndianCivilization, with the explicit goal of providing Hindu- or Indic-centered critiques of Western scholarship on Hinduism and ancient Indian history. One of the first public activities of the newly formed Educational Council of Indic Traditions of the Infinity Foundation was to send a letter to the National Endowment for the Humanities (NEH), which had funded a project to train high school teachers to teach the *Ramayana*. The letter protested the inclusion of one lesson (chapter 5, unit 25, lesson 2, 335–337), out of a total of around forty, in which the author, the anthropologist Susan Wadley, had used a contemporary Dalit song critical of the *Ramayana* to make the point that the ideology of caste was contested in India. Describing the Dalit author of the song as an "anti-Hindu activist," the ECIT letter made the case that many Americans were Hindus and therefore that it was the responsibility of teachers and scholars to be sensitive about how they were representing the religion in a multicultural classroom context: "It is irresponsible for any multicultural school to introduce a protest song against Hindus and Sikhs that includes hate speech. . . . What does this do to foster mutual respect and understanding among different ethnic and religious communities in America's sensitive tapestry, now represented in classrooms? Should Government funds be used to create such racially and religiously inflammatory teaching materials, denigrating to one's classmates' sensitivities, ironically in the name of multiculturalism?"[9]

Some Hindu activists, including Malhotra, also attended the annual meeting of the American Academy of Religion that year. In an article, "A Hindu View of the American Academy of Religion's Convention, 2000," which was widely circulated on Indian American Internet groups, Malhotra denounced the presentation of

Hinduism at the meeting, describing it as "Hindu-bashing" (Malhotra 2000a). In response to the concerns of the Hindu community about the academic study of the religion, the December 2000 issue of the *Journal of the American Academy of Religion (JAAR)* carried a special feature, "Who Speaks for Hinduism," with articles from a range of scholars. This issue was also severely criticized by Malhotra in a follow-up article.[10] His critique came to the attention of the editors of the international Hindu magazine *Hinduism Today,* and subsequently they too published a critique of the *JAAR* issue (see *Hinduism Today* 2001).

Particularly since the year 2000, influencing the presentation of Hinduism and Indian history in U.S. textbooks and within academia has become an important goal of many Hindu American groups. Hindu activists bombard scholars who are viewed as being critical of any aspect of Hinduism or of India with hostile e-mails[11] and have even gone to the extent of contacting the administration of their universities in an attempt to get them dismissed from their academic positions or to prevent them from being hired.[12] Supporters are also sent to attend public presentations on Hinduism and India, to dispute presentations or books that do not fit in with Hinducentric conceptions of history. Details regarding the presentation and the response of the scholars to the questions are then circulated within activist Hindu circles and the wider Hindu American community through e-mail bulletins, opinion pieces on Hindu Web sites, and Indian American newspapers. The e-zine *Sulekha.com* has featured several articles critical of Hinduism scholars in the United States.

The Kali's Child *Controversy*

One of the first of such mobilizations was against the book *Kali's Child*, by Jeffrey Kripal, published by the University of Chicago Press in 1995, which won a book award of the American Academy of Religion the same year. Using a psychoanalytical approach, Kripal argues that the mystical and visionary experiences of Ramakrishna, a revered nineteenth-century Bengali Hindu saint, were driven by his conflicted, latent, homoerotic impulses. Many Hindus who came to know about this book were angry and upset. The major fallout in the United States began primarily after 2000, however, when Swami Tyagananda, a member of the Ramakrishna order and the Hindu chaplain at Harvard University, produced a long, meticulously argued tract entitled *Kali's Child Revisited or Didn't Anyone Check the Documentation* (now archived at the Web site of the Infinity Foundation), which was distributed at the annual meeting of the AAR that year. Tyagananda argued that many of Kripal's interpretations were based on his lack of understanding of the nuances of Bengali language and culture. In 2001 a group of Hindu activists wrote to the religion department at the University of Chicago (where Kripal had written his dissertation on Ramakrishna) to protest the book and the role of the department in its development. In the spring of 2002, other Hindu groups also contacted the administration at Rice University (where Kripal was a candidate for a position) in an attempt to prevent him from being hired.[13] *Kali's Child* was additionally critiqued in the first issue of the Indian journal *Evam* (2002) and in several articles on *Sulekha.com.*

Although Kripal responded to his critics in each of these venues, his responses failed to satisfy Hindu American activists.

Attacks against Religions in South Asia Scholars

The Religions in South Asia (RISA) subsection of the American Academy of Religion, in response to criticisms from Hindu activists that became particularly pronounced after the events of 9/11, organized a panel entitled "Defamation/Anti-Defamation: Hindus in Dialogue with the Western Academy" at the annual American Academy of Religion meetings in November 2001. Malhotra, who was invited to be on the panel (as a representative of "practicing Hindus"), criticized what he characterized as the "five asymmetries in the dialog of civilizations" in his presentation and accused American scholars of Hinduism of "denying agency and rights to non-westerners," of "academic arson" or the "age-old 'plunder while you denigrate the source' process," and of "intimidating name-calling to effect censorship," concluding with the demand that Hindus in the diaspora be included as "dialog representatives" in a joint study of the tradition.[14]

The "tipping point" in the relationship between "the academic and faith community," according to the religious studies scholar Arvind Sharma (2004, 5), came in September 2002, when an article by Rajiv Malhotra (2002c) entitled "RISA Lila—1: Wendy's Child Syndrome" (the term "Lila" in Hinduism conventionally refers to divine play or the sport of the gods) was published on *Sulekha.com* and was widely read (it received over 20,000 hits). In the article, Malhotra launched a blistering attack against religious studies scholars such as Wendy Doniger of the University of Chicago (whom he refers to as the "Queen of Hinduism"), and others like Sarah Caldwell, Jeffrey Kripal, and Paul Courtright who adopt a psychoanalytical approach to the study of Hindu deities and saints. With quotations from the most sensational of such passages in each of their works to illustrate his arguments, Malhotra argued that the Freudian psychoanalytical approach had been discredited even among Western psychologists, that religious studies scholars had no training in psychoanalysis, and furthermore that the approach was not valid when it was applied to non-Western subjects. Claiming that Hinduism scholars want to "demonize it [Hinduism], in order to create Hindu shame amongst the youth," (Malhotra 2002c, 15), Malhotra continues, "history shows that genocides have been preceded by the denigration of the victims. . . . The time has come to ask: Are certain 'objective' scholars consciously conspiring, or unconsciously driven by their Eurocentric essences, to pave the way for a future genocide of a billion or more Hindus . . . ?" (ibid.). The article also included a brief discussion of the treatment of the elephant-headed deity Ganesha by Paul Courtright, which, as we shall see, became the basis for a series of subsequent events.

Another article on *Sulekha.com* later that month examined the article on Hinduism in Microsoft Corporation's Encarta encyclopedia (2002), written by Wendy Doniger. The author of the article, Sankrant Sanu, one of the advisors of the Infinity Foundation, argued, with excerpts from the respective articles, that Doniger's article on Hinduism was unsympathetic and negative, in contrast to the articles on

Islam and Christianity in the encyclopedia, which were respectful and positive in tone. Subsequently, in 2003, the Hindu American community was successful in getting Encarta to replace Doniger's article with an article on Hinduism by Arvind Sharma, professor of religion at McGill University and a practicing Hindu.

In the spring of 2003 the appointment of the well-known Indian historian Romila Thapar as the first holder of the Kluge Chair in Countries and Cultures of the South at the Library of Congress was announced. The announcement immediately provoked a flurry of activity within Hindu American discussion groups. A petition was circulated against her appointment, alleging that according such an honor to Thapar was a "great travesty," since she was a Marxist and an anti-Hindu who was engaged in a "war of cultural genocide" against Hindu civilization. The signatories numbered over two thousand, and many in their comments used invectives against her. In response, scholars and other intellectuals sent letters strongly supporting Thapar's appointment. The anti-Thapar petition had no impact on the decision by the Library of Congress, but Internet discussion groups provided details on the heckling Thapar received during her public talks in the United States.

The Courtright Issue

On October 6, 2003, a petition against the book *Ganesha: Lord of Obstacles, Lord of Beginnings,* by Paul Courtright of Emory University, launched by a Hindu group in Louisiana, started circulating on the Internet. Ganesha, the popular elephant-headed Hindu deity, is regarded with much affection by his devotees. The first edition of *Ganesha* was published in 1985 by Oxford University Press, but in 2001, an Indian edition was published with a picture of a nude baby Ganesha on the cover (Courtright was not involved in the selection of the picture). The Internet petition objected to the cover of the book and passages that applied a Freudian framework to analyze the stories about Ganesha found in Hindu texts. Excerpting a few of the passages that the authors of the petition considered to be the most offensive (such as the description of Lord Ganesha's trunk as a "displaced phallus" and of the deity as a "eunuch"), the authors demanded that the book be immediately withdrawn from circulation and that the author and publisher offer an apology to Hindus. The petition generated considerable anger in the worldwide Hindu community and received over four thousand signatures in the first few days. The book was quickly withdrawn by the Indian publisher, Motilal Banarsidas. Courtright even received death threats on the Internet site, at which point the petition was withdrawn by its originators. Hindu groups in Atlanta subsequently met with Emory University administrators to demand that the university stop defending Courtright and take action to address the misrepresentations in his book and, more broadly, to oversee the way academics portrayed other cultures and religions.[15] The Courtright issue was discussed in an article in the *Washington Post* (Vedantam 2004a),[16] and the book also came under severe attack on e-zines such as *Sulekha.com* (e.g., Agarwal and Venkat 2003a,b; Sanu 2003).

The issue of the academic portrayal of religion was taken up in a November 2003 roundtable at the American Academy of Religion, entitled "Creating Bridges: Dharma

Traditions and the Academy." The roundtable was organized by the Dharma Association of North America (DANAM), an organization discussed in chapter 7. According to one published report, the roundtable provoked a heated discussion, with RISA scholars agreeing that a "fair, respectful and thorough representation of their culture is 'non-negotiable' to Hindus in North America." They also insisted, however, that "respect for tenure and free exchange of ideas for the professors was just as 'non-negotiable.'" The report indicates that the latter point was "strongly countered" by Balagangadhara of the University of Ghent (the newly elected co-chair of the Hinduism unit of the AAR), who apparently argued that "misrepresentation of the Hindu culture to the point of destroying age-old spiritual experience is an act of violence" and that such misrepresentation was "unprofessional, non-negotiable and must stop" (Vijayakar 2003, A6).

The California Textbook Controversy

Hindu American mobilization against school textbooks began in the fall of 2004, when the school district in Fairfax, Virginia, put forward a new set of world history textbooks for public review. Hindu parents mobilized and were relatively successful in making some changes in the way Indian history was taught in their district. One textbook was rejected and eight others were revised (Glod 2005). Encouraged by this success, Hindu American groups decided to organize and turn their attention to school textbooks in other regions of the country. In the summer of 2005, the California State Board of Education opened up its process of textbook review for sixth-grade social studies to the public. Two Hindu American groups—the Vedic Foundation (VF), based in Austin, Texas, and the Hindu Education Foundation (HEF), a group made up of members from around the country and India—participated in the review process. The efforts of the VF and the HEF were backed by the Hindu American Foundation (HAF). The VF–HEF combine proposed more than 117 edits to the content on India and Hinduism covered by the books. Some of the edits corrected blatant errors or gratuitous insults, but the changes that became controversial fell into one of four categories paralleling objections that Hindu leaders had already been publicizing in the United States. First, material referring to the plurality of deities, beliefs, and forms of worship in Hinduism was redacted and the texts were revised to portray Hinduism as a monotheistic religion based on Vedic texts. Second, the caste system was dissociated from Hinduism, its hereditary nature was not mentioned, and passages describing its oppressive nature were modified. Third, references to patriarchy or the unequal treatment of women were erased. Finally, the Aryan invasion/migration argument was dismissed as having been "disproved" by contemporary evidence. Ninety-one of these edits were originally accepted by the curriculum commission, and these edits were to be presented and ratified at a meeting on November 9. In early November, however, an Indian graduate student in California, who had been approached by the Vedic Foundation for a signature for its petition, had notified Michael Witzel, professor of Sanskrit and Indian studies at Harvard University, and one of his coauthors, Steve Farmer, about the attempts of the groups to "rewrite" the textbooks. Witzel and Farmer spread word of the matter to other scholars of India via the Internet. On November 8, Witzel sent a letter to the California Board of Education with signatures from forty-six other prominent academics specializing in Indian studies. The letter urged the board to reject many of the edits proposed by the Hindu groups, since they were "not of a scholarly but of a religious-political nature . . . primarily promoted by Hindutva supporters." Witzel also pointed out that the same revisions that the Hindu groups were trying to make in California textbooks had been temporarily inserted in textbooks in India when the BJP was in power and had since been removed when that government had been voted out of power. Various Indian American groups—both those supportive of the edits and those opposed to the efforts of the VF-HEF-HAF combine (opponents included both scholars and secular Indian American and Dalit groups)—mobilized their respective constituencies. Through a spate of articles on Internet Web sites, discussion groups, newspapers, and magazines, both sides tried to get their views heard by a wider public. Articles by secular Indian American groups meticulously traced and publicized the links between the Vedic Foundation, Hindu Education Foundation, Hindu American Foundation, and Hindutva groups in the United States and India and denounced the changes as trying to promulgate a sanitized view of history, deny oppression, and argue that non-Hindus were outsiders (IPAC 2006; Maira and Swamy 2006). Groups supportive of the VF, HEF, and HAF denounced the scholars, secular Indian Americans, and Dalit groups as "anti-Hindu." They argued that the treatment of Hinduism in the California textbooks did not comply with the standards set by the California State Board of Education and that Hindus were merely demanding that Hinduism be treated with the same consideration and respect as other groups (Malhotra and Jhunjhunwala 2006, 2). Several of the pro-Hindu writers pointed out that Jewish, Muslim, and Christian traditions were presented respectfully, from the point of view of the practitioners of the religion, and even erroneously. In contrast, they argued that the treatment of Hinduism in the textbooks was so biased and focused on the negative that it was causing grievous psychological harm to Hindu American children (ibid. 2; Venkat 2005). Members of the California State Board of Education found themselves caught in the cross-fire between the two sides. After a series of public and private meetings, they finally voted to overturn most of the contentious changes proposed by the VF-HEF (but accepted the uncontroversial changes that had the support of both sides). In response, the Hindu American Foundation and an association of Hindu parents in California filed suit against the California State Board.

In early September 2006, the judge overseeing the case ruled that "the challenged texts comply with the applicable legal standards" for materials on religious and historical subject matter. But he also ruled that the California board had not complied with the regulations governing the textbook approval process and that it needed to prepare more detailed regulations for future textbook adoptions. On the basis of this ruling both sides claimed a victory. South Asian groups opposed to the edits pointed to the fact that the judge discussed and rejected each of the Hindu group's substantive challenges to the current texts; the Hindu American Foundation contended that the court had recognized procedural irregularities in the way the edits proposed by the Hindu groups had been challenged by the South Asian academics.

SOUTH ASIAN STUDIES VERSUS BRAND INDIA

Another long-standing emotional issue within the Indian American community is whether Indians should identify and be classified as "South Asians" in the United States. Those who argue for a South Asian identity make the case that forming coalitions to address common issues is advantageous to Indian Americans, who are minorities in this country. They argue that there are many cultural similarities between individuals of South Asian background and that in this country they also face common concerns and similar treatment as "brown-skinned" individuals. They also point out that policymakers do not see differences among South Asian groups. Though agreeing that there are many fundamental issues on which individuals belonging to different South Asian countries do not see eye to eye, they argue that it is still possible to forge alliances by understanding and respecting these differences (see Kurien 2003).

Hindu and Indic activists, however, have long been unhappy with this classification. Members of such groups describe themselves as proud Hindus and patriotic Indians who are trying to build community solidarity and inculcate individual and collective pride on the basis of an identity and culture that is thousands of years old. They maintain that it is disadvantageous for India to be lumped together with the other countries in South Asia, since India is much ahead of these countries in size and in terms of social and economic indicators. They further argue that the cultural and political gulf between members of these countries is too vast to bridge. Thus these groups contend that instead of trying to ignore these cleavages, Indian Americans ought to educate their children and the wider American society about the fundamental differences between the countries in South Asia. They characterize members of South Asian organizations as anti-Hindu and anti-Indian, a "deracinated group" with very little knowledge about Indian history and culture, who have bought into the "artificial" U.S. State Department construct of a homogeneous subcontinent (R. Rao 2003; Srinivasan 2000).

In a series of articles on *Rediff.com* between December 2003 and January 2004, Rajiv Malhotra (2003c,d, 2004a,b) elaborated on this latter viewpoint. He argued that U.S. universities play an important role in "India's brand positioning" by influencing the perspectives of the media, government, business, education, and Indian American identities, and claimed that compared with other major countries, a positive stance on India is underrepresented in American academia. In his view, this underrepresentation derived from South Asian studies programs that were run and staffed by Westerners hostile to Indian interests, by "Indian-American Sepoys," and by Indian Americans wanting to be white (2004a). Describing the latter two groups of Indian Americans as "career opportunists" and "Uncle Toms," he argued that "to become members of the Western Grand Narrative—even in marginal roles—these Indians often sneer at Indian culture in the same manner as colonialists once did" (ibid., 4). Thus, according to Malhotra, South Asian studies was undermining India by promoting "a perspective on India using worldviews which are hostile to India's interests" (2003c, 2),[17] and Indian American donors were being "hoodwinked" (ibid., 6) into thinking that they were supporting India through their monetary contributions to such programs.

Specifically, Malhotra referred to the "identities of victimhood with other Indians depicted as culprits" that he argued South Asianists promoted (2003c, 5).[18] He claimed that such scholarship undermined India "by encouraging paradigms that oppose its unity and integrity" (ibid.) and that South Asian scholars also played "critical roles, often under the garb of 'human rights' in channeling foreign intellectual and material support to exacerbate India's internal cleavages" such as the insurgencies in various parts of the country and the lower-caste movements (2004b, 3). Pointing out that 9/11 was unanticipated by South Asian scholars who were focused on Hindutva but not on the Taliban, Malhotra argued that there was a real chance that under a series of crises, separatist movements could tear India apart "with Indian-American sepoys abetting the process," which in turn could lead to the Talibanization of India and to the subsequent Talibanization of other Asian countries (ibid., 4). In addition to being devastating for the South Asian region, such a Talibanization would also have harmful consequences for the United States. Consequently the "divisive scholarship" (2004b) of South Asian studies was also "detrimental to U.S. strategic interests" (2004a, 1). Malhotra indicated that his goal in getting involved in the U.S. academy was to "reposition India's brand" by "challenging the India-bashing club" (2003c, 5) and emphasizing India's positive contributions. He concluded by calling for a "re-imagining [of] India" (2004b, 5) as a major partner of the United States, and for changing the depictions of India by "retraining" South Asian scholars in the new paradigm (ibid., 6).

In an article published in *Sulekha.com* in 2005 entitled "Geopolitics and Sanskrit Phobia," Malhotra goes on to develop the argument made by the Hindutva leader Savarkar ([1923] 1969, 92), about the importance of Sanskrit to "Sanskriti," or the common culture shared by Hindus. Calling South Asianist scholars who argued that Sanskrit frameworks were elitist and brahminical "house Indians," Malhotra repeats the charge that by denigrating Sanskrit, the scholars were also attacking Sanskriti or Indian culture, an attack "which might feed the subversion of sovereignty" of the country (Malhotra 2005, 30). Although Malhotra has repeatedly defined himself as a "non-Hindutva Hindu" and has sometimes spoken critically of the strategies pursued by Sangh Parivar groups in India, in this article he argues that even the anti-Hindutva position of South Asian scholars was antinational, because "underneath the attack on Hindutva lies a broader attack on Indian Sanskriti, and this, in turn, feeds the pipeline of separatist tendencies" (ibid., 22). Responding to a question about "non-Indic religions" and Sanskriti in the discussion following the article, Malhotra (comment posted on July 21, 2005) goes on to assert that "Islam/ Christianity become a part of Indian Sanskriti when they are disconnected from foreign nexuses. But they remain a foreign base in India as long as they derive their legitimacy, funding, appointments, authority etc. from other nexuses." We have seen that the FHA also similarly argued that under Hindutva, mosques and churches in India would not be allowed to obtain foreign resources. (This argument is often made by the Sangh Parivar about Christianity and Islam in India, and it too exhorts these religions to "indigenize.") It is interesting that Hindu American organizations and leaders who take this position with respect to minority religions in India would not accept such restrictions on Hinduism in the United States In fact, as we have seen, many of these organizations are actively forging links with Indian groups, institutions, and ideologies to legitimize their position as Hindu American representatives.

Conclusion

In this chapter we see the often simultaneous use of the model-minority and oppressed-minority discourses by Hindu American leaders in their quest for a place for Hindus in America's multicultural society. Although it may be too early to say what type of long-term effect Hindu American mobilization will have, Hindu American leaders have made significant headway in having their concerns heard by the entertainment industry, businesses, news media, and to some extent even by governmental institutions. Scholars specializing in Hinduism and India studies have been the particular targets of Hindu American ire. Several of the issues raised by Hindu leaders in this context are certainly important—intellectually, culturally, and socially. Undeniable Eurocentric biases in the academy that need to be corrected, and many remarkable Indian achievements of the past and present ought to be more widely acknowledged. Hindus and Indians should be able to take justifiable pride in their heritage, and Hindus should have the same right to a more positive portrayal of Hinduism as the practitioners of other religious traditions. At the same time, the effectiveness of the critiques launched by Hindu leaders are often diminished by their lack of understanding of the goals of the humanities and the social sciences as well as the organization of these disciplines, by the tendency of many of these leaders to indulge in sweeping generalizations and unsubstantiated allegations, and by their narrow view of Hinduism and their Hinducentric perspective of India.

The adoption of many elements of the Hindutva discourse by this group, such as the denigration of Abrahamic traditions, the aggrandization of Hinduism, and the diatribes against secularism and secular scholars, is a matter of particular concern. The reverse triumphalism of the Hindu American leaders and the fetishization of the doctrine of indigenousness (both of which can also be found in the Hindutva ideology) only undermine the demand for pluralism and for rights as new citizens of the United States. It is indeed an irony that Hindus who are arguing for a multiculturalist conception of American identity on the basis of its changing history and the backgrounds of the groups that form the nation should be simultaneously promoting a chauvinistic Indic-centrism based on a civilization that flourished in a section of northwestern India thousands of years ago. This conception of India ignores how its identity and culture has been irrevocably shaped by the variety of groups and cultures that have been part of the country for millennia, as well as the experiences of the past five thousand years.

As the numbers of immigrants increase in the United States and as the children of such immigrants grow to adulthood, there will undoubtedly be more challenges to American academia like those presented by Hindu Americans, particularly to humanities and social science scholarship dealing with non-Western traditions. How these challenges will be met and addressed will be crucial in determining the future contours of American society and culture.

PART III

The Relationship between Popular and Official Hinduism

CHAPTER 10

Being Young, Brown, and Hindu

STUDENT ORGANIZATIONS

Post-1965 immigrants have been challenging established American conceptions of race and ethnicity, since many of them hail from areas of the world where groups are categorized on the basis of very different criteria. For instance, many Hispanics and South Asians resist being located on the black-white racial axis (Bailey 2001; Kibria 1998), and Caribbean immigrants challenge conventional American definitions of blackness (Butterfield 2004). The implications of the new immigration for traditional American notions of race and ethnicity have been the subject of several studies (Bean and Stevens 2003, 224–249; Smelser, Wilson, and Mitchell 2001). Children of the post-1965 immigrants (termed the "new second generation"), whose patterns of sociocultural and economic incorporation will be pivotal in determining the racial and ethnic profile of the United States in the future, have been described as a "crucial cohort" to study (Mollenkopf, Kasinitz, and Waters 1995, 3), and much of the recent literature on immigrant incorporation has focused on this group (Kibria 2002; Portes and Rumbaut 2001; Rumbaut and Portes 2001; Waters 1999; Zhou and Bankston 1998).

This chapter is based on a case study of a Hindu Student Council (HSC) chapter at "Western University" in Southern California, and looks at how the attempts of second-generation Indian Americans to deal with issues of race and identity brought many of them to the organization but also produced conflicts and cleavages within it. Because Indian American youth are located at the interstices of conventional American categories of race and ethnicity, an examination of their identity choices and struggles demonstrates how and why these categories are often inadequate to understand the experiences of contemporary immigrants and their children. In addition, by overlooking the role of religious institutions in immigrant incorporation, the dominant sociological models of this process ignore the complex interplay between race, ethnicity, and religion in the identity construction of second-generation Americans. After providing a theoretical background, I discuss why the particular HSC chapter was formed and the goals of its founders, followed by an overview of the organization and its membership. Field observations of the discussions held in the organization, in-depth interviews, and an analysis of the group's Internet forum all help to elucidate the central concerns of the membership and the schisms within the group.

The literature on immigrant integration into the United States has generally distinguished between two models of immigrant incorporation—the "ethnic" model, characteristic of European immigrants who eventually were able to reconcile or merge their ethnic identity with their American identity, and the experiences of "colonized" racial minorities, whose racial identities had prevented them from becoming successfully incorporated into the American mainstream (Blauner 1994; Kibria 2002; Ogbu and Gibson 1991; Omi and Winant 1986). The "segmented assimilation" framework that currently dominates the sociological literature on post-1965 immigrant incorporation is an attempt to synthesize both of these models by recognizing the existence of several patterns (Portes and Rumbaut 2001; Waters 1999; Zhou 1997). Most scholars working within this tradition acknowledge that the "ethnic" model of the earlier wave of European immigrants who were able to successfully assimilate into the mainstream is probably not appropriate for the current wave of largely nonwhite immigrants, since racialization is likely to make such assimilation more difficult. Thus Alejandro Portes and Rubén Rumbaut (2001, 44–69) argue that the most successful strategy for such second-generation Americans to follow is a process of "selective acculturation," whereby they incorporate themselves into mainstream society while retaining some of their parents' culture and remaining embedded in family and community networks (which provide a shield against racism and help achieve upward mobility).

Portes and Rumbaut (2001, 284) contrast this selective acculturation with what they describe as "reactive ethnicity," a process wherein the home-country culture and traditions are reaffirmed and acquire a heightened significance as a self-defense mechanism against marginalization and discrimination. They maintain that although reactive ethnicization has positive collective consequences, such as the empowerment of the group, the individual consequences are less positive, because the adversarial stance toward mainstream society and its institutions can result in downward mobility. These authors conclude that selective acculturation is a better route to success (ibid., 284–285).

The multiculturalist context in the United States is crucial to understanding the process of identity formation of second-generation American youth. As we have seen, multiculturalism legitimizes the expression not only of "heritage preservation" and "ethnic pride" but also of "ethnic victimization" among minority groups (Berbrier 1998, 2002). In other words, using the segmented assimilation framework, we can see that multiculturalism encourages the development of a strategy of selective acculturation, whereby groups use a celebratory model-minority discourse of ethnic pride to maintain aspects of their ethnic culture. But multiculturalism also encourages the development of a reactive ethnicity, based on an adversarial, oppressed-minority discourse of ethnic victimization. The possibility that groups might develop dual or mixed strategies has not been adequately taken into account by the segmented assimilation model, and thus the causes and consequences of sociocultural and economic incorporation may be more complex and contradictory than the model suggests.

Sunaina Maira (2002) argues that Hinduism and "Indianness" become significant for second-generation Hindu Indian Americans in part because of the ethnic segregation on college campuses and in part because of a multiculturalism that demands a performance of authenticity. For these reasons, ethnic campus organizations play a signification role in identity formation. In such groups, Hindu Indian American college students hailing from a variety of subcultural backgrounds are faced with the challenge of constructing unitary versions of Indianness and Hinduness. These constructions are often somewhat different from those of the first generation. I found that secular ethnic associations of Indian Americans only organized social events and cultural programs a few times a year, compared with religious organizations, which met much more frequently and were also more study- and discussion-oriented. Thus I decided to focus on a religious organization, the Hindu Student Council, for my research. We will see how racism and the pressures of campus multiculturalism led the contrary discourses of Hindu American leaders discussed in previous chapters to develop within the HSC at Western University.

I chose a chapter of the HSC, rather than an independent campus organization, both because the HSC was a national organization and because it was linked to the VHPA. Some scholars have argued that many of the Hindu American youth who attend the VHPA's youth camps or are part of the HSC are drawn to the organization in their search for "roots" and are unaware of its political agenda (Mathew and Prashad 2000; McKean 1993; Rajagopal 2000). My goal was to see what Hinduism meant for the second generation and what, if any, influence the Hindutva movement had on them.

I attended the weekly discussion meetings and some of the other activities of the Western University HSC for a semester in the early 2000s. I introduced myself and my project at the first meeting of the semester, and most members seemed to be enthusiastic and pleased that their club had been chosen to be studied. I told them that besides attending the meetings, I would also be conducting in-depth interviews with "as many members as possible" and passed around a sheet asking for volunteers. Practically everyone in the room that day signed up (twenty-seven students) but because of scheduling difficulties and lack of time (mine and theirs) I was only able to conduct in-depth, audiotaped interviews of at least an hour each with twelve of its regular attendees, chosen to obtain a diversity of backgrounds and viewpoints. However, I talked to several more students informally during the semester. At the last meeting that I attended, I distributed a short survey with questions about the reasons for attending meetings and members' involvement in the different types of HSC activities, definitions of identity, and finally whether and how they kept in touch with current events in India. I received twenty-two surveys back. I also monitored the group's Web site and Internet discussion forum for almost two years, until it was closed down. This combination of methodologies helped me to gain a much better understanding of the central dynamics of the organization and the contradictions and schisms within it than I would otherwise have been able to observe. To supplement this primary case study, I conducted brief studies of two other Hindu student clubs (another branch of the HSC, and an independent, campus-specific organization). I attended a few meetings of these two clubs, talked to students informally, and interviewed the leadership (four students in all).

Western University HSC meetings were held from 6 to 7 P.M. every Tuesday in a classroom at the international center. Between fifteen and forty people attended every week during the period that I attended. Most attendees were university undergraduates who were second-generation Indian Americans from Hindu families, but several students from Jain backgrounds were also regular and active members. Two or three graduate students attended the meetings as well, including one regular member who was an economics student from India. There was a sprinkling of non-Indian students. Most of the time, there were about equal numbers of male and female members.

The meetings were organized and moderated by the two young women who were co-chairs for the year, Meena and Sheetal, and the discussion each week focused on a different issue. Meena and Sheetal would introduce the topic by summarizing an article or the central issue and would then facilitate the ensuing discussion. Some of the topics discussed in the semester that I attended included "the Hindu male"; an article (downloaded from the Internet) entitled "Why I Am Not a South Asian"; the concept of "desire" in the *Bhagavad Gita;* "nationalistic dharma"; a discussion of a magazine's write-up on homosexuality in Hinduism; and a presentation on the RSS (Rashtriya Swayamsevak Sangh, the Hindu nationalist organization in India) by some local Hindu activists.

My interviews with members of the HSC typically consisted of two parts. First, I asked them about their involvement with the HSC and the things about the club that they liked and did not like. Following this, I asked them to tell me about themselves and about growing up in the United States, to get a sense of what had brought them to the group. I asked how and when their parents had arrived in the United States; their experiences while growing up, particularly as they related to issues of identity; and religious and cultural practices. I also asked them about their future plans and their views on the Hindu nationalist movement in India.

RACE, MARGINALITY, AND THE TURN TO HINDU ORGANIZATIONS

I began my research with a fascinating conversation with two of the HSC chapter's founders, Ravi and Vijay, at a coffee shop on campus. At that time, the club had been in existence for one and a half years. Both Ravi and Vijay were second-generation Indian American science majors in their senior year. Ravi had already been accepted to law school for the following year, and Vijay was planning to go to graduate school for engineering. I was surprised and pleased to discover that Vijay had been part of the KHO and that I had been to his house to interview his father and his older brother as part of that research. Ravi told me that his involvement in the HSC had served as a "springboard" to found two other related types of campus organizations—a yoga club and a peace club—and to participate in an environmental organization.

Vijay described himself as an "activist" who was involved with the Asian American student organization on campus, as an Indian American representative.

Ravi, who arrived before Vijay, began the conversation by talking about how hard it had been to set up HSC chapters on the West Coast. There were roughly 800 students of Indian ancestry on campus, he said, but only 150 were even on the HSC mailing list. In the Northeast, because of the more established communities, identifying one's Hindu identity was not so problematic. "But here, people are ashamed to come out as Hindus. A few people faced racist comments from their white friends when they did. We can't even have a puja here since people don't want to be associated with 'idol worship.' " Ravi said that one of the main problems was that unlike other religious identities, to be a Hindu was a "vague" identity. "What does it really mean to be a Hindu? Most people haven't a clue." They decided to form the HSC club, organized around a weekly discussion session, so that Hindu students could talk about these issues. The founders of two other Hindu student organizations that I spoke to similarly made clear that the primary reason that they had formed the organizations was the racial and religious marginality experienced by many Hindu students (see also *Hinduism Today* 1997b).[1]

Ravi emphasized that the HSC was trying to create an "inclusive" and "pluralistic" culture and to invite Sikhs and Jains to become part of the club by pointing out that there was as much difference between some Hindu sects as there was between Sikhs and Hindus. "We are trying to convey the message that the Hindu identity is the indigenous Indian identity and that all these religious groups also shared in this identity. But the Sikhs have their own club. This is one problem here—there are so many clubs." He believed that most of these groups, like the Sikh club, were based on a "rejection identity"—an identity resulting from their being rejected by the wider society. But he said that the HSC, in contrast, was trying to create a "positive identity," one that stemmed from a "complete absence of self-hatred." Thus the official goal of that HSC chapter was "to bring to students' attention the glorious cultural/ social spiritual heritage which was Vedic or Hindu culture." Another central goal of the organization was to demonstrate that Hinduism was the indigenous culture of India and needed to be protected to ensure that it did not suffer the obliteration and extinction of many other indigenous cultures around the world. The HSC leadership brought an urgency to their appeal by drawing a parallel between the likely fate of Hindus in India (if the community did not mobilize to aggressively defend Hinduism) and that of Native Americans in the United States today, "who have lost their land, their culture, and their people."

Vijay had joined us by this time and he contrasted the HSC with the South Asian club (SAC), which he described as a "superficial, party club." Both Vijay and Ravi indicated that the SAC was trying to create an identity based on "South Asianness," something that they felt was a "false identity," an artificial and recent academic construct (see Kurien 2003). According to Ravi, the SAC, in its attempt to be inclusive, was swinging very far toward accommodating minorities and their viewpoints. "For instance, there are several Muslims in the club, who have an important voice, since the organizers want to make sure that they feel included. But it is not truly inclusive since they don't have people who are really Hindus. People like myself and Vijay."

Ravi and Vijay indicated that one of their goals for the HSC was to try to "intellectualize Hinduism," and to show that it provides a more holistic vision than the "conventional scientific paradigm" that carves disciplines like biology, quantum mechanics, and philosophy into distinct fields, each governed by different, often conflicting, paradigms. "Whereas in Hinduism . . . you have *ayurveda,* which promotes an integrated body/soul approach to medicine. Again, there are Hindu scholars like Subhash Kak [Kak gave a talk on campus that semester, as part of an HSC lecture tour], who are electrical engineers. They are also neuroscientists, they have a good understanding of physiology. At the same time, they are linguists and they have read the Vedas and they are scholars of the Vedas too. This is the level of integration that we are aiming at."

But they admitted that people in the club were not always open to such ideas. They spoke of their particular frustration with members who constantly drew parallels between Hindu and Judeo-Christian concepts because of their need to validate Indian culture by finding Western parallels. "Like, they will say, in Hinduism we have temples. Here there are churches. Here they have Jesus. There we have Krishna. The thread ceremony is like the confirmation of the Catholics. . . . but they are not parallel concepts at all. What they are doing is forcing parallels between completely different ideas." This need for external validation, according to Ravi and Vijay, stemmed from the self-hatred that many Indian Americans tended to have. "A lot of us internalize the way outside society looks at us—stereotypes that sometimes society imposes on us as minorities." Vijay went on passionately,

> The people I really . . . I won't say dislike . . . but the people I have had the worst experiences with are the people that consider themselves white. Some people tell me, there is no discrimination in America. I tell them, that's great that you haven't experienced any discrimination, but that does not mean it does not exist. Like there is this [Indian American] girl in the HSC, . . . , she has always dated white men. And she was saying, "I don't think I could ever be with an Indian guy." I said, Why? She said, Indian guys never listen. And then I just started laughing because I am like, Wait, first of all, what am I doing right now? And second of all, like in the HSC, the opinion of females is almost more valued than the opinion of males. Are you trying to tell me that if you were among a group of white guys, they would pay any attention to what you said?

Ravi and Vijay said that the students in the HSC who were directly from India were, if anything, even more alienated from their heritage and identity than the students who had been brought up in the United States. They often tended to be "iconoclasts for their own culture": "They are constantly bringing up the negative things about Hinduism. But if we even bring up something about some of the violence done in the name of religion in north India [by Muslims], the kids that came straight from India would be like, No, I don't believe it." The two co-founders said that they were then accused of being "right wing, hateful, fascist." Such accusations

made their relationship with the group "difficult." They were, they said, "just talking from our hearts about these ideas. And automatically, people are conditioned to
brand it a certain way."

Vijay talked at some length about the sociopolitical agenda of the organization.
He said that they wanted to "provide a club where we could examine ourselves, the
ideas and patterns that Hindu Americans have, and at the same time, work toward
social change, social justice." As an example of the activist orientation of the club,
he mentioned that they supported the cause of the Hindus in Kashmir, and that
they had joined the "*Xena* rally" in front of Universal Studios to protest the use of
Hindu deities in an episode of that television series. He said that members of the
club had become a big presence in campus activist circles, for instance, within the
Asian Pacific Students' organization, where Indian Americans had been underrepresented. Vijay indicated that HSC members were trying to raise the consciousness
of the student body to Indian American concerns. Two of the issues that he mentioned were the biases in historical accounts of India and the neglect of Indians
within Asian and Asian American studies programs. But the group was also trying
to raise the consciousness of Indian American students on campus regarding the
negative stereotypes about minorities that many in the community had. "We grow
up here as upper-middle-class kids and we tend to gloss over injustice. We don't see
that a lot of things that affect other minorities affect us as well, or will affect us in
the future as the immigration patterns get spread out. So we fall into this whole
model-minority pattern." For instance, Indian Americans often tended to be against
affirmative action, feeling that it hurt them. Vijay indicated that he was a strong
supporter of affirmative action and that he was trying to show Indian Americans
that though it might sometimes hurt them when it came to college admissions, it
does help in the workplace, "where discrimination against Indians is a reality."

Toward the end of the discussion, I asked Ravi and Vijay about their opinion of
the Hindu nationalist movement and whether they were in touch with what was
going on in India. Both said that they were not really in touch, but Vijay went on to
say, "The Hindu nationalist movement, because it is political in nature, it's going to
have certain political flaws. But the thing is that it isn't really calling for the expulsion
of Muslims or Christians or espousing violence. It is calling for an understanding
of the cultural ethos of India." Ravi continued, "It's really crazy that the movement
in India is being compared to the Nazi movement. It's sick." Vijay added, "Because
it's like, who are the victims of genocide. Who was the violence perpetuated [*sic*]
against. It's not against the minorities in India, that's for sure [he means that most
of the violence has been against Hindus] . . . there are some exceptions and all that,
but, really, no way."

Choosing my words carefully, I asked them about many Hindu Americans in the
United States who strongly emphasized the need for the Hindu Indian community
to maintain its culture and distinctness within this country, while at the same time
demanding that Muslims and Christians in India assimilate to Hindu culture. Both
Ravi and Vijay countered by arguing that the situations were not analogous, because
the "culture" that is now defined as "American" is not the indigenous culture.

So there was no legitimacy in the white American demand that minorities assimilate, because, they argued, "this is a land which is not, quote, theirs."

Keshav, a young man in the HSC who had come up to me after the first meeting to declare that "Hinduism is my passion," stated that there was a need for a group like the HSC which emphasized pride in Hinduism. Many Indian Americans, he said, have an "inferiority complex and are ashamed or scared" to express a Hindu identity because they feel that there is a stigma associated with being Hindu. He went on, "You know how in this society, Hinduism is associated with twelve armed gods and such." Chandan, the graduate student from India, made a similar point, saying that in his opinion, "Non-Christians in the U.S. are forced to act and behave as if they are white Christians. Because that is the only way you can get accepted in the society here. These people, all their lives, have never had the opportunity to think in public, in school, that they are Hindus. So this is a terrific forum for the resurgence of Hindu pride in them. Now a lot of these people go out and say, Hey, you know, I am Hindu."

These accounts indicate that experiences with racial and religious marginalization in the "wider society" drew members to the Hindu Student Council in search of a supportive community within which they could "learn about Hinduism and Indian culture," "build friendships," and experience a sense of empowerment. The secular South Asian club was not able to meet this need, being "too superficial" and party oriented, and thus these students turned to the Hindu Student Council. Yet, as we will see, the same issues of racialization and identity that brought them to the Hindu Student Council also produced fundamental cleavages within the group.

THE FACTIONS

When talking about things in the HSC that they did not like, every member that I interviewed referred to the increasing polarization between the two subgroups in the club. On the one hand there was the subgroup that was referred to variously as "hard core," "extremist," and "anti-Muslim" or as "pro-Hindu" and "pro-tradition," depending on which side was characterizing it. The other group was described as "moderate," "silent majority," "we should all get along" or "wishy-washy" and "passive," again depending on whether the person describing the group was a sympathizer or an opponent. Members indicated that this was a "split beyond the club," in that it also determined "who hung out with whom" outside the club. There was general agreement that the moderate group constituted the majority of the members of the club, but that those in the pro-Hindu group were "more knowledgeable" and therefore dominated the weekly discussions and, to a lesser extent, the Internet forum.

The clearly identifiable members (and those who self-identified as falling into this category) of the "pro-Hindu" group included the three co-founders of the club (Ravi, Vijay, and Atul), Ravi's two cousins (Kumar and Gopi), and a young woman, Preeti (who was elected as one of the chairpersons for the third year, and who was dating Atul). Another member, Alok, a young man of Jain heritage, self-identified as falling into this category. A few other men in the HSC who did not speak up at the meetings were also identified as being part of this group. So all the visible members of this faction, with the exception of Preeti, were male, and a substantial number were from south Indian Brahmin backgrounds.

Preeti told me passionately that she believed strongly that her generation had to hold on to its "awesome" and "amazing" tradition, because otherwise it would be lost to the next generation. She continued, "I think it is not doing it [tradition] justice if we assimilate into Western culture, which isn't really a culture. It's a blending of lots of different cultures. If you don't hold on to tradition, it becomes something that the Western media just commercializes. For instance, I find it so sacrilegious to see Ganesha on a T-shirt. If we let go of our religion, then people are going to wear our gods on T-shirts, on purses and skirts, and it becomes like nothing. It trivializes everything that our ancestors fought for." She said that the pro-Hindu group within HSC was not necessarily anti-Muslim, but that they "very much recognized the fact that Muslims have caused a lot of harm to Hindus. That right now in Kashmir, millions of Hindus are being killed."

Chandan, the graduate student from India, disputed Preeti's characterization of the pro-Hindu group and described a few people in the club as "fanatics." "If they had the power, they would make India a Hindu country, get rid of all the Muslims, whatever it took. . . . They have very militant ideologies." He added, "They don't say it directly but it seeps through." But, he pointed out, the most extremist views were generally expressed on the Internet discussion forum by people who used pseudonyms such as "Hindu fanatic." Who exactly these people were seemed to be a mystery to the HSC members with whom I spoke. The forum was accessible to outsiders, and so it is likely that some of the messages were posted by individuals who were not members of the club. At the same time, it was clear from the references in the messages that many of the people who used pseudonyms (including "Hindu fanatic") were insiders who had been present at the weekly meetings and knew the members of the HSC well. Were they part of the silent majority? Or were they part of the vocal minority who wrote under their own names but perhaps also under fictitious names? That was the mystery. Whoever these members were, they seemed to feel that they could not adopt some positions publicly.

The pro-Hindu group viewed the moderates as people who "don't know very much," who were "not really into religion," and who were trying to be "white." Preeti described them a little sarcastically as a group that felt "we should all get along, let's all just assimilate into Western culture." She complained that this faction seemed to be in the HSC only for social reasons. The pro-Hindu members wanted a club that focused primarily on discussing Hinduism and said that they did not like the more "cultural" turn the HSC had taken in the second year. From my survey, however, this opinion seemed to be held only by a minority, since only three students indicated that they preferred the religious discussions to the cultural. The majority (thirteen out of twenty-two) indicated that they liked both the religious and the cultural discussions equally.

Most of the people who identified themselves as "moderate," such as Meena, Sheetal, Rashmi, Chandan, Rekha, and Anita (all women, except for Chandan), or who separated themselves from the "extremist" group, readily admitted that they were not very well informed about Hinduism. But they said that they were in the club precisely for this reason, to learn about Hindu religion and culture. Chandan mentioned that he was one of those who vocally opposed the views of the "hard-core" group by constantly bringing up counterevidence from his knowledge and experience of India.

Although only a few members referred to it directly, a gender cleavage in the group was also evident. The group had started off as largely male, and had focused on philosophical discussions. More female members joined later, as the club got involved in sociocultural activities. When I asked the women why for two years in a row, the leadership had been predominantly female, even though it was still the males who dominated the discussions, all of them indicated that while the men were willing to "sit around and talk," they did not want to do any of the work that running and maintaining the club required (the men, on the other hand, just put it down to their being too busy or the women's being "more popular"). For instance, Preeti said acidly, "guys are all talk and no action" and went on to point out that it was always the women who ended up staying up late and working on the projects. "Like, we had this award ceremony and we had to turn in all these applications, and it was the girls who did all the work, except for Ashish." Sheetal similarly pointed out that a lot of work that went into running the club was "activities planning and things like that. Not to make stereotypes, but I think it is that girls are more interested in doing and organizing things whereas the guys are more interested in just discussing issues." Preeti, though she identified herself as being part of the "pro-Hindu" group, publicly disagreed with many of the things that people like Ravi and Vijay said (whereas the men in the pro-Hindu group generally supported and reinforced one another during the discussions), particularly when it came to issues like the status of women in Hindu or Indian culture. Several of the men in the group that I talked to indicated that they were upset at the way many of the women seemed to accept Western stereotypes about Indian women and always brought up negative examples at the meetings.

When it came to other potential cleavages such as caste, language, and region of origin in India, however, it seemed that the members of the club had managed to overcome many of the divisions of their parents' generation, since most indicated that these were not issues of importance to them.

From the comments of Preeti, Ravi, and Vijay, we see that one of the key issues differentiating the pro-Hindu and the moderate members of the organization was their view regarding the location of Hindu Indian Americans within the wider American society. All three characterized the moderates disparagingly as those who were "trying to be white" or to "assimilate" into American culture and who did not know about or value their Hindu identity enough to resist assimilation pressures. Preeti, who said, "I believe strongly that if our generation doesn't hold on to it [tradition], our children won't have it," expresses a fear of cultural and religious extinction as one of the reasons that she is motivated to adopt her pro-tradition position, a viewpoint echoed by her boyfriend, Atul, as well. The pro-Hindu group's characterization of the moderate members as those who did not "value" their Hindu identity is at odds with statements by the moderates, who made it clear that they had joined the HSC to learn more about Hinduism because they thought it was important to know about their heritage. Thus both groups saw Hinduness as a positive identity to be valued and preserved, but what differentiated the pro-Hindu group was its use of an adversarial, oppressed-minority discourse. Ravi, Vijay, and Keshav spoke about the "self-hatred" and the "inferiority complex" that racialization produces, and Preeti referred to the group's awareness that Muslims had caused "a lot of harm" to Hindus. What accounted for the divergence in the viewpoints of the two factions and between the men and women in the group? Why did the pro-Hindu group comprise almost entirely men and the moderate group almost entirely women?

Racialization and Identity Formation: Growing Up Hindu American

The twelve members of Western University's HSC whom I interviewed were all from upper-middle-class, professional families and were children of the "first wave" of contemporary immigrants, who had arrived in the United States between 1960 and 1970. Several students mentioned that they hailed from prominent families in India. However, interesting patterns differentiated the pro-Hindu from the moderate faction.

The Pro-Hindu Group

The men in the pro-Hindu group hailed from families who had emphasized the importance of knowing and practicing Hinduism, and who had been part of a religious or cultural Indian organization in the United States. They had also attended bala vihar classes for at least a few years. The common themes that they brought up in the interview were being conscious of their racial identity; being perceived as "unmanly," passive, and nonviolent (two of them said they were called "Gandhi") because they were Indians; being bombarded by Christian propaganda; and reaching a point where they wanted to learn more about Hinduism. All had read avidly on the subject at that point, seeking out both books and Internet Web sites. Although none kept in touch with what was happening in India on any regular basis, all had some knowledge about the Hindu nationalist movement and spoke positively about it.

In his interview, Ravi stressed several times that he had grown up with a total absence of self-hatred. He indicated that even when he was quite young, "I definitely knew what I was, racially, and religiously, and culturally." Racially, he said that he recognized that he was from India, and had a darker skin and, because of this, had an "affinity to black people." He said that his family was "culturally rich" and had exposed him to a variety of Indian and Western music and literature. His parents followed several cultural and religious practices from India, but unlike most Indian parents, knew what they were doing and could explain the practices to him. He grew up immersed in the Indian culture; his parents would talk to him in

Tamil all the time and his mother "would always trot out these references to heroic people in the Puranas. All the great inspiring stories, like Krishna's." She was able to make them real and show him that these ancient epics had relevance even today.

Ravi continued, saying that since he did not have the "phenomenon of self-hatred," he wouldn't look at Shiva, a purple-skinned god, "and be like, Hey that's strange, Jesus was white so why is my God a different color. I never had that complex. To me it was like white people have their God and I have mine and it's cool. And I *wish* everyone was like that. In my opinion, that's a very enlightened way to be. . . . So instead of struggling to reconcile the two [traditions], I was like, hey, Batman, Superman, I can beat that. I can give you one story from Krishna's life that will just . . . take the crap out of that." Although he had friends from several different backgrounds, his closest friends were and still continued to be Indian American Hindus, because "communication is furthered when you have people with the same interest and background." His mother was involved with the VHP when he was young, and he attended the VHP bala vihar when he was between ten and fifteen years of age. His parents left the VHP during the Ayodhya episode, because they were upset about the violence. But Ravi said that he had subsequently read up on it and had realized that the media had distorted a lot of what had really happened, so "we are all very pro-VHP and -RSS now."

Because Ravi indicated that he had only started thinking about his identity and Hinduism seriously in his late teens, I asked him whether there had been any particular trigger bringing this about. He replied with a half laugh, "I think it probably began when I started getting pulled over by cops all over the place, for no reason at all." Since he had found high school uninteresting, he had also started reading much more on his own. He described going to his school library and reading up on books on India, "about the Aryan invasion of India in 1500 B.C. and about how Krishna and Rama and all of our heroes were mythical characters. How the Mahabharata war was a lie. How the greatest thing that happened to India was when the Mughal invaders came to India and brought culture. And I was reading all of it." Ravi indicated that these were books written by European Indologists. He continued, "I had already read the *Upanishads* and the *Gita*. So, there was no way that you were going to convince me that a bunch of cattle herders that came with light skin and that were beating up on the dark-skinned little indigenous people were the ones that came up with the amazing Vedas. There's no way. It's just ridiculous."

Ravi said that it was at that point that he got himself "a spiritual shovel and started digging." He talked about how he and others in the Hindu movement (which he viewed as the "healing process for India" from the "disease of imperialism") were telling the so-called experts on Indian history, "We don't care what you say. We are going to read these books ourselves and are going to make our own judgments." At the end of the interview, Ravi reiterated a point that he had made earlier, that as second-generation Indians in the United States,

> we have almost a responsibility to be global. We've been blessed by India, we've been blessed by America. We've been blessed by everything. We are a very wealthy,

talented, global community and we should do progressive work and not just be career oriented. Then, that is the full flourishing of Hinduism, the Hindu ethos. And this is not just idealistic mumbo-jumbo. It's really happening. It happened with the Brahmo Samaj, the Arya Samaj. They branched out and look at the amazing work they did, like Ram Mohan Roy and Mahatma Gandhi. They gave rise to India's Independence movement. We are the new Mahatma Gandhis, the Ram Mohan Roys.

Vijay's story was somewhat different. Although he claimed to have always been "spiritual," he said that he got "turned on to Hinduism" only in his second year of college, after two trips to India. The group of friends that he had "hung out with" in his teen years (all non-Indian Americans) had started to break up around the middle of his first year of college, and so by the end of the year, he found himself "rootless." This is when he took a trip to India (after many years without a visit). He said that the trip got him connected to "an Indian method of thinking" and changed him from being "100 percent American to 20 percent Indian." A second trip the following summer completed the transformation, and he returned after that trip feeling "100 percent Indian. Everything here looked foreign to me. It was such a culture shock. That's when I really came on to Hinduism."

He had then welded his earlier antiestablishment and anti-imperial activism to his spirituality to form the HSC along with Ravi. Although he strongly supported the Hindutva movement, Vijay said that he had noticed that "a lot of members of the movement, not the movement itself, tended to use Hindutva as an excuse to perpetuate a misogynist, ethnocentric agenda," something that he was against.

Keshav, who seemed to be the most knowledgeable about the Hindu scriptures in the group, indicated that the foundation for his knowledge had been laid by his father, who was "very, very religious, almost saintly." But in his mid-teens he went through an "anti-Indian phase." He did not want to be Indian and cut himself off from his relatives and his Indian friends. All his friends in his Catholic school had a way to connect to each other since they went to Bible class together, but he, in contrast, felt "like an outsider." He was also being picked on for being Indian, and taunted with the epithet "Gandhi." Apparently Gandhi's nonviolent approach was seen as being "unmanly" by at least a subset of American teenage boys, and many people also viewed Indians as being passive and cowardly. Many times, according to Keshav, "I had to fight back, just to prove that we as a people are not weak." Then one night, he picked up the *Gita* and started reading. "And it was like a lot of things just started clicking . . . why people die, all my questions, a lot of them were answered. So I felt, if this thing could answer my questions, maybe there is more to it." That's when he got back into Indian culture and started reading up on Hinduism. He said that he read a lot of Indian philosophy, regularly scoured Internet sites on Hinduism, and was also a participant in Internet discussion groups such as the ones at www.hindunet.org. With respect to the Hindutva movement, Keshav believed that Hindus in India should have more of a voice, since India was a democracy and Hindus were the majority. But he did not want to see the Hindu "equivalent of an Islamic or a Christian nation. Either India should become totally secular, or it should apply the Hindu idea where there is a dominant religion in the state but it does not impede other religions."

Preeti was the only one in this group who had not been part of a bala vihar (something she said she very much regretted) and whose parents had not been "practicing" Hindus. She said this was primarily because they had "wanted us to be as American as possible" (until she got into her teens, when "all of a sudden they started imposing all these rules" on her, which they had not done for her brother), and to "speak English as well as possible." So her parents had downplayed their "Indianness," had talked to her in English, and had not taught her anything about Hinduism. Preeti said that she became conscious of her ignorance about her religion as she was being taught about Christianity in her Catholic high school. Because her parents did not seem to be able to answer her questions, she had taught herself about Hinduism by borrowing books from the library and by going onto the Internet.

The "Moderate" Group

The stories of the six members of this faction whom I interviewed were somewhat more diverse than those of the pro-Hindu group. But there were still some similarities in many of their stories. In most cases, their parents had not talked much about Hinduism and had not been able to provide satisfactory answers to many of the questions their children had raised. With the exception of Anita, none had attended a bala vihar. Unlike the pro-Hindu group, the moderates had not tried to read up on Hinduism to any great extent. They were in the club primarily to have their questions answered and to learn about Hinduism. With the exception of Chandan, the student from India (who said he supported the "moderate group" within the Sangh Parivar), none of the others had any real knowledge of the Hindu nationalist movement and so said that they did not feel ready to formulate an opinion about it.

Meena's and Rekha's stories were fairly typical of this group. Meena said that she had started thinking a lot about identity issues from the time she was about eleven or twelve. There had not been many Indians in her school, and all her friends were white. So she remembers thinking at one point, "What group do I really belong to?" Her mother told her to say that she was "Indo-American," when she was asked, "because you are both." Meena said that she had asked her parents about God in her early teen years. "They were honest and told me, I don't really know if God exists, but I believe in a greater energy. But they wouldn't put a name to it." The family went to the temple occasionally, not to do a puja but just because it was a "spiritual place." Occasionally, when she asked them, her parents would tell her some of the stories in the *Mahabharata* and the other epics. However, according to Meena, "they always said, This is the story. They never said, This is what we believe." They celebrated some Hindu festivals at home, but "only the cultural aspects, not the religious." Despite the lack of religion, Meena said that her family was "culturally very Indian." They always had Indian food at home, they were constantly exposed to Indian music and movies (her mother had a huge selection of cassettes and videos), and Meena and her sister learned to sing classical Indian music and to play some Indian instruments. Her mother was also very active in the local Indian association for some time.

Rekha said that her parents did not have much time for religion or to associate with other Indian families, because their main focus was on getting established. They attended an Indian function only one or two times a year. Earlier, her mother "did puja every day, now my sister does it." But the puja consisted only of doing the aarti. Her parents did tell her some of the stories from the epics, but did not discuss Hinduism any further. Until the beginning of high school Rekha indicated that she had not been a "practicing Indian." "I had Indian skin but American culture." In high school she became 75 percent American and 25 percent Indian. In college, Rekha defined herself as "Indian American" and as being "half, half."

Differences in the Narratives

Differences between the narratives of the pro-Hindu and the moderate members were apparent. With the exception of Preeti, all the pro-Hindu members came from families who stressed the importance of Hinduism and an Indian identity, taught their children about it, and sent them to bala vihar classes. Each of these students had also done independent reading and was thus fairly "knowledgeable" on the subject. With the exception of Anita, all the moderate members came from families who had not emphasized Hinduism or Indianness and who could not adequately answer their children's questions about these issues. None of the moderates had done any independent reading to learn about their religion or culture. There was a strong positive correlation between the experience or perception of social, racial, and religious marginality (even though this was often constructed in a positive way, as when Ravi emphasized his lack of "self-hatred") and the tendency to fall into the pro-Hindu faction. Turning to Hinduism and Indianness after an identity crisis—in Ravi's case being constantly pulled over by the police, and in Vijay's case being left "rootless" after losing his teenage circle of friends—was also a common theme in the narratives of the pro-Hindu members as well as in interviews I conducted with Hindu American youth who were part of my larger study. Although some members of the moderate group, such as Meena, mentioned racial difference, a distinctive feature was that none of these individuals emphasized racial or religious marginality, quite unlike the pro-Hindu members.

Patterned differences in the upbringing and the institutional and friendship networks of the two factions and, even more important, in the frameworks that the pro-Hindu members and the moderates used to make sense of their social location and their teenage experiences are thus evident. But why did these patterned differences affect the outlook of these groups on Hinduism and a Hindu identity? Perhaps ironically, those who were given a better understanding of Hinduism by their parents and by the bala vihar classes seemed to be more drawn toward Hindu nationalism than those who knew less about Hinduism. My larger research suggested that this was not necessarily because Hindu nationalism was taught at home or emphasized in the classes. Rather, it appeared that this early exposure to Hinduism set the stage for the religion's becoming an important and emotional part of the personal identity for these youth. Subsequent experiences of social and racial marginalization and encounters in which the religion was denigrated were interpreted as attacks on this core personal identity and led the teenagers to turn to Hindu nationalist groups, Web sites, and literature to seek answers to their identity crisis (see Kurien 2004). These sources provided them with the emotional and intellectual ammunition for the ethnic pride/ethnic victimization outlook of the pro-Hindu group. A Hindu identity was less freighted with emotionality for the "moderates" whom I interviewed, whose upbringing had not included a strong emphasis on Hinduism or an Indian identity and who had not researched it on their own. Thus it is likely that such youth did not have a clear framework or vocabulary with which to define their racial experiences, and turned to Hinduism in college when faced with a multiculturalism that demanded that they be aware of their heritage (see Maira 2002).

Gender Differences

Although only two of the women, Preeti and Meena were outspoken about and very critical of the gender inequality that they saw in their homes and within the Indian American community, all six of the women recognized the double standards that were prevalent in their families. The families had always moved to accommodate their fathers' career needs. Their mothers had done all or most of the housework regardless of whether they had also worked outside the home, and had quit working for several years to raise the children. In most cases, the father was also the dominant personality and decision maker in the house. The women who had brothers also noticed the difference between the rules that they and their brothers had to follow, particularly with respect to going out and dating. All six strongly emphasized that they wanted to have careers and recognized some of the difficulties that they would have to face in combining them with family life. All indicated that unlike their parents, they would like to have an "equal marriage," where their husbands shared in the household and child-care responsibilities and supported their careers (although only Preeti and Meena were vehement about this).

By and large, it was difficult to get men to talk about gender issues at any length (it could also be because I unconsciously probed the women more on these topics). Most seemed to think that their parents had a good, balanced relationship and that their mothers made many of the decisions in the home. Although two of the men acknowledged that their parents had applied different rules to them and their sisters, the greater lenience with the sons was explained as being due to the fact that their parents had "mellowed over time" (both sisters were older). When asked what type of marriage they wanted for themselves, they talked in general terms about "personal compatibility." Two men said that women were better with children and that it would probably be good if their wives stayed at home while their children were young, but most indicated that they had not thought seriously about these issues.

DIFFERENCES IN RELIGIOUS IDENTITY MANIFESTED:
THE DISCUSSIONS

The differences in these students' experiences and frameworks influenced the positions the pro-Hindu and the moderate groups adopted in the HSC group discussions and on their Internet forum. Pro-Hindu members stressed racial and social marginality and also adopted militant, anti-Muslim, and anti-Christian positions; the moderate members stressed pluralism and the common humanity of all groups. I draw on the HSC meetings that I attended as well as on the discussions on the Internet forum to bring out some of the issues of concern to the membership and to illustrate the way the pro-Hindu/moderate cleavage manifested itself.

Whenever it came to discussions on gender issues, there was a clear split between men and women, with the men usually arguing that men and women "were perfectly equal" in the Vedic period, and pointing out that there were several powerful female goddesses within Hinduism (to indicate that the Hindu tradition respected women). The women, in contrast, would refer to the gender inequalities they saw in their homes and their extended families, and would also cite other evidence to show that there was substantial gender inequality in contemporary India.

Nationalism and Politics

Two of the most interesting discussions in the semester I attended revolved around issues of nationalism, politics, and identity. The first was based on an Internet article "Why I Am Not a South Asian," written by an Indian American. In the article, the writer argued that it was disadvantageous for India to be lumped together with the other countries in South Asia, which were not as developed. The writer therefore urged Indians in the United States to be "nationalistic" and to resist the South Asian classification. All of the men in the pro-Hindu group who were at the meeting (Vijay, Ravi's cousins Kumar and Gopi, and Atul) said that they did not want to be called "South Asian" because they did not want to be classified along with Pakistan and Bangladesh. They argued that the Hindu culture of India and the Islamic culture of the other two countries had nothing in common. At this point, Chandan jumped in, asking the assembled students, "Have any of you guys ever hung out with Pakistanis?" No one had, so he continued, "Well, I have, and I didn't find any difference between them and me. We all had very similar cultures, food, and language." Chandan and some of the women argued that there were such large cultural differences between the different regions in India that it did not make sense to draw an arbitrary line between India and the other South Asian nations on the basis of culture. Chandan also pointed out that to talk about the Indian culture as purely Hindu was inaccurate and "segregational," since there were more Muslims in India than in Pakistan, "so we cannot exclude Muslims from the definition of Indian culture."

The discussion continued on the Internet forum, with Meena asking, "Many of us agree that the British were experts at the 'divide and conquer' doctrine. . . . By carrying on the anti-Muslim, anti-Pakistan 'tradition,' aren't we continuing the system? . . . I am asking for clarification on resolving the seeming paradox between being anti-imperialist and anti-Muslim." Atul rose to the challenge, writing a long, passionate reply, which seemed to only indirectly address Meena's question. He argued that India was "the land of one of the last indigenous cultures" and that he felt a responsibility to help particularly the "weak and poor" in India maintain their traditions and practices. He continued, "My two cents for a losing battle. Most likely in our lifetime the religious tradition and culture of India will be lost to economics and con-version. . . . Most Indians are too passive to even care when their kids are converted to another religion. Most of us here don't give a damn either, because we are too con-cerned about offending people who want us to 'vanish.'" When an anonymous writer told him that he was "being arrogant and assuming that all Indians are idiots" by belittling their ability to choose what they wanted for themselves, Atul replied, "Call me arrogant . . . but YES, I do think that Indians ARE IDIOTS . . . as they are quick to adopt Western culture out of their own insecurities of being brown and not white."

The second discussion of note that semester was on "nationalistic dharma" (obligations to the nation). Interestingly, in this discussion, everyone in the room seemed to understand that the "nation" in this case referred to India. Some people felt that just learning about India was a good start, and Alok also pointed out that the group had periodically collected money to send back to India. Keshav talked about the importance of getting involved in Indian American politics, so that Indian Americans could become a powerful lobby group, and influence United States policies toward India. Ravi and Alok spoke passionately about the need for members to network with one another and with other Hindu Americans (some-thing they had also brought up in the interviews); Ravi argued that "communities like the Jews have been successful because they are really networked."

At this point Sheetal raised the issue, "If we are Indo-Americans, what are we doing to help American society?" A few people felt that it was important to help the poor and homeless in this society, but the majority seemed to feel that their primary obligation was to India, since the people there were in a more desperate situation. Ravi added, "We work here, earn here, spend here, and pay taxes here. We make more for corpora-tions than they actually give us, so all of this is contributing to American society."

There were several discussions on the Internet forum about Indian politics, where, for instance, members of the pro-Hindu group extolled the Hindutva move-ment and organizations like the VHP and the RSS. But one of the most striking remarks concerning national identity came in a discussion regarding the relation-ship between Hinduism and India. To a question about what the difference between a Hindu and an Indian was, Gopi (Ravi's cousin) replied, "None," and then elabo-rated in a lengthy reply. After going over the familiar argument about Hinduism's being indigenous to India, something that Muslim and Christian Indians have to acknowledge, he continued by saying that he did not define India as a country that "spontaneously generated in 1947" but instead as a "product of thousands of years." The current Indian nation-state, however, seemed to be repudiating its spiritual heritage and had instead become a "nation that revels in accepting foreign ideolo-gies (Marxism, pseudo-secularism) as superior to its own." While he acknowledged that he could not officially claim to be Indian since he had been born and brought up in the United States, he insisted that he was "an Indian if you are talking about a cultural and spiritual entity, if you are talking about my skin color, my religion, my language, my family, my identity, my background."

In this discussion, Gopi, like many of the pro-Hindu members, was making a distinction between the Indian nation-state, which he considered to be a recent and artificially created entity, and Sanatana Dharma, an ethos that is thousands of years old and that is not necessarily geographically bound. He felt that in this sense, he was more true to the Indian or Hindu ethos than Indians in India. Such a prenational definition of Hinduism and Indianness allows diasporic Indians, particularly of the second and later generations, to make a distinction between their country of residence and citizenship (in this case, the United States) and their nationality (Hindu or Indian) and thereby affirm that they still belong to the Hindu nation.

Gender

Gender issues, and particularly the position of women in Indian or Hindu culture, were important topics of discussion within the group. Although the meeting focused on the "Hindu female" took place the semester before I started attending, I heard a great deal about it from members. There was also a follow-up discussion on the forum, primarily between Vijay and Meena (the moderator of the discussion at the meeting). Vijay began his e-mail by cautioning Meena about being careful not to fall into the trap of using stereotypes about Hindu culture, which "antagonistic elements" could exploit to further their anti-Hindu agenda, and about using an upper-middle-class Indian American woman's lens to view the "land of our ancestors." He also suggested that often young people brought up here tended to project their own problems onto "the culture over there." He continued:

> When we talk about Hindu women, do we ever have a discussion (a real one) about the role of Hindu women in Vedic times? How about Goddess worship, and how we are one of the last cultures to still do it, and how it empowers Hindu women more so than women of almost every other culture? . . . Instead we had (a few weeks ago) to focus our discussion on the sad fact of bride-burning, and the intensely negative expectations of (upper middle class) Indian-American women . . . I know this is the difficulty in moderating these discussions: as a female, you are coming into this situation with a certain perspective.

In her reply, Meena agreed that there were many negative stereotypes about India, but argued that it was important for Indian Americans to "acknowledge that there are flaws in our society, just as there are flaws in every society." Instead of discussions about women in the Vedic period, she said that she preferred to focus on the status of women in contemporary India and within the Indian American community, "who are still expected to eat after their men have, who are still expected to give up a Ph.D. in order to take care of their in-laws, who are still expected to produce male children to carry on the family name." She continued, "Perhaps we can have a 'real' discussion about the paradoxes in Hindu culture, wherein Goddesses are worshiped every morning for their powers and wives are expected to have a hot breakfast on the table for their husbands." In conclusion, Meena pointed out that Vijay also appeared to be operating with certain biases "as a male" in the meetings since he seemed reluctant to confront the "negative aspects of Hindu culture" that the women were bringing up.

In a subsequent e-mail, an anonymous author explodes,

Do you think women have it better in other parts of the world [than India]? In America, a woman is expected to put out by the time she finishes high school. If she doesn't, she's either a lesbian or a b****. . . . If a woman here isn't at least five or ten pounds underweight, she's ugly. . . . In Islamic states, well, do we even have to go there? Genital mutilation, murder, rape, veiling. . . .

The instances of dowry murder, etc. [in India] are symptoms of POVERTY, NOT HINDUISM/INDIAN CULTURE!!! When will some people get that into their [expletive] heads???

During the discussion on the "Hindu male," I noticed an interesting gender cleavage in the group, which I summarize below.

[ONE OR MORE] WOMEN: Indian men are very dominant and expect their wives to be submissive.
[ONE OR MORE] MEN: But isn't that true of all cultures in general?
W: Indian women are expected to do all the housework even if they are working.
M: But isn't that only true of the older generation?
W: No, we know several friends who are married here who are in that situation.
M: In Indian households, women have much more power because they do everything—they look after the household, they look after the children and they make the decisions about the children.
W: Not because they want to, but because they have to.
M: How do you define power, is it who does what in the house?
W: It is decision making.
M: Well, the mother makes most of the decisions, especially about the children. Isn't that power?
W: Often women want men to get more involved in their children's lives. They don't want to make all the decisions themselves.
M: [Two men argued] In our houses, our grandfathers are basically "useless." It is our grandmothers who do everything, including conducting all the ceremonies.

And so it went, round and round in this fashion for the rest of the discussion. At the end, the group addressed the question of whether things were going to change and whether Indian Americans were moving toward a more gender-equal society. Again the men seemed to be very positive, while many of the women were more skeptical.

Hindu Pride

Undoubtedly the most widely discussed and the most rancorous of issues had to do with the question of Hindu pride and who was a "true" Hindu. The e-mail by a "Hindu Fanatic" was typical of the pro-Hindu group's stance. This person began by saying that "no one" was even willing to admit being a Hindu, and charged that everyone was "scared of the label." He or she continued, saying that if no one was willing to proudly affirm this Hindu identity, "who is going to give a damn about the situation of Hindus in India, in Kashmir. Everyone is happy in their cozy houses, watching 'Friends' reruns etc. We don't want to be 'bothered' by the plight of starving people in the land of our ancestors—it might upset our stomachs after we've eaten our beef TV dinners." People in Hindu organizations such as HSC, the e-mail went on, "don't even know what they are. They think they are Muslims, or Christians or something." The writer wondered why Hindu American youth couldn't "focus on uplifting ourselves, our community, our religion. . . . Why is it that so many people will give money or donate clothes here in America but it is so hard for them to pick up a pen and write a check to IDRF [India Development and Relief Fund]."

Meena replied, saying, "Names, creeds, they don't matter. We're all human, we all hurt. Christian kids starve just as Hindu kids starve" and a person writing under the name "Humanitarian" similarly responded, "I was brought up to respect all cultures and all humans. To help those that are in need, whether he is a stranger, friend or foe . . . because he is a human being. . . . Doesn't sanatana dharma say that all the living *jivas* (beings) are part of the supreme personality of the godhead? If so, why are you trying to segregate your help?" Periodically, individual members on the forum (usually anonymously) challenged the moderate writers by asking them whether they considered themselves "true" Hindus. To one such query, Meena replied, "I certainly consider myself a Hindu, but I don't let myself be boxed into whatever someone else's definition of that term is."

Perhaps the denouement came when Ravi burst out in an e-mail on the forum, some time after I had left the group: "I think that its ridiculous how there are so many supporters of Islam and Christianity on the HSC forum, while on any of the Internet Islamic sites there are NO supporters of Hinduism or any other indigenous culture. I think that many of you self-hating Hindus should recognize that the other groups you want to emulate (white people, Christians, etc) often reject you!" He refused, he said, to merely be a "reject in the sociopolitical arena!" In his view, the others in the group, instead of paying attention to the "true voice" of their own "pristine being," were listening to the "tattered and homeless voice of the politically correct upper class academic establishment, that sees you as a commercial commodity!" He went on, "Instead of listening to what your South Asian studies textbooks preach, why not listen to what your inner, primal being is SCREAMING at you!" Ultimately he threatened to separate from these he called Philistines: "All you Hindus wearing green [a color identified with Muslims], you betray your yellow belly, your whitewashed exterior, and your emptiness within! I refuse to any longer be a leader of Philistines. Is there anybody out there to join my hand and alongside me, accept the bounty of creativity, expression, art and poetry which is our culture?"

This e-mail seemed to have polarized the group further, since several of the "hard-core" members, such as Vijay and Gopi, came out strongly in support of Ravi, while several of the moderate members criticized him. Some of the critiques were anonymous, but Chandan and Meena responded to Ravi using their own names.

Chandan argued, "I think you have *grossly* misunderstood some of us. We (or lets say me) are not supporting Islam and Christianity. We are saying that Hinduism not only tolerates but acknowledges other religions and beliefs. [Ravi] you are one of the people, who keeps showing up at the meetings with the banner which says, 'God is one, sages call him by different names.'" Christianity, Islam and many other religions, he said, "may beat up on all other religions; however, that doesn't mean we Hindus need to do the same with them. It is against the beliefs of Hinduism to not tolerate other religions." Perhaps drawing on his life experience in India, he also noted that "an important part of our heritage and our people are Muslims and Christians. Some of our best music, culture, food, poets, writers, scientists, etc, etc. come from these religions. Despite whatever Hindu Nationalist groups may lead you to believe, India is no longer "Hindustan"; it is now Hindu-Muslim-Christian-Sikh-Jain-manyOthers-Stan ('stan' means place in Hindi)."

Meena replied caustically to Ravi: "Interesting point of view. Is your view of Hinduism the absolute correct one? Where is Hinduism defined in the holy texts? I personally do follow my inner, primal being, which isn't screaming what you said: it's actually calmly reminding me that my own mind is what guides me, and not the frantic howlings of whoever is trying to force me to think their way—Christian, Muslim OR Hindu, because there are plenty out there who are egocentric and believe that they are right." She also wondered about his statement regarding Philistines, asking, "Who exactly is following you (if anyone is) that you consider a Philistine? Will you really keep anyone who wants to [be] alongside you, or will it be an elitist following, where those with their own minds will be cast aside in scorn?"

These exchanges vividly show the conflict and passion that discussions regarding issues of identity aroused in the group. As Ravi mentioned at my first meeting with him, it is not clear to many Indian Americans from a Hindu background what it really means to be a Hindu. But because of the prominence given to identity and "roots" in today's multicultural society, this definition becomes something that is important for them to know and to be able to articulate. Some students saw a Hindu identity as a means to set themselves apart from Christians and Muslims; and others saw it as a means to stress pluralism and the commonalities with these other two groups. A similar difference of opinion could be seen regarding the relationship between a Hindu identity and an Indian identity, with people like Gopi arguing that it was the same thing, since Hinduism was the indigenous identity and cultural ethos of India, and others, like Chandan and Meena, arguing that India had a multireligious society and culture.

Racially, what does it mean to be an American with "brown skin"? This issue is another that members of the group had to deal with, and here again, no clear answer emerged. From the many references to racial marginality that the students made, it seemed to be a painful reality for most members. HSC members like Vijay and Ravi argued that their marginalization meant that they had to identify with and form solidarities with other people of color. They had also criticized those who tried to cope with their racial marginality by avoiding the issue or pretending to be white. The pro-Hindu members frequently attributed the moderate group's inclusivist multiculturalism to their wanting "to adopt Western culture out of their . . . inse-curities of being brown and not white."

When it came to issues of gender, young Indian American men had to deal with the stereotypes of their white American peers who viewed them as "nerdy," sexually unattractive, passive, and weak. They were drawn to the HSC, which they felt would be a comfort zone where they could discuss these stereotypes and recover their wounded masculinity. So it is not surprising that they felt doubly betrayed when many of the women within the group accused them (i.e., Indian men) of being sex-ist oppressors. Indian American women are generally brought up to be repositories of Indian culture, and many were therefore drawn to a club that gave them the opportunity to showcase their talents by participating in cultural activities. At the same time, they were aware of the constraints and limitations that their mothers, sisters, and female cousins faced as women, accounting for the ambivalence that many of the women students manifested toward Hinduism and Indian culture.

CONCLUSION

With the coming of age of the "new second generation," many of whose members are located at the interstices of conventional American racial and ethnic categories, issues of identity are likely to come to the forefront in both the private and the pub-lic sphere. Although such issues may lead to more conflicts and challenges as these groups try to locate their place at the American multicultural table (e.g., Kurien 2006), on the positive side, such challenges could result in the development of a more open and fluid multiracial, multi-ethnic system.

Sociological paradigms of second-generation American identity formation have largely neglected religion. We have seen, however, the central role that religion plays in identity formation for Hindus. Because religion can be used to contest racial marginality (as in the case of the pro-Hindu faction) or to sidestep it (as perhaps some of the moderate members were trying to do), examining how participation in religious groups affects the process of immigrant incorporation becomes impor-tant. For instance, the reactive ethnicity of the pro-Hindu HSC members did not seem to have led them to turn away from mainstream American institutions, as Portes and Rumbaut (2001, 284–285) had predicted such individuals would. On the contrary, the pro-Hindu individuals were, if anything, even more academically suc-cessful than those who embraced a moderate ideology. They, like their parents, may have viewed professional education as a route to overcoming racial and ethnic bar-riers in the United States. Or possibly much of the hostility or "oppositional iden-tity" that the pro-Hindu group developed in reaction to their experience of racial marginality had come to be directed against Muslims rather than against main-stream America. This attitude could be seen particularly in the Internet forum, which over time degenerated into a platform for anti-Muslim hate speech and threats by anonymous posters. (The forum was closed down by its Internet host for this reason.) Thus the inclusion of religion greatly complicates the "segmented assimilation" model of immigrant incorporation.

As a club that was formed under the mandate and guidelines of campus multi-culturalism, the HSC was also influenced by the norms of American pluralism. As we have seen, racial marginality (largely ignored by multiculturalism's focus on cultural diversity) seems to promote the formation of a reactive and oppositional identity that is articulated through the victimization discourse legitimized by multiculturalism. "Indigenousness" comes to be fetishized as the touchstone of the "cultural authenticity" that is mandated by contemporary identity politics (Maira 2002; Rudrappa 2004, 132–146). That multiculturalism seems to reinforce diasporic nationalism and intergroup cleavages even for the second generation is particularly significant, indicating that such nationalism is not just a transitory immigrant phenomenon. The financial and moral support provided by the second generation to Hindu nationalist organizations only empowers such organizations to continue their divisive agenda in the United States and in India.

Certainly not all or even most of the HSC chapters are as politicized or as conflict ridden as the Western University HSC. The other HSC chapter that I studied was small, relatively cohesive, and strongly against involvement in politics. It appeared that the degree to which a particular chapter was tied to the national organization (the second, apolitical chapter had hardly any connection with the latter) was a crucial factor. The independent Hindu student organization that I also studied steered clear of politics as well (as seemed to be the case with many other such campus-specific organizations that I knew or heard about).[2] Even within the Western University HSC, a diversity of opinions prevailed and it was only a minority who were militantly Hinducentric.

It is unclear whether, as in the case of the immigrant generation, the Hinducentric group in the second generation will come to represent the voice of American Hinduism in the future and will similarly be made up of mainly of male, upper-caste, upper-class, highly educated professionals. As an Indian American newspaper reported, it is no secret that the second-generation leadership for American Hindu nationalist organizations "is being groomed in the Hindu Student Council" (Lakhihal 2001, 59). Although a minority, such members may be pushed to the forefront because of the social, intellectual, and financial backing they receive from the by now well-entrenched American Hindutva movement.

CHAPTER 11

The Development of an
American Hinduism

I have explored two types of Hinduism in the United States: popular Hinduism and official Hinduism. By "popular Hinduism" I mean the transmission and practice of local religious and cultural traditions. Individuals learn about the attributes and characteristics of the deities and possibly some of the history and theology of their tradition through the stories, legends, and scriptures of popular Hinduism. Family members, local groups, and temple priests teach Hindus how to worship and supplicate the deities by means of prayers, devotional songs, and ritual practices and also teach them the ethics, prohibitions, and prescriptions necessary to live a moral life. Through these institutions, individuals reproduce and transmit the language, clothing, food, and culture of their region of origin. Popular Hinduism also refers to the ways in which most Hindus understand and practice the religion in their everyday lives, whether it is performing a puja at home, celebrating a festival or a life-cycle rite, keeping a fast, observing the food codes and rules regarding auspiciousness and inauspiciousness, being part of a satsang, or going to the temple.

Popular Hinduism is generally transmitted informally in India, but as we have seen, more formal institutions and mechanisms are required elsewhere. The institutions of popular Hinduism in the United States, in addition to practicing and reproducing Hinduism, also become the means to create community; provide professional, educational, and economic support; understand and articulate identity; and provide a shelter from the racism and cultural misunderstanding that Hindus encounter in the wider society. The American context thus necessitates changes in traditional organizations like satsangs and temples, and leads to the development of new institutions such as bala vihars, Hindu student groups, and Hindu heritage summer camps.

"Official Hinduism" refers to the attempts of Hindu leaders to define Hinduism and Hindu interests and to develop a unified platform to mobilize on behalf of these interests. Because official Hinduism speaks for all of Hinduism, it tends to be abstract, universalistic, and antiritualistic, in contrast to popular Hinduism, which is regional, practice-oriented, and, in the United States, frequently congregational. We have seen that the spokespersons for Hinduism draw on central elements of the

Hindutva platform to define the distinctiveness and superiority of Hinduism with reference to other religions, to defend the religion from misrepresentations and criticism, and to attack other traditions for not being like Hinduism. They also define the position of Hindus in the world and in history, and articulate why Hindus are entitled to social, political, and economic resources on this basis. In the United States, Hindu American spokespersons affirm the estimable attributes of Hinduism to secure Hindus an honored place at the multicultural table.

What is the relationship between the everyday devotional Hinduism of most Hindu Americans and the political Hinduism of Hindu American leaders? The mass of Hindu devotees around the country are far removed from the small group of ideologues who head the Hindu umbrella organizations mentioned in this book. For the most part, "lay" Hindu Americans are uninterested in and to a large extent unaware of Hindutva politics. Only a small minority of Hindus in the United States can be described as Hindutva-vadis, that is, activists working for Hindu nationalist causes. At the same time, only a small minority of Hindu Americans actively work to oppose the Hindutva movement. Such individuals are mainly members of left-leaning, pluralist organizations who go out of their way to include Indian religious minorities and to develop coalitional alliances with them. Between these extremes lie the vast silent majority of Hindu Americans. Since the mid-1990s, however, tacit acceptance of many central tenets of the Hindutva platform has increased among this group, as lay Hindu teachers, parents, and members of the second generation have often turned to Hindutva organizations and Web sites for information.[1] Because few public challenges to the revisionist history propounded by these sources have been available, many individuals, even apolitical Hindu Americans, have gradually internalized many Hindutva ideas.[2]

As we have seen, Hindu umbrella groups in the United States organize several large religious and cultural festivals every year, where the message of Hindutva is delivered and lay Hindus are exposed to the ideas of official Hinduism. For instance, the Hindu Sangam in Northern California, billed as a "Grand Cultural Festival," drew an estimated ten to fifteen thousand people on July 21, 2001. Although the organizers of the event claimed not to have a political agenda, the chief guest was the head of the Rashtriya Swayamsevak Sangh and one of the most powerful leaders of the Sangh Parivar in India, K. S. Sudarshan (the VHP president, Ashok Singhal, who was to have been the chief guest, was not able to attend because he was indisposed). Prominent Hindutva sympathizers such as David Frawley and Koenraad Elst also spoke at the event (Shah 2001; Sundaram 2001). Despite the obvious Hindutva agenda of the Sangam, two of its three primary sponsors were Hindu temples in the area (the third was the Hindu Swayamsevak Sangh), and it was also supported by thirty-two other Bay Area organizations, including officially secular organizations such as the Federation of Indian Associations and the Federation of Indian Associations of the Bay Area, regional cultural groups such as the Maharastra Mandal, Kannada Koota, and the Gujarati Cultural Association of the Bay Area, and various Hindu organizations. Nonpolitical Hindu groups such as the BAPS and the Maata Amritanandamayi Ashram enthusiastically endorsed the conference (www.hindusangam.org/endorsements.html, retrieved July 23, 2001).

Through these methods of transmission, Hindu umbrella groups in the United States, as in India, have been able to erase the boundaries between the public and the private and thus have transformed Hindutva into an emotional, personal grievance for many ordinary Hindus (Geetha and Jayanthi 1995, 247). As Hinduism has become the axis around which community, ethnic pride, and individual identity revolves, organizations of popular Hinduism such as satsangs, bala vihars, and temples, though not necessarily directly supporting the call of Hindutva, have indirectly provided a receptive soil in which the seeds of the movement could be sown. For instance, while the leadership and most members of KHO, described in chapter 4, emphasized that they were against "Hindu fundamentalism," KHO was a registered member of the FHA in the 1990s, and FHA officeholders gave speeches promoting the Hindutva agenda at the KHO's function on the occasion of Onam, the most important Kerala Hindu festival, in the middle of that decade. The articles of FHA leaders were also published in the KHO annual Souvenir (yearbook) for two years during the same period. Similarly, although none of the devotees at the Malibu temple whom we interviewed were involved with Hindu umbrella organizations like the VHPA or the HSS, and all indicated that they were uninterested and uninvolved in politics (whether the politics of the board members at the temple or larger Indian politics), several still indicated support for some aspects of the Hindutva movement. As an example, Subhra, a south Indian computer programmer on an H1-B visa, felt that "we need some fanaticism but it should be controlled." He indicated that he liked to cultivate himself to be a "controlled fanatic as Hindus have been taking crap for some time from other minorities." Mrs. Sudha Ganeshan, a middle-aged Tamil Brahmin immigrant, asked, "What is so wrong in believing in the majority religion? When Vajpayee [the prime minister during the BJP government] talks about a Hindu nation, everybody is up in arms. It is not fair to call him a fundamentalist. We have double standards. There is no need to resort to violence but we should be proud Hindus." Vijaya, a young mother who came to the temple every week with her husband and child, similarly argued that "the Hindutva movement makes sense because Hindus have always been discriminated against for being Hindus." She continued, "We are not asking for favors. But, it really doesn't make much of a difference. Muslims and Christians will still have a special status [in India]. Instead, everybody should be given the same opportunity."

The BAPS group officially eschewed politics and most of its membership were completely apolitical, but scholars have pointed out that in the public presentations, of this Swaminarayan sect, it promoted several aspects of Hindutva worldview, such as pride in the Vedas as the source of all knowledge and the argument that Muslim rule in India was the reason for the development of many negative Indian practices such as female infanticide (see Mukta 2000, 461–462). Shukla (1997) has also argued that the BAPS portrayal of Hinduism at the Cultural Festival of India promoted many Hindutva ideas. This official discourse of the Swaminarayans is of particular relevance for the development of an American Hinduism, since the group is trying to project itself as the public face of Hinduism and of Indians in the West (Bhatt 2000, 588; Mukta 2000; Shukla 1997). Although the individual Hindu Student Council chapters studied varied in their orientation, the national organization has supported many of the ideas of official Hinduism, judging from its (constantly updated and changing) Web site and the issues discussed at its annual camps. The 2005 camp was no exception, with presentations on "Contributions of Hindus to Human Civilization," "Heroic Epochs of Hindu History," and "Hinduism in American Classrooms" (www.hscnet.org). In the American context, we have seen that the racism and marginality experienced by the first and second generations and the identity struggles of Indian American youth also further reinforce the discourses of official Hinduism in the United States. In addition, American multiculturalism also plays an important part in strengthening the power of official Hinduism.

MULTICULTURALISM AND OFFICIAL HINDUISM

The emphasis on the tolerance and pluralism of official Hinduism in the United States is carefully produced to fit in with American multiculturalism. But as I have argued, militant Hinducentricism and Hindu nationalism are also products of the same multiculturalism. The anti-Abrahamic and antidefamation campaigns, the attacks against scholars of Hinduism, and the sponsorship, support, and dissemination of revisionist Indian history have all been made in the name of multiculturalism and minority rights. Ajay Shah, the convener of AHAD, maintains, "In seeking the honor of Hindus and demanding they not be ridiculed . . . we are being good Americans. In our fight for Hindu dignity, we are championing American pluralism" (quoted in Pais 2001). The Infinity Foundation describes its mission as encouraging "contemporary society to rise above narrow cultural chauvinism and to appreciate the contributions to World civilization made by non-Western cultures," and its president, Rajiv Malhotra, has framed his critiques of Hinduism scholars in the United States as an attempt to prevent "hate speech" and to enlarge American multiculturalism.[3] The HICAD petition protesting the planned showing of two films critical of Hindu nationalism by the American Museum of Natural History in New York emphasized the need "to educate the cosmopolitan population of the greater New York area and the rest of the USA to respect all our neighbors who might be following diverse religions and traditions" (HICAD 2002).

Multiculturalist policies have reinforced Hindu nationalism in two other ways. The need to find "ethnic spokespersons" to represent the community in a multicultural society has led to the legitimization of many extremist Hindutva activists, with some achieving a sort of celebrity status, by mainstream American politicians at the behest of Hindu umbrella groups. For instance, Narain Kataria, RSS worker and senior figure in the militant Hindu Unity group (see also Murphy 2001) discussed in chapter 7, which advertised on its Web site that it wanted to get Muslims and Christians out of India "by whatever means possible," received a Declaration of Honor from Helen Marshall, president of the borough of Queens, New York. Marshall also declared March 12, 2003, to be "Narain Kataria Day."[4] Moorthy Muthuswamy, nuclear physicist and director of the Hindutva-oriented Indian American Intellectuals Forum (see their Web site at www.saveindia.com), who argued in an article that

Indian Muslims should be banned from employment and business in India and prevented from voting unless they "reverted to Hinduism"(Muthuswamy 2003), was part of a delegation that met with U.S. Counterterrorism Section officials of the Justice Department on the issue of cross-border terrorism, a fact he touted while making the argument that he was an "expert" on Islamic terrorism. Gilles Kepel (1997, 110) has similarly noted that in the United Kingdom, multiculturalism has encouraged the rise of community leaders who act as intermediaries between their communities and the state and strengthen the sense of "otherness" and separatism felt by the communities.

The need to bring the homeland into prominence in a multicultural society where resources are tied to the recognition of ethnicity can also explain the enthusiastic response of many Indian Americans to the nuclear testing of the BJP government. Scholars argue that this enthusiasm was due to the fact that nuclearization brought India into the limelight as a country with the technological ability to develop nuclear weapons and the willingness to stand up to American double standards (Mathew and Prashad 2000, 528; Rajagopal 2000, 486–487).

CONTRADICTIONS WITHIN AMERICAN MULTICULTURALISM

Why do contemporary multiculturalist policies seem to promote two contradictory self-presentations—genteel multiculturalism and militant nationalism—among Hindu American leaders? A common critique of multiculturalism from the Left is that although the pressure for multiculturalism in the United States grew out of the demands of racial minorities for a more inclusive culture and society, it has currently become a way to sidestep the issue of racism and unequal structures by focusing on cultural diversity. The premise of Western multiculturalism is that there is no longer a dominant culture and that society is made up of a "mosaic" of equally valued cultures. The reality, of course, is very different.

Faced with the discourse of multiculturalism, and the reality of Eurocentricism and racism, Hindu Americans develop a two-sided strategy for recognition that on the one hand emphasizes their success as model ethnics, but on the other hand stresses a history of oppression. Recall that the dual strategy of "ethnic pride" and "ethnic victimization" is typical of groups seeking to be recognized as "minorities" within the contemporary multiculturalist framework (Berbrier 1998, 2002). Not surprisingly, in the Indian American case, this dual strategy is modeled on Jewish Americans—a minority religious group which has achieved integration with the white majority. Hindu Americans also frequently draw on black and feminist discourses to point to similar experiences of marginalization and to argue both for the importance of a positive presentation of Hinduism and Indian culture and for more "practicing Hindu" scholars to be represented in academia.

The combination of a multiculturalism that demands the celebration of ethnicity and a racism that denigrates non-Western cultures makes Hindu Americans very sensitive to perceived or real "slights," a sensitivity that may explain the emotional intensity of the antidefamation campaigns. Both multiculturalism and racism also heighten the importance of a positive reconstruction of homeland culture. Indian immigrants construct an idealized past because they recognize that the present is problematic.[5] Rajagopal (2001, 267) quotes the president of the VHPA as saying, "Every time they go to India, they feel disgusted—they see the dirty streets and the dirty bathrooms. They don't want to identify with India. But they can take pride in Hindutva [which rests on being part of an ancient civilization]." To the extent that professional Indian Americans internalize the value placed on material progress, scientific development, and gender equality in contemporary America, these attributes become central elements in the glorious past that they invoke. They also recognize that it is at least partly the sophistication and antiquity of a group's ancestral culture that rank it within America's stratified system. Thus the characterizations of ancient India as the "cradle of civilization" (Feuerstein, Kak, and Frawley 1995) and the homeland of the Aryans are means for Indian Americans to distinguish themselves from other American minority groups by demonstrating their ancestral racial and cultural ties with Europeans.

Official Hinduism performs important functions for Hindus in a multicultural context like that of the United States. It provides the resources for Hindu Americans to know about, articulate, and be proud of their heritage. It offers a convenient, short-hand, intellectualized comparison with and criticism of Abrahamic religions and also acknowledges and publicizes the racism and Eurocentricism that many Hindus suffer and resent. Most important, Hindu American umbrella organizations take measures to redress some of these grievances by fighting for Hindu rights and respect. In the long run, however, the quest of community leaders for a prominent place for Hindus at the American multicultural table may be compromised by some of the fundamental contradictions within official Hinduism.

Contradictions within Official American Hinduism

Armand Mauss (1994) points out that new religions in the United States have always had to maintain a delicate balancing act between assimilating to established American patterns of religious organization and expression and maintaining their separateness and distinctiveness. If they accommodate too much, they are in danger of losing their distinctiveness and disappearing. If they remain too distinctive or militant, they face hostility and repression. Official Hinduism in the United States has also had to perform this balancing act between accommodation and resistance. Pressures to assimilate to Western culture in both the colonial and the immigrant contexts led Hindu leaders to construct an organized, monotheistic, textually and historically based Hinduism (e.g., the Ram Janmabhumi mobilization and the preoccupation with trying to date the Vedas and historically validate the various incidents in the epics) that emulates the Abrahamic religions they criticize. However, we have seen that when Hindu leaders want to distinguish themselves from these religions, they celebrate the polytheism and the fluid, pluralistic, nonhistorically bound nature of the religion.

The shifts in the way the concept of Hindu tolerance has been interpreted in the United States are a particularly good example of the dilemma faced by Hindu

American leaders. Nancy Fraser points out (1997, 16) that in a multicultural society, "recognition claims often take the form of calling attention to, if not performatively creating, the putative specificity of some group and then affirming its value." Thus Hindus in the United States, following the precedent laid in India's colonial period by leaders such as Swami Vivekananda, have long defined and celebrated tolerance as the central distinctive feature of Hinduism. But when tolerance was interpreted to mean that all religions were true, the question arose, as Frank Morales (2005) argues, of why parents and Hindu leaders should object to second-generation Hindus' converting to other religions. In response, many Hindu American leaders now reject the concept of radical universalism. It remains to be seen what new attribute of Hinduism will be defined as constituting the "specificity" and superiority of Hinduism in the future.

As I have shown, most of the leaders and umbrella groups that currently represent Hindu Americans have direct or indirect links to Hindu nationalism. We have also seen that the aggrandization of Hinduism in the Hindu nationalist platform largely rests on celebrating the putative achievements of ancient Vedic civilization and on attacking other religious and secular traditions. Particularly as the militant side of Hindu nationalism becomes apparent, Hindu American leaders and their claims of pluralism and tolerance may begin to lose credibility in the wider American society. Even if the goals that they are striving for in the United States are legitimate, the endeavor of such leaders could be undermined by critics pointing to their links with extremist ideologies or groups in India.

Besides the discrepancies between the rights that many of the leaders demand for Hindus in the United States and those that they would like minorities in India to have, I have also mentioned the contradiction between demanding an inclusive multiculturalism in the United States, based on a dynamic model of national identity, while promoting a static, assimilationist, monocultural model for India. When pressed, some leaders offer the justification that Ravi and Vijay provided in the last chapter, saying that the two situations are not equivalent, since Hindus are indigenous to India while Euro-Americans are migrants in the United States. This claim and the corresponding argument that minorities in India should not therefore have the same rights as minorities in the United States is not likely to be accorded much credence by American policymakers or by members of the wider society. Such a distinction is also dangerous in that it opens the door for other essentialist constructions of citizenship and national belonging (e.g., arguments that earlier migrants have greater social and political entitlements than more recent ones), which would marginalize Hindus in the United States and in the other countries where they have settled.

A fundamental problem is the attempt by Hindu American leaders to create a singular, monolithic religion by ignoring the vast differences between the various traditions within Hinduism (see Edelmann 2004). Groups that practice other versions of Hinduism are marginalized, and individuals or groups that question some of the interpretations of Hinduism offered by these leaders or that attempt to offer alternative interpretations are subjected to vitriolic attacks.[6] For instance, while most Hindu American leaders argue that Dalits and tribals should be considered to be Hindu and should be educated about their Hindu heritage by groups like the VHP, Dalits and lower-caste groups that criticize the upper-caste Hindu interpretations of Hindu texts and doctrines offered by spokespersons of Hinduism are frequently attacked on Internet discussion groups as "anti-Hindus." Similarly, while these spokespersons argue that women are given equal rights within Hinduism, they deny women any agency to interpret or shape Hinduism. Thus women who criticize any aspect of Indian or Hindu culture are attacked as "becharis," or as Westernized "feminists." Although there is a long tradition of women's activism in India, DasGupta and Dasgupta (1996, 385) argue that because of the efforts of Hindu American leaders, "the role of the *virangana* [brave warrior woman struggling against injustice] . . . has been wiped out in Indian American communities" (see also Bhattacharjee 1992). The California textbook case demonstrated the ways in which such monolithic constructions of community identity could be undermined by the mobilization of marginalized groups and showed that the interpretations of the self-appointed Hindu American spokespersons were not acceptable to all Hindus in the United States. Thus the edits of the HEF-VF combine were challenged by members of Dalit groups, who objected to the attempts to erase the exploitative nature of the caste system and to argue that caste oppression no longer took place in contemporary India. Similarly women's organizations protested the attempts to recast the history of patriarchy in India. Both types of groups argued that these erasures hid all the struggles of the past and the present by lower castes and women to obtain equal rights. Secular and pluralist Indian American groups similarly attacked the edits for promoting a narrow, Hinducentric perspective of Indian history. The California textbook controversy also indicated that anti-Hindutva groups were becoming more organized in the United States. Since such groups are also able to use the multicultural context to legitimize their claims of oppression, how the balance between Hindutva and anti-Hindutva forces plays out in the future bears watching. This relationship will be crucial in shaping the further development of an American Hinduism.

What are the broader impacts of the pronouncements and activities of Hindu American leaders on the community? As I have mentioned, the ethnic nationalism that these leaders promote provides the resources for Hindus to network and mobilize, to resist prejudice, and consequently to be successful in multicultural America. Yet, ethnic nationalism only sidesteps, and does not alter, the reality of racism and subordination. Further, it may divert the attention of ethnic leaders from the substantive concerns of Hindu Americans. As aggressive Hinduness has become the means to obtain status within the Indian American community and visibility outside the community, dozens of individuals and organizations claiming their mission to be the defense of Hinduism have tried to garner publicity for themselves by finding a Hindu cause to champion, most often by attacking companies and, more recently, scholars who have allegedly insulted Hinduism through their portrayals of Hindu deities and icons. Thus issues such as the treatment of immigrants and immigration laws, health care, schooling, and discrimination, which affect Indian Americans in more serious ways, are neglected. The discourse of "authenticity" of both multiculturalism and ethnic nationalism puts great pressure on members to conform to the celebratory version of culture that is on display. Community activists, however, point out that the model-minority image that Indian American leaders like to maintain prevents them from acknowledging and addressing the problems of working-class Indian immigrants. Indian American feminists similarly argue that the gender equality and family values that are said to distinguish Indians from other groups suppress the reality of patriarchy as well as the diversity and dissent that exist within many Indian American families (Abraham 2000; Bhattacharjee 1992; DasGupta and Dasgupta 1996).

Recently Indian Americans have been trying to translate their affluence and their prominence in the fields of information technology and health care in the United States into political clout, recognizing that successful incorporation into the political system is critical to becoming a prominent player in multicultural America. James M. Lindsay, vice president of the Council on Foreign Relations, has noted that Indian Americans contributed an estimated $8 million to federal election campaigns in the three elections prior to 2004 and identified the Indian American lobby group as most "likely to emerge as a political powerhouse in the U.S." over the next few years (Lindsay 2002). Indian Americans have also been able to develop one of the largest ethnic caucuses on the Hill: right before the 2006 mid-term elections, the Congressional India Caucus, founded in 1993, had 186 members, and the newer India caucus in the Senate had 35 members. The geopolitical significance of the Indian subcontinent as a result of the nuclearization of India and Pakistan and the events of 9/11 has meant that the U.S. administration is now well aware of the need to balance carefully the competing interests of these two countries. The rise of India as a key economic player in what Thomas Friedman (2005) describes as a "flat world" is a further reason that Indian Americans have been gaining influence on the Hill. Not surprisingly, Indian American political mobilization has been deeply imbricated by Hindutva politics.

We have seen that Hindu American leaders frequently claim to speak for all Indian Americans and are trying to obtain recognition as representatives of the larger ethnic community.[7] If Hindu nationalists become accepted as the public voice for all people of Indian ancestry in the United States, a variety of consequences are possible. Since these leaders are often hostile to other Indian groups (whether they be Muslims, Christians, or secularists), these communities will obviously be negatively affected. Tensions created within the Indian American community over the efforts of Hindutva leaders to define and articulate "Hinduness" but also "Indianness" could also spill over to the wider society as all sides in the conflict (Hindu, Muslim, and Christian Indian Americans) form alliances with other American groups, leading to the exacerbation of religious tensions within the United States and the development of competing ethnic lobbies (Kurien 2001). These schisms and challenges may undermine the efforts of Hindu Americans to oppose their racialization and obtain a position of respect in the United States as Hindus and as Indians. In the long run, therefore, it will be crucial to have credible, independent leaders who will forge coalitional alliances with other Indian and non-Indian groups to achieve these goals.

The Impact of American Hinduism on India

Because of their educational and economic standing and their location in the United States, Hindu Indian Americans wield considerable influence among the leadership and masses in India and among other diasporic Hindu communities and will undoubtedly shape the face of global Hinduism. Thus the types of satsangs, bala vihars, Hindu summer camps, Hindu student groups, and ecumenical temples developed within the American context may become popular in India and in Hindu communities around the world. The contribution of Hindu Americans to the Hindutva movement in India has received much scholarly attention. In addition to Hindu Americans' financial contributions, there are some indications that they have made important contributions to the ideological platform of the Hindutva movement as well, from the contemporary formulation of the concept of "Hindutva" by Mihir Meghani (see chapter 7), to the "Hinduism under siege" discourse and the fears of being reduced to a minority (Thapar 2000a, 608–609), to the syncretic Hinduism that the VHP began to promote in the 1980s (Rajagopal 2000, 471; 2001, 245–246). Some writers suggest that it may not be a coincidence that the VHP emerged as a Hindu nationalist organization in India only in the 1980s, after a decade during which it had been primarily active overseas (Rajagopal 2001, 245–246; van der Veer 1994, 134–137). We have also seen that Hindu American revisionist scholarship has had a significant impact on the "history wars" taking place in India. Thus well-known Indian historian Irfan Habib (2001, 15–17) comments caustically that the claims regarding the extreme antiquity of the Vedas and the scientific achievements of ancient Indians are "truly a case of genuine 'Indian Tradition' . . . manufactured in the United States. The inventions grow apace so rapidly that one is not surprised when one reads that though the Vedic Indians did not build any Pyramids here, they yet taught the Pharaohs of Egypt to build them!" The close ties between American and Indian Hindutva organizations can be seen by the fact that the parallel between the Native American and Hindu positions first drawn by Hindu Indian Americans (see chapter 10) was subsequently picked up by the Rashtriya Swayamsevak Sangh. Indian American newspapers reported that the RSS chief, K. S. Sudarshan, had discussions with Native Americans during his visit to the United States and Canada in August 2001, apparently in a bid to emphasize the similarities between the two groups. Sudarshan is reported to have said, "Hindu and native American cultures have many things in common and probably these two cultures originated from the same root" (*India Post* 2001b).

Diasporic Hindu nationalism has already had profound impacts on Indian society and politics and will be a crucial factor in determining the success of the Hindutva movement and the future of religious minorities in India. The rise of Hindu nationalism may also have serious international implications, as the nuclearization of India and Pakistan (a by-product of the competing religious nationalisms of the two countries) has demonstrated. On the positive side, however, Hindu nationalism has also influenced individuals to establish and support various social service and humanitarian projects in India. The politicization of Indian Americans (largely through the Hindutva movement) has also resulted in a significant shift in American foreign policy as the U.S. government has adopted a significantly more pro-India position than in the past.

CONCLUSION

As opposed to the symbolic, costless, and voluntarily chosen ethnicity of third- and fourth-generation white ethnics, the ethnicity of immigrants of color such as Indians is very different (see Waters 1990). It is difficult for second-generation Indian Americans, even those who do not maintain their ethnicity, to be easily accepted as "mainstream Americans." Therefore the religio-ethnic organizations of Indian Americans, far from being the means of achieving individual feelings of being special and of belonging that prevail among white ethnics (Waters 1990, 151), are group efforts to provide support in an alien and frequently hostile environment. Youth associations and religious groups in colleges and universities are becoming important venues for second-generation Indian Americans to meet fellow ethnics, celebrate ethnicity, and discuss its meaning and significance. Their importance is likely to increase over time.

Because of both the distinctiveness and fluidity of Hinduism as a religion and the racial identity of Indian Americans, it seems unlikely that either Hinduism or Hindu Indian communities in the United States will disappear in the near future. Since Hinduism, at least to some extent, seems to be serving as a substitute for an Indian racial identity, its future also depends largely on how race and racial politics evolve in this country. The evidence from countries around the world with long-established Hindu Indian communities, such as Southeast Asia (Mearns 1995), Fiji (Kelly 1991), Africa (Bhachu 1985), and the Caribbean (Vertovec 1992, 1994), where the communities remain distinct, suggests that Hindu Indian ethnicity in the United States will continue to play a substantial role in shaping the lives of its members for a long time to come, although the content of that ethnicity will undoubtedly be much modified.

In the twenty-first century, American ethnic groups remain important in shaping the contours of religion, society, and politics in the United States as well as the international arena. The case of Hindu Indian Americans highlights the dilemmas faced by multicultural societies trying to institutionalize pluralism. Policies aimed at facilitating the integration of immigrants and winning their loyalty have focused on the positive acknowledgment of cultural difference. As Tariq Modood argues (1998), religion has been the blind spot of multiculturalism. This missing perspective, of course, changed after the events of September 11, 2001, and the summer 2005 bombings in London. These tragedies showed that religious identity frequently trumps cultural and national background and that religion as a force of community solidarity urgently needs official recognition and attention. Because these events led to a greater tendency to categorize non-Western groups in Western countries in religious terms and, for the groups themselves, a greater need to "manage" and positively represent their religious identities in the public sphere (Purkayastha 2005, 174), the importance of religion as an organizing principle is only likely to increase in the future. The 2005 riots in Paris and the summer bombings in London in the same year also raised the troubling question of how radical extremism could be nurtured within the bosom of liberal, multicultural Western societies. Most of the research on multiculturalism and non-Christian groups in the West has been undertaken since 9/11 and has focused on Muslim communities in Europe (AlSayyad and Castells 2002; Fetzer and Soper 2005; Hunter 2002; Modood 2005). Although the economic and social marginality of the individuals involved in the riots in Paris and the summer bombings in London seemed to provide an obvious explanation for the participants' militancy, the Hindu American case shows that even well-placed, highly educated, "model-minority" groups in multicultural societies can develop feelings of estrangement and turn toward ethnic nationalism. This case study thus underscores the problems in current approaches to cultural identity and difference.

Steven Vertovec (2001) argues that recent commissions in the United States and the United Kingdom have promoted newer versions of multiculturalism that have attempted to move away from the bounded, cultural essentialism of previous Western approaches to recognize the multiplicity of individual identities. He points out, however, that the reality of a transnational world has not been suitably recognized by these newer versions of multiculturalism, and thus that what he describes as the "container" model of the nation-state has still been largely retained. Vertovec (2001) therefore calls for the concept of multiculturalism to be "loosened" in order to recognize the complexity of globalization, transnationalism, and a diversity of attachments (see also Bauböck 1994; Laguerre 1998; Ong 1999; Soysal 1994). I would argue further that such a loosening alone will not be enough, because a multiculturalism that does not address religious difference and the deeper issues of racialization and inequality is likely merely to legitimize the development of modular cultural nationalisms among ethnic and racial groups. What is crucial will be the development of a reconstructed multiculturalism that addresses these issues and thereby helps bring about a genuine change in the conception, treatment, and position of nonwhite and non-Western ethnic communities.

Notes

PREFACE

1. Information on scholars who have been harassed obtained through private conversations with several scholars. See also the Web site of the Hindu Unity organization, which has a Black List (earlier called a Hit List) of people critical of Hindutva (www.hinduunity.org/hitlist.html, retrieved June 4, 2001). Romila Thapar, an Indian historian, Paul Courtright, professor of religion at Emory University, Jeffrey Kripal, professor of religious studies at Rice University, and Michael Witzel, professor of Indology at Harvard have all written and spoken publicly about experiencing such harassment and threats.

2. I later discovered that this referred to the Pew Charitable Trusts and the Center for the Study of Religion at Princeton University, from whom I received funding.

3. This report was subsequently archived on the Hindu Vivek Kendra Web site (www.hvk.org/articles/0301/113.html).

4. According to the Hindutva perspective, all contemporary non-Hindus in India are converts, although Indians of Muslim and Christian background have lived in India for well over 1,200 years.

CHAPTER 1 — THE TRANSFORMATION OF HINDUISM IN THE UNITED STATES

1. Raymond Williams, who was one of the first to use the term "American Hinduism," uses it to refer to the fact that the Hindu American community and their religious organizations are "made in the U.S.A." by the assembling "of Hindu traditions in the United States from imported components by relatively unskilled labor (at least unskilled by traditional standards) and adapted to fit new designs to reach a new and growing market" (Williams 1992, 230).

2. From the turn of the twentieth century, immigration from Asian countries to the United States was virtually banned through exclusion acts. From the 1920s immigration was restricted on the basis of national origin, and quotas were set that favored immigrants from northern and western Europe. The 1965 Immigration Act dismantled the national-origins quotas and the Asian exclusion provisions and for the first time permitted immigration from countries around the world.

3. These organizations are also found among many other Hindu communities outside India.

4. Satsang groups have become more widespread in India since the 1980s (see *Hinduism Today* 1998; Narayanan 1999a, 43–44), because of the resurgence of Hinduism there and frequently in imitation of diasporic satsang groups.

5. Most households have a small area in the home where pictures or images of deities are enshrined, and where they conduct regular puja.

6. The GHEN Web site was rated number one among religious sites by Lycos, and was selected as one of the best Web sites of the year in 1998 by Yahoo Internet Life Magazine.

7. "Focus, Activities, Structure and Programs" (www.vhp-america.org/activities.htm).

8. According to the HSC Web site, the organization became independent of the VHPA in 1993. However the VHP Web site listed the HSC as one of its programs even in 2001.

CHAPTER 2 — HINDUISM IN INDIA

1. The anthropologist Frits Staal (1983) notes that some elaborate rituals described in the later Vedic texts were still being performed by some Nambudri Brahmins in Kerala in the contemporary period.

2. Vac is described in the following way in one of the Brahmanas: "This, [in the beginning] was only the Lord of the universe. His Word was with him. This Word was his second. He contemplated. He said, 'I will deliver this Word so that she will produce and bring into being all this world' " (*Tandya Maha Brahmana*, XX, 14, 2, quoted in Panikkar 1977, 107).

3. The "linga" or "lingam" is often translated as "phallus," but it literally means "distinguishing mark." In this case, the distinguishing mark of Shiva, the male principle, is the phallus.

4. According to this doctrine, the human soul is part of the one divine power, Brahman, and has no separate existence. Salvation is obtained when the individual through meditation and enlightenment realizes this and merges with God.

5. Ramanuja accepts that the soul and God are of the same essence, but argues that the soul has its own individuality and can thus have a relationship with God.

6. The creation of the world is dated at 1,972,947,101 B.C.E. according to traditional Hindu sources (Klostermaier 1989, 415).

7. According to Genesis, the dispersal took place because of the confusion that ensued when a multitude of languages developed among a hitherto monolingual population (God's punishment because people had built the Tower of Babel in defiance of his wishes). This perspective viewed Indians as some of the descendants of Noah's son Ham (the black sheep of the family, whom Noah had cursed).

8. In Müller's usage, however, the term "race" had not acquired the biological essentialism it would acquire only a few decades later as "racial science" was formulated. As the obsession with the "Aryan race" issue (at least partly growing out of Müller's Aryan race theory and his shifting use of the term) enveloped Europe, Müller remonstrated, "again and again . . . if I say Aryas, I mean neither blood nor bones, nor hair nor skull. . . . How many misunderstandings and how many controversies are due to what is deduced by arguing from language to blood-relationship or from blood-relationship to language" (Müller 1887, 120). But by this time it was too late and his clarification was largely ignored (Bryant 2001, 33).

9. According to Gail Omvedt (1993, 9–10), at the all-India level, the upper castes (the top three varnas) constitute only 15 percent of the population. The Mandal Commission report of 1980 determined that in addition to Scheduled Castes and Scheduled Tribes, who together constituted 22.5 percent of the Indian population, another 52 percent could be classified as "Backward," that is, eligible for caste-based affirmative action in some form. Thus, according to this report, the Forward or upper castes constituted 25.5 percent of the Indian population.

CHAPTER 3 — TRANSPLANTING HINDUISM IN THE UNITED STATES

1. The term "Hindu" was introduced as a census category in 1930. It disappeared in the 1950 schedule but appeared again in 1960, when enumerators for the census were instructed to classify those who identified as "Indian" in the race item as "Hindu" (Gupta 1999, 86).

2. Indian customs were followed only when the men died. Sikh and Hindu men were cremated and the appropriate death rituals were performed (Leonard 1992, 129).

3. The number of H-1B visas issued to people from India jumped from 2,697 in 1990 to 55,047 in 2000 (www.iacfpa.org/press/census515.htm). Reports indicate that through the 1990s about half of all the H-1B visas issued went to Indians.

4. The Harvard Pluralism Project provides two estimates for 2000: 1,285,000 from the 2000 World Almanac, and 1,032,000, from the 2000 Britannica Book of the Year (www.pluralism.org/resources/statistics/tradition.php). Regional, nonrandom surveys of the religious distribution of the Indian American population conducted at different periods have estimated that Hindus constituted from 65 percent in Atlanta and Queens, New York (Fenton 1988, 28; Min 2003, 129) to around 77 percent in Chicago (Rangaswamy 2000, 132), and 81 percent in Pittsburgh (Clothey 1983).

5. The same is true (though to a much lesser extent) in the cases of men who married non-Indian women or Indian women from a different subcultural background.

6. The significant exception to this pattern is in the immigration of nurses from India. As a consequence of Indian gender norms, most individuals who work in this profession are women. Because of the interaction of ethnicity and gender, a significant proportion of Indian nurses (both in India and overseas) are Christians from Kerala state. The shortage of nursing professionals in the United States served as the stimulus for the immigration of the group, who subsequently sponsored their husbands (see George 2005; Joseph 1992).

7. A good example is the work by Jain (1989), who studied the community in 1963 and 1987 and came to this conclusion.

8. The satguru is quoted as noting with pride that the group had "created a global publication to advance the cause of Hindutva" (Melwani, n.d. "The Story of Hinduism Today," www.hinduismtoday.com/about_us.shtml).

9. In his book *Living with Siva* (excerpted in the November/December 2001 issue of *Hinduism Today*), the satguru restricts women's activities to the home sphere, instructs them to worship their husbands as Siva, exhorts them to be the first up and the last to retire, to eat only after their husband and family have eaten, and to practice menstrual taboos. He also advocates arranged marriages and forbids divorces.

10. For instance, in August 1997, 121 Vedic priests (81 from India) conducted an Adi Rudra Maha Yajna to Lord Shiva for eleven days in Pennsylvania (reported in *Hinduism Today*, December 1997). In April 1999, a Maruti Mahayagna was conducted for three days in Southern California (reported in *India Post*, May 7, 1999), and in August 2001, a nine-day Gayatri Katha was organized in Chicago.

11. "Desi" is a term for those hailing from the Indian subcontinent.

12. The Indicorps was formed in mid-2001 by three siblings to provide Indian American youth the opportunity to do social work in India. See www.indicorps.org.

CHAPTER 4 — "WE ARE BETTER HINDUS HERE"

1. Because it was not considered seemly for women to make separate dishes for their own consumption, in practice this meant that they could not eat much of the food that they prepared for their families.

2. In two cases, both the man and the woman had arrived in the country independently and married later. Only in one case did the woman come first as a medical student and then subsequently sponsor her husband.

3. Two studies, both based on interviews with Bengali-speaking Indian women in New Jersey, found, however, that the respondents felt that the effect of migration on their lives had been mostly negative, due to the loss of their "female world" that had provided emotional intimacy and social support in India (S. S. Dasgupta 1989, 159; Ganguly 1992, 42).

4. Marriage to black Americans was generally strictly taboo.

5. As far as I know, this workshop never materialized.

6. He was based in Southern California for the last few years of his life and died in 1992 in San Diego.

7. This statement was challenged by the Narayans, who asserted that it did not apply to the Tamil bala vihar. Because my fieldwork there was shorter and confined mainly to participant-observation of the monthly meetings, I do not have direct evidence to support my claim. However, it seemed to me more than a coincidence that all the members seemed to be well placed and to have children in top schools and universities (see my discussion of this later in the chapter). The overwhelming upper-class atmosphere and the constant talk about economic and professional achievements were also alluded to by several members, and two members who had been well placed in the past but had recently experienced some economic misfortunes told me that such talk made them uncomfortable.

8. Significantly, the only time when there were men on the stage was during the speeches of the KHO president and the chief guest of the function, both of whom were men.

CHAPTER 5 —— THE ABODE OF GOD

1. Although government supervision does have its supporters, this policy has also led to a great deal of resentment among temple functionaries and among Hindus at large, who feel that it is discriminatory for the government to regulate only the religious institutions of Hindus (non-Hindu groups are allowed to manage their institutions without state interference).

2. The TTD official who met with the HTSSC stipulated that the murti in Malibu could not be taller than the murti in Tirupathi.

3. The latter are sometimes directly appointed by the administrative government officer in charge of the temple (after applicants are solicited by public announcements). In other cases, the government officer appoints regional committees to select trustees (Presler 1987, 67–69). Sometimes a combination of these procedures is used, with the regional committees coming up with a list of names from which the administrative officer makes the appointment.

4. Hinduism has no official conversion ceremony, and traditionally a Hindu is defined as someone born into a Hindu family. Recognizing the needs and financial contributions of American believers like Will, however, the Malibu temple defines Hindus as those who "have faith in Hinduism." Some American believers also go through a ceremony conducted by priests in which they take Hindu names; the manager told me that it was possible that this might have taken place at the Malibu temple as well.

5. This is not to say that such conflicts do not take place in India. In fact, they have a long history there (see Presler 1987).

6. In the United Kingdom, for instance, "Ministers of Religion" are now required to pass a high-level English-language test before their visas can be approved. Hindu leaders in that country are requesting an exemption from this rule for temple priests, arguing that their role is purely devotional and not pastoral ("UK Hindus Appeal Visa Restrictions on Priests," Hindu Press International (HPI), July 7, 2005).

7. Several of the major Hindu temples in India are officially open only to Hindus. Some, like the Aiyappa shrine in Sabarimala, south India, are not open to women who are in the reproductive age group.

8. With the inauguration of a sprawling thirty-acre cultural complex in Delhi in November 2005, featuring exhibition halls focusing on India's cultural heritage and Indian moral values, the BAPS is also likely to become a major public face for Hinduism in India as well.

9. One of the teenage boys in the Los Angeles temple talked about how Pramukh Swami had told his father to sell everything in California in the 1980s. "My father followed his directions and a year after he sold everything, the recession hit California. We could have lost everything. We felt very lucky for that." The man later started a business in a midwestern city that was flourishing.

CHAPTER 6 — FORGING AN OFFICIAL HINDUISM IN INDIA

1. Van der Veer (1996, 258) argues that the "hierarchical relativism" of Hindu doctrine (that there are many paths to God but some are better than others) was reinterpreted by Hindu reformers in the nineteenth and twentieth centuries "in orientalist terms, as 'tolerance.'" Pinch (1996) similarly points out that the emphasis on tolerance was a strategy developed by Hindu pandits and reformers as a way to organize and counter Western hegemony. "Tolerance reconciled the variant religious traditions of the colonized subcontinent into a serviceable theological whole by the late eighteenth century, while pacifism was Gandhi's way of turning a Jain and bhakti-driven aversion to sacrificial violence into a weapon with which to mount a civilizational attack on the West" (Pinch 1996, 141).

2. Quotation from the Trust Deed of the Brahmo Samaj, cited in Flood (1996), 253.

3. See the documentation and discussion of such literature in Hasan (1996), 200–202.

4. From the title page of *Hindutva*, 4th edition, quoted in Pandey (1993), 248.

5. Gandhi's death in 1948 at the hands of a Hindu nationalist, Nathuram Godse, was partly responsible for this development.

6. S. Gopal, *Jawaharlal Nehru*, 3:172, cited in Jaffrelot (1996), 103–104, note 123.

7. "The Birth of Vishwa Hindu Parishad," *Hindu Vishwa*, July 1982, 3, cited in van der Veer (1994, 131).

8. *Organizer*, Diwali Special (1964, 15), cited in Jaffrelot (1996, 197).

9. *Organizer*, June 11, 1967, 14, cited in Jaffrelot (1996, 201).

10. *Hindu Vishva*, March–April 1979, 89, cited in Jaffrelot (1996, 348).

11. "Why You Should Work for Vishwa Hindu Parishad," in *Shraddhanjali Smarika*, 69, cited in Jaffrelot (1996, 202).

12. Vishwa Hindu Parishad, *The Hindu Awakening—Retrospect and Promise* (New Delhi, n.d.), 28, cited in Jaffrelot (1996, 351).

13. See also Anderson (1998, 73); Mathew (2000); Mathew and Prashad (2000, 529–530).

14. Cassette marked VHP–New Delhi, entitled Ram Shila Puja, cited in Jaffrelot (1996, 396).

15. Cited in Nandy et al. (1995, 53).

16. G. Lodha, *How Long Shri Ram Will Be Insulted in Ayodhya?*, VHP, n.p., n.d., cited in Jaffrelot (1996, 402). See also Gyanendra Pandey (1993a, 10). Both Jaffrelot and Pandey stress that such claims are false.

17. Sarkar (2002) and other scholars (e.g., Basu 2000) have argued that rape of Muslim women has been enjoined upon Hindu men as a religious duty, right from the beginning of Hindu nationalism (for instance, in the writings of Sarvarkar).

18. http//iic.nic.in/vsiic/piocard.htm.

19. Basu (1995, 1996); Fuller (2001); Geetha and Jayanthi (1995); Hansen (1999), esp. 188–196.

20. For instance, see the essays in Sarkar and Butalia (1995). See also Basu (1996); Chhachhi (1994); Datta (2002); Sarkar (1991).

CHAPTER 7 — FORGING AN OFFICIAL HINDUISM IN THE UNITED STATES

1. Berbrier (1998, 2002) shows how ethnic identification has become such an important and acceptable source of cultural capital in contemporary America that ethnic activists from groups as diverse as deaf individuals, gays, and white supremacists have reinvented themselves as cultural minorities by invoking the tropes of "heritage preservation" and "ethnic pride," on the one hand, and of "victimization," on the other.

2. Interestingly, I noticed that by 2005 (when I checked the Web site again), the article appeared on the BJP Web site without mentioning the name of the author (at www.bjp.org/philo.htm). But the same article appeared with the name of the author at www.bjp.org/history/htvintro-mm.html.

3. With help from Dipa Gupta and Sujatha Ramesh.

4. Statement made by Prithvi Raj Singh, president of FHA, at a banquet organized to raise money for the construction of a local temple (Saberwal 1995, DSW6). Despite the FHA's professed goal, it could not maintain internal unity and in late 1998, a section of the organization broke away to form a parallel organization—the American Hindu Federation (AHF).

5. They claim that around 20,000 people attended their Diwali-Dussera function in 1999 (FHA 1999).

6. In 1997 the parent company added two Indian American television news programs, one from San Francisco and the other from New York, further expanding its reach and influence within the Indian American community.

7. François Gautier (http:www.mantra.com/holocaust/HinduHolocaustMuseum), retrieved June 26, 2003.

8. For instance, see the Nation of Hindutva Web site (http:www.geocities.com/Capitol Hill/Lobby/9089/links/organizations.html, retrieved May 12, 2003). This site has gone off the Web now; Hindu Unity has a link to it, but the link is no longer active.

9. From the Web site of the Hindu Unity organization (http://www.hinduunity.org), retrieved June 23, 2003.

10. This sentiment has been voiced on some of the Internet discussion groups.

11. An independent study conducted in the United Kingdom came to much the same conclusion about Hindu organizations in that country. See the report by Jonathan Miller of Channel Four in Britain (http:www.channe14.com/news/homez/stories/20021212/guj/html, retrieved December 12, 2002).

12. See the description on the Web site of the Dharam Hinduja Institute of Indic Research (DHIIR) at the University of Cambridge, www.divinity.cam.ac.uk/CARTS/dhiir/ default.html.

13. See description of the conference at www.lokvani.com/lokvani/article.php?article_id=410, retrieved November 2, 2004.

CHAPTER 8 — RE-VISIONING INDIAN HISTORY

1. The best example is the attack in January 2004 on a well-known center for historical research, the Oriental Institute in Pune, near Bombay, which had been mentioned in the acknowledgments of a book on Shivaji (2003) by an American professor, James W. Laine. The militants responsible for the attack subsequently held public meetings at which they threatened to arrest "every Indian named in the book's acknowledgements" (Dalrymple 2005).

2. Quotations from article in *Indian Express,* December 20, 2001, cited by the Delhi Historians' Group (2001), 9.

3. Article in *Hindu,* October 23, 2001, cited by the Delhi Historians' Group (2001), 5.

4. Hindu sadhus traditionally wear saffron robes, and thus the term "saffron" has come to be associated with the Hindutva movement.

5. See Bryant (2001) and Witzel (2001) for a detailed discussion of the work of these scholars.

6. Because there does not seem to be any Indian influence on the language in contrast to the loan words in Sanskrit derived from non-Aryan Indian sources.

7. This generally indicates that the items were unfamiliar to the Indo-Aryan speakers and that they were a largely nomadic people who encountered settled agriculture in India.

8. This characterization is based on a sentence excerpted from one of his letters to his wife, where he says, "This edition of mine . . . the Veda . . . will hereafter tell to a great extent on the fate of India . . . it is the root of their religion, and to show them what that root is, is the only way of uprooting all that has sprung up from it during the last 3000 years" (Müller 1902, 63–64, quoted in Bryant 2001, 289).

9. N. S. Rajaram is now based in India but has over twenty years of teaching experience in universities in the United States.

10. See the discussion of the AMT versus the OIT scholars and their interpretation of the IVC in Bryant (2001).

11. Skeptics of this argument like Michael Witzel, however, argue that the ability to read this code in the Vedas is due more to the creativity of Kak, rather than to the actual evidence in the text (e.g., see Witzel 2001, 61).

12. See the compilation of evidence on the Web site www.atributetohinduism.com, for instance, or in the work of Stephen Knapp (2000).

13. It was subsequently picked up by the Arabs in the seventh or eighth century C.E. and reached Europe through them in the twelfth century. See the article "Indic Mathematics: India and the Scientific Revolution" by David Gray, n.d., on the Web site www.infinityfoundation.com, retrieved July 10, 2002.

14. See the series of articles on Indic "inner science" on the Web site www.infinity foundation.com.

15. E.g., the *Satpatha Brahmana* 3.41.2 and the *Brihadaranyaka Upanishad* 6.4.18, cited in Thapar (2001).

16. H. D. Sankalia, "The Cow in History," in *Seminar*, May 1967, 93; and B. B. Lal, *Ancient India* nos. 10 and 11 (1954–55), 14, cited in Thapar (2001).

17. The book was subsequently published in London by Verso Books in 2002 under the title *The Myth of the Holy Cow*.

18. Internet articles include "Hindu Kush Means Hindu Slaughter" by Shrinandan Vyas, and those on Hindutva Web magazines like *Sword of Truth* (www.swordoftruth.com). Sita Ram Goel was an amateur historian and publisher of the Voice of India publishing house. François Gautier is a French journalist, married to an Indian, who has lived in India for decades. Arun Shourie is an Indian journalist with a Ph.D. in economics.

19. E.g., see the accounts of Eaton (2000), Keay (2000), Metcalf and Metcalf (2002), and Stein (1998).

20. E.g., Rajiv Malhotra of the Infinity Foundation.

21. In the colonial period, British men and women were colloquially referred to as "Sahib" and "Memsahib" by Indians.

22. Brian K. Smith (1994) argues that the varna system was a mapping onto the social universe of principles that Vedic religious leaders believed organized the universe as a whole, and that therefore this classification of society was considered to be a part of a primordial and universally applicable order of things.

23. Kumkum Sangari and Sudesh Vaid point out that sometimes such laws were counterproductive, due to caveats or clauses in them that actually reinforced the practices they sought to abolish (Sangari and Vaid 1990, 15–17).

24. Sarkar (2001, 224), citing a newspaper article, *Dainik O Samachar Chandrika,* January 14, 1891.

25. Sarkar points out that he tended to vacillate between liberalism and conservatism (2001, 135–162).

26. Bankimchandra Chattopadhyay, "Kamalakanter Daptar," *Bankim Rachanabali,* vol. 2 (Calcutta, 1954), cited in Sarkar (2001), 203.

27. Nationalists, reformists, and colonialists, as Lata Mani points out (1990), to different degrees, all created a new colonial discourse of knowledge by canonizing brahmanical religious texts as the precepts guiding the everyday behavior of all Hindus.

28. In addition to Punjab in India, and the adjoining states of Haryana, Himachel Pradesh, and Delhi, colonial Punjab included a core part of current-day Pakistan.

29. These are usually cases where the groom's family continues to demand cash or consumer goods after the marriage and the bride's family is unable to meet these demands. Such women are often killed by being burned through contact with the kitchen fire (so that the death can be described as being a result of a "cooking accident"). The murder of the bride paves the way for the man to marry again and obtain another dowry.

30. E.g., see the report on the 2005 conference in Houston, Texas, by the Hindu Press International (HPI), September 28, 2005 (www.hinduismtoday.com/hpi2005/9/28.shtml).

CHAPTER 9 — CHALLENGING AMERICAN PLURALISM

1. The texts of these talks were posted on Indictraditions on September 25, 2001 and October 4, 2001. The texts were subsequently combined and archived by HICAD, "Lessons from Gita on Fighting Terrorism," by Rajiv Malhotra (www.hicad.org/gita.htm). A modified version, "Gita on Fighting Terrorism," was also posted on the Infinity Foundation Web site (www.infinityfoundation.com/mandala/s_es/s_es_malho_gita.htm).

2. Reported at http://www.infinityfoundation.com/mandala/s_es/s_es_rao-r_govt.htm.

3. One was on a Dalit critique of the *Ramayana* and the other a critical look at the Hindu nationalist movement in India.

4. http://www.petitiononline.com/AMUSEUM, retrieved January 23, 2002.

5. This information is based on eyewitness reports by people who attended the film showings.

6. See www.hinduamericanfoundation.org/Content/Achievements.html, retrieved August 8, 2005.

7. Press Release, October 20, 2004, archived at www.hinduamericanfoundation.org.

8. See www.infinityfoundation.com/people.shtml.

9. From "Complaint against Anti-Rama Song in Secondary Schools," www.infinityfoundation.com/ECITnehletterframe.htm, retrieved December 16, 2001.

10. Rajiv Malhotra, "Who Speaks for Hinduism? A Critique of the Special Issue of the Journal of the American Academy of Religion," www.infinityfoundation.com/mandala/s_es/s_malho_critiq.htm.

11. This issue has been frequently discussed on the Religions in South Asia list-serv (RISA-L).

12. E.g., as indicated in note 1, Preface.

13. Archived at www.infinityfoundation.com/mandala.s_rv_misce_feed.htm, retrieved July 15, 2004.

14. Material for this paragraph was taken from an Internet report on the panel (including the papers presented), John Stratton Hawley, "Defamation/Anti-defamation: Hindus in Dialogue with the Western Academy," http://www.web.barnard.columbia.edu/religion/hindu/malhotra_defamation/html.

15. The controversy and the presentations of the group are archived under the title "Animal House: The South Asian Religious Studies Circus," jitnasa.india-forum.com.

16. The *Washington Post* coverage of the issue resulted in another angry round of articles as writers like Rajiv Malhotra wrote to argue that the writer was biased and had actually been commissioned to write the article by a public relations firm working for Emory University. (See the discussion in Malhotra 2004c, d; Sanu 2004; Vedantam 2004b.)

17. He gives as examples the exotic of anthropology, colonial or Marxist frameworks in history, U.S. foreign policy interests in South Asian studies, and non-Indian categories in religious studies (Malhotra 2003c, 4).

18. For instance, Western feminists telling Indian women that they are victims of Indian culture, Dalit (lower-caste) activists being sponsored to blame Brahmins, and the Aryan theory used to create a separate Dravidian identity and blame Aryan north Indians as foreign imperialists.

CHAPTER 10 — BEING YOUNG, BROWN, AND HINDU:

1. In a later interview Vijay said that they had decided to be a chapter of the HSC rather than an unaffiliated Hindu campus organization because they realized the advantages of being part of a national organization. Ravi was a close family friend of the person who had founded an earlier chapter of the organization on another Southern California campus. This friend, Murali, had been involved with the VHP all his life and had pointed Ravi in the direction of the HSC. Although Ravi and Vijay indicated that the HSC had since become completely independent of the VHP and other Sangh Parivar organizations, local VHP and RSS members were present for at least two of the meetings during my semester of fieldwork and one of them was a constant presence on the HSC discussion forum.

2. However, a few years later I found that the independent Hindu student organization had developed a Web site that included an exposition of Hindutva, in this case defining it as an outlook "upholding righteousness and fighting ignoble attitudes."

CHAPTER 11 — THE DEVELOPMENT OF AN AMERICAN HINDUISM

1. I have noticed a big increase in the number of people who support some aspects of the Hindutva movement between the time I started my research in 1994 and the present time.

2. Some of these ideas include the following: (1) Hinduism is the oldest continuously existing religion and that the Vedas and the Vedic period represents the purest and highest stage; (2) Hinduism suffered a decline in the medieval period under the Mughals and in the modern period under the British; (3) many of the problems seen in Hinduism from the medieval period on, such as the presence of the caste system and a decline in the status of women, were due to the impact of Muslim rule and to a corruption of Hindu ideals and are not an inherent part of Hinduism; (4) the government of India (including the former BJP-led government) under the pretext of secularism discriminates against Hindus and favors Muslims and Christians; (5) the reason that the Muslims and the British were able to gain control over India was because of the lack of unity and passivity of Hindus; (6) it is time that Hindus united and asserted themselves using the model of Rama and other deities who were willing to fight to protect justice or dharma; (7) the greatest problem facing India today is Islamic terrorism and Christian evangelism; (8) unless India becomes strong, Indians will not get respect in the United States.

3. See the "Complaint against Anti-Rama Song in Secondary Schools," http:www. infinityfoundation.com/ECITnehletterframe.htm, retrieved December 16, 2001.

4. "March 12 Proclaimed Narayan Kataria Day in Queens," *India Post*, April 11, 2003, 6.

5. The rapid development of many metropolitan areas in India over the past decade following liberalization and the IT boom has greatly increased the pride Indian immigrants take in contemporary India.

6. For instance, see the attack on Professor Madhav Deshpande, who criticized some of the edits proposed by the VF and HEF in the California textbook case (Kalyanaraman 2006).

7. For instance, in 2004, when it was formed, the Hindu American Foundation claimed that it represented the "2 million strong" Hindu American community. But since the total number of Indian Americans in the country was only 1.7 million in the year 2000, this number could have been obtained only by assuming that all of them were Hindu and by projecting the increase for that population over the intervening years.

Glossary

aarti. Ritual in which a flame is moved clockwise in front of a picture or statue of a deity

abishekham. Ritual bath of deity

Agamas. Scriptures

ahimsa. Nonviolence; a concept championed by Mohandas Gandhi

ashram. Monastery

asura. Demon

avatars. incarnations

Bajrang Dal. Militant activist group

bala vihar. Educational group for children

bhajan. Devotional song

bhaktha. Devotee

bhakti. Loving devotion

Bharat. Indigenous term for India

Bharatanatyam. South Indian dance

Bharatiya Janata Party (BJP). Indian People's Party

Brahman. The one great cosmic power

Brahmin. Priestly caste

candala. Lowest of the Untouchable groups

Dalit. Term adopted by mobilized members of former Untouchable castes

darshan. Visual communion with a deity

desi. Someone hailing from the Indian subcontinent

deva. Deity or divine power

dharma. Righteousness, duty, a moral and social obligation; prescribed duties; moral order

Dharma Shastras. Codes of law

Ghadar. Radical movement originating in Northern California, whose mission was the violent overthrow of British rule in India

gramadevata. Village deity

gunas. Qualities

guru. Spiritual guide or teacher

hari mandir. Type of Swaminarayan Temple, converted from a building used for other purposes

Hindu Swayamsevak Sangh (HSS). Parallel organization to the RSS

Hindutva. Hinduness

ishtadeva. Chosen deity

karma. Actions in the previous life; the idea that every action has consequences for the individual

Kshatriya. Warrior caste

mantra Chant

maryada. Honor, rights of precedence in temples

mela. Religious fair

moksha. Liberation

murti. Image of a deity

papa. Sins resulting from deviations from dharma

pativrata. Devoted wife

prasadha. Consecrated food offering

puja. Worship

punya. Merits brought by following dharma

Ram Janmabhumi/Janmabhoomi. Movement for the liberation of Rama's birthplace in Ayodhya in north India

Rama Rajya. Kingdom of Rama

Ram-raj. Rule of Rama, king of Ayodhya

Ram Shila Pujas. Pujas to sacralize the bricks of the Ram Temple for the Lord Ram

rashtra. Nation

Rashtriya Swayamsevak Sangh (RSS). National Volunteer Corps

sabha. Assembly

sadhu. Ascetic religious seeker

sampradaya. Religious tradition

samaiyo. Sacred festival celebration

samsara. Cycle of reincarnation

samskara. Life-cycle rite

Sanatana Dharma. Name that some Hindus give to Hinduism, meaning "eternal faith"; the eternal law manifested in the Vedas

Sangh Parivar. Family of Hindu organizations

sannyasin. World-renouncing ascetic

Sanskriti. Indian culture

sanstha. Subsect

sant. Saint

satguru. "True" guru

satsang. Local worship group

satyagraha. Truth-force; a concept championed by Mohandas Gandhi

Shaivism. The tradition that worships Lord Shiva

shakhas. Local branches of swayamsevaks

shakti. Power, also conceptualized as a female principle

Shaktism. Traditions that worship Devi, the mother goddess

Shankaracharya. Head of a monastic order tied to a particular Hindu philosophical schools

shastras. Ancient Sanskrit texts or scriptures

shikarabadda mandir. Type of Swaminarayan Temple made of limestone and marble, built from the ground up following guidelines in the scriptures, with domes or spires over the central shrines.

shilpis. Artisans who make sculptures

shuddi. Purification

smriti. "Remembered" scriptures which are authored by humans but still considered to be inspired texts

sruti. "Revealed" scriptures which are considered to be authorless and thus enshrine eternal truth

sthapathi. Traditional temple architect

Sudra. Service worker caste

sumangali. A woman whose husband is alive

swadeshi. Indigenously made goods; a movement led by Mohandas Gandhi to boycott British-made goods

swayamsevaks. Group of young men committed to serving the cause of Hindu unity and defense

upanayana: Initiation

Vaishya. Merchant caste

Vaishnavism. Tradition that worships Lord Vishnu as the primary deity

varna. Four caste categories

varnashrama dharma. Moral code governing the behavior of men of the four varnas in the four stages of life

Vishwa Hindu Parishad (VHP). World Hindu Council

Vishwa Hindu Parishad of America (VHPA). American branch of the World Hindu Council

vrata. Votive observance usually characterized by partial fasts (i.e., abstaining from certain foods)

yatra. March or a religious procession

References

Abraham, Itty, and Samip Mallick. 2004. "RSS Public Diplomacy2." www.sas.upenn.edu/~dludden/RSS%20Public%Diplomacy2.htm. Retrieved August 18, 2005.

Abraham, Margaret. 2000. *Speaking the Unspeakable: Marital Violence among South Asian Immigrants in the United States.* New Brunswick, NJ: Rutgers University Press.

Agarwal, Purshottam. 1995. "Sarvarkar, Surat and Draupadi: Legitimizing Rape as a Political Weapon." Pp. 29–57 in *Women and the Hindu Right: A Collection of Essays,* edited by T. Sarkar and U. Butalia. New Delhi: Kali for Women.

Agarwal, Priya. 1991. *Passage from India: Post-1965 Indian Immigrants and Their Children.* Palos Verdes, CA: Yuvati Press.

Agarwal, Vishal, and Kalavai Venkat. 2003a. "When the Cigar Becomes a Phallus. Part I." *Sulekha.com,* December 8. http://www.sulekha.com/expressions/articledesc.asp?cid=307042.

———. 2003b. "When the Cigar Becomes a Phallus. Part II." *Sulekha.com,* December 15. http://www.sulekha.com/expressions/articlesdesc.asp?cid=307053.

Ahmad, Mumtaz. 1991. "Islamic Fundamentalism in South Asia: The Jamaat-I-Islami and the Tablighi Jamaat." Pp. 457–530 in *Fundamentalisms Observed,* edited by M. Marty and R. S. Appleby. Chicago: University of Chicago Press.

Ahmed, K. 1997. "South-Asian American Adolescent Girls: Integrating Identities and Cultures." Paper presented at the South Asian Women's Conference, Los Angeles.

Ahmed, Patricia. 2001. "The Dialectic between Discourse and Collective Action Revisited: The Case of the Hindu Nationalist Movement in the Central Provinces: 1908–1945." Presentation at the annual meeting of the American Sociological Association, Anaheim, Calif.

Allen, James P., and Eugene Turner. 1997. *The Ethnic Quilt: Population Diversity in Southern California.* Northridge, CA: Center for Geographical Studies, Department of Geography, California State Northridge.

AlSayyad, Nezar, and Manuel Castells. 2002. *Muslim Europe or Euro-Islam? Politics, Culture, and Citizenship in the Age of Globalization.* Oxford: Lexington Books.

Altekar, A. S. 1959. *The Position of Women in Hindu Civilization: From Prehistoric Times to the Present Day.* Delhi: Motilal Banarsidass.

Anderson, Benedict. 1998. "Long Distance Nationalism." Pp. 58–76 in *The Spectre of Comparisons: Nationalism, Southeast Asia, and the World,* by Benedict Anderson. London: Verso.

Andezian, S. 1986. "Women's Roles in Organizing Symbolic Life: Algerian Female Immigrants in France." Pp. 254–266 in *International Migration: The Female Experience*, edited by R. J. Simon and C. B. Brettell. Totowa, NJ: Rowman and Allanheld.

Appadurai, Arjun. 1981. *Worship and Conflict under Colonial Rule: A South Indian Case.* Cambridge: Cambridge University Press.

———. 1996. *Modernity at Large: Cultural Dimensions of Globalization.* Minneapolis: University of Minnesota Press.

Babb, Lawrence A. 1975. *The Divine Hierarchy: Popular Hinduism in Central India.* New York: Columbia University Press.

Bacon, Jean. 1996. *Life Lines: Community, Family, and Assimilation among Asian Indian Immigrants.* New York: Oxford University Press.

Bailey, Benjamin. 2001. "Dominican-American Ethnic/Racial Identities and United States Social Categories." *International Migration Review* 35:677–708.

Bailly, Jean-Sylvain. 1777. *Letters sur l'origine des sciences et sur celle des peuples de l'Asie.* Paris: Frères Debure.

Balagangadhara, S. N. 1994. *"The Heathen in His Blindness . . .": Asia, the West, and the Dynamic of Religion.* Leiden: E. J. Brill.

Banerjee, Aditi. 2003. "Hindu American: Both Sides of the Hyphen." *Silicon India,* December 30. www.siliconindia.com.

Banerjee, Kanchan. 2003. "What Is Dharma, What is Religion." Global Dharma Conference, July 25–27, Edison, NJ. Brochure.

Basch, Linda, Nina Glick Schiller, and Cristina Szanton Blanc. 1994. *Nations Unbound: Transnational Projects, Postcolonial Predicaments, and Deterritorialized Nation-States.* Basel: Gordon and Breach.

Basham, A. L. [1967] 1993. *The Wonder That Was India: A Survey of the History and Culture of the Indian Sub-continent before the Coming of the Muslims.* Calcutta: Rupa and Co.

Basu, Amrita. 1995. "Feminism Inverted: The Gendered Imagery and Real Women of Hindu Nationalism." Pp. 158–180 in *Women and the Hindu Right: A Collection of Essays,* edited by T. Sarkar and U. Butalia. New Delhi: Kali for Women.

———. 1996. "Mass Movement or Elite Conspiracy? The Puzzle of Hindu Nationalism." Pp. 55–80 in *Contesting the Nation: Religion, Community, and the Politics of Democracy in India,* edited by D. Ludden. Philadelphia: University of Pennsylvania Press.

———. 2000. "Engendering Communal Violence: Men as Victims, Women as Agents." Pp. 265–285 in *The Interplay of Gender, Religion, and Politics in India,* edited by J. Leslie and M. McGee. New Delhi: Oxford University Press.

Bauböck, Rainer. 1994. *Transnational Citizenship: Membership and Rights in International Migration.* Aldershot, England: Edward Elgar.

Bayly, Susan. 1989. *Saints, Goddesses, and Kings.* Cambridge: Cambridge University Press.

Bean, Frank D., and Gillian Stevens. 2003. *America's Newcomers and the Dynamics of Diversity.* New York: Russell Sage Foundation.

Berbrier, Mitch. 1998. " 'Half the Battle': Cultural Resonance, Framing Processes, and Ethnic Affectations in Contemporary White Separatist Rhetoric." *Social Problems* 45:431–450.

———. 2002. "Making Minorities: Cultural Spaces, Stigma Transformation Frames, and the Categorical Status Claims of Deaf, Gay, and White Supremist Activists in Late Twentieth Century America." *Sociological Forum* 17:553–591.

Bernstein, Carl. 1992. "The Holy Alliance." *Time,* February 24, pp. 28–35.

Bhatia, Zen S. 1997. "Letter to the editor: Symposium on human rights under Islam." *India West,* July 18, pp. A5–6.

Bhatt, Chetan. 1997. *Liberation and Purity: Race, New Religious Movements, and the Ethics of Postmodernity.* London: University College of London.

————. 2000. "*Dharmo rakshati rakshitah:* Hindutva movements in the UK." *Ethnic and Racial Studies* 23:559–593.

Bhattacharjee, Annanya. 1992. "The Habit of Ex-Nomination: Nation, Woman, and the Indian Immigrant Bourgeoisie." *Public Culture* 5:19–44.

Bhattacharyya, Somnath. 2002. "Kali's Child: Psychological and Hermeneutical Problems." *Sulekha.com,* December 14.

Bhutani, S. D. 1994. "A Study of Asian Indian Women in the U.S.: The Reconceptualization of Self." Ph.D. dissertation, Department of Education, University of Pennsylvania.

Bilimoria, Purushottama. 2001. "The Making of the Hindu in Australia: A Diasporic Narrative." Pp. 3–34 in *Hindu Diaspora: Global Perspectives,* edited by T. S. Rukmani. New Delhi: Munshiram Manoharlal.

Blauner, R. 1994. "Colonized and Immigrant Minorities." Pp. 149–160 in *From Different Shores: Perspectives on Race and Ethnicity in America,* edited by R. Takaki. Oxford: Oxford University Press.

Bowen, David. 1987. "The Evolution of Gujarati Hindu Organizations in Bradford." Pp. 15–31 in *Hinduism in Great Britain: The Perpetuation of Religion in an Alien Cultural Mileu,* edited by R. Burghart. London: Tavistock Publications.

Breckenridge, Carol A., and Peter van der Veer. 1993. "Orientalism and the Postcolonial Predicament." Pp. 1–19 in *Orientalism and the Postcolonial Predicament,* edited by C. A. Breckenridge and P. van der Veer. Philadelphia: University of Pennsylvania Press.

Bryant, Edwin. 2001. *The Quest for the Origins of Vedic Culture: The Indo-Aryan Migration Debate.* Oxford: Oxford University Press.

Burghart, Richard. 1987a. "Introduction: The Diffusion of Hinduism to Great Britain." Pp. 1–14 in *Hinduism in Great Britain: The Perpetuation of Religion in an Alien Milieu,* edited by R. Burghart. London: Tavistock Publications.

————. 1987b. "The Perpetuation of Hinduism in an Alien Cultural Milieu." Pp. 224–251 in *Hinduism in Great Britain: The Perpetuation of Religion in an Alien Cultural Milieu,* edited by R. Burghart. London: Tavistock.

Busto, Rudy V. 1996. "The Gospel According to the Model Minority?: Hazarding an Interpretation of Asian American Evangelical College Students." *Amerasia Journal* 22:133–147.

Butterfield, Sherri-Ann. 2004. "Challenging American Conceptions of Race and Ethnicity: Second Generation West Indian Immigrants." *International Journal of Sociology and Social Policy* 24:75–102.

Caglar, Ayse S. 1997. "Hyphenated Identities and the Limits of 'Culture.' " Pp. 169–185 in *The Politics of Multiculturism in the New Europe: Racism, Identity, and Community,* edited by T. Modood and P. Werbner. London: Zed Books.

Carman, John, and Vasudha Narayanan. 1989. *The Tamil Veda: Pillan's Interpretation of the Tiruvaymoli.* Berkeley: University of California Press.

Casanova, Jose. 1994. *Public Religions in the Modern World.* Chicago: University of Chicago Press.

Chai, Karen J. 1998. "Competing for the Second Generation: English-Language Ministry at a Korean Protestant Church." Pp. 295–332 in *Gatherings in Diaspora: Religious Communities and the New Immigration,* edited by R. Stephen Warner and Judith G. Wittner. Philadelphia, PA: Temple University Press.

————. 2001. "Beyond 'Strictness' to Distinctiveness: Generational Transition in Korean Protestant Churches." Pp. 157–180 in *Korean Americans and Their Religions: Pilgrims and Missionaries from a Different Shore,* edited by K. Ho-Young, K. C. Kim, and R. S. Warner. University Park: Pennsylvania State University Press.

Chatterjee, Partha. 1993. *The Nation and Its Fragments: Colonial and Postcolonial Histories.* Princeton, NJ: Princeton University Press.

———. 1995. "History and the Nationalization of Hinduism." Pp. 103–128 in *Representing Hinduism: The Construction of Religious Traditions and National Identity*, edited by V. Dalmia and H. von Stietencron. Thousand Oaks, CA: Sage Publications.

Chhachhi, Amrita. 1994. "Identity Politics, Secularism, and Women: A South Asian Perspective." Pp. 74–95 in *Forging Identities: Gender, Communities, and the State in India*, edited by Z. Hasan. New Delhi: Kali for Women.

Clothey, Fred. W. 1983. *Rhythm and Intent: Ritual Studies from South India*. Madras: Blackie & Son.

Cohn, Bernard S. 1996. *Colonialism and Its Forms of Knowledge: The British in India*. Princeton, NJ: Princeton University Press.

Coward, Harold. 1998. "The Religions of the South Asian Diaspora in Canada." Pp. 775–795 in *A New Handbook of Living Religions*, edited by J. R. Hinnells. New York: Penguin.

Crossette, Barbara. 2002. "Indian Starts a Campaign against Cash for Militants." *New York Times*, August 18, p. 15.

Dalrymple, William. 2005. "India: The War over History." *New York Review of Books*, April 7. www.nybooks.com/articles/17906.

Das Gupta, Monisha. 1999. "Identities, Interests and Alternative Spaces: A Transnational Perspective on South Asian Political Participation in the US." Ph.D. dissertation, Department of Sociology, Brandeis University.

Dasgupta, S. S. 1989. *On the Trail of an Uncertain Dream: Indian Immigrant Experience in America*. New York: AMS Press.

DasGupta, Sayantani, and Shamita Das Dasgupta. 1996. "Women in Exile: Gender Relations in the Asian India Community in the U.S." Pp. 381–400 in *Contours of the Heart: South Asians Map North America*, edited by S. Maira and R. Srikanth. New York: Asian American Writers' Workshop.

Dasgupta, Shamita Das, and Sayantani DasGupta. 1996. "Public Face, Private Space: Asian Indian Women and Sexuality." Pp. 226–243 in *Bad Girls, Good Girls: Women, Sex, and Power in the Nineties*, edited by Nan Bauer Maglin and Donna Perry. New Brunswick, NJ: Rutgers University Press.

Datta, Nonica. 2002. "Gujarat and Majority Women." *The Hindu*, June 15. www. hinduonnet.com.

Davids, T. W. Rhys. 1880. *Buddhist Birth Stories or Jataka Tales*. London: Trubner and Company.

Dekmejian, R. Hrair, and Angelos Themelis. 1997. "Ethnic Lobbies in the U.S. Foreign Policy: A Comparative Analysis of the Jewish, Greek, Armenia, and Turkish Lobbies." Institute of International Relation, Athens, Greece.

Delhi Historians' Group, eds. 2001. *Communalization of Education: The History Textbooks Controversy*. Delhi.cyber_bangla0.tripod.com/Delhi_Historian.html.

Derné, Steve. 1995. *Culture in Action: Family Life, Emotion, and Male Dominance in Benares, India*. Albany: State University of New York Press.

Desai, Nirav S. 2003. "Forging a Political Identity: South Asian Americans in Policymaking." *The Subcontinental: A Journal of South Asian American Political Identity* 1:10.

di Leonardo, M. 1984. *The Varieties of Ethnic Experience: Kinship, Class, and Gender among California Italian Americans*. Ithaca, NY: Cornell University Press.

Dirks, Nicholas B. 1989. "The Invention of Caste: Civil Society in Colonial India." *Social Analysis* 25:42–52.

———. 1992. "Castes of Mind." *Representations* 37:56–78.

———. 2001. *Castes of Mind: Colonialism and the Making of Modern India*. Princeton, NJ: Princeton University Press.

Dumont, Louis. 1980. *Homo Hierarchicus: The Caste System and Its Implications*. Chicago: University of Chicago Press.

Dusenbery, Verne. 1995. "A Sikh Diaspora? Contested Identities and Constructed Realities." Pp. 17–42 in *Nation and Migration: The Politics of Space in the South Asia Diaspora*, edited by P. van der Veer. Philadelphia: University of Pennsylvania Press.

Eastmond, M. 1993. "Reconstructing Life: Chilean Refugee Women and the Dilemmas of Exile." Pp. 35–53 in *Migrant Women: Crossing Boundaries and Changing Identities*, edited by G. Buijs. Oxford: Berg.

Eaton, Richard. 2000. *Essays on Islam and Indian History*. New Delhi: Oxford University Press.

Ebaugh, Helen Rose, and Janet Saltzman Chafetz. 2000. *Religion and the New Immigrants: Continuities and Adaptations in Immigrant Congregations*. Walnut Creek, CA: Altamira Press.

Eck, Diana L. 2001. *A New Religious America: How a "Christian Country" Has Now Become the World's Most Religiously Diverse Nation*. San Francisco: Harper Collins Publishers.

Edelmann, Jonathan B. 2004. "Some Problems in the Hinduism and Science Dialogue." *Metanexus Chronos*, September 17. www.metanexus.net.

Eikelman, Dale F., and James Piscatori. 1990. "Social Theory in the Study of Muslim Societies." Pp. 3–28 in *Muslim Travellers: Pilgrimage, Migration, and the Religious Imagination*, edited by D. F. Eikelman and J. Piscatori. Berkeley: University of California Press.

Elst, Koenraad. 1992. *Negationism in India: Concealing the Record of Islam*. New Delhi: Voice of India.

Espiritu, Y. Le. 1992. *Asian American Pan-ethnicity: Bridging Institutions and Identities*. Philadelphia: Temple University Press.

———. 1995. *Filipino American Lives*. Philadelphia: Temple University Press.

Espiritu, Y. Le, and D. L. Wolf. 2001. "The Paradox of Assimilation: Children of Filipino Immigrants in San Diego." In *Ethnicities: Children of Immigrants in America*, edited by R. G. Rumbaut and A. Portes. Berkeley: University of California Press.

Faist, Thomas. 2000. *The Volume and Dynamics of International Migration and Transnational Social Spaces*. Oxford: Oxford University Press.

Falcone, Jessica. 2004. "Putting the 'Fun' in Fundamentalism: Religious Extremism at Hindu Summer Camps in Washington D.C." Unpublished.

———. 2005. "'I Spy . . .' The (Im)possibilities of Ethical Participant Observation with Religious Extremists." Unpublished article.

Falk, Nancy Auer. 2006. *Living Hinduisms: An Explorer's Guide*. Belmont, CA: Thomson Wadsworth.

Federation of Hindu Associations (FHA). 1995a. *Directory of Temples and Associations of Southern California and Everything You Wanted to Know about Hinduism*. Artesia, CA: N.p.

———. 1995b. "Support to Separatism 'Pseudo-secularism' Condemned." *India Post*, November 24, p. A4.

———. 1997a. "A Hindu Center." *India Post*, January 24, p. B3.

———. 1997b. "FHA Memorandum." *India West*, February 21, p. C20.

———. 1997c. "A Call of Dharma Raksha." *India Post*, August 8, p. A15.

———. 1997d. "How to Be a Good Hindu." *India Post*, August 8, p. A15.

———. 1997e. "Ideal Hindu Temple." *India Post*, August 29, p. A27.

———. 1999. "FHA Is Overwhelmed." *India Journal*, November 26, p. A7.

———. N.d.a. *Hinduism Simplified*. Diamond Bar, CA: N.p.

———. N.d.b. *Bhagwan's Call of Dharma Raksha*. Diamond Bar, CA: N.p.

Fenton, John Y. 1988. *Transplanting Religious Traditions: Asian Indians in America*. New York: Praeger.

————. 1992. "Academic Study of Religion and Asian Indian-American College Students." Pp. 258–277 in *A Sacred Thread: Modern Transmission of Hindu Traditions in India and Abroad*, edited by R. B. Williams. Chambersburg, PA: Anima.

Fetzer, Joel S., and Christopher Soper. 2005. *Muslims in the State in Britain, France, and Germany*. Cambridge: Cambridge University Press.

Feuerstein, Georg, Subhash Kak, and David Frawley. 1995. *In Search of the Cradle of Civilization*. Wheaton, IL: Quest Books.

FHA. *See* Federation of Hindu Associations.

Fishman, Joshua. 1985. "The Ethnic Revival in the United States: Implications for the Mexican-American Community." Pp. 309–354 in *Mexican-Americans in Comparative Perspective*, edited by Walker Connor. Washington D.C.: Urban Institute:

Flood, Gavin. 1996. *An Introduction to Hinduism*. Cambridge: Cambridge University Press.

Foner, N. 2002. *From Ellis Island to JFK: New York's Two Great Waves of Immigration*. New Haven, CT: Yale University Press.

Fraser, Nancy. 1997. *Justice Interruptus: Critical Reflections on the 'Postsocialist' Condition*. New York: Routledge.

Friedman, Thomas. 2005. *The World Is Flat: A Brief History of the 21st Century*. New York: Farrar, Straus and Giroux.

Frykenberg, Robert E. 1989. "The Emergence of Modern 'Hinduism' as a Concept and as an Institution: A Reappraisal with Special Reference to South India." Pp. 29–50 in *Hinduism Reconsidered*, edited by G. D. Sontheimer and H. Kulke. New Delhi: Monohar Publications.

————. 1993. "Hindu Fundamentalism and the Structural Stability of India." Pp. 233–255 in *Fundamentalisms and the State: Remaking Polities, Economies, and Militance*, edited by M. E. Marty and R. S. Appleby. Chicago: University of Chicago Press.

Fuller, C. J. 1984. *Servants of the Goddess: The Priests of a South Indian Temple*. Cambridge: Cambridge University Press.

————. 1992. *The Camphor Flame: Popular Hinduism and Society in India*. Princeton, NJ: Princeton University Press.

————. 2001. "The 'Vinayaka Chaturthi' Festival and Hindutva in Tamil Nadu." *Economic and Political Weekly*, May 12. www.epw.org.in.

————. 2003. *The Renewal of Priesthood: Modernity and Traditionalism in a South Indian Temple*. Princeton, NJ: Princeton University Press.

Ganguly, K. 1992. "Migrant Identities: Personal Memory and the Construction of Selfhood." *Cultural Studies* 6:27–50.

Gans, Herbert. 1979. "Symbolic Ethnicity: The Future of Ethnic Groups and Cultures in America." *Ethnic and Racial Studies* 2:1–20.

Gautier, François. 2003. "Heed the New Hindu Mood." *Rediff.com*, March 11. www.letindia develop.org/news/RediffMarch112003.html.

Geetha, V., and T. V. Jayanthi. 1995. "Women, Hindutva, and the Politics of Caste in Tamil Nadu." Pp. 245–269 in *Women and the Hindu Right: A Collection of Essays*, edited by T. Sarkar and U. Butalia. New Delhi: Kali for Women.

George, Rosemary M. 1997. " 'From Expatriate Aristocrat to Immigrant Nobody' ": South Asian Racial Strategies in the Southern California Context." *Diaspora* 6:30–61.

George, Sheba. 1998. "Caroling with the Keralites: The Negotiation of Gendered Spaces in an Indian Immigrant Church." Pp. 265–294 in *Gatherings in Diaspora: Religious Communities and the New Immigration*, edited by R. S. Warner and J. G. Wittner. Philadelphia: Temple University Press.

————. 2005. *When Women Come First: Gender and Class in Transnational Migration*. Berkeley: University of California Press.

Ghamari-Tabrizi, Behrooz. 2001. "The Postmodern Condition and the Emergence of Islamism." Talk at the Department of Sociology, University of Southern California, December 5.

Glod, Maria. 2005. "Wiping Stereotypes of India Off the Books." *Washington Post,* April 17, P. C07.

Goel, Sita Ram. 1991. *Hindu Temples: What Happened to Them.* Vol. 1. New Delhi: Voice of India.

———. 1993. *Hindu Temples: What Happened to Them.* Vol. 2. New Delhi: Voice of India.

Gold, Daniel. 1991. "Organized Hinduisms: From Vedic Truth to Hindu Nation." Pp. 531–593 in *Fundamentalisms Observed,* edited by M. E. Marty and R. S. Appleby. Chicago: University of Chicago Press.

Golwalkar, M. S. 1939. *We, or Our Nationhood Defined.* Nagpur: Bharat Prakashan.

Gordon, Avery F., and Christopher Newfield. 1996. "Introduction." Pp. 1–16 in *Mapping Multiculturalism,* edited by A. F. Gordon and C. Newfield. Minneapolis: University of Minnesota Press.

Gupta, Monisha, D. 1999. "Identities, Interests and Alternative Spaces: A Transnational Perspective on South Asian Political Participation in the U.S." Ph.D. Dissertation, Sociology. Brandeis University.

Habib, Irfan. 2001. "The Rewriting of History by the Sangh Parivar." Pp. 14–21 in *Communalization of Education: The History Textbooks Controversy,* edited by the Delhi Historians' Group. Delhi: Delhi Historians' Group.

Haddad, Yvonne Yazbeck. 1991. *The Muslims of America.* New York: Oxford University Press.

Handlin, Oscar. 1951. *The Uprooted: The Epic Story of the Great Migrations That Made the American People.* Boston: Little Brown and Company.

Haniffa, Aziz. 2003. "IDRF Not Funding Hate, Says 'Friends of India.' " *India Abroad,* March 14. www.letindiadevelop.org/news/IndiaAbroad/March132003.html.

Hansen, Thomas Blom. 1999. *The Saffron Wave: Democracy and Hindu Nationalism in Modern India.* Princeton, NJ: Princeton University Press.

Hanson, Richard Scott. 2001. "Sri Maha Vallabha Ganapati Devasthanam of Flushing, New York." Pp. 349–366 in *Hindu Diaspora: Global Perspectives,* edited by T. S. Rukmani. New Delhi: Munshiram Manoharlal.

Hasan, Mushirul. 1996. "The Myth of Unity: Colonial and National Narratives." Pp. 185–208 in *Contesting the Nation: Religion, Community, and the Politics of Democracy in India,* edited by D. Ludden. Philadelphia: University of Pennsylvania Press.

———. 1997. *Legacy of a Divided Nation: India's Muslims since Independence.* Delhi: Oxford University Press.

Hawley, John Stratton. 1981. *At Play with Krishna: Pilgrimage Dramas from Brindavan.* Princeton, NJ: Princeton University Press.

Heller, Agnes. 1996. "The Many Faces of Multiculturalism." Pp. 25–42 in *The Challenge of Diversity: Integration and Pluralism in Societies of Immigration,* edited by R. Baubock, A. Heller, and A. R. Zolberg. Aldershot, England: Avebury.

Helweg, Arthur W., and Usha M. Helweg. 1990. *An Immigrant Success Story: East Indians in America.* Philadelphia: University of Pennsylvania Press.

Herberg, Will. 1960. *Protestant, Catholic, Jew: An Essay in American Religious Sociology.* Garden City, NY: Doubleday.

HICAD. *See* Hindu International Council against Defamation.

Hiltebeitel, Alf. 1987. "Hinduism." Pp. 337–360 in *The Encyclopedia of Religion.* Vol. 6. Edited by M. Eliade. New York: Macmillan.

The Hindu (Special Correspondent). 2001. "Book on beef-eating runs into trouble." August 9.

Hindu International Council against Defamation. 2001. "A Petition from American Hindus to President Bush: Subject: Why do you exclude Hindus from your prayers?" http://www.hicad.org/bush.htm.

———. 2002. "Screening of Politically Motivated Marxist Films in the Exhibition 'Meeting God: Elements of Hindu Devotion.'" http://www.petitiononline.com.

Hinduism Today. 1977. "Precious Precepts: A Basic Blueprint to Guide the Passing of Dharma to the Next Generation." July:30–33.

———. 1985. "Hindu Federation of America Launches Bold Effort for Unity." November. http://www.hinduismtoday.com.

———. 1993. "10,000 Rally in Washington D.C. to Honor Vivekananda." October. http://www.hinduismtoday.com.

———. 1997a. "Cues and Clues: Keys to Hindu Protocol for Novices and Western Pilgrims to the Holy Land." September:30–33.

———. 1997b. "Searching for Our Roots." October. www.hinduismtoday.com.

———. 1998. "Middle Class, Middle Path." February:20–23.

———. 2000. "Nine Questions." May/June:34–41.

———. 2001. "Who Speaks for Hinduism? Commentary by the Editors." September/October http://www.hinduismtoday.com.

Hindustan Times. 2002. "We'll Repeat Gujarat: Togadia." http://www.hindustanstimes.com/news/printedition/161202/detNATs.html.

Hirchman, C., J. Dewind, and P. Kasinitz. 1999. *The Handbook of International Migration: The American Experience.* New York: Russell Sage.

Hobsbawm, Eric. 1987. *The Age of Empire, 1875–1914.* New York: Pantheon Books.

Hofrenning, S. K., and B. R. Chiswick. 1999. "A Method for Proxying a Respondent's Religious Background: An Application to School Choice Decisions." *Journal of Human Resources* 34:193–207.

Hondagneu-Sotelo, P. 1994. *Gendered Transitions: Mexican Experiences of Immigration.* Berkeley: University of California Press.

Hunter, Shireen T. 2002. *Islam, Europe's Second Religion: The New Social, Cultural, and Political Landscape.* Westport, CT: Praeger.

Huntington, Samuel P. 2004. *Who Are We Now: The Challenges to America's National Identity.* New York: Simon and Schuster.

Hurh, Won Moo, and Kwang Chung Kim. 1990. "Religious Participation of Korean Immigrants in the United States." *Journal for the Scientific Study of Religion* 29:19–34.

Ifrah, Georges. 2000. *The Universal History of Numbers: From Prehistory to the Invention of the Computer.* New York: John Wiley & Sons.

Iliah, Kancha. 1996. *Why I Am Not a Hindu.* Calcutta: Samya Publications.

Inden, Ronald. 1990. *Imagining India.* Oxford: Blackwell Publishers.

India Journal. 1999a. "Separate Department to Be Created for NRI's: Vajpayee." October 22, p. A3.

———. 1999b. "Indo-Americans Now Wield Great Influence in U.S. Politics." August 15, p. A3.

India Post. 1995. "Hindu Philosophy Has no Place for Caste System Says FHA." March 17, p. A6.

———. 1999. "US Visa Facility for Skilled Workers Being Abused: Report." May 14, p. 38.

———. 2000. "NRIs Behind Surge in Indo-U.S. ties." October 6, p. 4.

———. 2001a. "New Vedic City Aims to Create Ideal Municipality." June 1, p. B14.

———. 2001b. "RSS Bid to Forge Ties with Native Americans." August 31, p. 69.

———. 2003. "Hindu Alliance Launches India Development Center." May 23, p. 6.

India West. 1998. "Singh Asks NRIs to Stand by India in Critical Hour." June 19, p. A30.

———. 2005. "Malibu Temple Celebrates 21st Anniversary." May 20, p. B15.

Infinity Foundation. 2000. "Complaint against Anti-Rama Song in Secondary School." http://www.infinityfoundation.com/ECITnehletterframe.htm.

IPAC (Indian American Public Education Advisory Council). 2006. "Section VI: Timeline of the Hindutva California Textbook Campaign and the Academic/Indian American Community's Response." http://indiatruth.com. Retrieved February 21, 2006.

Islam, Naheed. 1993. "In the Belly of the Multicultural Beast I Am Named South Asian." Pp. 242–245 in *Our Feet Walk the Sky: Women of the South Asian Diaspora*, edited by the Women of the South Asian Descent Collective. San Francisco: Aunt Lute Books.

Jackson, Carl T. 1994. *Vedanta for the West: The Ramakrishna Movement in the United States.* Bloomington: Indiana University Press.

Jacobson, Mathew Frye. 1995. *Special Sorrows: The Diasporic Imagination of Irish, Polish, and Jewish Immigrants in the United States.* Cambridge, MA: Harvard University Press.

Jaffrelot, Christophe. 1996. *The Hindu Nationalist Movement in India.* New York: Columbia University Press.

Jain, Usha R. 1989. *The Gujaratis of San Francisco.* New York: AMS Press.

Janmohamed, Zahir Sajad. 2002. "The Sangh Parivar in our Backyard." *Communalism Combat*, July 18. http://www.sabrang.com.

Jha, Ajit K. 1993. "Saffron Sees Red: Secular Groups Pose a Challenge to the Hindutva Brigade." *India Today*, August 15, p. 56.

Jha, D. N. 2001. *The Holy Cow: Beef in Indian Dietary Traditions.* New Delhi: Matrix Books, an imprint of CB Publishers. After being banned in India, published as *The Myth of the Holy Cow*, London: Verso, 2002.

Jha, Lalit K. 1997. "Anthropological Survey of India Releases Finding." *India West*, December 19, p. C14.

Jha, N., and N. S. Rajaram. 2000. *The Deciphered Indus Script.* New Delhi: Aditya Publications.

Jones, William. 1807. *The Works of Sir William Jones.* 13 vols. London: John Stockdale and John Walker.

Joseph, Ramola B. 1992. "Perceived Change of Immigrants in the United States: A Study of Kerala (Asian Indian) Immigrant couples in Greater Chicago." Ph.D. dissertation, Department of Sociology and Anthropology, Loyola University of Chicago.

Juergensmeyer, Mark. 1979. "The Ghadar Syndrome: Immigrant Sikhs and Nationalistic Pride." Pp. 173–190 in *Sikh Studies: Comparative Perspectives on a Changing Tradition*, edited by M. Juergensmeyer and N. G. Barrier. Berkeley: Graduate Theological Union.

———. 1988. "The Logic of Religious Violence: The Case of Punjab." *Contributions to Indian Sociology* 22:65–88.

Kak, Subhash C. 1993. "The Structure of the Rgveda." *Indian Journal of History of Science* 28:71–79.

———. 1994. *The Astronomical Code in the RigVeda.* Delhi: Aditya Prakashan.

———. 2001. "Light or Coincidence." http://infinityfoundation.com/mandala/t_es/t_es_kak-s_light.htm.

———. 2003. "The Date of the Mahabharata War." *Sulekha.com.* www.sulekha.com/column.asp?cid=305835.

Kalyanaraman, Srinivas. 2006. "Gunga Din Comes to Michigan." *India Forum*, January. www.india-forum.com.

Kandiyoti, D. 1988. "Bargaining with Patriarchy." *Gender and Society* 2:274–290.

Keay, John. 2000. *India: A History.* New York: Grove Press.

Kelley, Ron. 1993. "Ethnic and Religious Communities from Iran in Los Angeles." Pp. 81–157 in *Irangeles: Iranians in Los Angeles,* edited by Ron Kelley, Jonathan Friedlander, and Anita Colby. Berkeley: University of California Press.

Kelly, John D. 1991. *A Politics of Virtue: Hinduism, Sexuality, and Countercolonial Discourse in Fiji.* Chicago: Chicago University Press.

Kepel, Gilles. 1997. *Allah in the West: Islamic Movements in America and Europe.* Stanford, CA: Stanford University Press.

Khandelwal, M. 2002. *Becoming American, Being Indian: An Immigrant Community in New York City.* Ithaca, NY: Cornell University Press.

Kibria, Nazli. 1998. "The Racial Gap: South Asian American Racial Identity and the Asian American Movement." Pp. 69–78 in *A Part, yet Apart: South Asians in Asian America,* edited by L. D. Shankar and R. Srikanth. Philadelphia: Temple University Press.

———. 2002. *Becoming Asian American: Second Generation Chinese and Korean American Identities.* Baltimore: John Hopkins University Press.

———. 2006. "South Asian Americans." Pp. 206–227 in *Asian Americans: Contemporary Trends and Issues,* edited by P. G. Min. Thousand Oaks, CA: Pine Forge Press.

Kim, Hanna Hea-Sun. 2000. "Being Swaminarayan: The Ontology and Significance of Belief in the Construction of a Gujarati Diaspora." Ph.D. dissertation, Department of Anthropology, Columbia University.

Klostermaier, Klaus K. 1989. *A Survey of Hinduism.* Albany: State University of New York.

Knapp, Stephen. 2000. *Proof of Vedic Culture's Global Existence,* Detroit: World Relief Network.

Kopytoff, I. 1990. "Women's Roles and Existential Identities." Pp. 75–98 in *Beyond the Second Sex: New Directions in the Anthropology of Gender,* edited by P. R. Sanday and R. G. Goodenough. Philadelphia: University of Pennsylvania Press.

Kripal, Jeffrey. 1998. *Kali's Child: The Mystical and the Erotic in the Life and Teachings of Ramakrishna.* Chicago: University of Chicago Press.

———. 2002. "The Tantric Truth of the Matter." *Sulekha.com.* September 20.

Krishna, Nanditha. 2000. *Balaji-Venkateshwara: Lord of Tirumala-Tirupathi, an Introduction.* Mumbai: Vakil & Sons.

Krishnakumar, V. E., and L. Prashanth. 2000. "Clinton Wishes Indians First Ever Diwali Greetings." *India Post,* November 3, p. 22.

Krutch, J. W. 1962. *Thoreau: Walden and Other Writings.* New York: Bantam.

Kulkarni, Beth. 2003. "Indic Culture and Traditions Seminars—Sharing Our Dharma." Global Dharma Conference, July 25–27, Edison, NJ: Brochure.

Kundnani, Arun. 2002. "An Unholy Alliance? Racism, Religion, and Communalism." *Race and Class* 44:71–80.

Kurien, Prema A. 1993. "Ethnicity, Migration, and Social Change: A Study of Three Emigrant Communities in Kerala, India." Ph.D. dissertation, Department of Sociology, Brown University, Providence.

———. 1996. "Gendering Ethnicity: Creating a Hindu Indian Identity in the United States." Paper presented at the Twenty-fifth Annual Conference on South Asia, Madison, WI. October.

———. 1998. "Becoming an American by Becoming Hindu: Indian Americans Take Their Place at the Multicultural Table." Pp. 37–70 in *Gatherings in Diaspora: Religious Communities and the New Immigration,* edited by R. S. Warner and J. G. Wittner. Philadelphia: Temple University Press.

———. 1999. "Gendered Ethnicity: Creating a Hindu Indian Identity in the U.S." *American Behavioral Scientist* 42:648–670.

———. 2000. "Different Patterns for Different Groups: Explaining the Political Behavior of American Religious Organizations." Paper presented at the annual meeting of the American Sociological Association. Washington, DC.

———. 2001a. "'We Are Better Hindus Here': Religion and Ethnicity among Indian Americans." Pp. 99–120 in *Building Faith Communities: Asian Immigrants and Religions,* edited by J. H. Kim and P. G. Min. Walnut Creek, CA: Altamira Press.

———. 2001b. "Religion, Ethnicity and Politics: Hindu and Muslim Indian Immigrants in the United States." *Ethnic and Racial Studies* 24:263–293.

———. 2002. *Kaleidoscopic Ethnicity: International Migration and the Reconstruction of Community Identities in India.* New Brunswick, NJ: Rutgers University Press.

———. 2003. "To Be or Not to Be South Asian: Contemporary Indian American Politics." *Journal of Asian American Studies* 6:261–288.

———. 2004. "Multiculturalism, Immigrant Religion, and Diasporic Nationalism: The Development of an American Hinduism." *Social Problems* 51:362–385.

———. 2005. "Hindu Temples in the U.S." Paper presented at the annual meeting of the American Academy of Religion. Philadelphia.

———. 2006a. "Mr. President, Why Do You Exclude Us from Your Prayers? Hindus Challenge American Pluralism." Pp. 119–138 in *A Nation of Religions: The Politics of Pluralism in Multireligious America,* edited by S. Prothero. Chapel Hill: University of North Carolina Press.

———. 2006b. "Multiculturalism and the Incorporation of Hindu Indian Americans." *Social Forces* 85:723–742.

Laguerre, M. S. 1998. *Diasporic Citizenship: Haitian Americans in Transnational America.* London: Macmillan.

Laine, James W. 2003. *Shivaji: Hindu King in Islamic India,* New York: Oxford University Press.

Lakhihal, Prashanth. 2001. "Sudershan to Salute Hinduism's Growth." *India Post,* pp. 1, 59, 60.

Lakra, Yash Pal. 1997. "Let Us Call Ourselves 'Hindu Americans.'" *Hinduism Today,* October, p. 9.

Lal, Vinay. 1999. "The Politics of History on the Internet: Cyber-Diasporic Hinduism and the North American Hindu Diaspora." *Diaspora* 8:137–172.

Lal, Vinay, et al. 1995. "Shame of Award to Thackerey." *India West,* June 23, p. A5.

Leonard, Karen. 1992. *Making Ethnic Choices: California's Punjabi Mexican Americans.* Philadelphia: Temple University Press.

———. 1993. "Ethnic Identity and Gender." Pp. 165–180 in *Ethnicity, Identity, Migration: The South Asian Context,* edited by M. Israel and N. K. Wagle. Toronto: Center for South Asian Studies, University of Toronto.

———. 1998. *The South Asian Americans.* Westport, CT: Greenwood Press.

Lessinger, Johanna. 1995. *From the Ganges to the Hudson: Indian Immigrants in New York City.* Boston: Allyn and Bacon.

Levitt, Peggy. 2001. *The Transnational Villagers.* Berkeley: University of California Press.

Linda, Mary. 2001. "Constructing Identity: Hindu Temple Production in the United States." Pp. 387–396 in *Hindu Diaspora: Global Perspectives,* edited by T. S. Rukmani. New Delhi: Munshiram Manoharlal.

Lindsay, James. 2002. "Getting Uncle Sam's Ear." *Brookings Review.* Winter.

Lopez, David, and Yen Le Espiritu. 1990. "Pan-ethnicity in the United States: A Theoretical Framework." *Ethnic and Racial Studies* 13:198–224.

Lorenzen, David N. 1999. "Who Invented Hinduism." *Comparative Studies in History and Society* 41:630–659.

Ludden, David. 2004. "RSS Public Diplomacy." www.sas.upenn.edu/~dludden/RSS%20Public%20Diplomacy.htm. Retrieved August 18, 2005.

Mahmood, Cynthia Keppley. 1996. *Fighting for Faith and Nation: Dialogues with Sikh Militants.* Philadelphia: University of Pennsylvania Press.

Maira, Sunaina Marr. 2002. *Desi's in the House: Indian American Youth Culture in New York City.* Philadelphia: Temple University Press.

Maira, Sunaina Marr, and Rajini Srikanth. 2002. *Contours of the Heart: South Asians Map North America.* Philadelphia: Temple University Press.

Maira, Sunaina Marr, and Raja Swamy. 2006. "History Hangama: The California Textbook Debate." *Siliconeer* 7. http://siliconeer.com/past_issues/2006/february2006.html.

Malhotra, Rajiv. 2000a. "A Hindu View of the American Academy of Religions Convention 2000." www.infinityfoundation.com/ECITAAR2000frame.htm.

———. 2000b. "The Ethics of Proselytization." Paper presented at the Cornell University Conference on Human Rights and Religion. November 8. Archived at www.infinityfoundation.com/ECITproselytizationframeset.htm.

———. 2001a. "The Asymmetric Dialog of Civilizations." *Sulekha.com*, December 3.

———. 2001b. "A Business Model of Religion—1." *Sulekha.com*, December 31.

———. 2002a. "A Business Model of Religion—2." *Sulekha.com*, April 24.

———. 2002b. "The Case for Indic Traditions in the Academy." Paper presented at the colloquium *Completing the Global Renaissance: The Indic Contributions*, New York. July. Paper revised July 24, 2002, and archived at www.infinityfoundation.com/indic_colloq/person_malhotra.htm.

———. 2002c. "RISA Lila—1: Wendy's Child Syndrome." *Sulekha.com*, September 6.

———. 2003a. "Problematizing God's Interventions in History." *Sulekha.com*, March 19.

———. 2003b. "RISA Lila 2: Limp Scholarship and Demonology." *Sulekha.com*, November 17.

———. 2003c. "Does South Asian Studies Undermine India." *Rediff.com*, December 4.

———. 2003d. "Repositioning India's Brand." *Rediff.com*, December 9.

———. 2004a. "America Must Re-discover India." *Rediff.com*, January 20.

———. 2004b. "Preventing America's Nightmare." *Rediff.com*, January 21.

———. 2004c. "Washington Post and Hinduphobia." *Sulekha.com*, April 20.

———. 2004d. "Ten Challenges to Washington Post." *Sulekha.com*, April 26.

———. 2004e. "Dialog on Whiteness Studies." *Sulekha.com*, September 20.

———. 2004f. "Myth of Hindu Sameness." *Sulekha.com*, November 18.

———. 2005. "Geopolitics and Sanskrit Phobia." *Sulekha.com*, July 5.

Malhotra, Rajiv, and David Gray. 2001. "Global Renaissance and the Roots of Western Wisdom." *IONS Review*, vol. 56. http://www.noetic.org?Ions/publications/r56Malhotra.htm.

Malhotra, Rajiv, and Vidhi Jhunjhunwala. 2006. "Academic Hinduphobia." *Outlookindia.com*, February 10.

Malhotra, Rajiv, and Robert Thurman. 2002. "Completing the Global Renaissance: The Indic Contributions, Overview of Mission." http://www.infinityfoundation.com/indic_colloq/colloq_mission_long.htm.

Mani, Lata. 1990. "Contentious Traditions: The Debate on Sati in Colonial India." Pp. 88–126 in *Recasting Women: Essays in Indian Colonial History*, edited by K. S. Sangari and S. Vaid. New Brunswick, NJ: Rutgers University Press.

Marty, Martin E., and Scott Appleby. 1991. *Fundamentalisms Observed*. Chicago: University of Chicago Press.

Mascaro, Juan. 1962. *The Bhagavad Gita*. London: Penguin Books.

Mathew, Biju, 2000. "Byte-Sized Nationalism: Mapping the Hindu Right in the United States." *Rethinking Marxism* 12:108–128.

Mathew, Biju, and Vijay Prashad. 2000. "The Protean Forms of Yankee Hindutva." *Ethnic and Racial Studies* 23:516–534.

Mauss, Armand I. 1994. *The Angel and the Beehive: The Mormon Struggle with Assimilation*. Urbana: University of Illinois Press.

Mazumdar, Sanjoy. 1989. "Race and Racism: South Asians in the United States." Pp. 25–39 in *Frontiers of Asian American Studies*, edited by G. Nomura, R. Endo, S. H. Sumida, and R. C. Leong. Pullman: Washington State University Press.

Mazumdar, Shampa, and Sanjoy Mazumdar. 2003. "Creating the Sacred: Altars in the Hindu American Home." Pp. 143–158 in *Revealing the Sacred in Asian and Pacific America,* edited by J. N. Iwamura and P. Spickard. New York: Routledge.

McKean, Lise. 1993. "Political Capital and Spiritual Camps: The Vishwa Hindu Parishad in the United States." Paper presented at the Twenty-second Annual Conference on South Asia. Madison, WI.

———. 1996. *Divine Enterprise: Gurus and the Hindu Nationalist Movement.* Chicago: University of Chicago Press.

Mearns, David James. 1995. *Shiva's Other Children: Religion and Social Identity amongst Overseas Indians.* New Delhi: Sage Publications.

Mehra, Beloo. 2003. "Pride and Probe: Political Coming-of-Age for Indian-Americans." *Sulekha.com,* June 17.

Melwani, Lavina. 2004. "Mr Jindal Goes to Washington." *Little India,* December. http://www.littleindia.com/december2004/JindalGoestoWashington.htm.

Metcalf, Barbara D., and Thomas R. Metcalf. 2002. *A Concise History of India.* Cambridge: Cambridge University Press.

Michell, George. 1988. *The Hindu Temple: An Introduction to Its Meaning and Forms.* Chicago: University of Chicago Press.

Milner, Murray Jr. 1994. *Status and Sacredness: A General Theory of Status Relations and an Analysis of Indian Culture.* Oxford: Oxford University Press.

Min, Pyong Gap. 1992. "The Structure and Social Functions of Korean Immigrant Churches in the United States." *International Migration Review* 26:370–394.

———. 2000. "Immigrants' Religion and Ethnicity: A Comparison of Korean Christians and Indian Hindu Immigrants." *Bulletin of the Royal Institute for Inter-Faith Studies* 2:121–140.

———. 2002. *Mass Migration to the United States,* Walnut Creek, CA: Altamira Press.

———. 2003. "Immigrants' Religion and Ethnicity: A Comparison of Korean Christian and Indian Hindu Immigrants." Pp. 125–143 in *Revealing the Sacred in Asian and Pacific America,* edited by J. N. Iwamura and P. Spickard. New York: Routledge.

Misir, Deborah N. 1996. "The Murder of Navroze Mody: Race, Violence, and the Search for Order." *Amerasia Journal* 22:55–76.

Misra, V. N. 1992. *The Aryan Problem: A Linguistic Approach.* New Delhi: Munshiram Manoharlal.

Modood, Tariq. 1997. "Introduction: The Politics of Multiculturalism in the New Europe." Pp.1–26 in *The Politics of Multiculturalism in the New Europe: Racism, Identity, and Community,* edited by T. Modood and P. Werbner. London: Zed Books.

———. 1998. "Anti-Essentialism, Multiculturalism, and the 'Recognition' of Religious Groups." *Journal of Political Philosophy* 6:378–399.

———. 2005. *Multicultural Politics: Racism, Ethnicity, and Muslims in Britain.* Minneapolis: University of Minnesota Press.

Moffat, Michael. 2000. "Devotional Hinduism in New Jersey: The Bochasanwasi Akshar Purushottam Swaminarayan Sanstha." Department of Anthropology, Rutgers University, New Brunswick, NJ.

Mohaiemen, Naeem. 2003. "Bangladeshi New Yorkers: Beyond Token." *The Subcontinental: A Journal of South Asian American Political Identity* 1:89–96.

Mollenkopf, J., P. Kasinitz, and Mary Waters. 1995. "The Immigrant Second Generation in Metropolitan New York." Research proposal to the Russell Sage Foundation.

Morales, Frank Gaetano. 2005. "Does Hinduism Teach That All Religion Are the Same." *Sulekha.com,* January 7.

Mukta, Parita. 2000. "The Public Face of Hindu Nationalism." *Ethnic and Racial Studies* 23:442–466.

Müller, Friedrich Max. 1847. "On the Relation of the Bengali to the Arian and Aboriginal languages of India." *Report of the British Association for the Advancement of Science*, pp. 319–350.

———. 1854. "The Last Results of the Researches Respecting the Non-Iranian and Non-Semitic Languages of Asia and Europe, or the Turanian Family of Languages." Pp. 263–472 in *Outlines of the Philosophy of University History, Applied to Language and Religion*, edited by C.C.J. Bunsen. London: Longmans, Brown, Green, and Longmans.

———. 1883. *India: What Can It Teach Us?* London: Longmans.

———. [1887] 1985. *Biographies of Words and Home of the Aryas*. New Delhi: Gayatri.

———. 1902. *The Life and Letters of the Right Honourable Friedrich Max Müller. Vol. 1.* London: Longmans.

Mullins, Mark. 1987. "The Life Cycle of Ethnic Churches in Sociological Perspective." *Japanese Journal of Religious Studies* 14:320–334.

Murphy, Dean E. 2001. "Two Unlikely Allies Come Together in Fight against Muslims." *New York Times*, June 2, pp. B1, B6.

Muthuswamy, Moorthy. 2003. "Islam's Weakness." *Sulekha.com*, July 24.

Nagel, Joane. 1994. "Constructing Ethnicity: Creating and Recreating Ethnic Identity and Culture." *Social Problems* 42:152–176.

———. 1995. "American Indian Ethnic Renewal: Politics and the Resurgence of Identity." *American Sociological Review* 60:947–965.

Nanda, Antara. 1999. "1998 : A Year of NRI Confidence in India." *India Post*, January 1, pp. 1, 36.

Nanda, Tanmaya K. 2003. "Dharma for the New Generation." *Rediff.com*, July 26.

Nandy, A., S. Trivedy, S. Mayaram, and A. Yagnik. 1995. *Creating a Nationality: Ramjanmabhumi Movement and the Fear of the Self.* Delhi: Oxford University Press.

Narayanan, Vasudha. 1992. "Creating South Indian Hindu Experience in the United States." Pp. 147–176 in *A Sacred Thread: Modern Transmission of Hindu Traditions in India and Abroad*, edited by R. B. Williams. Chambersburg, PA: Anima Publications.

———. 1996. "The Hindu Tradition." Pp. 12–133 in *World Religions: Eastern Traditions*, edited by W. G. Oxtoby. New York: Oxford University Press.

———. 1998. "Hinduism." Pp. 126–161 in *The Illustrated Guide to World Religions*, edited by M. D. Coogan. Oxford: Oxford University Press.

———. 1999a. "Brimming with Bhakti, Embodiments of Shakti: Devotees, Deities, Performers, Reformers, and Other Women of Power in the Hindu Tradition." Pp. 25–77 in *Feminism and World Religions*, edited by A. Sharma and K. K. Young. Albany: State University of New York Press.

———. 1999b. " 'Victory to Govinda Who Lives in America': Hindu Rituals to Sacralize the American Landscape." Paper presented at the annual meeting of the American Academy of Religion, Boston.

———. 2000. "Diglossic Hinduism: Liberation and Lentils." *Journal of the American Academy of Religion* 68:761–780.

Newfield, Christopher, and Avery F. Gordon. 1996. "Multiculturalism's Unfinished Business." Pp. 76–115 in *Mapping Multiculturalism*, edited by A. F. Gordon and C. Newfield. Minneapolis: University of Minnesota Press.

Nielsen, François. 1985. "Toward a Theory of Ethnic Solidarity in Modern Societies." *American Sociological Review* 50:133–149.

Nimbark, Ashakant. 1980. "Some Observations on Asian Indians in an American Educational Setting." Pp. 247–271 in *The New Ethnics: Asian Indians in the United States*, edited by P. Saran and E. Eames. New York: Praeger.

Oak, P. N. 1969. *Tajmahal—The True Story: The Tale of a Temple Vandalized.* Houston: Ghosh.

O'Flaherty, Wendy Doniger. 1981. *The Rig Veda: An Anthology.* London: Penguin Books.

Ogbu, J., and M. Gibson. 1991. *Minority Status and Schooling: A Comparative Study of Immigrant and Involuntary Minorities.* New York: Garland.

Oldenburg, Veena Talwar. 2002. *Dowry Murder: The Imperial Origins of a Cultural Crime.* Oxford: Oxford University Press.

Olender, Maurice. 1992. *The Languages of Paradise: Race, Religion, and Philology in the Nineteenth Century.* Cambridge, MA: Harvard University Press.

Olzak, Susan. 1992. *The Dynamics of Ethnic Competition and Conflict.* Stanford, CA: Stanford University Press.

Omi, M., and H. Winant. 1986. *Racial Formation in the United States.* New York: Routledge.

Omvedt, Gail. 1993. *Reinventing Revolution: New Social Movements and the Socialist Tradition in India.* Armonk, NY: M. E. Sharpe.

Ong, Aiwa. 1999. *Flexible Citizenship: The Cultural Logic of Transnationality.* Durham, NC: Duke University Press.

Orum, Anthony M. 2002a. "Circles of Influence and Chains of Command: A Structural Perspective on How Ethnic Communities Influence Host Societies." Unpublished paper, Department of Sociology, University of Illinois, Chicago.

———. 2002b. "A Neo-Weberian Perspective on Questions of Immigration and Incorporation: New Insights and Theoretical Opportunities." Paper presented at the annual meeting of the American Sociological Association, Chicago.

Østergaard-Nielsen, Eva Kristine. 2001a. "The Politics of Migrants' Transnational Political Practices." http://www.transcomm.ox.ac.uk.

———. 2001b. "Transnational Political Practices and the Receiving State: Turks and Kurds in Germany and the Netherlands." *Global Networks* 1:261–281.

Padilla, Feliz M. 1985. *Latino Ethnic Consciousness: The Case of Mexican Americans and Puerto Ricans in Chicago.* Notre Dame, IN: Notre Dame University Press.

Padmanabhan, Anil, and Ishara Bhasi. 2003. "Fund Fracas." *India Today,* March 24.

Pais, Arthur. 2001. "A First Line of Defense." *Beliefnet.com,* September 4.

Pandey, Gyanendra. 1993a. "The Civilized and the Barbarian: The 'New' Politics of Late Twentieth Century India and the World." Pp. 1–23 in *Hindus and Others: The Question of Identity in India Today,* edited by G. Pandey. New Delhi: Viking.

———. 1993b. "Which of Us Are Hindus." Pp. 238–272 in *Hindus and Others: The Question of Identity in India Today,* edited by G. Pandey. New Delhi: Viking.

Panikkar, Raimundo. 1977. *The Vedic Experience, Mantramanjari: An Anthology of the Vedas for Modern Man and Contemporary Celebration.* Berkeley: University of California Press.

Park, Robert E. 1921. "Immigrant Heritages." Pp. 492–497 in *Proceedings of the National Conference of Social Work, 1921.* Chicago.

Parpola, Asko. 1994. *Deciphering the Indus Script.* Cambridge: Cambridge University Press.

Patel, Kanti B. 1998. "Incomplete Work of Partition." *India West,* April 3, pp. A5–A6.

Patel, Raju. 2002. "UK Media Use of the Term 'Asian' Causes Confusion." Hindu Press International (HPI), November 17.

Pinch, William R. 1996. "Soldier Monks and Militant Sadhus." Pp. 140–161 in *Contesting the Nation: Religion, Community, and the Politics of Democracy in India,* edited by D. Ludden. Philadelphia: University of Pennsylvania Press.

Pluralism Project. 2004. "Statistics by Tradition: Hinduism Statistics." http://www.pluralism. org/resources/statistics/tradition/php#Hinduism.

Portes, Alejandro. 1999. "Conclusion: Towards a New World: The Origins and the Effects of Transnational Activities." *Ethnic and Racial Studies* 22:463–477.

Portes, Alejandro, and D. MacLeod. 1996. "What Shall I call Myself? Hispanic Identity Formation in the Second Generation." *Ethnic and Racial Studies* 19:523–547.

Portes, Alejandro, and Rubén G. Rumbaut. [1990]. 1996. *Immigrant America: A Portrait.* Berkeley: University of California Press.

———. 2001. *Legacies: The Stories of the Immigrant Second Generation.* Berkeley, and New York: University of California Press and Russell Sage Foundation.

Potts, Michael. 2002. "A Historical Overview of the FIAs of Southern California: 3 Separate Republic Day Events Planned by 3 FIAs." *India West,* January 25, p. A28.

———. 2003. "SAN, Activists Raise Voices against INS Policy." *India West,* April 4, p. A28.

Prasad, B.S.V. 2003. "Some Arguments in Favour of an Early Date for the Mahabharata War." *Sulekha.com,* July 4.

Prashad, Vijay. 1997. "Culture Vultures." *Communalism Combat* 30:9.

———. 1998. "Crafting Solidarities." In *A Part, yet Apart: South Asians in Asian America,* edited by L. D. Shankar and R. Srikanth. Philadelphia: Temple University Press.

Prashanth, L., and V. E. Krishnakumar. 2000. "Indian Americans Blast Delhi over Dual Citizenship Denial." *India Post,* December 8, p. A1.

Presler, Franklin A. 1987. *Religion under Bureaucracy: Policy and Administration for Hindu Temples in South India.* Cambridge: Cambridge University Press.

Prothero, Stephen. 2001. "Mother India's Scandalous Swamis." Pp. 418–432 in *Religions of the United States in Practice,* vol. 2, edited by C. McDannell. Princeton, NJ: Princeton University Press.

———. 2002. "Hinduphobia and Hinduphilia in American Culture." Unpublished paper, Department of Religion, Boston University.

Raheja, Gloria Goodwin. 1988. *The Poison in the Gift.* Chicago: University of Chicago Press.

Rai, Amit S. 1995. "Indian On-line: Electronic Bulletin Boards and the Construction of a Diasporic Hindu Identity." *Diaspora* 4:30–57.

Raj, Dhoolekha Sarhadi. 2000. "Who the Hell Do You Think You Are? Promoting Religious Identity among Young Hindus in Britain." *Ethnic and Racial Studies* 3:535–558.

Rajagopal, Arvind. 1995. "Better Hindu than Black? Narratives of Asian Indian Identity." Presentation at the Annual Meetings of the Society for the Scientific Study of Religion, St. Louis. October.

———. 2000. "Hindu Nationalism in the United States: Changing Configurations of Political Practice." *Ethnic and Racial Studies* 23:467–1496.

———. 2001. *Politics after Television: Hindu Nationalism and the Reshaping of the Public in India.* Cambridge: Cambridge University Press.

Rajaram, Navaratna S. 1993. *Aryan Invasion of India.* New Delhi: Voice of India.

———. 1995. *The Politics of History.* New Delhi: Voice of India.

Rajaram, Navaratna S., and David Frawley. 1995. *Vedic "Aryans" and the Origins of Civilization.* Quebec: W. H. Press.

Rajghatta, Chidanand. 2002. "India Tops China in Student Inflow to U.S." *India West,* November 22, p. A35.

———. 2003. "U.S. Probing Saffron Links of Charity." *The Times of India,* February 17. http://www.timesofindia.indiatimes.com/cms.dll/html/uncomp/articleshow?artid=37701036.

Ramaswamy, Sumathi. 1997. *Passions of the Tongue: Language Devotion in Tamil India, 1891–1970,* Berkeley: University of California Press.

Ramesh, Sujatha. 2000. "Negotiating Arranged Marriages in the Swaminarayan Congregations." Paper presented at the annual meeting of the Society for the Scientific Study of Religion, Houston, TX.

Rangaswamy, Padma. 1996. "The Imperatives of Choice and Change: Post-1965 Immigrants from India in Metropolitan Chicago." Ph.D. dissertation, Department of History, University of Illinois, Chicago.

————. 2000. *Namaste America: Indian Immigrants in an American Metropolis.* University Park: Pennsylvania State University Press.

Rao, Ramesh. 2003. "It Is India, not South Asia." *The Subcontinental: A Journal of South Asian American Political Identity* 1:27–40.

Rao, Ramesh, Narayan Komerath, Beloo Mehra, Chitra Raman, Sugrutha Ramaswamy, and Nagendra Rao. 2003. "A Factual Response to the Hate Attack on the Indian Development and Relief Fund (IDRF)." http://www.letindiadevelop.org/thereport/synopsis .html.

Rao, S. R. 1991. *Dawn and Devolution of the Indus Civilization.* New Delhi: Aditya Prakashan.

————. 1999. *The Lost City of Dvaraka.* New Delhi: Aditya Prakashan.

Ravu, Lakshmi. 2005. Report on the Dharma Summit 2005. August 22. www.dharmacentral.comdharmasummit.htm.

Rayaprol, Aparna. 1997. *Negotiating Identities: Women in the Indian Diaspora.* Delhi: Oxford University Press.

Raychaudhuri, Tapan. 1988. *Europe Reconsidered: Perceptions of the West in Nineteenth-Century Bengal.* Delhi: Oxford University Press.

Rediff.com. 2002. "'Hindu Rastra' in Two Years: Togadia." *Rediff.com,* December 15.

Reitz, Jeffrey G. 2002. "Host Societies and the Reception of Immigrants: Research Themes, Emerging Theories, and Methodological Issues." *International Migration Review* 36: 1005–1019.

Roosens, Eugeen E. 1989. *Creating Ethnicity: The Process of Ethnogenesis.* Newbury Park, CA: Sage Publications.

Rosser, Yvette C. 2001. "Stereotypes in Schooling: Negative Pressures in the American Educational System on Hindu Identity Formation." Pp. 193–212 in *Hindu Diaspora: Global Perspectives,* edited by T. S. Rukmani. New Delhi: Munshiram Manoharlal.

————. 2002–2003. "The Groan: Loss of Scholarship and High Drama in 'South Asian' Studies." *Sulekha.com.* Five-part series.

Roy, Raja Ram Mohan. 1999. *Vedic Physics: Scientific Origin of Hinduism.* Toronto: Golden Egg Publishing.

Rudert, Angela C. 2004. "Inherent Faith and Negotiated Power: Swaminarayan Women in the United States." M.A. thesis, Department of Religion, Cornell University, Ithaca, NY.

Rudner, David West. 1994. *Caste and Capitalism in Colonial India: The Nattukottai Chettiars.* Berkeley: University of California Press.

Rudolph, Susanne Hoeber, and James Piscatori, eds. 1997. *Transnational Religion and Fading States.* Boulder, CO: Westview Press.

Rudrappa, Sharmila. 2004. *Ethnic Routes to Becoming American.* New Brunswick, NJ: Rutgers University Press.

Rumbaut, Rubén, and Alejandro Portes. 2001. *Ethnicities: Children of Immigrants in America.* Berkeley: University of California Press.

Saberwal, S. 1995. "FHA Unity Banquet Raises $20,000 for Norwalk Temple, Support Emphasized at Sangeet Sandhya." *India Post,* July 28, p. DSW6.

Sabrang Communications Private Limited. 2002. *The Foreign Exchange of Hate: IDRF and the American Funding of Hindutva.* Mumbai: Sabrang.

Sangari, Kumkum, and Sudesh Vaid. 1990. "Recasting Women: An Introduction." Pp. 1–26 in *Recasting Women: Essays in Indian Colonial History,* edited by K. Sangari and S. Vaid. New Brunswick, NJ: Rutgers University Press.

Sanu, Sankrant. 2002. "Are Hinduism Studies Prejudiced? A Look at Encarta." *Sulekha.com,* September 24.

————. 2003. "Courtright Twist and Academic Freedom." *Sulekha.com,* December 20.

————. 2004. "The Post and Manufacturing Consent." *Sulekha.com,* May 4.

Sarabhai, M., and C. Mathur 1995. "'I Do Not Have the Luxury of Being Apolitical': A Conversation with Mallika Sarabhai by Chandana Mathur." *Samar* (South Asian Magazine for Action and Reflection), pp. 23–29.

Saran, P. 1985. *The Asian Indian Experience in the United States.* Cambridge, MA: Schenkman.

Sarkar, Tanika. 1991. "The Woman as Communal Subject: Rashtrasevika Samiti and the Ram Janmabhoomi Movement." *Economic and Political Weekly,* August 31.

———. 1993. "Women's Agency within Authoritarian Communalism: The Rashtrasevika Samiti and Ramjanmabhoomi." Pp. 24–45 in *Hindus and Others: The Question of Identity in India Today,* edited by G. Pandey. New Delhi: Viking.

———. 2001. *Hindu Wife, Hindu Nation: Community, Religion, and Cultural Nationalism.* Bloomington: Indiana University Press.

———. 2002. "Semiotics of Terror: Muslim Children and Women in Hindu Rashtra." *Economic and Political Weekly,* 2872–2876.

Sarkar, Tanika, and Urvashi Butalia, eds. 1995. *Women and the Hindu Right: A Collection of Essays.* New Delhi: Kali for Women.

Savarkar, V. D. [1923] 1969. *Hindutva: Who Is a Hindu.* Bombay: S. S. Savarkar.

Schiffauer, W. 1999. "Islamism in the Diaspora: The Fascination of Political Islam among Second generation German Turks." http://www.transcomm.ox.ac.uk.

Seidenberg, A. 1983. "The Geometry of the Vedic Rituals." Pp. 95–126 in *The Vedic Ritual of the Fire Altar,* edited by F. Staal. Berkeley: Asian Humanities Press.

Sekhar, Radhika. 2001. "Authenticity by Accident: Organizing, Decision Making, and the Construction of Hindu Identity." Pp. 307–328 in *Hindu Diaspora: Global Perspectives,* edited by T. S. Rukmani. New Delhi: Munshiram Manoharlal.

Sen, A. K. 2002. "Deflections to the Right." *OutlookIndia.com,* July 22.

Shah, Rupal. 2001. "Hindu Sangam Cultural Festival Attracts 15,000." *India West,* pp. B1, B31.

Shaikh, S. I., and M. Abraham. 1997. "Domestic Violence in the South Asian Community." Paper presented at the South Asian Women's Conference, Los Angeles.

Shain, Yossi. 1999. *Marketing the American Creed Abroad: Diasporas in the U.S. and Their Homelands.* Cambridge: Cambridge University Press.

Shankar, Lavina Dhinga, and Rajini Srikanth. 1998a. "Introduction: Closing the Gap? South Asians Challenge Asian American Studies." Pp 1–24 in *A Part, yet Apart: South Asians in Asian America,* edited by L. D. Shankar and R. Srikanth. Philadelphia: Temple University Press.

———, eds., 1998b. *A Part, Yet Apart: South Asians in Asian America.* Philadelphia: Temple University Press.

Sharma, Arvind. 2000/2001. "Perspectives from the Indic Religious Traditions." Internet columns from 2000–2001 archived at www.infinityfoundation.com.

———. 2002. "An Indic Contribution Towards an Understanding of the Word 'Religion' and the Concept of Religious Freedom." Paper presented at the conference "Completing the Global Renaissance: The Indic Contributions." July 24–29, New York. http://www.infinity foundation.com/indic_colloq/papers/paper_sharma.2.pdf.

———. 2004. "Hindus and Scholars." *Religion in the News,* June 24. Leonard Center, Trinity College, Hartford, CT.

Sheffer, Gabriel. 2003. *Diaspora Politics: At Home Abroad.* Cambridge: Cambridge University Press.

Shinagawa, Larry Hajime. 1996. "The Impact of Immigration on the Demography of Asian Pacific Americans." Pp. 59–126 in *The State of Asian Pacific America: Reframing the Immigration Debate, A Public Policy Report,* edited by B. O. Hing and R. Lee. Los Angeles: LEAP Asian Pacific American Public Policy Institute, UCLA Asian American Studies Center.

Shukla, Sandhya. 1997. "Building Diaspora and Nation: The 1991 'Cultural Festival of India.'" *Cultural Studies* 11:296–315.

Sil, Narasingha P. 1997. *Swami Vivekananda: A Reassessment.* Cranbury, NJ: Associated University Presses.

Singer, Milton. 1972. *When a Great Tradition Modernizes: An Anthropological Approach to Indian Civilization.* Chicago: University of Chicago Press.

Singh, Prithvi Raj. 1996a. "The 'Fighting Machine' and Hindus, Letter to the editor." *India Post,* October 11, p. A26.

———. 1996b. "Can 'Hindutva' Be Indian Nationalism?" *India Post,* August 16, pp. A28–29.

———. 1997a. "Discussing religious role models, Letter to the editor." *India Post,* March 14, p. A26.

———. 1997b. "A Time of Agony and a Time for Joy." *India Post,* August 15, pp. A9, A26.

Singhal, Ashok. 2004. "RSS: Embodiment of Vivekananda's Teachings." *Organiser,* February 1. www.organiser.org.

Singhvi, L. M. 2000. "NRIs Should Mean National Reserve of India." *India Post,* September 29, p. A64.

Smelser, N. J., W. J. Wilson, and F. Mitchell, eds. 2001. *America Becoming: Racial Trends and Their Consequences.* Chicago: University of Chicago Press.

Smith, Brian K. 1994. *Classifying the Universe: The Ancient Indian Varna System and the Origins of Caste.* New York: Oxford University Press.

Smith, Jane. 1999. *Islam in America.* New York: Columbia University Press.

Smith, Michael Peter, and Luis Eduardo Guarnizo. 1998. *Transnationalism from Below.* New Brunswick, NJ: Transaction Publishers.

Smith, Timothy. 1978. "Religion and Ethnicity in America." *American Historical Review* 83:1155–1185.

Smith, Tim W. 2002. "Religious Diversity in America: The Emergence of Muslims, Buddhists, Hindus and Others." *Journal for the Scientific Study of Religion* 41:577–585.

Smith, Tony. 2000. *Foreign Attachments: The Power of Ethnic Groups in the Making of American Foreign Policy.* Cambridge, MA: Harvard University Press.

Smith, Wilfred Cantwell. 1962. *The Meaning and End of Religion.* New York: Macmillan.

Sorin, Gerald. 1997. *Tradition Transformed: The Jewish Experience in America.* Baltimore: John Hopkins University Press.

South Asian Network. 2003. "Stop the Detention, Stop Attacks on Immigrants' Rights." *India West,* January 3, p. A17.

Soysal, Yasmin N. 1994. *The Limits of Citizenship: Migrants and Postnational Membership in Europe.* Chicago: University of Chicago Press.

Springer, Richard. 1995. "Poverty Persists amid Indo-American Wealth." *India West,* April 18, p. C-1.

———. 1997. "Indians Jump to Third Place in Immigration to U.S." *India West,* May 2, p. A22.

Srinivasan, Rajeev. 2000. "Why I Am Not South Asian." *Rediff.com,* March 20.

Srirekha, N. C. 2001. "Survey Finds Americans Ignorant about Hinduism." *India Post,* p. 80.

———. 2003. "200,000 NRI Millionaires in US." *India Post,* pp. 16, 19.

Staal, Frits. 1983. *AGNI: The Vedic Ritual of the Fire Altar.* 2 vols. Berkeley: University of California Press.

Stafford, Susan B. 1987. "The Haitians: The Cultural Meaning of Race and Ethnicity." Pp. 131–158 in *New Immigrants in New York,* edited by N. Foner. New York: Columbia University Press.

Stein, Burton. 1998. *A History of India.* Oxford: Blackwell Publishers.

Stietencron, Heinrich von. 1989. "Hinduism: On the Proper Use of a Deceptive Term." Pp. 11–28 in *Hinduism Reconsidered,* edited by G. D. Sontheimer and H. Kulke. New Delhi: Manohar Publications.

Stratton, Jon, and Ien Ang. 1998. "Multicultural Imagined Communities: Cultural Difference and National Identity in the USA and Australia." Pp. 135–162 in *Multicultural States: Rethinking Difference and Identity*, edited by D. Bennett. London: Routledge.

Subbarayappa, B. V. 1970. "India's Contribution to the History of Science." Pp. 47–66 in *India's Contribution to World Thought and Culture*, edited by Lokesh Chandra, et al. Madras: Vivekananda Rock Memorial Committee.

Sundaram, Viji. 2001. "Concern for Others' Welfare Is Dharma: RSS Chief." *India West*, pp. B1, B32, B33.

Sweetman, Will. 2001. "Unity and Plurality: Hinduism and the Religions of India in Early European Scholarship." *Religion* 31:209–224.

Takaki, Ronald. 1989. *Strangers from a Different Shore: A History of Asian Americans.* Boston: Little, Brown and Company.

Tatla, Darshan Singh. 1999. *The Sikh Diaspora: The Search for Statehood.* Seattle: University of Washington Press.

Taylor, Charles. 1992. "The Politics of Recognition." Pp. 25–74 in *Multiculturalism and the Politics of Recognition*, edited by A. Gutmann. Princeton, NJ: Princeton University Press.

Thapar, Romila. 1989. "Imagined Religious Communities? Ancient History and the Modern Search for a Hindu Identity." *Modern Asian Studies* 23:209–231.

———. 2000a. "On Historical Scholarship and the Uses of the Past (interview with Parita Mukta)." *Ethnic and Racial Studies* 23:594–616.

———. 2000b. "A Historical Perspective on the Story of Rama." Pp. 1055–1078 in *Cultural Pasts: Essays in Early Indian History*, edited by R. Thapar. New Delhi: Oxford University Press.

———. 2000c. "The Tyranny of Labels." Pp. 990–1014 in *Cultural Pasts: Essays in Early Indian History*, edited by R. Thapar. New Delhi: Oxford University Press.

———. 2001. "Propaganda as History Won't Sell." In *Communalization of Education: The History Textbooks Controversy*, edited by Delhi Historians' Group. http://cyber_bangla0.tripod.com/Delhi_Historian.html.

Trautmann, Thomas R. 1997. *Aryans and British India.* Berkeley: University of California Press.

Tu, Wei-Ming. 1994. *The Living Tree: The Changing Meaning of Being Chinese Today.* Stanford: Stanford University Press.

Tweed, Thomas A. 1997. *Our Lady of Exile: Diasporic Religion at a Cuban Catholic Shrine in Miami.* New York: Oxford University Press.

van der Veer, Peter. 1994. *Religious Nationalism: Hindus and Muslims in India.* Berkeley: University of California Press.

———. 1995. "Introduction: The Diasporic Imagination." Pp. 1–16 in *Nation and Migration: The Politics of Space in the South Asian Diaspora*, edited by P. van der Veer. Philadelphia: University of Pennsylvania Press.

———. 1996. "Writing Violence." Pp. 250–269 in *Contesting the Nation: Religion, Community, and the Politics of Democracy in India*, edited by D. Ludden. Philadelphia: University of Pennsylvania Press.

Vedantam, Shankar. 2004a. "Wrath over a Hindu God: U.S. Scholar's Writings Draw Threats from Faithful." *Washington Post*, April 10, p. A01.

———. 2004b. "In Response to Rajiv Malhotra's Column." *Sulekha.com*, April 23.

Venkat, Kalavai. 2005. "The California Textbook Trial." *Sulekha.com*, December 6.

Verma, Harsh. 2003. "The Leftist Attack on IDRF, Harsh Verma's Blog." *Sulekha.com*, January 17.

Vertovec, Steven. 1992. *Hindu Trinidad: Religion, Ethnicity, and Socio-Economic Change.* London: Macmillan.

———. 1995. "Hindus in Trinidad and Britain: Ethnic Religion, Reification, and the Politics of Public Space." Pp. 132–156 in *Nation and Migration: The Politics of Space in the*

South Asian Diaspora, edited by P. van der Veer. Philadelphia: University of Pennsylvania Press.

———. 1996. "Multiculturalism, Culturalism, and Public Incorporation." *Ethnic and Racial Studies* 19:49–69.

———. 2000. *The Hindu Diaspora: Comparative Patterns.* London: Routledge Press.

———. 2001. "Transnational Challenges to the 'New' Multiculturalism." http://www.transcomm.ox.ac.uk.

Vickerman, Milton. 1999. *Crosscurrents: West Indies Immigrants and Race.* New York: Oxford University Press.

Vijayakar, Mona. 2003. "Western Scholars vs. Hinduism." *India West,* December 12, pp. A5, A6.

Visweswaran, Kamala, and Ali Mir. 1999/2000. "On the Politics of Community in South Asian–American Studies." *Amerasia Journal* 25:97–108.

Vivekananda, Swami. 1893a. "Response to Welcome at the World's Parliament of Religions." Presentation at the World Parliament of Religions. Chicago: www.hindunet.org/vivekananda/chicago/response_welcome.

———. 1893b. "Paper on Hinduism." Presentation at the World Parliament of Religions. Chicago. www.hindunet.org/vivekananda/chicago/paper_hinduism.

———. 1893c. "At the Final Session." Presentation at the World Parliament of Religions. Chicago. www.hindunet.org/vivekananda/chicago/final_session.

———. 1895. "India's Gift to the World, Lecture Delivered in Brooklyn, 1895, Published in the Brooklyn Standard Union, February 27, 1895." In *Complete Works of Swami Vivekananda.* Vol. 2, *Reports in American Newspapers.* www.ramakrishnavivekananda.info/vivekananda/volume_2/vol_2_frame.htm.

———. 1897. "First Public Lecture in the East." *Complete Works of Swami Vivekananda.* Vol. 3, *Lectures from Columbo to Almora.* www.ramakrishnavivekananda.info/vivekananda/volume_3/vol_3_frame.htm.

———. N.d. "The Mission of the Vedanta." In *Complete Works of Swami Vivekananda.* Vol. 3, *Lectures from Columbo to Almora.* Internet edition, Same URL as for Vivekananda 1897.

Wadley, Susan, S. 1992. "Women and the Hindu Tradition." Pp. 111–136 in *Women in India: Two Perspectives,* edited by D. Jacobson and S. S. Wadley. Columbia, MO: South Asia Publications.

Waghorne, Joanne P. 1999. "The Hindu Gods in a Split-Level World: The Sri Siva-Vishnu Temple in Suburban Washington, D.C." Pp. 103–130 in *Gods of the City: Religion and the American Urban Landscape,* edited by R. Orsi. Bloomington: Indiana University Press.

———. 2004. *Diaspora of the Gods: Modern Hindu Temples in an Urban Middle-Class World,* New York: Oxford University Press.

———. 2006. "Spaces for a New Public Presence: The Sri Siva-Vishnu and Murugan Temples in Metropolitan Washington, D.C." Pp. 103–127 in *American Sanctuary: Understanding Sacred Spaces,* edited by L. Nelson. Bloomington: Indiana University Press.

Waldman, Amy. 2002. "A Secular India, or Not? At Strife Scene, Vote Is Test." *New York Times,* p. A18.

Walzer, Michael. 1992. *What it Means to Be an American.* New York: Marsilio Publishers.

Warner, Stephen R. 1993. "Work in Progress toward a New Paradigm for the Sociological Study of Religion in the United States." *American Journal of Sociology* 98:1044–1093.

———. 1998. "Immigration and Religious Communities in the United States." Pp. 3–36 in *Gatherings in Diaspora: Religious Communities and the New Immigration,* edited by S. Warner and J. Wittner. Philadelphia: Temple University Press.

———. 1994. "The Place of the Congregation in the American Religious Configuration." Pp. 54–99 in *American Congregations,* Vol. 2, *New Perspectives in the Study of Congregations,* edited by James P. Winder and James W. Lewis. Chicago: University of Chicago Press.

Warner, Stephen R., and J. G. Wittner, eds. 1998. *Gatherings in Diaspora: Religious Communities and the New Immigration.* Philadelphia: Temple University Press.

Waters, Mary C. 1990. *Ethnic Options: Choosing Identities in America.* Berkeley: University of California Press.

———. 1999. *Black Identities: West Indian Immigrant Dreams and American Realities.* Cambridge, MA: Harvard University Press.

Waters, Mary, and Karl Eschbach. 1999. "Immigration and Ethnic and Racial Inequality in the U.S." In *Majority and Minority: The Dynamics of Race and Ethnicity in American Life,* edited by N. R. Yetman. Needham Heights, MA: Allyn and Bacon.

Weightman, Simon. 1997. "Hinduism." Pp. 261–309 in *A New Handbook of Living Religions,* edited by J. R. Hinnells. Oxford: Blackwell Publishers.

Wellmeier, Nancy J. 1998. "Santa Eulalia's People in Exile: Maya Religion, Culture, and Identity in Los Angeles." Pp. 97–122 in *Gatherings in Diaspora: Religious Communities and the New Immigration,* edited by S. Warner and N. J. Wellmeier. Philadelphia: University of Pennsylvania Press.

Wildman, Sarah. 2001. "All for One." *New Republic,* December 24. http://www.thenewrepublic. com/122401/diarist122401.html.

Williams, Raymond B. 1988. *Religions of Immigrants from India and Pakistan: New Threads in the American Tapestry.* Cambridge: Cambridge University Press.

———. 1992. "Sacred Threads of Several Textures." Pp. 228–257 in *A Sacred Thread: Modern Transmission of Hindu Traditions in India and Abroad,* edited by R. Williams. Chambersburg, PA: Anima Press.

———. 2001. *An Introduction to Swaminarayan Hinduism.* Cambridge: Cambridge University Press.

Witzel, Michael. 2001. "Autochthonous Aryans? The Evidence from Old Indian and Iranian Texts." *Electronic Journal of Vedic Studies* 7:1–111.

Witzel, Michael, and Steve Farmer. 2000. "Horseplay in Harappa." *Frontline,* October 13, pp. 4–14.

Wolpert, Stanley. 1991. *India.* Berkeley: University of California Press.

Xenos, P., H. Barringer, and M. J. Levin. 1989. "Asian Indians in the United States: A 1980 Census Profile (No.111)." East-West Population Institute, Honolulu, HI.

Yang, Fenggang. 1999. *Chinese Christians in America: Conversion, Assimilation, and Adhesive Identities.* University Park: Pennsylvania State University Press.

Yang, Fenggang, and Helen Rose Ebaugh. 2001. "Transformations in New Immigrant Religions and Their Global Implications." *American Sociological Review* 66:269–288.

Zaidi, Akbar S. 2002. "Who Is South Asian." http://www.dawn.com/2002/09/090p.htm#2.

Zhou, M. 1997. "Segmented Assimilation: Issues, Controversies, and Recent Research on the New Second Generation." *International Migration Review* 31:975–1008.

———. 2001. "Straddling Different Worlds: The Acculturation of Vietnamese Refugee Children." Pp. 187–228 in *Ethnicities: Children of Immigrants in America,* edited by R. Rumbaut and A. Portes. Berkeley: University of California Press.

Zhou, M., and Carl L. Bankston III. 1998. *Growing Up American: How Vietnamese Children Adapt to Life in the United States.* New York: Russell Sage.

INDEX

About the Author

Prema A. Kurien is an associate professor in the Sociology Department at Syracuse University. Her first book, *Kaleidoscopic Ethnicity: International Migration and the Reconstruction of Community Identities in India* (Rutgers University Press, 2002), was cowinner of the 2003 book award from the Asia and Asian America section of the American Sociological Association. She is currently researching transnationalism and the generational transmission of religion among a group of Indian American Christians, and Indian American lobby groups.